As one of the world's longest esta
and best-known travel b
Thomas Cook are the experts in

For more than 135 yea
guidebooks have unlocked the se
of destinations around the w
sharing with travellers a wealth of
experience and a passion for travel.

**Rely on Thomas Cook as your
travelling companion on your next trip
and benefit from our unique heritage.**

Thomas Cook **driving** guides

CALIFORNIA

Maxine Cass and Fred Gebhart

Your travelling companion since 1873

Written by Maxine Cass and Fred Gebhart, updated by Maxine Cass
Original photography by Maxine Cass and Fred Gebhart

Published by Thomas Cook Publishing
A division of Thomas Cook Tour Operations Limited
Company registration no. 3772199 England
The Thomas Cook Business Park, Unit 9, Coningsby Road,
Peterborough PE3 8SB, United Kingdom
Email: books@thomascook.com, Tel: + 44 (0) 1733 416477
www.thomascookpublishing.com

Produced by Cambridge Publishing Management Limited
Burr Elm Court, Main Street, Caldecote CB23 7NU
www.cambridgepm.co.uk

ISBN: 978-1-84848-329-3

© 2005, 2007, 2009 Thomas Cook Publishing
This fourth edition © 2010
Text © Thomas Cook Publishing
Maps © Thomas Cook Publishing/PCGraphics (UK) Limited

Series Editor: Karen Beaulah
Production/DTP: Steven Collins

Printed and bound in India by Replika Press Pvt Ltd

Cover photography: © Dennis Frates/Alamy

About the authors

Maxine Cass is a rare specimen, a California native. Since she was born on the Stanford University campus in Palo Alto, Maxine has studied Medieval Studies and History at the University of California, Santa Barbara, lived in Greece and Senegal, and become a widely published photojournalist and author. Maxine is the author of the *AAA Photo Journey to San Francisco*, *Time for Food: San Francisco*, and other guidebooks to Florida, Western Canada, the Pacific Northwest, India and Mexico. She contributes to travel and business publications in Europe, the US, Canada and Asia. Between research trips around the world, Maxine gardens at the home in San Francisco she shares with her husband and title co-author, Fred Gebhart.

Fred Gebhart has lived in California for more than 40 years, interrupted by extended sojourns in Europe and West Africa that have eventually sent him back to his adopted state. He has logged thousands of miles in California, as a child as well as an adult, travelling by foot, horseback, balloon, bicycle, sailing boat, RV and car. A freelance photojournalist for more than 25 years, Fred covers California and the Western United States for publications in Asia and Europe while focusing on Australasia for US readers. With his wife, Maxine Cass, Fred has written a number of Thomas Cook titles, including *On the Road Around California*, *Must See Florida*, and *Drive Around Guides Vancouver* and *British Columbia*.

Acknowledgements

The authors and publishers would like to thank the following people and organisations for their assistance:
Laurie Armstrong, San Francisco CVB; Molly Blaisdell; Kate Buska & Joe Timko, San Diego CVB; Calaveras Visitors Bureau; Kelly Chamberlain; Lara Chanley, Santa Monica CVB; Chris Chrystal, Nevada Commission on Tourism; Ellen Clark & Geoffrey Williams; Delaware North Companies; Robert Deuel, the Disneyland® Resort; Bob Fish, USS *Hornet*; Kris Fister, Sequoia & Kings Canyon National Parks; Lee Foster; Lou Gebhart; Mark Graves, Palm Springs Desert Resort Communities CVA; Elizabeth Harryman & Paul Lasley; Kenny Karst, DNC Parks & Resorts at Yosemite; Brian M Logan, BLM Arcata; Carol Martinez, LA, Inc.; Paul & Virginia McCarthy; Mendo & Panther; Monterey Bay Aquarium; John Poimiroo; Mary Ellen Quesada; Sharon Rooney; Sue Russell, El Dorado County Chamber of Commerce; San Diego Zoo's Wild Animal Park; San Diego Zoological Society; Fred Sater; Stanford Inn by the Sea; Lucy Steffens, Sacramento CVB; Richard Stenger, Humboldt County CVB; Town & Country Hotel; Marilyn Wagner; Keith Walklet; Welk Resort Center; Whale Watch Inn.

Contents

Above
The stark beauty of the desert

About driving guides

Thomas Cook's driving guides are designed to provide you with a comprehensive but flexible reference source to guide you as you tour a country or region by car. This guide divides California into touring areas – one per chapter. Major cultural centres or cities form chapters in their own right. Each chapter contains enough attractions to provide at least a day's worth of activities – often more.

Ratings
To make it easier for you to plan your time and decide what to see, every area is rated according to its attractions in categories such as Architecture, Beaches and Children.

Chapter contents
Every chapter has an introduction summing up the main attractions of the area, and a ratings box, which will highlight the area's strengths and weaknesses – some areas may be more attractive to families travelling with children, others to wine lovers visiting vineyards, and others to people interested in finding castles, churches, nature reserves or good beaches.

Each chapter is then divided into an alphabetical gazetteer, and most chapters feature a suggested tour. You can select whether you just want to visit a particular sight or attraction, choosing from those described in the gazetteer, or whether you want to tour the area comprehensively. If the latter, you can construct your own itinerary, or follow the authors' suggested tour, which comes at the end of most area chapters.

The gazetteer
The gazetteer section describes all the major attractions in the area – the villages, towns, historic sites, nature reserves, parks or museums

Symbol key
ℹ️ Tourist information centre

🔄 Advice on arriving or departing

🅿️ Parking locations

🔄 Advice on getting around

🏛 Sights and attractions

🌙 Accommodation

🍴 Eating

🛍 Shopping

🏅 Sport

🎭 Entertainment

Practical information

The practical information in the page margins, or sidebars, will help you locate the services you need as an independent traveller – including the tourist information centre, car parks and public transport facilities. You will also find the opening times of sights, museums, churches and other attractions, as well as useful tips on shopping, market days, cultural events, entertainment, festivals and sports facilities.

that you are most likely to want to see. Maps of the area highlight all the main places mentioned in the text. Using this comprehensive overview of the area, you may choose just to visit one or two sights.

One way to use the guide is simply to find individual sights that interest you, using the index or overview map, and read what our authors have to say about them. This will help you decide whether to visit the sight. If you do, you will find plenty of practical information, such as the street address, the telephone number for enquiries and opening times.

Alternatively, you can choose a hotel, perhaps with the help of the accommodation recommendations contained in this guide. You can then turn to the overall map on pages 8–9 to help you work out which chapters in the book describe those cities and regions that lie closest to your chosen touring base.

Driving tours

The suggested tour is just that – a suggestion. The routes are designed to link the attractions described in the gazetteer section, and to cover outstandingly scenic coastal, mountain and rural landscapes. The total distance is given for each tour, as is the time it will take you to drive the complete route, but bear in mind that this indication is just for the driving time: you will need to add on extra time for visiting attractions along the way.

Many of the routes are circular, so that you can join them at any point. Where the nature of the terrain dictates that the route has to be linear, the route can either be followed out and back, or you can use it as a link route, to get from one area in the book to another.

Accommodation and food

In every chapter you will find lodging and eating recommendations for individual towns, or for the area as a whole. These are designed to cover a range of price brackets and concentrate on more characterful small or individualistic hotels and restaurants. The price indications used in the guide have the following meanings:

$ budget level
$$ typical/average prices
$$$ de luxe

BRYCE CANYON

ZION CANYON

GRAND CANYON

UTAH

ARIZONA

Page 272

Tonopah

Fallon

Basalt

Bridgeport

Lakeview

Reno

Carson City

South Lake Tahoe

Twain Harte

Alturas

Page 112

Susanville

Page 120

SACRAMENTO

Stockton

Quincy

Oroville

Marysville

Page 224

Medford

Klamath Falls

Yreka

Mt Shasta

Burney

Chester

Chico

Yuba City

Clearlake

Antioch

Oakland

Page 244

Pages 152

Redding

Red Bluff

Willows

Page 174

Page 144

San Rafael

Grants Pass

Ashland

Brookings

Crescent City

Garberville

Willits

Ukiah

Cloverdale

Healdsburg

Santa Rosa

Page 184

Arcata

Eureka

Fortuna

Fort Bragg

Mendocino

Page 194

Introduction

Above
Mission Carmel: San Carlos
Borromeo del Rio Carmel
Mission

California is an asylum where the inmates have permanent control and the rest of the world is clamouring to get in. It's a hypermarket of people, places and experiences, from the vast horizons of the northeast to the teeming streets of Los Angeles and San Diego, from manicured vineyard rows to trackless forests that have never been properly mapped.

It's a land rife with myths, half-truths and outright lies stirred together to create a morality tale that is part admonition and part salacious entertainment. Even the handful of Californians who were born here can't always discern one tale from another. Most don't care. When Californians heard that 'perception is reality', they took it to heart as their own reality. California is a land of change, always moving towards an ever-better future. From that shared belief has sprung the California Dream, an ever-evolving mix of fact, fantasy and hope that suffuses the Golden State in a golden glow of arrested adolescence.

Named after a mythical land and nourished by generations of dreamers and schemers, California has come to epitomise a place where anything can happen – and usually does. Fortunes have been won, lost and won again by every means imaginable. More than a few sprang full-grown from the minds of men whose ambition overreached their good sense. Avarice, lust and fraud are as much part of the California Dream as peace, love and happiness. What all six share is an unshakeable faith in the positive power of change, a maniacal belief that tomorrow *will* be a better day.

Until the arrival of steamships and transcontinental railways, simply travelling to California required an unhealthy dose of optimism. The journey from the Atlantic Coast of North America offered the prospect of gruelling physical hardship by land or gnawing boredom by sea, both leavened by the very real prospects of death by disaster, disease or foul play along the way. Rugged terrain and treacherous coastal shoals made travel up and down the state equally problematic. Despite the obvious difficulties, California has been portrayed as the Golden State – a paradise on earth – since it was first viewed by Europeans more than four centuries ago. It didn't seem to matter that just getting to California required either an extraordinary leap of faith or an equally extraordinary act of desperation. Once arrived, fame and fortune somehow seemed assured.

Generations of stubborn determination have turned that impenetrable faith in the future into a self-fulfilling prophecy that feeds upon itself and infects legions of newcomers from around the globe. The soaring spires of the Yosemite Valley and the cathedral silence of a grove of redwood trees wreathed in mist and spotlit by beams of sunlight are as much a part of modern California as the imagination, engineering and sheer sweat that created Disneyland, Industrial Light & Magic and generations of silicon chips.

California is a study in contradictions. It's the most populous state in America, yet has vast tracts of untouched wilderness. It produced the cult of youth, beauty and health that is sweeping the globe, yet has one of America's fastest-growing populations of retired persons. It's a land built by immigrants whose political leaders fan the flames of anti-immigrant sentiment at election time. It's among the richest economies on earth, yet it refuses to feed, house and educate a growing minority of its population.

None of this is news to Californians. They revel in quirks and contradictions. Most of them are here by choice, not by birth. That they remain only reinforces the optimism that drew them, or their parents, here in the first place. One of the seldom-acknowledged joys of California is that everything that is said about the place is both true and untrue at the same time.

Below
Golden Gate Bridge,
San Francisco

Travel facts

Accommodation

Thousands of chain hotels and motels provide the most reliable accommodation. Expect to pay $100–$250 per night in major cities, $70–$150 in smaller towns, single or double occupancy. Enquire if an unadvertised or group membership discount is on offer and request the least expensive rate when booking accommodation.

Camping pitches and RV sites must be booked in advance for popular national, state and local parks. RV parks are common in rural areas but rare in cities (*see Recreational vehicles, page 19*). Bed & Breakfast is often among the most expensive options; several hundred are listed on the California Association of Bed and Breakfast Inns, *www.cabbi.com*. Fax or use the toll-free telephone numbers for booking; you can also book via email or a website. Local tourist offices usually have lists of area accommodation and some make bookings.

Airports

Heightened airport security in the US may mean delays and unpredictable waits. Plan plenty of time to make connections, and be prepared to remove footwear and laptop computers at security checkpoints, where cabin baggage may also be hand-searched. Before departure for the United States, check at *www.tsa.gov* for current restrictions on liquids, food, beverages and medication that may be hand-carried on to an aircraft. Most international visitors fly into Los Angeles International Airport (LAX) or San Francisco International Airport (SFO). Luggage trolleys are free for international arrivals; expect to pay $3 at domestic terminals. For flight information and bookings, contact individual airlines. Major airports have foreign exchange, banking services and cash machines (ATMs) as well as car-hire facilities. Secondary airports may be less congested.

Children

Most attractions offer children's rates. Many hotels and motels can arrange for babysitters, a pricey service. Children up to 18 stay free in their parents' room with many motel chains.

Picnics offer mealtime flexibility. So does a small cooler filled with cold drinks and snacks. Most towns have roadside restaurants with long hours, cheap children's menus and familiar names.

Currency

US dollars, all the same size, come in denominations of $1, $2 (rare), $5, $10, $20, $50 and $100. Older versions of $50 and $20 and the other denominations are all the same colour, green and white. Updated bills have added colours to designs. All bills have a different US president on the front and design on the back. There are 100 cents to the dollar. Coins are: 1 cent (penny), 5 cents (nickel), 10 cents (dime), 25 cents (quarter), 50 cents (half-dollar – rare), and a rarely seen gold-coloured dollar. Oversized silver dollar coins are common in Nevada.

The safest forms of money are traveller's cheques and credit or debit cards. Carry at least one, preferably two, major credit cards such as **Access** (MasterCard), **American Express** or **Visa**. Car-hire companies, hotels and motels require a credit card or a substantial cash deposit, even if the bill has been prepaid or will be settled in cash.

Banks can exchange foreign currency or traveller's cheques, but expect delays at small town branches. US dollar traveller's cheques from well-known issuers such as Thomas Cook are acceptable almost everywhere.

Customs allowances

Allowances can change. Before travelling, check with the US Department of Homeland Security, Customs and Border Protection, *tel: (877) 227-5511, international: (703) 526-4200; www.cbp. gov/xp/cgov/travel.* Non-resident visitors to the US may bring 1 litre of spirits, beer or wine, 200 cigarettes and 100 non-Cuban cigars and up to $100 worth of gifts duty-free. The minimum age for alcohol is 21 and 18 for tobacco. Be aware that the state of California enforces a strict smoking ban in all public places, including outdoor restaurants.

Check with customs officials at home for returning duty-free allowances. Alcohol, tobacco, perfume, electronics and similar items are cheaper at supermarkets and department stores than at airport and downtown duty-free shops.

Disabled travellers

Federal and state laws require that public businesses and services be readily accessible by persons with disabilities. Hotels, restaurants, offices, shops, cinemas, museums, post offices and other buildings must have access ramps and toilets designed for wheelchairs. Most cities also have kerb ramps at street corners. Major parks have at least a few sealed pathways for disabled visitors. For specific information, contact **SATH** (Society for Accessible Travel & Hospitality), *347 5th Ave, Suite 605, New York, NY 10016; tel: (212) 447-7284; www.sath.org* or **RADAR**, *12 City Forum, 250 City Rd, London EC1V 8AF; tel: (020) 7250-3222; www.radar.org.uk.* California State Parks are access friendly; *tel: (916) 445-8949; access@parks.ca.gov; http://access.parks.ca.gov*

Above
Lunching alfresco in San Francisco's North Beach

Opposite
Native American-style art in Grand Canyon National Park

Electricity

America uses 110 volt 60 hertz current with two- or three-prong plugs. Power and plug converters are seldom available.

Beware of buying electrical equipment – it probably won't operate on your voltage at home. Exceptions are battery-operated items such as radios, cameras and portable computers.

Be equally wary of DVDs. DVD players are designated by region. The US is in region D1, the UK and Western Europe are region D2. Look for a 'region-free' DVD, otherwise it's unlikely the DVD will play on your DVD player. America uses the NTSC format, most other countries use PAL or SECAM. Make sure you check your home country High Definition (HD) equipment standard for compatibility if you plan to shop in the United States.

Drinking laws

The drinking age is 21 and it is strictly enforced. Beer, wine and spirits can be purchased in food, drug- and convenience stores as well as in liquor stores. Licensed establishments, bars, lounges, saloons and pubs may open between 0600 and 0200 in California and any hours in Nevada. Laws against drinking and driving are severe and are also strictly enforced (*see Drinking and driving, page 23*).

Earthquakes

Most of the 5,000-plus earthquakes that shake California yearly are too small to be noticed. If the tremor is mild, i.e. dishes aren't rattling, treat it like an amusement park ride and thrill friends at home with tales of terror.

If it becomes difficult to stand or items fall from shelves, take cover beneath the nearest solid table. If there's no table, brace yourself in an interior doorway. Stay away from windows, bookcases or anything else that could collapse. *Don't* run outside, where glass, masonry and power lines could be falling.

If driving, pull off the road and stop on solid ground – you can't drive safely when the road is moving. If you are about to cross a bridge or flyover, stop, or get to the other side as quickly as possible. Then get ready for the next shake. There are always aftershocks, sometimes as strong as the mother quake.

Eating out

Expect to eat too much. The US periodically indulges in fad diets, touting fad-related dishes on menus. Otherwise, an 'American breakfast' combines bacon, sausages or ham, hash browns, eggs, pancakes or French toast and toast. English muffins (crumpets), waffles, bagels, fresh fruit, yoghurt, porridge and cereal are other possibilities. A 'continental breakfast' is juice, coffee or tea and bread or a pastry.

Lunch and dinner menus feature appetisers, salads, soups, pastas, entrées and desserts. Salads come at the beginning of the meal. Sunday brunch, self-service buffets piled high with hot and cold dishes, can be good value for hearty eaters (usually served 1100–1400).

Many fast-food outlets have drive-up windows. Look for A&W, Arby's Roast Beef, Burger King, Carl's Jr, In-N-Out Burger, Jack-in-the-Box, KFC (Kentucky Fried Chicken), McDonald's, Pizza Hut, Quiznos Sub, Subway and Taco Bell.

Chain restaurants, ubiquitous along freeways, include Applebee's, Denny's (both American), Chevy's (Mexican), Fresh Choice (salads, soups and pastas), Olive Garden (Italian), Red Lobster (seafood) and Sizzler (American).

Above
Rock climbing in Joshua Tree
National Park

Entry formalities

Eligible citizens or nationals of some countries with machine-readable passports can travel to the US for pleasure or business for less than 90 days under the Visa Waiver Program (VWP). An electronic application must be filed (see *https://esta.cbp.dhs.gov*) and approved through the Electronic System for Travel Authorization (ESTA) prior to boarding a US-bound airplane or vessel. Check details at *www.customs.gov/xp/ cgov/travel/id_visa/business_pleasure/vwp/vwp.xml*. Requirements and approved countries change frequently. An ESTA is effective for two years unless the passport expires sooner. A valid visa may still be accepted for entry under certain circumstances. To search for common questions and answers about the process, see *www.cbp.gov/xp/cgov/travel/id_visa/esta*. Weapons, narcotics, many foodstuffs and certain pharmaceutical products may not be imported. Carry documentation such as a doctor's prescription to prove that medications are legitimate.

Health

Museums

Most museums are closed one day per week, usually Monday or Tuesday. Rural museums may open only at weekends or during the busy summer season. Most charge an entry fee.

In the event of a life-threatening emergency, telephone 911 for an ambulance. If a life is at stake, treatment will be swift and professional, with payment problems left for later. For more mundane problems, urban areas and most rural communities have 24-hour walk-in clinics.

Because US medical providers do not accept non-US health plan coverage, health insurance is mandatory to ensure provision of non-emergency health services. Most travel agents who sell international travel offer travel insurance policies covering US medical costs.

Bring prescription medication for the entire trip plus a few extra days, and a copy of the prescription for emergencies. As names of drugs vary from country to country, the prescription should show the generic (chemical) name and formulation, not just a brand name.

California is basically a healthy place. No inoculations are required and common sense is enough to avoid most health problems. Eat normally and don't drink water that hasn't come from the tap or a bottle. Most groundwater is contaminated with *giardia* and other intestinal parasites. Check the US Centers for Disease Control website (*www.cdc.gov*) for recommended repellents and precautions against Lyme Disease (deer tick-borne) and West Nile virus (mosquito-borne).

Sunglasses, broad-brimmed hats and sunblock help prevent sunburn, sunstroke and heat prostration. Be sure to drink plenty of non-alcoholic liquids, especially in hot weather.

Information

California Travel & Tourism Commission, *PO Box 1499, Sacramento, CA 95812-1499; tel: (800) 862-2543 or (916) 444-4429; www. visitcalifornia.com.* California has 17 **California Welcome Centers**, listed

Opening hours

Standard office hours are Mon–Fri 0900–1700. Some tourist offices are open weekends. Most banks are open Mon–Thur 1000–1600, Fri 1000–1800, Sat 0900–1300. ATMs are open 24 hours.

Shopping malls usually open at 0900 or 1000 and close between 2000 and 2200, with shorter hours on Sun. Many restaurants, theatres and museums are closed Mon or Tue, but cinemas and most tourist attractions are open seven days a week.

Opening times and services in missions and places of worship vary widely. Call before visiting if possible.

Climate

Expect sunshine in Southern California, fog along the coast and heat inland, but uneven terrain creates a patchwork of weather patterns which cannot be explained. Summer fog can hang heavy or burn away to reveal deep blue skies and a blistering sun. Winter temperatures generally drop with altitude and the further north you go, with snow above 5,900ft. In summer, look for increasing heat inland and to the south.

with links to each location and its region, at *www.visitcwc.com*. **Nevada Commission on Tourism**, *401 N. Carson St, Carson City, NV 89701; tel: (775) 687-4322 or (800) 638-2328; www.travelnevada.com*. Annual California and Nevada visitor guides are online at the states' respective websites.

For national park, monument and seashore information, contact **National Park Service, Pacific West**, *Regional Office, 1111 Jackson St, Ste 700, Oakland, CA 94607; tel: (510) 817-1300; www.nps.gov*

For California State Parks and Beaches, contact **State of California Department of Parks and Recreation**, *1416 9th St, Sacramento, CA 95814 or PO Box 942896, Sacramento, CA 94296; tel: (916) 653-6995 or (800) 777-0369; www.parks.ca.gov*. For state park camping reservations, first check *www.parks.ca.gov* for current regulations, then contact **Reserve America CA**; *tel: (800) 444-7275; www.reserveamerica.com*

For Nevada State Parks, contact **Nevada Division of State Parks**, *901 S. Stewart St, Ste 5005, Carson City, NV 89701-5248; tel: (775) 684-2770; www.parks.nv.gov*

Packing

Take half as many clothes and twice as much money as you expect to need. Anything you can imagine is sold in California, plus some items you never thought of. Apart from a few restaurants which require business attire, dress is casual and informal, particularly in Southern California. It is a good idea to dress in layers as temperatures can change dramatically during the day, especially in the mountains and near the ocean.

Postal services

Every town has at least one post office. Most are open Monday–Friday 0900–1700 and may operate Saturday morning, closed Sunday. For stamps, consult the telephone book blue government pages under US Postal Service. Some hotels and supermarkets also sell them. Letters or parcels sent abroad should go airmail to avoid delays. Domestic letters should arrive in three to seven days.

Public holidays

The following public holidays are observed in California and Nevada: New Year (1 January); Martin Luther King Jr Day (third Monday in January); Presidents' Day (third Monday in February); Easter (Sunday in March/April); Cesar Chavez Day (31 March in California); Memorial Day (last Monday in May); Independence Day (4 July); Labor Day (first Monday in September); Nevada Day (31 October, observed last Monday in October); Thanksgiving Day (last Thursday in November and Friday following); and Christmas (25 December).

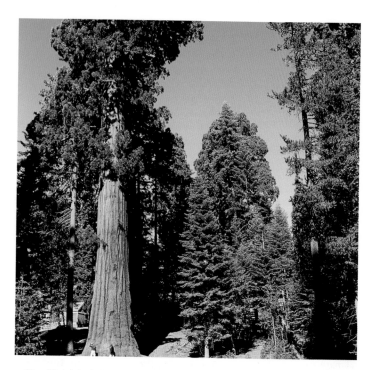

Right
Giant redwoods in Sequoia
National Park

Unofficial holidays such as the lunar Chinese New Year and Cinco de Mayo (5 May, Mexican victory against French troops) are celebrated with as much gusto as official days off.

Post offices and government offices close on public holidays, as do some businesses. Department stores hold huge holiday sales. Tourist attractions frequently have longer holiday hours. Accommodation is heavily booked in advance except for Easter, Thanksgiving and Christmas, which are usually celebrated at home.

Reading

- *Adventuring in the California Desert*, by Lynne Foster, 1997, Sierra Club Books, San Francisco.
- *California Wildlife Viewing Guide*, by Jeanne Clark, 1996, Globe Pequot/Falcon, Guilford, CT.
- *The Complete Nevada Traveler*, by David W Toll, 2008, Gold Hill Publishing Co, Virginia City, NV.
- *Moon California Hiking*, by Tom Stienstra and Ann Marie Brown, 2008, Avalon Travel Publishing, Emeryville, CA.
- *Discover Historic California: The Official Travel Guide to State Historic Landmarks and Other Historic Sites*, by George and Jan Roberts, 2004, Gem Guides Book Co, Baldwin Park, CA.

Tipping

Tipping is standard except in the very rare restaurant where a service charge is added and a tip may still be expected! Servers expect 15–20 per cent of the food and drink charge; bartenders at least $1 per drink. The traditional reward for poor service is two pennies.

Hotel porters get $1 per bag and the bellperson who shows you to your room several dollars more. Expect to pay $1–$5 for valet parking each time your car is delivered. Don't tip ushers in cinemas, theatres and similar establishments.

Casino employees depend on tips for survival. If you win, be generous with the dealer, croupier or slot-machine change person. They can't help you beat the odds, but the dealer's attitude makes the difference between a good time and simply losing money.

For casino shows without reserved seating, $5–$20 to the maître d' usually gets better seats. If you want to change, ask discreetly, bill in hand, before sitting down. Showroom servers get $5–$10 per couple for a cocktail show, $10–$20 for a dinner show.

- *The Grapes of Wrath*, by John Steinbeck, multiple editions.
- *Haunted Houses of California: A Ghostly Guide to Haunted Houses and Wandering Spirits*, by Antoinette May, 2006, World Wide Publishing/Tetra, San Carlos, CA.
- *Humbugs and Heroes*, by Richard Dillon, 2003, James Stevenson Publisher, Fairfield, CA.
- *The Laws Field Guide to the Sierra Nevada*, by John Muir Laws, 2007, Heyday Books, Berkeley, CA.
- *The Mountains of California*, by John Muir, 2008, multiple editions.
- *The Painted Ladies Guide to Victorian California*, by Elizabeth Pomada and Michael Larsen, 1991, Dutton Studio Books, New York.
- *Roughing It*, by Mark Twain, multiple editions.
- *Two Years Before the Mast*, Richard Henry Dana, multiple editions.
- *The Ultimate Hollywood Tour Book*, by William A Gordon, 2007, North Ridge Books, El Toro, CA.

Recreational vehicles

Recreational vehicles, or RVs (camper vans and caravans), are an increasingly popular way to travel. The higher cost of hiring and operating an RV is offset by savings on accommodation and meals and the convenience of not packing and unpacking at every stop. RVs are cramped, and savings evaporate if you give in to the temptation of high-priced hotels and fancy restaurant meals.

Get operating manuals and a full demonstration for *all* systems before leaving the hire company. Buy a pair of sturdy rubber washing gloves to handle daily sewer chores. Pack old clothes to wear while crawling beneath the vehicle to hook up and disconnect at each stop.

For RV information, contact **Recreation Vehicle Industry Association**, *1896 Preston White Dr, Reston, VA 20191; tel: (703) 620-6003; www.rvia.org or www.gorving.com*, and/or **Recreational Vehicle Rental Association**, *3930 University Dr, Fairfax, VA 22030-2515; tel: (703) 591-7130; www.rvra.org*

Safety and security

Dial 911 on any telephone for free emergency assistance from police, fire and medical authorities. Use normal common-sense precautions.

Safe travelling

Never discuss travel plans or valuables in public. Use the same caution in rural areas as in cities, driving, parking and walking only in well-lit areas. Don't wear expensive jewellery when walking about. A wallet in a back pocket or an open handbag are invitations to theft. Take precautions – carry bags and camera cases across your chest and keep them between your feet or on your lap in restaurants.

Above
Embarcadero Center, San Francisco

Stores

Major department store chains: Bloomingdale's, JC Penney, Macy's, Neiman Marcus, Nordstrom, Saks Fifth Avenue and Sears. Discount chains: Ross, Target and Wal-Mart. For the best prices, check the Sunday newspapers.

Time

California and Nevada are on Pacific Standard Time (PST), GMT −8. Both states jump ahead to Pacific Daylight Time (PDT), GMT −7, from the second Sun in Mar until the first Sun in Nov.

Insurance

Travel insurance should cover your belongings and your holiday investment. Buy cover for delayed or cancelled flights as well as weather problems and evacuation in case of medical emergencies.

Unwatched luggage can vanish in an instant. Some airports and bus or train stations have lockers; guard the key and memorise the locker number. Hotel bell staff may keep guest luggage for a few days, but always get receipts.

If attacked, hand over your bag or money. Resistance is likely to provoke physical harm. Report incidents to local police immediately, if only to get a report for your insurance company.

Safe driving

Car-hire counter personnel should recommend a safe, direct route on a clear map. Lock all valuables and luggage in the boot or glove box. Keep car doors and windows locked. Don't drive into unlit areas or neighbourhoods that seem unsafe. If told by a passing motorist or pedestrian that something is wrong with your car, *do not stop*. If you must stop, wait for a well-lit or populated area.

If your car breaks down, turn on the flashing emergency lights, raise the bonnet and wait inside the vehicle. Lights on emergency vehicles are red or red and blue; never stop for flashing white lights.

Have your keys out to unlock car doors before entering a car park. Check the surrounding area and inside the vehicle before entering.

Don't pick up hitchhikers or leave the car with the engine running.

Safe sleeping

Lock room doors, windows and sliding glass doors from the inside. Ground-floor rooms are convenient but easier to break into. When leaving the room at night, leave a light on to deter prowlers.

When someone knocks at the door, use the peephole to see who it is. If someone claims to be on the hotel staff, check with the front desk. Money, cheques, credit cards, passports and keys should be with you or in the hotel safe-deposit box.

Safe documents

Photocopy the important pages of your passport, visas and tickets. Carry the copies and extra passport photos separately from the documents themselves. If you are robbed, you will have identification and a head start on replacing crucial documents. To replace a passport, apply to your nearest consulate, probably in Los Angeles or San Francisco.

Shopping

Souvenirs include local wines; almonds, walnuts, dates and other dried fruits; sourdough French bread; and prepared mustards, oils and condiments. Clothing is a bargain, especially at discount stores and

National and state parks

State parks charge daily entry fees, national parks charge by the week. Camping fees are extra. If visiting several national parks, national wildlife refuges, Bureau of Land Management lands, and national forests, it would be economical to purchase a **National Parks and Federal Recreational Lands Annual Pass** for $80. *Tel: (888)-ASK-USGS (press 1); http://store.usgs.gov/pass.* California's **Annual Day Use Pass** is $125. *Tel: (866) 417-2757; www.store.parks.ca.gov/passes.aspx*

Festivals

California celebrates everything from independence (from England, 4 Jul) to garlic (Gilroy Garlic Festival, Jul) and homosexuality (Gay Pride Week, San Francisco and other cities, Jun). California Tourism lists major festivals, or check with local visitor bureaux. Street fairs and Farmers' Markets thrive on sunny weekends.

Above
The entrance to Zion National Park (Utah)

factory outlets. California state sales tax is 8.25 per cent, applicable to all purchases except food and pharmaceuticals. Local taxes can add up to 2 per cent.

Sport

San Francisco, Los Angeles and San Diego have professional sports teams. Baseball, American football, basketball, hockey and football are major draws. Cities like Anaheim, Oakland, Sacramento and San Jose also have pro teams. Tickets may be available at short notice; ask at your hotel. Tickets for training games (late summer for American football, spring for baseball) are considerably cheaper than regular season tickets. Better still are small-town minor league baseball games. The minor leagues (called Triple A or farm teams) let you see tomorrow's stars at reasonable prices in small stadiums and a relaxed atmosphere.

Telephones

Public telephones (payphones), becoming rare in the mobile phone era, are usually marked by a white telephone on a blue background. Dialling instructions are posted on the telephone or in the telephone directory. Most payphones do not accept incoming or return calls. Local calls generally cost 50¢ to $1; toll-free (800, 866, 877 and 888 area codes) and 911 (emergency) calls are free. To talk to an operator, dial 0. To locate local numbers, dial 411. For long-distance information, dial 1-(area code)-555-1212. There is a charge for all information calls. Some areas require a 1 before dialling, even for local calls.

Many hotels and motels add steep surcharges to the cost of phone calls from rooms; use a payphone in the lobby. Few phonecards or calling cards issued outside the US are accepted by US phone companies, but prepaid calling cards are widely available at supermarkets, post offices, convenience stores and tourist offices.

For international enquiries or assistance, dial 00. For international calls, dial 011 (access code) + country code + city code (omit the first zero if there is one) + local number. To call inner London, for example, dial 011-44-207-local number. If your call does not connect, check the three-digit area code in the telephone directory white pages, or dial an information telephone operator.

Fax numbers are being used less and less in this technology-savvy area. Internet cafés are widely available in urban areas and around colleges and universities. Yet so many people have or travel with computers, it may be easier to travel with your own computer or with a locally compatible, web-enabled mobile phone. Many public areas, including coffee shops, airports, hotels and convention centres – even some cities – have wireless remote connections.

Driver's guide

Automobile clubs

There are no reciprocal agreements between the AA and RAC, and the equivalent AAA in the United States. You should ensure that you purchase sufficient insurance when you hire a car.

Autoroutes and bridges

California has several toll roads: the Seventeen Mile Drive, plus others in Orange County, Southern California, and one near the Mexico border. Most bridges charge a toll in one direction, although a carpool may use a special toll-free non-stop lane. Cash is fine, but no credit cards or traveller's cheques can be used. California has a FasTrak® pass system for commuters that deducts the toll automatically when an enrolled car passes through the tollbooth area.

Documents

A national driving licence is valid in California. It must be in your possession at all times. The minimum driving age, with driver training, is 16, or 18 years of age without training. Provisional licences are not

Accidents

You must STOP after any accident. You can be in serious trouble if you don't. *Never* leave the site of the accident before contacting the required authorities and exchanging information on who is involved, addresses, telephone numbers, automobile make, licence number and registration, and insurance details. Safeguard against a secondary accident. Hazard lights, warning triangles or red emergency flares signal to other traffic that there is a problem. Call the California Highway Patrol (CHP) or local police if there are injuries or obvious damage to any vehicle. The universal emergency number is 911 to alert the police authorities or to call an ambulance or the Fire Department. On some freeways, free emergency roadside telephones are located at approximately one-mile intervals. Show police your driving licence, vehicle registration, proof of insurance and contact information. Get the names of any witnesses. Note as many details as you can – photographs can be helpful later. Death or injury must be reported to the police or the CHP within 24 hours of the accident. Collisions in California resulting in death, injury or property damage over $750 must be reported – whether or not you caused the accident – to the California Department of Motor Vehicles (DMV) within ten days on California Accident Report Form SR1. DMV offices are listed in the telephone book blue government pages under California Government. In Nevada, report collisions resulting in death, injury or over $750 in property damage to police or the Nevada Highway Patrol and to the Nevada Department of Motor Vehicles within ten days.

If your vehicle collides with a parked vehicle, leave a note with your name and contact information securely affixed to the other vehicle. For a collision with an animal, do not try to move it, but call the nearest humane society, animal control department or the police. With any accident, inform your insurers as soon as possible.

Breakdowns

If you have a breakdown, stop your vehicle on the hard shoulder, getting it as far to the right as possible. On ordinary roads, consider using the verge but beware of roadside ditches. Turn hazard lights on and raise the bonnet. Place one or more reflective warning triangles where they can be seen by other drivers travelling in the same direction. (Remember, it can be very dangerous to walk on the hard shoulder of any freeway or highway.) You and your passengers may be valid. Car-hire companies require that all drivers be at least age 25. The vehicle registration, proof of liability and collision insurance cover, with any rental care contracts, must be in the car and accessible at all times.

Drinking and driving

DUI, Driving Under the Influence of alcohol (or any other drug), is illegal. The blood alcohol concentration (limit) is not to exceed .08 per cent (.01 per cent if under 21 years of age), and is strictly enforced. Drivers suspected of drunk driving have a choice of a breath, blood or urine test; police are also likely to ask any suspect to get out of the vehicle and walk in a straight line. Refusing a test is an admission of guilt. Penalties include imprisonment for 48 hours to 6 months, a large fine and the vehicle may be impounded for six months. The law requires attendance at a DUI programme and fees for insurance and other documents.

Police establish random checkpoints, sometimes in unmarked vehicles and sometimes parked in less obvious places. Roads near winery tasting rooms and popular restaurants are closely monitored.

Essentials

You should travel with three red reflective warning triangles, road flares, a torch, a first-aid kit and a jack for tyre repair. If the vehicle has a spare tyre, make sure that it is properly inflated.

safer out of the vehicle and well up the verge away from the traffic, but for security, stay in the locked car if you are in an isolated area, it is night-time, or it is hard to see for any reason.

If you need assistance on a freeway, you may use one of the free roadside telephones to connect you with the police. You may ring for a breakdown lorry, called a tow truck, which is usually dispatched from a local petrol (gas) station. Breakdown insurance is strongly recommended and one phone call is all it takes to hand the whole problem over to an operator who is expert in sorting things out. Your insurance company may call a towing service it has under contract for emergency roadside assistance repairs or towing to a repair garage. You are responsible for payment or for signing the form that affirms to your insurance company that you have had the service. Most car-hire companies either pay for repairs directly or reimburse the cost shown on repair receipts. If a hire car is going to be out of service for more than a few hours, ask the hire company for a replacement vehicle.

Caravans and campervans (trailers and RVs)

RVs are a popular way to move around the countryside and seek the best seasonal weather. Motorhomes are just that – popular year-round with retired people, and may be ideal for holidaymakers with families on a budget, planning to have some meals in or not wanting to change lodging every night. The cost of petrol may be a consideration.

California permits motorhomes up to 45ft long on most roads and the United States has a fairly extensive system of private RV parks. Woodall's (*www.woodalls.com*) is *the* reference for 15,000 camping spots, and publishes a comprehensive guide to US facilities. Most state and national parks and national forests have RV or trailer pitches (spaces) that should be reserved as far in advance as possible. Pitches may include a small barbecue grill and a picnic table with benches. Unless otherwise marked, it is generally legal to *park* an RV or trailer along the side of a road or on city streets (although not necessarily to stay in it), but the vehicle must always be pulled off the roadway and should only be parked in a safe, preferably well-lit place in view of passers-by. Thefts and break-ins are not unknown. Official California highway rest stops permit stays of up to eight hours, but overnighting is illegal and may be dangerous. Depending on local laws, it may *not be legal to occupy a vehicle parked overnight on the side of the road or on a city street.* Check in advance with local tourism offices or the police authorities. It is always safest to spend the night in an RV park or booked camping pitch.

Maintenance takes time and attention away from touring, but it must be done. Check the RV inside and out for its condition and understand its driving controls and systems maintenance before leaving the car park. For sanitary and environmental reasons, California requires that sewage system disposal be done at authorised dump stations.

Fines

Drivers can be fined for moving violations like speeding, illegal turns or other infractions, for parking violations, and for DUI, Driving Under the Influence (of alcohol or illegal drugs). Police authorities or the highway patrol will issue a citation, commonly called a ticket, on the spot. The citation specifies the police authority, jurisdiction (city, town, county, state), legal code reference number, a short description of the violation, the vehicle reference, the police officer's badge number (identification) and name, your information if it is a moving violation, and where and how the ticket can be paid or challenged.

On-the-spot fine payments are *never* made, and anyone offering to pay a fine when cited may be assumed to be offering a bribe to a police officer, an extremely serious offence.

Citations are registered in a computer database by car licence that is linked to the vehicle identification number. The car- or RV-hire company will be notified of any citations issued to its vehicles.

Lights

All traffic must use headlights in rain, fog, snow, or when visibility is poor or unclear, i.e. less than 1,000ft ahead. Lights must be on from one half-hour after sunset to one half-hour before sunrise. Having lights on is always sensible on small country

Motorhomes, towed vehicles and any vehicle with more than two axles pay more for bridge tolls. RVs and trailers are legally considered trucks and must observe truck speed limits and other road directions, including warnings on road declines and inclines.

RVs are blown about by wind more than cars and are more subject to rollover. Taller and wider dimensions can create hazards at petrol stations, tollbooths, car parks, and with low-hanging trees and signs.

Driving in California

Sightseers take to the roads on public holidays and during the June–August school summer break.

The US has several common types of road: highways (that can be Interstate Highways or within the state); freeways (designed to speed traffic flow, although in urban areas like Los Angeles or the San Francisco Bay Area freeways do anything but); state routes (fewer traffic lanes than highways or freeways and often a more scenic way to transit between areas); rural routes (which seldom have tourist attractions); and city streets. In large cities, expect one-way streets in downtown areas.

Generally, roads are numbered, with odd numbers running north–south and even numbers going east–west. In the Los Angeles area, some freeways, though numbered, are referred to by names like the Hollywood Freeway (Hwy 101 in the Los Angeles region) or San Diego Freeway (I-405).

Interstate 5 (I-5) starts in San Diego, goes through Orange County and Los Angeles, and continues north up California's Central Valley to Oregon and beyond, an efficient route without much scenic value. I-8 from San Diego roughly follows the Mexican border. I-10, east of LA, is the way to Palm Springs and Phoenix, Arizona. From San Diego, I-15 heads north before turning northeast to wind through the desert to Las Vegas. I-80 connects San Francisco, Sacramento and Reno.

Hwy 1 is the coast route; the narrow lanes and twisting coast along Big Sur may be California's most famed scenic route. Hwy 101, the old Spanish El Camino that connected the string of 21 missions, follows some coast, but winds inland, too, for a variety of scenery from Hollywood to Crescent City. Hwy 49 serpentines through California's Gold Country.

California has almost every difficult driving condition imaginable outside the tropics. For desert travel, the air conditioner and heater should be in perfect condition. Carry extra water, food, warm clothing and a torch. Rare desert rains can cause flash floods, turning dry river beds into churning torrents in seconds. A sand- or snowstorm can reduce visibility to zero; if caught, pull off the road to a high spot and wait it out. Many passes over the Sierra Nevada Mountains are closed November–June. Open highways in snow country post signs indicating when chains must be used. The petrol tank should always or mountain roads. Driving only with parking lights is illegal. Most motorcycles will have headlights on at all times, and most cyclists will wear reflectors or have them on the bike; wearing a helmet is compulsory for both.

Mobile phones

Mobile or cell(ular) phone use while driving is illegal in California. A hands-free device is legal. A mobile phone can be useful to call for breakdown assistance, or 911 in an emergency.

Road information

For California road conditions, including closures, call Caltrans, *tel: (800) 427-7623*, for recorded information keyed to highway numbers, or check *www.dot.ca.gov/hq/roadinfo*. In some regions, such as in the San Francisco Bay Area, *tel: 511; www.5ll.org*, for travel information. For Nevada Department of Transportation Road Information, *tel: 511* or *(877) 687-6237* or check *http://safetravelusa.com/nv*. Local radio stations broadcast weather and driving information.

Seat belts

The driver and all passengers must wear seat belts. Children under the age of 6 or weighing less than 60lb must ride in National Highway Traffic Safety Administration-approved child safety seats. Infants up to 20lb or I year should have the safety seat secured to the

be half full, and winter travellers should carry warm clothing, food and water in case of traffic delays. Fog and dust storms cause massive chain-reaction collisions in the Central Valley each year. Slow down and turn the headlamps on low beam for better visibility.

Driving rules

Traffic drives on the right in the United States. Where streets meet and vehicles arrive at close to the same time, priority belongs to the vehicle on the right, and proceeds anticlockwise. Traffic already on a roundabout (traffic circle or rotary) has the right of way, and those waiting launch in whenever they can. Unless otherwise posted, in California, a vehicle can turn right from the right-hand lane. Before turning, the driver signals the intended direction, although in practice, many drivers don't bother. Horns are seldom used.

Interstate highways, highways and freeway entrances are clearly marked with green and white signs. Heavily used freeways will have a signal light to control traffic flow on to the roadway. In populous areas, the left-hand freeway lane will be marked with a white diamond for HOV (High-Occupancy Vehicle) and accommodate car pools, groups of two, three or more in a vehicle, as signposted by that fast-flow lane.

On city streets and occasionally on country roads, bicycle paths are marked as a separate lane on the right where bikes have the right of way. Buses stopping at the right side of the road and pulling out into traffic go first. A school bus stopped with flashing lights and lights at a railway crossing stop traffic as long as the lights flash.

Roadways are marked with a solid white line for 'do not pass', and with a broken line where passing is permitted. Blind curves are not infrequent, dictating slower speeds and no passing on curves.

Police use radar, lasers and aeroplanes to track, stop and cite speeding drivers. In California, pedestrians always have the right of way.

Fuel

Petrol (and diesel) is sold at gas stations in US gallons (about four litres per gallon). Most vehicles take unleaded gas, which comes in regular, premium and super grades. Buy regular unless the car-hire company or the vehicle operation manual specifies otherwise. Most gas stations are self-service, although some offer a higher-priced full-service alternative. Pump prices include all taxes. Gas stations generally accept cash, credit cards, debit cards and $20 traveller's cheques. Due to counterfeiting and safety concerns, gas station clerks will not accept $50 or $100 bills. Fuel is cheapest at budget chains and at some discount stores (usually not in tourist areas), and there is some competition, so prices can vary. Prices are reasonable off highway exits and highest in the cities where traffic flow is high and stations are back seat and be facing the rear of the vehicle. Safety seats can be hired with the car or purchased for under $100 at a discount store. In an RV, passengers riding behind the driver's seat need not wear belts, but should be safely seated when the vehicle is in motion.

Speed limits

California and the rest of the United States choose miles over metric. Kilometres appear alongside mileage on occasional highway and national park signs.

Interstate Highways – 60, 65 or 75mph (as posted)

Highways and freeways – 65mph (55mph for RVs and trailers)

In cities or towns – 25mph unless posted otherwise

Poor driving conditions – keep to a safe speed.

Road signs

European-style road signs are widely used, but not universally. *Red* signs indicate 'stop', 'do not enter' or 'wrong way'. *Yellow* signs are warnings or direction indicators. *Orange* means road repairs (roadworks) or detours (diversions). *White* shows speed limits and distances, almost always in miles. *Brown* indicates parks, camping and other recreation opportunities. *Blue* gives non-driving information such as services in a nearby town.

scarce. The cost is always shown with .9 at the end of the number, as $439.9 or $398.9. Chain gas stations stay open long hours daily, and in urban areas may operate 24 hours.

Information

The AAA has the widest map coverage in the US, though local auto club map designs mean that maps are not consistent between areas. Rand McNally also publishes map series. Local Chambers of Commerce or Convention and Visitors Bureaux will have local maps of varying quality and detail for free or for a small charge.

Parking

Street parking in downtown areas can be scarce; San Francisco has only a fraction of parking spaces per resident, and that does not include workers who commute into the city centre. Multi-storey car parks, called 'garages', indicated by a white P on a blue background, are one choice in downtown areas but can be exorbitant in major cities, as much as $20 per hour. Prices are posted at the car park entrance.

Kerbside parking time is usually limited, by either posted signs or coin-operated parking meters. Kerbs may be colour coded: *red* means no stopping or parking at any time; *white* is for passenger loading/unloading only; *green* is limited parking, usually 10 minutes; *yellow* is a commercial loading zone; and *blue* is disabled parking. Parking is not allowed within 15ft of a fire hydrant, within 3ft of a disabled kerb ramp, in bus stops, zebra crossings (crosswalks), on pavements (sidewalks) or on freeways. Fines vary from a few dollars to several hundred, depending on the infraction and jurisdiction. No police authority accepts cash on the spot to take care of the fine. Fines levied against hire cars are charged against the hirer's credit card.

Security

Sensible care should be taken, particularly where vehicles are left for long periods in vulnerable places such as tourist site car parks. Do not leave items on view inside the car. Even if you know they are of little or no value, a potential thief does not. Park in well-lit areas and double-check that the vehicle is locked.

In the large cities, it is wise to keep car doors locked and windows up. If hot weather means you must have the window open, be sure that handbags, wallets, cameras, etc. are well out of sight and reach and, above all, never on a passenger's lap. Check for intruders before getting in, especially at night and in an RV any time. Never leave the vehicle engine running when the driver isn't behind the wheel.

Should you have the misfortune to become a victim of crime, your insurers will require you to report the circumstances to the police and obtain a police report that you have done so.

TYPICAL ROAD SIGNS IN CALIFORNIA

INSTRUCTIONS

Stop	Give way	Wrong way - often together with 'No entry' sign	No right turn	No U-turn

One-way traffic | Two-way left turn lanes | Divided highway (dual carriageway) at junction ahead | Speed limit signs: maximum and maximum/minimum limits

WARNINGS

Crossroads	Junction	Curve (bend)	Winding road

Stop ahead	Two-way traffic	Divided highway (dual carriageway)	Road narrows on right	Roadworks ahead

 Railway crossing

 No-overtaking zone

Getting to California

Unless you already live within driving distance of California, flying is the most practicable way to get there. Transcontinental train and motor coach travel is slow, cramped and unpredictable, although AMTRAK operates popular coastal services from San Diego to Seattle, Washington (*www.amtrak.com*). Air travel is even more cramped, but travel time is counted in hours rather than days.

Don't undertake a full day's touring after a long flight. Los Angeles and San Francisco may be only 10–12 air hours from much of Europe and 12–14 hours from Asia, but jet lag intensifies the effects of long-distance air travel. Expect to arrive fatigued, disoriented, short-tempered and otherwise *not* ready to drive.

Night-time flights are attractive because they seem to offer an extra day of sightseeing upon arrival. Resist the temptation. Most travellers do better by timing their flights to arrive in the late afternoon or early evening, then getting a good night's sleep before tackling the sights. Since many airport-area hotels and motels offer free shuttle service to and from the airport, you can take a shuttle to the hotel, recover from the flight and pick up your hire car the next morning at no additional cost.

Many fly-drive programmes offer what looks like an easy first-day drive, such as Los Angeles International Airport to the Disneyland® area in Anaheim. It's a 45-minute jaunt that can stretch to hours in heavy rush-hour traffic. Better to rest the first night and hit the road refreshed in the morning – especially if you are not accustomed to urban traffic or driving on the right side of the road.

The reverse is equally true. Don't plan a tight schedule that gets you into Los Angeles or San Francisco and to the airport the requisite three hours before an international departure. Unexpected traffic can leave you stranded on a freeway as your plane takes off overhead. Check current security and luggage requirements with your airline before departure, and verify document requirements again, before travelling. Allow a safety margin by spending your last night in California near the departure airport, or at least in the same city. Wear comfortable clothing and shoes that can be removed for airport security inspection.

Luggage trolleys are free in the international arrivals area; in domestic terminals, a major credit card like Visa or Access/MasterCard will allow you to hire a trolley.

Currency exchange facilities will be obvious upon arrival in international airport terminals, though numerous ATMs offer the best currency exchange rates and never close. Star and Circus are the most common international ATM networks. US dollar traveller's cheques from Thomas Cook and other major issuers are accepted almost everywhere, but traveller's cheques in other currencies must generally be cashed at a bank. Personal cheques drawn on banks outside the United States are usually not accepted. Major hotel registration desk staff will usually exchange major currencies with unfavourable rates – convenient only as a last resort.

California airports don't have duty-free shopping for incoming travellers. Prices for alcohol and other duty-free items are almost always lower in California supermarkets and discount stores than in duty-free shops. The same goes for other goods. Airport prices are higher than in similar shops nearby and the selection is smaller. Airport fast-food outlets are comparable to chain outlets anywhere, but airport restaurants are generally higher in price and vary in quality, although some are memorably good.

A few car-hire companies have desks located near airport luggage-claim areas, but nearly all require that you take a coach to an off-airport facility to pick up your car. Follow terminal signs for Rental Cars to the proper coach or van loading area.

Once at the car-hire location, have your booking number, passport, credit card and driving licence ready. Everyone who might drive the vehicle must show his or her driving licence and be listed on the rental contract. Drivers must generally be at least 25 years old, although some companies allow younger drivers for an additional fee.

Setting the scene

The lure of California is as much mythical as real, but even the reality of the place borders on the unbelievable. The state, a bent rectangle 900 miles long by 200 miles wide, holds every climatic zone on earth except tropical rainforest and arctic wastes. The highest point in North America, Mount Whitney (14,494ft), and the lowest, Death Valley (282ft below sea level), are just 60 miles apart in southeastern California, but the winding 120-mile road trip between the two can take most of the day.

The state is a patchwork of awkward but awesome terrain, formed by tens of millions of years of earthquakes that have rent the landscape into a mosaic of mountains and fault lines. The biggest patch of flat land, the **Central Valley**, is 400 miles long by 50 miles wide. Nearly everything else is vertical.

California's entire coastline of 1,264 corrugated miles is hemmed in by the **Coast Range**. Southern slopes are cloaked in explosively flammable brush, northern mountains by dense forests. **San Francisco Bay** is the only break in this natural wall.

The eastern side of the state is guarded by the **Sierra Nevada Mountains**, which rise gently from the Central Valley through the rolling hills of **Gold Country** to drop precipitously down eastern slopes into the Nevada deserts. A series of east–west ranges connects the Coast Range with the Sierra, making north–south travel a slow and tortuous task before the advent of modern roads. Fifty feet and more of snow blankets the Sierra every winter, closing most mountain passes from November until June. Each spring, the run-off roars through canyons up to 5,000ft deep.

The climate is officially Mediterranean, even though the winter rain/summer drought pattern more resembles North Africa than Greece or Italy. Annual rainfall varies from less than an inch in the southeast deserts to more than 100in in the northwest. Coastal redwood forests drip with accumulated mist while the deserts wither under scorching sun and some of the highest temperatures on earth.

In the beginning

The veil of myth and hyperbole that colours California was first woven in Spain. A 1510 Spanish romantic novel created Queen Califa, ruler of an island somewhere to the west of Europe, a land filled with black Amazons who rode griffins into battle and fought with weapons of pure gold. A few years later, Spanish conquistadores ventured north after subduing Native empires in Central and South America, hoping for more conquests, more gold and more glory.

Above
Joshua Tree National Park is named after these striking trees, so called because they resemble Joshua raising his arms to heaven

What they found instead was the peninsula of lower, or Baja, California. The locals were hostile, the landscape barren and gold nowhere to be found. The would-be conquerors named the unpromising peninsula 'California', hoping that fiction would serve better than truth.

The first European to see Alta, or upper, California died there. **Juan Rodríquez Cabrillo** landed at San Diego in 1542, then broke his leg on San Miguel Island, now part of **Channel Islands National Park**, and died there, probably of gangrene. His crew sailed north as far as Oregon, then retreated back to Mexico. Spain called Cabrillo's voyage a failed and futile expedition.

Francis Drake, English privateer and later admiral, was the first European to make his fortune in California. Like many who followed, his scheme was not entirely legal but eminently successful.

Drake hunted Manila galleons, the lumbering Spanish treasure ships that sailed east from Manila each year laden with the plunder of Asia and the Philippines. The galleons sailed east to California, then turned south to Mexico and safety. Those that survived the trip were unloaded in Acapulco and other Mexican ports, their treasures transhipped to the east coast of Mexico, then sent through the Caribbean and on to Spain. Drake found the lightly armed galleons such easy prey that his ship, the *Golden Hinde*, was soon splitting from the weight of Spanish booty.

In 1579, he beached the *Hinde* for repairs, probably landing at Drakes Bay, now part of **Point Reyes National Seashore**, just north of San Francisco. Drake and his crew left a few undeniably English silver pennies behind for modern archaeologists. An engraved copper plaque claiming the land for Queen Elizabeth may or may not be authentic. Drake then sailed home to a knighthood while Spain ignored California for another 200 years.

Spain's neglect was a final reprieve for California's Native American population. Rugged terrain limited travel, but the climate was mild and food plentiful. Acorns were the staple, usually made into porridge or bread. Deer and small game were abundant. Rivers and bays were so rich in shellfish that coastal clans left heaps of discarded shells 30ft high. When the Spanish arrived in 1769, the Native American world quickly collapsed beneath the combined weight of disease, slavery and Christianity.

Gaspar de Portolá and a Franciscan friar, **Junípero Serra**, led an expedition from Baja California north to San Diego. Serra stayed in San Diego to tend the sick and establish the first of 21 missions that stretched north to Sonoma. Portolá explored north along what would become **El Camino Real**, 'The King's Highway', better known today as Hwy 101. The Spanish Empire had come to California.

An advance party climbed a ridge between today's cities of Pacifica and Millbrae and found their way blocked by an immense bay. Portolá gave up and turned south again. Juan Crespi, a monk, recorded in his diary the sighting of a bay big enough to hold all the fleets of Europe. It was the first recorded description of **San Francisco Bay**.

Portolá later sailed north with Serra from San Diego to Monterey, supposedly a fine harbour. Portolá built a presidio, or fort; Serra built another mission. More missions were founded, including San Francisco in 1776, the year the United States declared independence from England.

Spain's empire declined during the early 19th century, but the California missions prospered. Vineyards, orchards, herds and maize fields flourished. Buildings began to assume a familiar form: whitewashed stone or brick churches topped by red clay tiles and bordered by arched colonnades. Fountains cooled lush central gardens.

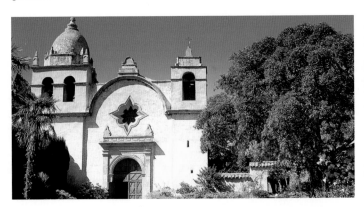

Right
Mission Carmel: San Carlos
Borromeo del Rio Carmelo
mission church

Above
Trail riders in Grand Canyon
National Park

Californios

Ecclesiastical prosperity was short lived. Mexico gained independence
from Spain in 1821. Thirteen years later, Mexico secularised and sold
the vast mission estates to cattle ranchers (*Californios*). The Church's
loss was California's gain.

The *rancho*, or ranch, became the basic social, cultural and
economic unit. This gave California a rose-tinted heritage of dashing
caballeros, gentlemen landowners, and swirling señoritas, glamorous
young women. They created one of the largest and most prosperous
pastoral societies the world has ever seen.

Californios sold 75,000 cattle hides yearly at $2 each to Yankee
traders. With no enforceable taxes, plentiful food supplies and no
need for armies, everything went to luxury imports. The caballeros
raised cattle and bought them back as Boston-made boots. Señoritas
slipped into fine Cantonese silk gowns to dance on floors of packed
dirt. English and American merchants, most of them former sailors
who had jumped ship, managed the trade.

The foreigners also managed the fur and whaling trade. New
Englanders hunted whales migrating between Alaska and Baja
California, nearly destroying every species of whale in the Pacific
Ocean, while Russians hunted sea otters to the brink of extinction
from their base at **Fort Ross**, north of San Francisco.

Furs lured English and American adventurers overland, and the
Hudson's Bay Company began California operations in 1829. In 1832,
mountain man **Christopher 'Kit' Carson** helped map a trail from
Santa Fe, New Mexico, to a lawless, dusty village called **Los Angeles**.

The first American overland immigrants arrived in 1841, the first wagon train in 1844. Then came the Donner Party, which had the misfortune to follow a guidebook written by an explorer who had never actually been to California. The party were snowbound in the Sierra near Donner Summit, on what is now I-80, from November 1846 to February 1847. Forty of the eighty-seven would-be pioneers survived by eating their livestock and their comrades.

Donner survivors arrived to find a new flag. Earlier settlers had been unhappy with a succession of weak Mexican governors, and when American Captain John Frémont 'happened' to appear in 1846 with a troop of 68 heavily armed soldiers, California's foreign population revolted. The rebels raised a flag over Sonoma carrying a star and a bear (which contemporaries said looked more like a pig) and declared the California Republic. Their new republic lasted one month.

The US declared war on Mexico in May; by July, naval units had occupied every California port and taken control of what little provincial government existed. The transition to American rule proceeded smoothly. *Californios* still ruled society and local government, foreign merchants ran the economy and there was land to spare for immigrants.

Above
Re-enacting the Gold Rush at Columbia State Historic Park

The Gold Rush

The discovery of gold in January 1848 changed California forever. The population mushroomed from 10,000 to 100,000 in two years. San Francisco metamorphosed from a windy, flea-bitten village into a city of 25,000. Gold, the first significant supply the world had seen since Spain had looted the Aztec, Inca and Maya Empires in the 16th century, gave California the economic muscle to escape exploitation by New York and London financiers. The land nurtured its own collection of robber barons and a reputation as a place of eternal opportunity.

Americans of the era seized upon California gold as evidence of Divine favour and their right to rule the continent. After all, Spain and Mexico, the world's most experienced mining countries, had owned California for 300 years without finding significant deposits of the precious metal. American James Marshall spotted nuggets in a water-wheel raceway just days before America paid Mexico $18.25 million for the entire southwestern quadrant of the continent. Miners pulled more than 30 times that much gold from California alone in less than a decade.

Most of the **49ers** sought their fortunes in what is now called Gold Country, the Sierra Nevada foothills along Hwy 49. When military officials called a constitutional convention in 1849, delegates split along regional lines. The South opposed joining the United States, rightly fearing that land, not mines, would be taxed. The North wanted statehood in order to assure a stable gold market. The northern faction won and California became a state in 1850.

The Gold Rush brought fortune to lucky miners and merchants who supplied the mines. The influx of miners from around the globe created shortages in everything from tea to tin. The American majority discriminated openly and violently against Chinese, Roman Catholics, Mexicans, Indians and anyone else who had the misfortune to be both non-American and successful.

Gold also destroyed the *Californios*. Inflation ravaged their finances as drought devastated their herds. Newly arrived Americans demanded title to the millions of hectares owned by a few hundred *Californio* families. Dubious land commissions awarded most acreage to American claimants whose best arguments were their nationality and ability to speak English.

The California Dream never faltered. As the goldfields played out, a tide of silver from Nevada brought new riches. The Comstock Lode beneath **Virginia City** produced $400 million for San Francisco mining companies before deposits were mined out in the 1880s.

Railways were even better moneyspinners. **Mark Hopkins, Collis Huntington, Leland Stanford** and **Charles Crocker,** Sacramento merchants who backed the 1863 Transcontinental Railroad, became The Big Four. The quartet built fortunes on marginal land schemes and outright fraud, but California boomed. San Francisco ruled a commercial empire that stretched from China to Utah and Alaska to Mexico.

Even the weather contributed. As gold and silver lost their lustre, farmers realised that California was the one part of North America where rain fell only in winter. Agriculture flourished, from the vegetable farms that fed the cities to the vineyards that kept them drunk. With later irrigation schemes, the pattern of summer drought and winter water made the state an agricultural powerhouse in everything from apples and cotton to potatoes and marijuana.

In the 1880s, the railway, by then called 'The Octopus' for its many-tendrilled influence in state and local politics, decided that California needed more people. Transcontinental fares fell to $1 per person just as farmers, real estate developers and the city of Los Angeles began extolling the virtues of sunny Southern California. Nature provided the sunshine, but California business designed the message, complete with alluring 'California Girl' posters.

The advent of the automobile and the fortuitous discovery of oil made the move west even easier. The burgeoning population demanded water, particularly in the desert that was most of Southern California. In 1913, Los Angeles built an aqueduct to pull water from the Owens Valley, east of the Sierra Nevada Mountains, to the parched city. The scheme was ridden with unscrupulous behaviour, corruption and scandal, as depicted in the film *Chinatown*, which was produced half a century later, but Los Angeles had the water it needed to continue growing.

Agricultural interests saw the same future in irrigation; aqueducts carried water from the Colorado River to Southern California and the Central Valley. The Great Depression of the 1930s brought waves of migrant farmers into California from dusty, drought-plagued Oklahoma and Arkansas. Many joined indigenous Mexican farmworkers who migrated to harvest seasonal crops from Southern California to the Canadian border.

When World War II erupted, California became a wartime induction and shipping centre. Thousands of men passed through San Francisco, Los Angeles and San Diego on the way to battlefields in the Pacific, while naval operations brought an influx of military personnel and support services that remained through the 1990s.

After the war

With the war over, soldiers and sailors returned in droves to settle in California's alluring coastal cities. The GI Bill provided free university education for veterans, many of whom attended the University of California in Berkeley, where much of America's atomic bomb research had been conducted. The new life and easy climate helped breed a new movement of artistic protest as beatniks flocked to the coffee houses in San Francisco's **North Beach**.

The protest movement that the Beats began spread to other segments of the population. By the early 1960s, agricultural workers, most of them originally from Mexico, began to organise against backbreaking working conditions, while university students in Berkeley began demanding more freedom of speech.

By the mid-1960s, the first post-war generation was coming of age. Higher education received state funding and was no longer the reserve of the elite. Free thinking, free speech, free sex, free drugs, free everything came together in the hippy movement, while tie-dyed clothing, flowers, beads, incense, bare feet and jeans became the trademarks of a generation. Marijuana was the popular choice of drug, eclipsing the traditional favourites – alcohol and tobacco. Music recording studios in London suddenly had to contend with serious competition from Los Angeles and San Francisco.

Escalation of America's war in Vietnam in the late 1960s again brought thousands of soldiers pouring through California. Antiwar protesters from campuses state-wide took to the streets to demonstrate against the war even as the state's aerospace, communications and electronics industries grew wealthy from military spending.

The end of the Vietnam conflict in 1973 brought yet another wave of immigration, this time from Indochina. Political turmoil in Central and South America sent new waves of Hispanic immigrants heading towards California.

Above
Golden Gate Bridge – San Francisco's world-famous engineering masterpiece

Political turmoil at home created its own refugees. In 1978, California voters approved a ballot initiative, Proposition 13, which sharply cut taxes on homes and other real estate. Government revenues plummeted. Some mental sanatoriums were emptied, homeless shelters were reduced in size or closed and funding for education, libraries, museums and other public services was slashed. Government spending was brought into line, but the number of homeless people living on California streets skyrocketed.

The decline of the Cold War in the late 1980s and early 1990s brought stagnation and economic contraction to once-booming aerospace companies, but technology firms emerged to take their place. A bucolic agricultural area near San Jose, south of San Francisco, gradually lost its old name, 'Valley of Heart's Delight'. The name by which it is now known, **Silicon Valley** (which has started to appear on maps), comes from the time when the area was home to a large number of silicon chip innovators and manufacturers. Today it is the centre of the high-tech world, as the computer revolution that began in a Palo Alto garage continues to ricochet around the globe.

Home to a vibrant electronics industry since the early 20th century, Silicon Valley is now home to many companies, including Google and eBay, featured in the Fortune 1000 – the list of America's largest companies in terms of revenue alone. Right at the heart of the valley, in Cupertino, is Apple Inc., famous for its Macintosh computers, iPod portable media players and, more recently, its iPhone.

The same combination of university research, entrepreneurial drive, venture capital and willingness to succeed that brought Silicon Valley to life also ignited other business booms: the biotechnology sector was born when an ambitious businessman, Robert Swanson, and a biology researcher, Herbert Boyer, came together to found South San Francisco's Genentech in 1976.

California corporate upstarts have emerged to challenge the likes of IBM and Microsoft. Los Angeles-based automobile designers helped Volkswagen, Nissan and Toyota to knock some of the wind out of the sails of America's own car manufacturers in Detroit.

In the real world, there's no way to know just how long the string of successes and superlatives can continue. In the half-real, half-mythical allure of California, almost no one bothers to wonder, at least not in public.

California's population has nearly doubled every generation since the Gold Rush. The reasons to come change from one generation to the next – gold, silver, farms, oil, jobs – but the hopeful waves of immigrants keep coming, certain that the California Dream will come true for them too, as it did for Austrian-born, ex-actor, Arnold Schwarzenegger, California's recent and most famous governor.

Highlights

One of the best experiences of travel is tailoring an itinerary to match your own interests and tastes. Here are some suggestions for itineraries that will show you different aspects of California, depending on how much time you have at your disposal.

The top 10 sights

Not the top 10 places currently receiving the most visitors, but the 10 that we recommend not to miss.

Anza-Borrego Desert State Park *(page 88)* California's most accessible desert.
Big Sur and the Central Coast *(page 212)* Spectacular drive along golden, surf-baptised cliffs.
Grand Canyon National Park *(page 275)* After the IMAX®, feast your imagination on the real place.
Hearst Castle® *(page 216)* Megalomania unhampered by good taste.
Greater Las Vegas *(page 262)* The ultimate theme park where the casino *always* wins.
Napa/Sonoma Wine Country *(page 152)* Scenic home to some of the world's best wines.
The Redwoods *(page 194)* The biggest living things on earth (Sequoia National Park) and the tallest (Redwood National and State Parks).
San Diego Zoo's Wild Animal Park *(page 57)* The best place in California to see exotic animals.
San Francisco *(page 132)* Everybody's favourite city.
Yosemite National Park *(page 232)* Mountain scenery so stunning it overawes you.

The best of California

These two circular tours start and end in Los Angeles, but you can reverse them or pick them up in San Francisco or elsewhere. Suggested overnight stops are in **bold type**.

Two weeks
Marathon driving in 14 days!
Day 1: Arrive in **Los Angeles**.
Day 2: LA to Barstow, Baker, Shoshone and **Death Valley**.
Day 3: Death Valley to Lone Pine, Whitney Portal and **Bishop**.
Day 4: Bishop to Lee Vining, Mono Lake and **Yosemite National Park** (Hwy 120 to Yosemite closed in winter).
Day 5: **Yosemite**.
Day 6: Yosemite to Gold Country (Mariposa, Sonora, Columbia) and **South Lake Tahoe**.
Day 7: Loop to Genoa, Carson City, Virginia City, Reno and **South Lake Tahoe**.
Day 8: Squaw Valley, Tahoe City, Sacramento and **San Francisco**.
Day 9: **San Francisco**.
Day 10: Loop to Muir Woods, Point Reyes, Jenner, Guerneville, Healdsburg and **San Francisco**.
Day 11: San Francisco to Monterey, Carmel, Hearst Castle® (advance tour booking needed) and **San Luis Obispo**.
Day 12: San Luis Obispo to Santa Maria, Solvang and **Santa Barbara**.
Day 13: Santa Barbara to Ojai, Malibu and **Los Angeles**.
Day 14: Home.

Three weeks
See most of California, Grand Canyon National Park and Las Vegas in 21 fast-paced days.

Day 1: Arrive in **Los Angeles**.
Day 2: **Los Angeles**.
Day 3: Los Angeles to **Palm Springs**.
Day 4: Palm Springs to Blythe and **Prescott, Arizona**.
Day 5: Prescott to Sedona, Flagstaff and **Grand Canyon National Park**.
Day 6: Grand Canyon to Cameron, Marble Canyon, Kanab and **Bryce Canyon National Park, Utah**.
Day 7: Bryce to **Zion National Park** (the road into Zion Canyon, Zion Canyon Scenic Drive, is closed to private traffic but accessible by free shuttle from April to October).
Day 8: Zion to St George and **Las Vegas, Nevada**.
Day 9: Las Vegas to Pahrump and **Death Valley National Park**.
Day 10: Death Valley to Lone Pine and **Bishop**.
Day 11: Bishop to Lee Vining, Mono Lake and **Yosemite National Park** (Hwy 120 to Yosemite closed in winter).
Day 12: **Yosemite**.
Day 13: Yosemite to Gold Country (Mariposa, Sonora, Columbia) and **South Lake Tahoe**.
Day 14: Loop to Genoa, Carson City, Virginia City, Reno and **South Lake Tahoe**.
Day 15: Squaw Valley, Tahoe City, Sacramento and **San Francisco**.
Day 16: **San Francisco**.
Day 17: Loop to Muir Woods, Point Reyes, Jenner, Guerneville, Healdsburg and **San Francisco**.
Day 18: San Francisco to Monterey, Carmel, Hearst Castle® (advance tour booking needed) and **San Luis Obispo**.
Day 19: San Luis Obispo to Santa Maria, Solvang and **Santa Barbara**.
Day 20: Santa Barbara to Ojai, Malibu and **Los Angeles**.
Day 21: Home.

Wine country

California has produced wine since Spanish mission days, and with Napa Valley marketing and world-judged quality in many wine regions, California is second to none in tasting-room accessibility. Microclimates produce distinctive bouquets in a vintage appellation system of AVAs (American Viticultural Areas).

San Francisco is the gateway to the **Napa Valley** and the multiple valley **Sonoma Wine Region**, and to **Mendocino**'s wineries, a further 2 hours' drive north. South of **San Francisco**, **Monterey** and **Santa Cruz** wineries can be found amid redwoods and coastal mountains. The **Sierra Foothills**, **Amador** and **El Dorado**, off Hwy 49 in Gold Country, produce rich, dry wines from volcanic soil and winter snow.

An east–west mountain range funnels fog and ocean breezes far inland to create a long, cool-climate growing season for Southern California's best vintages from **Santa Barbara** wineries, north of Santa Barbara via Hwys 154 and 246 in the Santa Ynez Valley, and the **Santa Maria Valley**, north on Hwy 101. **Edna Valley** white wines, south of **San Luis Obispo**, and **Paso Robles**'s heady reds and rich dessert wines, north of San Luis Obispo, create the flavour of summer heat in California's Central Coast region. **Temecula**, 60 miles north of San Diego, provides easy access to wine-tasting rooms amid rugged mountains enshrouded with morning fog, but gets congested at weekends.

Los Angeles

Ratings

Art	●●●●●
Museums	●●●●●
Shopping	●●●●●
Food and drink	●●●●○
Nightlife	●●●●○
Architecture	●●●○○
Children	●●●○○
Historical sights	●●●○○

A s your plane approaches Los Angeles International Airport, the flat sprawl which houses 9.9 million souls within Los Angeles County ends only at the great Pacific Ocean.

The denizens of the amorphous neighbourhoods, urban villages, slums, beach towns and creative colonies coexisting as Angelenos are an upbeat, eternally optimistic mix. Forty-eight per cent are Latino, many from Mexico; 9.4 per cent are African American; and 13 per cent have an Asian or Pacific Island heritage.

Los Angeles has a relentless beat, a constant music of car horns, computer keys tapping away in cafés, thrumming generators, beeping signs, the whoosh of espresso coffee machines, mechanised leafblowers, and the hiss of water wastefully washing pavements in this desert. Angelenos call their home El-Lay, short, snappy, abbreviated, sassy, an entertaining name, like themselves. Often faintly visible through 'haze', Los Angeles's mountains rise startlingly to the north and east. (*For Long Beach, Santa Monica and the beach cities between, see Route 4, pages 68–75.*)

Getting there and getting around

Metro *Tel: (800) 266-6883; http:// metro.net. One-day pass $5; www.metro.net/around/fares, with required $2 TAP card; www.metro.net/around/fares/ get-tap-card*

LA Inc., The Los Angeles Convention and Visitors Bureau *Tel: (213) 624-7300; www.discoverlosangeles.com* **Downtown Los Angeles Visitor Information Center** *685 S. Figueroa St between Wilshire Blvd and 7th St; tel: (213) 689-9822. Open Mon–Fri 0830–1700.*

Los Angeles International Airport (LAX) (*tel: (310) 646-5252; www.lawa.org/lax*), is 17 miles southwest of downtown. LAX Bradley International Terminal expansion continues through 2012. A taxi to downtown, fare for up to eight passengers, is $46.50. All outbound transport is on the Lower Level/Arrivals islands outside arrival baggage carousels. LAX to downtown door-to-door van service is $16 (single). The non-stop FlyAway (bus; *www.lawa.org/flyaway*) goes from LAX to Downtown Union Station, $7; Westwood, $5; Van Nuys (San Fernando Valley), $7, all cash only; and Irvine (Orange County), $25. There are free shuttles to car-hire locations and airport hotels.

AMTRAK (*tel: (800) 872-7245; www.amtrak.com*) trains pull into Union Station, where **Metrolink** (*tel: (800) 371-5465; www. metrolinktrains.com*) has weekday commuter train routes north to Oxnard, south into San Diego County, Irvine in Orange County, Riverside, San Bernardino and the San Fernando Valley. For Los Angeles County transport, there's **Metro**.

San Fernando Valley
Skirball Cultural Center
The Getty Center
VENTURA FREEWAY
SHARMAN OAKS
STUDIO CITY
Universal Studios®
Museum of the American West
VENTURA FREEWAY
GLENDALE
PASADENA
Griffith Park
Museum of Tolerance
WEST HOLLYWOOD
Hollywood
HOLLYWOOD
Santa Monica Mountains
Topanga State Park
Petersen Automotive Museum
BEVERLY HILLS
LACMA
Page Museum/ La Brea Tar Pits
Angels Flight
Elysian Park
DOWNTOWN
Grand Central Market
The Getty Villa
Will Rogers State Historical Park
Annenberg Space for Photography
Armand Hammer Museum of Art
Music Center
LA Fashion District
SANTA MONICA
PACIFIC COAST HIGHWAY
SANTA MONICA FREEWAY
Walt Disney Concert Hall
MOCA
Santa Monica Bay
California Science Center
The GRAMMY Museum
COMMERCE
VENICE
CULVER CITY
Marina del Rey
BELL

Los Angeles

Attraction
Important Building
Park
Main Road
Other Road
Railway

0   4km
0   2 miles

ℹ Hollywood Los Angeles Visitor Information Center

6801 Hollywood Blvd; tel: (323) 467-6412. Open Mon–Sat 1000–2200, Sun 1000–1900.

Port of Los Angeles Visitor Information Center Berth 93, Pacific Cruise Ship Terminal, San Pedro; tel: (310) 514-9484. Visitor Information Centers sell half-price theatre tickets, Hollywood CityPass®, etc.

◉ Go Los Angeles™Card $$

Tel: (866) 652-3053 or (617) 671-1000; www. golosangelescard.com. Discounts admission to approximately 40 attractions.

Parking

Parking meters are widely available, take change, and can be a good bargain if parking for less than one or two hours. Hourly restrictions are posted on detailed signs on the kerb and expired parking meters garner hefty fines. Downtown and in posh areas, car parks may charge several dollars per hour. For dining in any popular area, especially at night, valet parking is de rigueur, and costs $5–$20.

Driving

Traffic flows slowly during rush hour on most LA area freeways, so it may be more efficient to take major surface streets (arterials).

While much of the LA region is served by the **Metro** bus system including the five-line Metro Rail light rail and subway, not all routes are convenient for visitors; most journeys take several hours. The $0.25 **DASH** (*www.ladottransit.com/dash*) bus routes make frequent stops around Downtown LA, a terrific bargain for sightseeing – one DASH shuttle goes to the Griffith Park Observatory at weekends.

Listen to local radio stations for traffic reports, especially in the rush hours. You will also get regular weather checks.

Sights

CityPass® $$ *Tel: (888) 330-5008 or (208) 787-4300; www.citypass.com.* Offers booklets of discounted attractions for Southern California and Hollywood.

Bradbury Building *304 S. Broadway; tel: (213) 626-1893. Open to first landing daily 0900–1700.*

Angels Flight $ *Between Hill and Olive Sts, up to Bunker Hill; http:// angelsflight.com. Operates 0645–2200. 25 cents.*

Annenberg Space for Photography *2000 Avenue of the Stars, Century City; tel: (213) 403-3000; www.annenbergspacefor photography.org. Open Wed–Sun 1100–1800. Free.*

Armand Hammer Museum of Art $ *10899 Wilshire Blvd; tel: (310) 443-7000; www.hammer.ucla.edu. Open Tue, Wed, Fri & Sat 1100–1900, Thur 1100–2100, Sun 1100–1700. Free Thur.*

Downtown

Whimsical design and classic elegance got lost for decades before Downtown Los Angeles underwent extensive redevelopment and a clean-up. Once shunned as dingy and crime-ridden, today's civic centre has soaring skyscrapers, a pillar-like City Hall, a restored railway station and a wealth of architecture. The **Los Angeles Conservancy $** (*tel: (213) 623-2489; www.laconservancy.org*) offers tours of the notable monoliths, bank buildings and fine Art Deco, marble and terracotta architecture.

Stroll through the ornate Spanish Renaissance-style lobby of the three-tower 1923 **Millennium Biltmore Hotel** (*506 S. Grand Ave; tel: (213) 624-1011*), across from Pershing Square's geometric sculptures and fountain. Stop at the **Bradbury Building**, five skylit levels of graceful, intricate ironwork and an exposed lift accented by marble, tilework and polished wood. This fanciful $500,000, 1893 masterpiece is a frequent film location; Harrison Ford and androids battled here in *Blade Runner* (1982).

Shimmering white **City Hall** (*200 N. Spring St*) served as Superman's Daily Planet Building in the 1950s television series. The 1939 Spanish Mission exterior of **Union Station** (*800 N. Alameda St*) encloses the cavernous marble mosaic-lined hallway of a railway station with LAX and regional transport connections. The **Cathedral of Our Lady of the Angels $** (*555 W. Temple St; tel: (213) 680-5200; www.olacathedral. org*) is a spare, minimalist entry on the architectural scene, with free organ concerts on Wednesdays. Architect Frank O Gehry designed the curving, sweeping, stainless steel-panelled walls of downtown's most obvious landmark, the **Walt Disney Concert Hall** (*111 S. Grand Ave; www.laphil.com/philpedia/wdch-overview.cfm*), the home of the Los Angeles Philharmonic (*www.laphil.com*). The Los Angeles Opera (*www.losangeles opera.com*) performs at the Dorothy Chandler Pavilion (*135 N. Grand Ave*).

Angels Flight

The 1901 orange funicular, reopened to riders in 2010, ascends 298ft up steep Bunker Hill to the California Plaza skyscrapers, many of which have been used as action film locations.

Annenberg Space for Photography

A modern building in the midst of skyscrapers, which houses the LA cultural capital's newest, free photography display. Major exhibits change several times a year.

Armand Hammer Museum of Art

The museum houses the late entrepreneur-philanthropist's third art collection: Old Masters, Impressionist and Post-Impressionist paintings, Dürer, satirist Daumier's lithographs, and special exhibitions. The museum opens into the heart of Westwood, the **University of California, Los Angeles** (UCLA) shopping and entertainment area.

The Paley Center for Media $$$
465 N. Beverly Dr;
tel: (310) 786-1000;
www.paleycenter.org. Open
Wed–Sun 1200–1700.

California Science Center
(Exposition Park) 700
Exposition Park Dr; tel: (323)
724-3623;
www.californiasciencecenter.
org. Open daily 1000–1700.
Free except for a couple of
special rides.

Beverly Hills

Beverly Hills is a town and a state of mind, doing business within the aptly named Golden Triangle, an area bordered by N. Rexford Dr and Wilshire and Santa Monica Blvds. **Rodeo Drive's** three blocks of ultra-posh boutiques, where there are more tourists than shoppers, drip with sophistication. **Two Rodeo's** winding street of designer stores and quaint streetlamps offers a microcosm of la crème de la crème.

The film *Pretty Woman* (1990) put the **Four Seasons Beverly Wilshire** hotel (9500 Wilshire Blvd; tel: (310) 275-5200) on the must-see map. The **Paley Center for Media** is the best spot outside of the museum's New York City venue to view classic films and hear current television casts and entertainers talk about their lives and work.

California Science Center

The California Science Center and adjacent IMAX® theatre are in Exposition Park, south of Downtown Los Angeles, within walking distance of the **LA Memorial Coliseum**, central site for the 1932 and 1984 Olympiads, the **California African American Museum** (tel: (213) 744-7432; www.caamuseum.org) and the **Natural History Museum of Los Angeles County** (tel: (250) 763-3466; www.nhm.org). At the California Science Center, magenta light bathes a multi-storey entry pavilion hung with 1578 gold-leaf and palladium globes. You can balance on a bicycle suspended on a highwire, or tackle the Cliff Climb climbing wall. Check out the inner workings and appropriate sound effects of BodyWorks, featuring a 50ft-long anatomically correct female body model, named 'Tess', who discusses teenage physical strains. Explore the Ecosystems exhibit's Forest, River, Island and Extreme Zones.

Below
The California Science Center

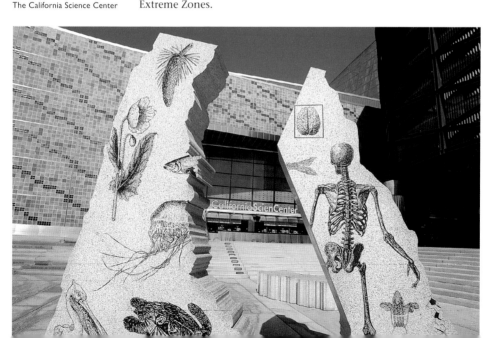

**LA Fashion
District** *(Downtown)
7th St to I-10 (Santa Monica
Fwy), Spring and Main Sts,
and San Pedro St; tel: (213)
488-1153;
www.fashiondistrict.org*

The Getty Center
*1200 Getty Center Dr,
exit from I-405; tel: (310)
440-7300; www.getty.edu.
Open Tue–Fri, Sun 1000–
1730, Sat 1000–2100. Free.
Parking $5.*

The Getty Villa
*17985 Pacific Coast Hwy,
Pacific Palisades (Malibu);
tel: (310) 440-7300;
www.getty.edu. Open
Wed–Mon 1000–1700.
Advance, timed individual
tickets required. Free.
Parking $5.*

The GRAMMY Museum
*$$ Corner of Olympic Blvd
and Figueroa St at L.A. LIVE;
tel: (213) 765-6800;
www.grammymuseum.org.
Open Sun–Fri 1130–1930,
Sat 1000–1930.*

L.A. LIVE *(Downtown)
Olympic Blvd, Figueroa St
and 11th St; www.lalive.com.
A sprawling entertainment
'campus' with live music at
the NOKIA Theatre and
Conga Room; the ESPN
Zone; GRAMMY Museum;
hotels, restaurants and the
STAPLES Center nearby.*

**Grand Central
Market** *(Downtown)
317 S. Broadway; tel: (213)
624-2378; www.grandcentral
square.com. Open daily
0900–1800. One hour free
parking with a $10
purchase.*

LA Fashion District

Vendors of everything to do with clothing and accessories sell wholesale to the trade and retail to the public. The many shops in this 90-block district offer a peek into a $24 billion industry. Merchants and designers operating from posh upper-floor shopfronts or street-level outlets employ local residents, many immigrants, to design, pattern, sew, display and sell garments, buttons, zippers, coats, dresses, scarves, bolts of cloth and almost anything that can be used to adorn the body or decorate a house. **California Market Center** (*110 E. 9th St; tel: (213) 630-3600; www.californiamarketcenter.com*) offers wide variety, as does the morning-only **LA Flower Market** (*Wall St between 7th and 8th Sts; tel: (213) 627-3696; http://laflowerdistrict.com*), the country's largest. Mannequins lurch surreally into the walkway of **Santee Alley** (*between Santee St and Maple Ave, Olympic Blvd and 12th St; tel: (213) 746-6776; www.thesanteealley.com*). The best day to find bargains is Saturday, but some wholesalers also sell samples on the last Friday of the month.

The Getty Center

Dazzling white among the brown mountains above Los Angeles, this $1 billion art museum is free and has a pleasant tram ride up, a shimmering pool in the courtyard, a stream through a central garden, inexpensive dining and an eclectic collection ranging from photographs to illuminated medieval manuscripts, paintings and decorative arts, covering 12 centuries of Western art.

The Getty Villa

Classical Greek, Roman and Etruscan art is arranged in a Greek-style villa and surrounding formal gardens above the Pacific Ocean. Advance reservations for a free visit to see more than 1,200 of the collection's 44,000 antiquities from as early as 6500 BC are required.

The GRAMMY Museum

The GRAMMY Museum is part of the **L.A. LIVE** entertainment, shopping and hotel complex near the Los Angeles Convention Center that includes the NOKIA Theatre and STAPLES Center (L.A. Lakers basketball venue). Four floors of music-related exhibits tout music technology and the winners of GRAMMY Awards.

Grand Central Market

Since 1917, Angelenos have shopped here for Mexican, Thai, Japanese, Chinese, Vietnamese, Armenian and Italian ingredients for their kitchens at home, finding exotic spices, candy and pastries, grains, rice and pastas, meat, fish, tortillas and other produce among more than 40 shops, restaurants and juice bars which wrap or dish up the freshest staples of ethnic life. Look for the bronze pig heads at the Broadway entrance, and the Angels Flight funicular across from the other S. Hill St entrance.

Griffith Park *(Griffith Park Ranger Visitor Center), 4730 Crystal Springs Dr; tel: (323) 913-4688; www.laparks.org/dos/parks/griffithpk/gp_info.htm*

Griffith Observatory *(Griffith Park) 2800 E Observatory Rd; tel: (213) 473-0800; www.griffithobs.org. Open Tue–Fri 1200–2200, Sat–Sun 1000–2200. Weekend shuttle from downtown – see website. Free. Admission for shows in the Leonard Nimoy Event Horizon theatre and the Samuel Oschin Planetarium $$.*

Travel Town Transportation Museum *5200 Zoo Dr; tel: (323) 662-5874; www.laparks.org/grifmet/tt. Open summer Mon–Fri 1000–1600, Sat–Sun 1000–1800, rest of year Mon–Fri 1000–1600, Sat–Sun 1000–1700. Free.*

Los Angeles County Museum of Art (LACMA) $$ *5905 Wilshire Blvd; tel: (323) 857-6000; www.lacma.org. Open Mon, Tue & Thur 1200–2000, Fri 1200–2100, Sat–Sun 1100–2000. Pay what you wish after 1700.*

LACMA West $$ *6867 Wilshire Blvd. Online catalogue: http://collectionsonline.lacma.org*

Griffith Park

More than 4,000 acres of green space in the Santa Monica Mountains above Hollywood are devoted to recreation and serious culture: cowboy-style at the **Museum of the American West** (*see page 46*); or pop/folk music-style at the outdoor **Greek Theatre $$$** (*Griffith Park, 2700 N. Vermont Ave; tel: (323) 665-5857; http://greektheatrela.com*). There is free science and splendid sunset-watching above the Los Angeles sprawl at the copper-domed **Griffith Observatory**. The equestrian trail paradise is augmented by the 77-acre **Los Angeles Zoo $$** (*5333 Zoo Dr; tel: (323) 644-4200; www.lazoo.org*), and fascinating railway carriages, equipment and firefighting gear at the **Travel Town Transportation Museum**. Golf courses and a merry-go-round top off the mix in this urban park.

Hollywood

This district, its name emblazoned across the dry hills, always evokes the magic of film. Stars of film, television, radio, music and the stage have been celebrated with more than 2,400 pink **Hollywood Walk of Fame** stars, embedded in the pavement on Hollywood Blvd from La Brea Ave to Vine St. Bright murals, neon lights and colourful, risqué shop windows brighten the neighbourhood and add a touch of whimsy to the pavement clutter. Hand- and footprints lure visitors to try out the stars' autographed imprints before the exotic pagoda façade of **Grauman's Chinese Theatre** (*6925 Hollywood Blvd*). (*See Route to the Stars, page 60, for more on Hollywood.*)

Los Angeles County Museum of Art (LACMA)

The western US's largest art museum always has an outstanding special exhibition. A redesign by architect Renzo Piano created an airy atrium and added the **Broad** (pronounced 'Brode') **Contemporary Art Museum** (BCAM) wing, easy to spot on Wilshire Blvd with 202 elegant lampposts installed by artist Chris Burden. The one-storey, naturally lit, glass roof-covered **Resnick Pavilion** is purpose built for special exhibitions. LACMA shares a huge block with the **Page Museum** and **La Brea Tar Pits** (*see page 47*). Among LACMA's powerhouse collections are Textiles and Costumes, a world-renowned Egyptian and Southeast Asian Art Collection, one of the most significant Islamic art collections, and the Japanese Pavilion in a building designed in the shape of a pagoda. Large outdoor sculptures whet the appetite for what's inside.

LACMA West, a transformed department store building, is a fine example of the 1930s Steamline Moderne deco architecture for which the Wilshire Blvd **Miracle Mile** is known. More than 70,000 LACMA artefacts are catalogued online.

Melrose Avenue

A decade of ultra-cool restaurants and Generation X boutique shopping has worn slightly thin around the edges of this punk-hair, black-garbed

🏛 Museum of the American West $$
(Griffith Park) 4700 Western Heritage Way; tel: (323) 667-2000; http://theautry. org. Open Tue–Fri 1000–1600, Sat–Sun 1100–1700.

Southwest Museum of the American Indian
http://theautry.org. Galleries closed for renovation until 2013.

Museum of Contemporary Art (MOCA) $$ Tel: (213) 626-6222; www.moca.org. Three locations: **MOCA Grand Avenue** 250 S. Grand Ave and **The Geffen Contemporary at MOCA** 152 N. Central Ave are open Mon & Fri 1100–1700, Thur 1100–2000, Sat–Sun 1100–1800. **MOCA Pacific Design Center** 8687 Melrose Ave, W. Hollywood. Open Tue–Fri 1100–1700, Sat–Sun 1100–1800. Free, all MOCA venues free Thur 1700–2000.

area between La Brea and Fairfax Aves. Evening dining means posh prices and handsome valets to park your auto – unless you opt for the ubiquitous American fast-food chains. Business façades sport half-sphere mirrors, shocking pink and aqua colours and flowerpot shards.

Museum of the American West

This Griffith Park museum offers a vibrant, honestly captioned collection of Western US art, artefacts and cowboy film memorabilia. Film star Gene Autry, 'The Singing Cowboy', amassed an extensive collection of cinema props, saddles, posters, cowboy costumes, boots, spurs and related 1950s-era outfits and toys for children. From the first Spanish conquerors to American wagon train expansion West, the museum doesn't shrink from the violence implied by the roomful of Colt firearms, the narrative diorama of the 'Shootout at the O.K. Corral', or descriptions of the decimation of Native Americans and buffalo. The **Southwest Museum of the American Indian**, part of the Autry National Center but closed for renovations (to be completed by 2013), has fine collections of indigenous people's artefacts amassed over 90 years that represent cultures from Alaska to South America.

Museum of Contemporary Art (MOCA)

MOCA Grand Avenue downtown venue at California Plaza (*250 S. Grand Ave*) presents an overview of the last 70 years of modern art. Large sculpture, abstract paintings, prints, multimedia and video presentations are in lower-level galleries. The cheerful brick-red building entrance is flanked by an arch. The museum's second venue, **The Geffen Contemporary at MOCA** (*152 N. Central Ave*) in a warehouse-like converted garage, is accessible from **Little Tokyo**, the heart of Los Angeles's Japanese-American community. **MOCA Pacific Design Center** (*8687 Melrose Ave, West Hollywood*) is MOCA's third venue.

Right
MOCA

🏛 Museum of Tolerance $$ *9786 W. Pico Blvd; tel: (310) 553-8403; www.museumof tolerance.com. Advance reservation suggested, tel: (310) 772-2505. Open Apr–Oct Mon–Fri 1000–1700; Sun 1100–1700; Nov–Mar Mon–Thur 1000–1700, Fri 1000–1530, Sun 1100–1700; closed Jewish and public holidays.*

Music Center *(Downtown) 135 N. Grand Ave/717 W. Temple St; tel: (213) 972-7211; www.musiccenter.org. Free tours, tel: (213) 972-4399.*

El Pueblo de Los Angeles Historical Monument *Tel: (213) 485-6855; http://elpueblo.lacity.org. Open daily 1000–1900. Sepulveda House Visitors Center open daily 0900–1500. Avila Adobe open daily 0900–1600. Plaza Firehouse Museum open Tue–Sun 1000–1500. Los Angelitas del Pueblo, 130 Paseo de la Plaza; tel: (213) 628-1274; www.lasangelitas.org/freetours.htm, offers free walking tours of the park Tue–Sat 1000, 1100, 1200.*

Chinese American Museum $ *425 N. Los Angeles St; tel: (213) 485-8567; www.camla.org. Open Tue–Sun 1000–1500.*

Page Museum/La Brea Tar Pits $$ *5801 Wilshire Blvd; tel: (323) 934-7243; www.tarpits.org. Open daily 0930–1700. Free first Tue of the month.*

Right
La Brea Tar Pits

Museum of Tolerance

The museum is a gripping introduction to – or reminder of – the effects of racism and intolerance. The World War II Holocaust is the final presentation after graphic interactive exhibits of Bosnian and Rwandan ethnic cleansing and the closer-to-home 'Final Solution' to the Jews' extermination.

Music Center

The performing arts centre is in the heart of downtown. The **Dorothy Chandler Pavilion** hosts dance companies and the Los Angeles Opera (*www.laopera.com*) while Center Theater Group cutting-edge theatre is presented in the **Mark Taper Forum** along with Broadway plays and mainstream theatre performed at the **Ahmanson Theatre**. A Jacques Lipchitz 'Peace' fountain in the courtyard constantly varies its water flow, creating the illusion of an erratic brook in the city centre. The Los Angeles Philharmonic (*www.laphil.org*) is ensconced in the modernistic, white Frank Gehry-designed **Walt Disney Concert Hall**.

Olvera Street

The pedestrian street at the heart of downtown is the centrepiece of **El Pueblo de Los Angeles Historical Monument**, where the first Spanish settlers arrived in 1781. Among the park's 27 buildings is LA's oldest, the 1818 **Avila Adobe**, perfectly restored and furnished as an 1850s *rancho*, and the **Plaza Fire House Museum**. A Mexican-style **open-air shopping arcade** has well-crafted leather goods and Mexican tourist trinkets. Restaurants serve modest, authentic Mexican food. The **Chinese American Museum**, in the only surviving structure (1890 Garnier Building) from Los Angeles's original Chinatown, is Southern California's major Chinese history museum with settlement and ethnic exhibits. The **Italian American Museum of Los Angeles**

(*http://italianhall.org*) may open in the historic Italian Hall building in 2011.

Page Museum/La Brea Tar Pits

This Hancock Park museum belies the feeling of late 20th-century construction that characterises LA. Ice Age fossils around 40,000 years old have been found in bubbling tar pits once mined for natural asphalt. After the Age of Dinosaurs, giant ground sloths, sabre-toothed cats, wolves, and at least one human, La Brea Woman, roamed the once-lush, rich land. More

ℹ **Pasadena
Convention and
Visitors Bureau** *300 E.
Green St, Pasadena; tel:
(800) 307-7977 or (626)
795-9311;
www.visitpasadena.com.
Open Mon–Fri 0800–1700,
Sat 1000–1600.*

ℹ **Gamble House $$**
*4 Westmoreland Pl,
Pasadena; tel: (626) 793-
3334; www.gamblehouse.org.
Open Thur–Sun
1200–1500, for tours.*

Norton Simon Museum
*$ 411 W. Colorado Blvd,
Pasadena; tel: (626) 449-
6840; www.nortonsimon.org.
Open Wed, Thur & Sat–Sun
1200–1800, Fri 1200–2100.*

**Huntington Library,
Art Collections and
Botanical Gardens $$$**
*1151 Oxford Rd, San
Marino; tel: (626) 405-
2100; www.huntington.org.
Open Mon, Wed–Fri
1200–1630, Sat–Sun
1030–1630, Memorial
Day–Labor Day Wed–Mon
1030–1630. Free first Thur
of the month, advance
tickets required.*

**Petersen Automotive
Museum $$** *6060 Wilshire
Blvd; tel: (323) 930-2277;
www.petersen.org. Open
Tue–Sun 1000–1800.*

**Skirball Cultural
Center $$** *2701 N.
Sepulveda Blvd; tel: (310)
440-4500; www.skirball.org.
Open Tue–Fri 1200–1700,
Sat–Sun 1000–1700.
Advance, timed-entry tickets
required for Noah's Ark at
the Skirball; check website
for procedure.*

than a million bones and several million more plant and invertebrate fossils have been recovered just outside the museum building; visible excavations of Pit 91 are ongoing in summer. A bas-relief around the building exterior depicts the world of gigantic birds, sloths, cats and mammoths. Inside, exhibits surround a garden planted with ferns and simple Ice Age-era flora. The current work of the palaeontology laboratory scientists is on view year-round.

Pasadena

Pasadena, northeast of Downtown LA (on the Metro Gold Line), is beamed into millions of homes on New Year's Day with the televised **Rose Parade** (*tel: (626) 449-4100; www.tournamentofroses.com*), which precedes the Rose Bowl American football game.

Wealthy Midwestern settlers spent the early 20th century building mansions in the balmy, orange-blossom-scented climate. The perfectly proportioned **Gamble House**, designed with dark woods and stained glass, is Craftsman architecture at its finest. This style of architecture, popularised by Gustav Stickley (1858–1941), represents a conscious departure from the excessive ornamentation of the Victorian era, and is characterised by large porches, straight lines and dark interior woods. The 1927 **Pasadena City Hall** (*100 N. Garfield Ave*) would look at home in Spain. Find designer wear and casual dining at **One Colorado** complex (*Colorado Blvd and Fair Oaks Ave; tel: (626) 564-1066; www.onecolorado.net*), one block of twenty-two in Old Pasadena.

The **Norton Simon Museum**, with its wealth of collections ranging from Picasso masterpieces to Hindu and Buddhist statues from India, Tibet and Nepal, is the marriage of a millionaire's exquisite taste with gallery display. In San Marino, close by, the **Huntington Library**, Art **Collections and Botanical Gardens** showcases fine art, medieval manuscripts, lovely gardens, a conservatory and Liu Fang Yuan (the Garden of Flowing Fragrance), a classic Chinese garden.

Petersen Automotive Museum

One of the most complete car museums chronicles LA's love affair and dependence upon the automobile. Cars of the stars, hot rods, sports cars, roadside cafés, service stations – it's all here.

Skirball Cultural Center

Known as the Skirball, this Jewish cultural centre has museum exhibits, music, film showings, live theatre and a popular café. The indoor-outdoor wooden **Noah's Ark at the Skirball** takes children and families through the biblical flood story with puppets and other depictions of 186 animal species made from recycled material.

Accommodation and food

Rooms can be found everywhere in this world metropolis. The LACVB (*see page 40*) lists a hotel reservations service but does not make bookings. To conserve time and energy, base yourself close to attractions you intend to see. Downtown, the Westside (Bel Air, Beverly Hills, West Hollywood) and Santa Monica are pricey; some Hollywood area hotels and motels, and those in less touristic neighbourhoods, are more moderate. Always ask for secure parking.

If there's a cuisine you haven't tried, LA has a restaurant that prepares it. Local newspapers and the free monthly *Where Los Angeles* magazine (*http://wherela.com*) list restaurants and review trendy newcomers.

Mel's Drive-in $ *8585 Sunset Blvd; tel: (310) 854-7201; www.melsdrive-in.com*. Serves quintessential American diner food along Hollywood's Sunset Strip 24 hours a day.

Original Pantry Café $ *877 S. Figueroa St; tel: (213) 972-9279; www.pantrycafe.com*. A downtown LA old-timer with traditional American comfort food at good prices is open 24 hours.

Chan Dara $$ *11940 W. Pico Blvd, West LA and other locations; tel: (310) 479-4461; http://chandarawestla.com*. Scrumptious Thai food – especially pad Thai noodles.

Entertainment

The Entertainment Capital of the World is rich with amusements, from high culture to pop culture to pornography. Look in the free weekly newspapers – *LA Weekly* (*www.laweekly.com*), *Los Angeles Independent* (*www.laindependent.com*), *Los Angeles Downtown News*

Right
Hollywood Boulevard

Above
Walt Disney Concert Hall,
Los Angeles

(*www.ladowntownnews.com*), *Entertainment Today* (*www.entertainmenttoday.net*) and the mainstream *Los Angeles Times* (*www.latimes.com*). Pick a neighbourhood, refer to the listings and gamble that it will be good; many of the world's best and most industrious actors, artists, musicians, comedians and creative people live in the Los Angeles area to be where the action is.

LA Stage Alliance offers half-price theatre tickets up to seven days in advance for performances around the region. See what's available and purchase tickets at *www.lastagetix.com*

Sunset Strip, Sunset Blvd in trendy West Hollywood, still offers **Whisky A Go Go** (*8901 Sunset Blvd; tel: (310) 652-4202; www.whiskyagogo.com*), with other star-making (Bruce Springsteen, Bob Marley) music venues such as **The Roxy** (*9009 W. Sunset Blvd; tel: (310) 278-9457; http://theroxyonsunset.com*) or American roots music at the **House of Blues® Sunset Strip** (*8430 Sunset Blvd; tel: (323) 848-5100; www.hob.com/venues/clubvenues/sunsetstrip*). Gay clubs are a few blocks south in West Hollywood along Santa Monica Blvd. Most comedians learn to swim upstream to live audiences in LA clubs such as **The Laugh Factory** (*8001 Sunset Blvd; tel: (323) 656-1336; www.laughfactory.com*), **The Improv** (*8162 Melrose Ave; tel: (323) 651-2583; www. symfonee.com/improv/hollywood/home/index.aspx*) and **The Comedy Store** (*8433 Sunset Blvd; tel: (323) 650-6268; www.thecomedystore.com*). Like the district, Hollywood clubs can be a little raw, attracting an audience of after-work slummers and devotees who seldom see daylight.

One of LA's best bargains is free tickets to live tapings of major television network talk shows and dramas. Book ahead online with **Audiences Unlimited** (*www.tvtickets.com*). Occasionally, location film shoots will permit visitors to watch, or filming may take place on city streets. **Warner Bros VIP Studio Tour $$$** (*3400 Riverside Dr, Burbank; tel: (818) 972-8687; www2.warnerbros.com/vipstudiotour*) and **Universal Studios Hollywood Studio Tour $$$** (*tel: (800) 864-8377; www.universalstudioshollywood.com/attraction_studio_tour.html*) offer behind-the-scenes tours.

Shopping

If it's made anywhere in the world, you can find it in Greater LA.

Dressing down and casual is almost a science. **Rodeo Drive** or the **Beverly Center** (*Beverly Blvd between La Cienega and San Vicente Blvds; www.beverlycenter.com*) in Beverly Hills are starting places for posh-conservative with touches of Academy Award gown thrown in. Other Westside hotspots are **The Grove** (*www.thegrovela.com*) and the old-fashioned, but ever-hip, produce, flower and food market with café dining, the original **Farmers' Market** (*www.farmersmarketla.com*). For the raw materials, visit the **LA Fashion District** (*see page 44*).

For art and books on cowboys and the West, the **Museum of the American West** (*see page 46*) is unparalleled. **Melrose Ave** is where the trendoids shop to be 'bad'. **Robertson Blvd** is a hip place to shop. In Venice, **Abbot Kinney Blvd** stocks boutiques with vintage clothing and one-of-a-kind togs. Hollywood Blvd at Wilcox Ave is the centre for costumes, exotic shoes, and costume and film poster shops. Peruse 'in' furniture along La Brea Ave south of Sunset Blvd and search out antiques in **Old Pasadena**. The Downtown **Toy District** (*3rd, 5th, Los Angeles and San Pedro Sts*) is crammed with toys, costume jewellery, silk flowers, DVDs and other 'finds'. Also Downtown, the **Arts District** (*6th, Wilson-Mill and Violet Sts, and the Los Angeles River*), best enjoyed in daylight for safety, is filled with warehouses and lofts, some converted into galleries, furniture and fashion designer studios, and eateries. Join the galleries' **Downtown Art Walk** (*www.downtownartwalk.com; second Thur of the month 1200–2100*). **Third Street Promenade** in **Santa Monica** (*www.thirdstreetpromenade.org/visitors/index.html*) has upmarket shops and a Farmers' Market patronised by film stars incognito within whiffing distance of the Pacific Ocean.

Suggested tours

Downtown, the **Los Angeles Conservancy Tours $** (*523 W. 6th St, Suite 826; tel: (213) 623-2489; www.laconservancy.org*) cover Art Deco, Biltmore Hotel, Broadway Movie Theatres, City Hall, Little Tokyo (Japantown), Union Station and local architecture on guided walking tours.

Drive-by tours of the stars' homes are on offer via limousine or open-top double-decker bus.

Right
Shops in Olvera Street,
El Pueblo de Los Angeles

Southern California Theme Parks

Ratings

Children	●●●●●
Theme parks	●●●●●
Architecture	●●●●○
Food and drink	●●○○○
Parks and gardens	●●○○○
Shopping	●●○○○
Wildlife	●●○○○
Art	●○○○○

If optimism and fantasy are Southern California's forte, the upbeat attitude is nowhere more evident than at amusement parks, lands of wonder for children of all ages. The secret is not to choose a park because it's famous, but because its attractions fit your interests.

Theme parks are geared for children. Disneyland® Resort, Knott's Berry Farm® and Universal Studios® Hollywood have oversized cartoon, television and film personalities strolling around the park to greet children, pose for pictures and give 'character' autographs. Baby buggies are ubiquitous, drinking fountains and other facilities are built to accommodate younger visitors, and some rides have safety in mind with posted size restrictions. Jurassic Park exists, but only as a water-soaked, high-spirited roller-coaster ride at Universal Studios® Hollywood. San Diego Zoo's Wild Animal Park is more an entertaining wildlife refuge than a traditional theme park à la Disneyland®, the Granddaddy of them all.

DISNEYLAND® RESORT

Disneyland® Resort
$$$ *1313 Harbor Blvd, Anaheim; tel: (714) 781-4565; http:// disneyland.disney.go.com. A 30-minute drive southwest of Downtown Los Angeles. Check the website for driving and parking instructions.*

Theme parks are would-be kingdoms; most conduct mandatory bag checks for security and to ensure that outside food and beverages are not consumed inside.

In 1955, Walt Disney took his flair for cinematic animation and dogged entrepreneurship beyond the Mickey Mouse film empire. Vast orange groves in Anaheim were turned into Uncle Walt's rosy-coloured concept of nostalgia, patriotism, innovation, fairy tale and adventure. More than half a century on, the original Disneyland® has grown into the Disneyland® Resort, combining two theme parks, Disneyland® and Disney's California Adventure®; a public entertainment-shopping-dining area, Downtown Disney®; and a collection of hotels.

Disneyland®

Just beyond the Main Entrance lies **Main Street, U.S.A.®**, an idealised version of small-town America from the early 20th century. Disney's first Mickey Mouse cartoon, the 1928 *Steamboat Willie*, plays at the **Main Street Cinema**. The steam locomotive-powered **Disneyland® Railroad** circles the park areas, offering a 20-minute park preview.

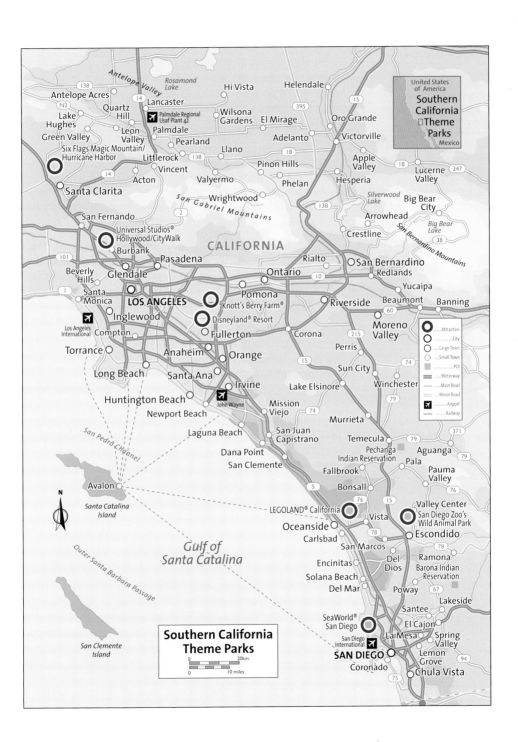

Southern California Theme Parks

Coping with queues

Summer is a hot, crowded time to visit a Southern California theme park, with long queues for rides, attractions, theme-park restaurants, refreshment stands and souvenir shops. Pack for an outing in the country or an imaginary safari, with comfortable shoes, sunhats, sunblock and a large closed bag for your camera and souvenirs. Most parks discourage or forbid outside food or drink; non-alcoholic drinks are widely available in concession to the desert-like climate and cement construction.

Adventureland stars the **Indiana Jones™ Adventure**, a spin-off from the Steven Spielberg films, that features a rough ride through an archaeological temple dig protected by the malevolent Eye of Mara – it's hard not to gulp when a boulder heads straight for your car. The **Jungle Cruise** offers a nostalgic glimpse of 1950s technology with mechanical hippos and elephants.

Fantasyland is the fairy tales come to life, anchored by Disney's signature **Sleeping Beauty Castle**. **Peter Pan's Flight, Mad (Hatter's) Tea Party** and **Pinocchio's Daring Journey** vie with dolls cavorting to the theme music of 'it's a small world'. **Frontierland** evokes the 19th century of Mark Twain with the paddle wheel Mark Twain Riverboat, rafts to **Pirate's Lair** on **Tom Sawyer Island** where children can run around, and the replica sailing ship *Columbia*.

Mickey's Toontown has attractions for the youngest. Weasels chase the macho hero bunny in **Roger Rabbit's Car Toon Spin**. **New Orleans Square** is a small land with the ghostly, old-fashioned humorous horrors of the **Haunted Mansion** and **Pirates of the Caribbean**, with an Audio-Animatronics® Captain Jack Sparrow.

Tomorrowland was rebuilt in 1998 with a retro-future look beneath an imposing Leonardo da Vinci astrolabe design transformed into a moving sculpture. **Space Mountain**, an enduring indoor coaster, **Star Tours**, Star Wars misadventures through interstellar space, and **Finding Nemo Submarine Voyage**, a yellow submarine descent into the Tomorrowland Lagoon, are the most popular attractions.

Evening parades down Main Street with fireworks over Sleeping Beauty Castle are worth waiting for, but find a vantage point early.

Disney's California Adventure® (DCA)

This Disney park is based on California, from the Golden Gate Bridge spanning the entrance to a make-believe beachfront boardwalk.

Golden Gateway is a life-sized picture-postcard entrance with California's most famous landmarks. **Soarin' Over California** puts you in a hang-glider soaring from the giant redwood forests of Northern California to the deserts of Palm Springs. On hot days, crowds head for **Grizzly River Run**, a white-water river raft ride that no one escapes dry.

a bug's land includes a popular 3-D production, *It's Tough to Be a Bug*, with rides and activities for younger children.

Paradise Pier idolises the amusement arcades that once framed beaches from San Diego to Santa Cruz. A visual icon of Disney's California Adventure® is the 150ft **Mickey's Fun Wheel**, a dual-circle Ferris wheel with Mickey Mouse's head at the centre. **Maliboomer**, a 180-ft free-fall ride, and **California Screamin'**, a wooden roller coaster that blasts from a standstill to freeway speeds in under 4 seconds, provide the adrenalin rush. Narrated by film characters, the **Toy Story Mania!** ride below the coaster pairs competitors wearing 3-D glasses to interactively take on 4-D targets.

Hollywood Pictures Backlot offers a classic Hollywood entrance beneath gilded elephants, à la D W Griffith, and 1940s-style

Disneyland's own hotels are close to the park, reflected in higher lodging prices. It may be better value to pay more for accommodation to avoid traffic congestion close to park entrances.

Parks charge $14 and up for parking, usually in covered car parks. Note your vehicle's location in the car park; it's easy to get disoriented after a long park visit. Most parks have kennel arrangements to keep pets cool and safe while their families enjoy the park.

streetscapes. **Playhouse Disney-Live on Stage!** combines 20 minutes of cartoon characters, human helpers and effects in a clubhouse stage show for little ones. **Turtle Talk with Crush** uses *Finding Nemo* film animation for a question-and-answer session with the film turtle character, Crush.

Arrive early near the Pacific Wharf area for the night-time Electrical Parade with Disney characters.

The Twilight Zone Tower of Terror™ is a thrill ride with weird apparitions who may have died in a violent storm that hit a Hollywood hotel decades ago, temperature effects, narration by the original *Twilight Zone* narrator Rod Serling, and a lurching ride up and down 13 storeys in a simulated elevator (lift) shaft.

Downtown Disney District
Disney's entertainment, shopping and dining arcade is open to the public. The winding promenade separates Disneyland from DCA and links three Disney hotels. **East Garden** is devoted to café dining and shopping. The **Wine Bar District** is filled with outdoor bar and restaurant seating. **Center Plaza** throbs with music and food from Cuba, New Orleans and Italy. **West Side Garden** features a multiplex cinema, sports bar and more cafés.

Accommodation and food in Disneyland®

Disney presents a complete holiday package with hotel and special park passes (*tel: (714) 520-7070; http://disneyland.disney.go.com*). A variety of lodging offers choices, but the trade-off for not staying at one of three official Disneyland® Resort Hotels, the **Disneyland® Hotel $$$, Disney's Paradise Pier® Hotel $$$** and **Disney's Grand Californian Hotel® $$$** (*tel: (714) 956-6425*), may be a long wait in traffic to access the park area. Hotel chains and Disney packages abound. Ask for all available discounts upon arrival.

The 'no outside food or drink' policy virtually mandates dining on pricey park fare. All lands except Toontown have at least one vegetarian outlet. The official hotels offer children **Character Dining $$$**, including **Minnie & Friends – Breakfast in the Park**.

KNOTT'S BERRY FARM®

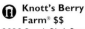
Knott's Berry Farm® $$
8039 Beach Blvd, Buena Park; tel: (714) 220-5200; www.knotts.com

America's first theme park started as a 1930s move by a berry farm family to survive the Great Depression. Chicken dinners with all the trimmings and pies are still served – more than 1.5 million annually – in a park well stocked with adrenaline-charged roller coasters, Americana and some history education. Knott's Berry Farm® includes Soak City, a summertime water park, a shopping and eating area called

Above
One of the rides at
Knott's Berry Farm®

Making the most

The cost of park admission, food, drink and souvenirs may range from $40 to $60 per person a day. It pays to research discounts on multiple-day or multiple-park passes, family discounts, senior/ pensioner discounts or auto touring club rates in advance. Various programmes include: Southern California **CityPass**® (*www.citypass.com*) for Southern California covers a combined 28 per cent discount on admission to Disneyland®, Disney's California Adventure®, Universal Studios® Hollywood, SeaWorld®, and a choice of the San Diego Zoo or San Diego Zoo's Wild Animal Park, over 14 days. If time or energy is limited, enquire if the park of your choice has guided VIP tours, a higher-priced admission which allows access to major attractions without queuing up. Behind-the-scenes views of attractions, entertainment studios, live filming and other pampering may be included.

Knott's MarketPlace, and a replica of Independence Hall, where the US Declaration of Independence was signed in 1776.

Knott's Berry Farm® has six areas. **Ghost Town** puts visitors in the Wild West, or at least a West with cowboys, gold panning, stagecoaches and *bandito* hold-ups of the **Ghost Town Calico Railroad**. The **Pony Express** coaster with a horse team theme reaches 38mph in 3 seconds. A 50ft plunge down a waterfall climaxes **Timber Mountain Log Ride**. GhostRider®, one of the longest and tallest wooden roller coasters in the world, drops 108ft over 4,533ft of track.

Wilde Water Wilderness area's **Bigfoot Rapids**® is a damp white-water river ride adjacent to a **Nature Center** which delves into Bigfoot/Sasquatch lore. Native American people present a narrative of magic and origins at **Mystery Lodge**®.

Fiesta Village has the twisting Mayan/Aztec **Jaguar**® roller coaster and **Montezooma's Revenge**®, accelerating to 55mph in 3 seconds. The South of the Border theme includes sombrero dances.

The Boardwalk Theme Park at Knott's has a roller coaster called **Boomerang** that launches riders back and forth along a half-sphere path. The biggest adrenalin charge is **Supreme Scream**®, where strapped-in riders rise 254ft skywards, then plunge to earth in 3 seconds. At 50mph, **Perilous Plunge** is a wet boat ride down a water chute. XCELERATOR™ rockets 205ft high in 2.3 seconds, then twists 90° to drop back to earth. The Charles M Schulz Theatre capitalises on the comic-strip artist's characters with a Snoopy ice show and other flash productions.

The little ones have Peanuts characters in **Camp Snoopy**®. Animals and tamer rides are reassuring, even the mini-Supreme Scream, **Woodstock's Airmail**, a 19ft rise with an air-cushioned return.

Accommodation and food at Knott's Berry Farm®

Lodging abounds because of Disneyland's proximity and Anaheim's numerous conventions. The **Anaheim/Orange County Visitor and Convention Bureau** (*800 W. Katella Ave, Anaheim; tel: (714) 765-8888; www.anaheimoc.org*) has an accommodation booking service (*tel: (800) 901-9655*).

Mrs. Knott's Chicken Dinner Restaurant $ is a park institution, the place to try fried chicken, broiled chicken, barbecued beef ribs or chicken-fried steak, veggies, rhubarb, mashed potatoes, salad or soup, endless rolls and the obligatory boysenberry pie. A steakhouse, barbecue spot, Mexican restaurant and a diner, serving pizzas and snacks, are sit-down dining alternatives.

Knott's Berry Farm Resort Hotel $$ (*7675 Crescent Ave, Buena Park; tel: (866) 752-2444 or (714) 995-1111; www.knottshotel.com*) is within the resort.

LEGOLAND® CALIFORNIA

🅛 LEGOLAND®
California $$$
*Near I-5 and Cannon Rd
interchange, Carlsbad;
tel: (877) 534-6526 or
(760) 918-5346; www.
legoland.com/california.htm*

**SEA LIFE™ Aquarium
at LEGOLAND® $$**
*Tel: (760) 918-5346; www.
sealifeus.com/carlsbad.*
The LEGO®-themed
LEGOLAND® Water Park
(www.legolandwaterpark.com)
is the latest addition.

The Danish plastic brick LEGO® Company's theme park is specifically for children aged 2 to 12. More than 40 million LEGO® bricks decorate the Carlsbad site, a beach town famed for exclusive spas and colourful flower fields. Among the main attractions are **Miniland USA**, with miniaturised versions of Las Vegas and the Daytona International Speedway, Washington, D.C., New Orleans, New York, San Francisco and the California coast; **Imagination Zone**, a LEGO® block, technology rides and play area; **Castle Hill** with **The Dragon**, a medieval-themed roller coaster, and simulated jousting and gem panning; and child-size cars, boats and helicopters in **Fun Town**, including a Volvo Driving School. **Dino Island's Coastersaurus** twists around dino models at 20mph – perfect for an introduction to roller coasters! **Pirate Shores** has a **Splash Battle** and a water drenching. Nineteen-twenties Egypt with a LEGO® Pharaoh and camel is the **Land of Adventure** theme, with lasers blasting in **Lost Kingdom Adventure**. A separate admission **SEA LIFE™ Aquarium**, with LEGO® models amid exhibits, displays water residents from the Sierra Nevada to local coastal waters in aquaria, and features numerous species feedings, including seahorses and rays.

SAN DIEGO ZOO'S WILD ANIMAL PARK

**🅛 San Diego Zoo's
Wild Animal Park**
$$ *15500 San Pasqual
Valley Rd, Escondido;
tel: (760) 747-8702; www.
sandiegozoo.org/park.*
Open-top, safari-style
Photo Caravan tours
(tel: (619) 718-3000) get
within a few feet of
animals, a superb
photographic experience
for an additional charge.

When to come

Check on opening hours.
Some parks, such as Six
Flags Magic Mountain, close
for most of the winter
season; occasionally parks
are hired for private
groups. Weekdays are less
crowded than weekends.
Arrive when the park opens
to avoid long queues and
ask for a park map for each
member of your party.
Head instantly for the most
popular attractions.

In the midst of rugged, rocky mountains 30 miles north of San Diego, lush savanna vegetation creates a scenario of blooming plants where African and Asian wildlife and birds live, relatively uncaged. Careful landscaping and the lack of obvious bars make this 1,800-acre wildlife preserve a fascinating experience on foot.

The 25-minute motorised **Journey into Africa Tour** is an excellent introduction before setting out for a gentle hike around the park. Shows include elephants, birds and rare species. Extensive botanic gardens with fuschias, epiphyllums, succulents, bonsai, native plants and conifers are connected by paths centred around the **Kupanda Falls Botanical Center** at the north end.

A large pond area shelters pink Chilean flamingos, African and other exotic birds. Gibbons, lowland gorillas, meerkats and red-ruffed lemurs have their own enclosures. The 2-mile **Kilimanjaro Safari Walk** features elephants, rhinos and other African species.

At the entrance to the stunningly accurate **Heart of Africa savanna**, pick up the brochure, a challenging guide to identification of species appearing along the route down to the main area. This is not a walk for the squeamish – fresh animal kills are consumed in front of gawking park visitors. The twisting path ends near the **Okavango Outpost**, where cheetahs loll as

Above
Grazing giraffe at San Diego
Zoo's Wild Animal Park

giraffes and other exotic species wander nearby. The **Lion Camp** savanna puts the big cats, antelope and giraffe on one side and pedestrians on the other side of a 40ft-long glass panel for mutual viewing. **Condor Ridge** shows how North America's largest bird has been saved from extinction.

SeaWorld® San Diego

SeaWorld® San Diego $$$
Mission Bay, San Diego;
tel: (800) 257-4268;
www.seaworld.com.
SeaWorld® organises same-day reservations for **Beluga** or **Dolphin Interaction** or **Dolphin Encounter** programmes for an additional fee, *tel: (800) 257-4268.*

Denizens of the oceans are in residence here, anchored by the orca (killer whale) **Believe** show, with special effects to enhance performances by Shamu and crew. Dolphins, exotic birds and human acrobats leap and fly in SeaWorld®'s latest show, **Blue Horizons.** **Journey to Atlantis** is a 6-minute ride through the lost-continent myth, eight storeys up without any sense of displacement, while accompanied by the vocalisations of a dolphin spirit guide. At the end, protected black and white Commerson's dolphins from the tip of South America are on view. On **Wild Arctic**, a simulated helicopter takes off in San Diego and lands in a North Pole scenario with polar bears, beluga whales and walruses going about their business. A plastic viewing tube protects visitors from the inhabitants of **Shark Encounter**. Bottlenose dolphins, pilot whales, sea lions, river otters and large birds perform routines, and aquaria introduce less tractable species.

Six Flags Magic Mountain/Hurricane Harbor

Six Flags Magic Mountain $$$, Six Flags Hurricane Harbor $ *Both via I-5, Magic Mountain Parkway, Valencia; tel: (661) 255-4100; www.sixflags.com.* Ask for combo tickets if visiting both parks and check for economical online specials.

These adjacent parks offer roller coasters and a water park in the Santa Clarita Valley, a half-hour's drive north of Downtown Los Angeles, but are open daily only in summer, some weekends the rest of the year.

Magic Mountain's themes include Warner Bros Superheroes and Looney Tunes cartoon characters. Want weightlessness and G force? Try **Superman: The Escape**'s 7-second acceleration to 100mph. The **Viper** loops three times vertically, flips riders over seven times, corkscrews and drops. Six Flags' thrills include X2, a roller coaster with wing-shaped cars that spin 360° as

Right
Pacific ray touch tank

riders loop and rocket through fire, fog and sound effects on a massive 3-D maze of tracks and girders, and **Déjà Vu**, which sends riders forwards and backwards along a twisted, looping inverted steel track – not recommended for the queasy. **Scream!** is another coaster with seven 360° turns, with a claim to fame that its cars are floorless. Stand up for **The Riddler's Revenge** coaster. **Tatsu** speeds at 62mph over 3,600ft of track, looping all around the park. For a breather in summer, try the **Hurricane Harbor**'s raft rides, water slides, tubing and pools.

UNIVERSAL STUDIOS® HOLLYWOOD/CITYWALK

Universal Studios®
Hollywood $$$
100 Universal City Plaza,
Universal City; tel: (800)
864-8377; www.
universalstudioshollywood.com

Metro Red Line
(www.metro.net) rail
service extends from
Downtown Los Angeles via
Hollywood to Universal City.
$1.25.

One of the world's oldest film studios is surrounded by a cinema-themed amusement park, and, unique in the Western US, includes an extensive **Studio Tour** in trams. Don't miss the perfect singing and showmanship of **The Blues Brothers® Show** concert from which the stars depart in a siren-wailing cop car.

The **Simpsons™ Ride** 6-minute motion simulator plunge through Krusty the Clown's Krustyland theme park is a 3-D everything-goes-wrong take-off from the animated television show. Dinosaurs run amok in **Jurassic Park® – The Ride**; prepare to get soaked when an enormous *Tyrannosaurus rex* dunks the ride's car. **Backdraft** re-creates the heat and fright of a raging fire. **Terminator 2® 3-D** offers a stunning integration of stunt actors, film and special effects to save the human race from cyborg imperialism. **Shrek 4-D™**, in OgreVision, uses wide-coverage glasses to show wild movements by the beloved characters of the ogre, his princess, Fiona, and the ever-talking sassy Donkey. **Revenge of the Mummy – The Ride** uses the modern *Mummy* films' creepy villain, the Egyptian priest Imhotep, and his tomb as the theme for lots of back and forth on the indoor roller coaster, darkness, and 450lb mummies in simulated freefall almost dropping on to riders. **King Kong 360 3-D** is the latest thrill, created by *Lord of the Rings* director Peter Jackson.

Universal
CityWalk $$ *Tel:*
(818) 622-4455;
www.citywalkhollywood.com.
Some clubs have a cover
charge.

Outside the park entrance gate is the free (with parking) CityWalk, a pedestrian walking, shopping, dining and entertainment complex and a multiplex cinema area. **Jillian's $$** serves burgers, pizza and comfort-food sports-bar dishes – the sports are billiards and bowling. Karaoke is often on the nightly music menu. If it catches your eye, look for the price tag – every piece of art on display is for sale. The **Hard Rock Cafe Hollywood $$** green and white guitar looms near the domed white restaurant building close to the car park entrance. The **Saddle Ranch Chop House $$** serves up steaks, a dance floor, live music, an outdoor patio for barbecuing and 100 screens for viewing the latest sports matches. The car park fee may be refundable with purchase of a cinema ticket. **Gibson Amphitheatre** (*tel: (818) 622-4440*) is the place to take in top pop bands and headliners.

Route to the Stars

Ratings

Star-spotting ●●●●●

Scenery ●●●●○

Architecture ●●●○○

Beaches ●●●○○

Children ●●●○○

History ●●●○○

Museums ●●●○○

Shopping ●●○○○

Star-struck! Hollywood conjures up images of sleek blonde starlets in form-fitting satin gowns wearing enormous sunglasses, impossibly handsome actors in evening wear, tyrannical directors, champagne, red convertibles and black limousines, Oscars, larger-than-life heroes and an industry that conveys eternal life upon the chosen. Hollywood, the place, can be shockingly unkempt.

The film (and television) industry has never been physically limited to Hollywood; it has worked, lived and played all over Southern California. The chances of seeing a 'movie' star are best at a location shoot in the Greater Los Angeles area, and probably worst during the popular guided tours of the Homes of the Stars. Like everyone else, stars like to eat, drink and dance at trendy restaurants and clubs, shop for bargains, stroll in supermarkets and walk in parks. Most tolerate autograph seekers only when they are 'on', made up and dressed to meet their fans and satisfy the needs of a publicity circus to promote their careers. Don't overlook luck and chance – a star may run through the airport to catch a flight or go flower shopping at a local Farmers' Market – providing you with your personal sighting and a unique story to take home.

BEVERLY HILLS

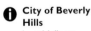 **City of Beverly Hills**
www.beverlyhills.org

Beverly Hills Conference and Visitors Bureau 239 S. Beverly Dr, Beverly Hills; tel: (800) 345-2210; www.beverlyhillsbehere.com

L.A. Westside Tourism Partnership (Beverly Hills, Marina del Ray, Santa Monica, West Hollywood)
www.westla.com

Beverly Hills has mansions, shopping and an aura of luxury few communities can match (*see Los Angeles, page 40*). **The Paley Center for Media** (*495 N. Beverly Dr; tel: (310) 786-1000; www.paleycenter.org*) covers the television and live performance industry, but star buffs will enjoy the **Polo Lounge** at the **Beverly Hills Hotel** (*9641 Sunset Blvd; tel: (310) 276-2251; www.beverlyhillshotel.com*) for the feeling of *luxe* and the power of moneymen doing deals for films. The **Four Seasons Beverly Wilshire** hotel (*9500 Wilshire Blvd; tel: (310) 275-5200*) was the setting for *Pretty Woman*.

Rodeo Drive Shops have back doors for stars' privacy, but hotel spas and hair salons cater to everyone, guests, patrons and celebrities alike. Well-heeled and celebrity shoppers find vintage designer clothing used by stars for the Academy Awards ceremony from **Lily et Cie** (*9044 Burton Way; tel: (310) 724-5757*) – *not* for casual shoppers or browsers!

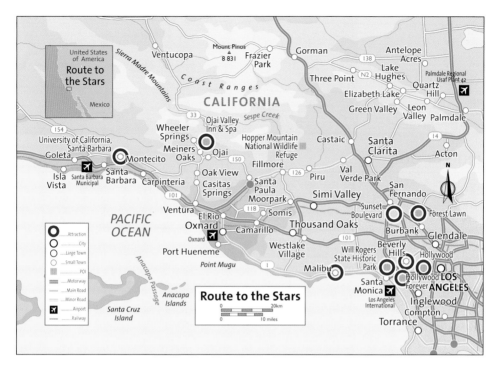

Westwood Village Memorial Park and Mortuary (*1218 Glendon Ave at Wilshire Blvd, behind a car park, Westwood; tel: (310) 474-1579*) is a peaceful cemetery where Marilyn Monroe and other stars are interred.

FOREST LAWN AND HOLLYWOOD FOREVER

Forest Lawn Memorial Park Hollywood Hills 6300 Forest Lawn Dr, Los Angeles; tel: (800) 204-3131; www. forestlawn.com. Open daily 0800–1700.

Hollywood Forever 6000 Santa Monica Blvd, Hollywood; tel: (323) 469-1181; www.hollywoodforever.com

Forest Lawn Memorial Park Hollywood Hills is another spot to see the stars, or rather their memorial tablets and a few opulent crypts. Bette Davis's (*Courts of Remembrance*) white marble maiden belies the crusty epitaph, 'She Did It The Hard Way'.

Hollywood Forever cemetery has buried entertainment industry folk for more than a century, including Rudolph Valentino, Cecil B DeMille, Douglas Fairbanks, Sr and Jayne Mansfield. **Cinespia** (*www.cinespia.org*) holds summertime cemetery alfresco screenings of classic films, free (parking $5) for picnickers who bring their own blankets, pillows, food and drink.

Right
Dolores del Rio, one of the many Hollywood stars that never die

HOLLYWOOD

Metro Red Line
(www.metro.net) rail service extends from Downtown Los Angeles via Hollywood to Universal City.

Holly Trolley
(www.ladottransit/other/ trolley) designed for Hollywood clubbing, operates Thur–Sat 1830–0230. $1.

LA INC., The Los Angeles Convention and Visitors Bureau Tel: (800) 228-2452; www. discoverlosangeles.com
Hollywood Los Angeles Visitor Information Center 6801 Hollywood Blvd, Hollywood and Highland complex, Hollywood; tel: (323) 467-6412. Open Mon–Sat 1000–2200, Sun 1000–1900.

Hollywood Chamber of Commerce 7018 Hollywood Blvd, Hollywood; tel: (323) 469-8311; www.hollywoodchamber.net

L.A. Westside Tourism Partnership (Beverly Hills, Marina del Rey, Santa Monica, West Hollywood)
www.westla.com

Tinseltown's glitter still shines some, but don't expect to see stars hanging out on Hollywood Boulevard. Politicos, businesspeople and developers have begun pouring money into Hollywood as a spot where history museums offer more than thin T-shirts, Maps of the Stars' Homes and a bus-bound whirl outside the gates of purported stars' mansions. Several historic Art Deco theatres have been restored and reopened as film palaces; Hollywood history-related museums supplement the oddity carnivals presented by Guinness®, Ripley's and the inevitable wax museum.

The **Capitol Records Building** (*1750 Vine St*) is a 1956 landmark, 13 storeys piled like long-playing records on a turntable. It has gold records on display in the lobby, but offers no tours.

The **Egyptian Theatre** (*6712 Hollywood Blvd; tel: (323) 466-3456; www.egyptiantheatre.com; tours tel: (323) 461-2020*) was Hollywood's original 1922 Art Deco film palace, taking fanciful advantage of interest in the Near East in the year Howard Carter discovered King Tutankhamen's tomb. American Cinematheque's two film theatres show avant-garde, career tribute, foreign and independent films. The Egyptian hosted Hollywood's first film premieres. Filmgoers can admire the elaborate Egyptian décor until portable acoustic walls move into place as films begin. *Forever Hollywood*, a documentary film, is screened sporadically, usually at weekends.

El Capitan Theatre (*6838 Hollywood Blvd; tel: (818) 845-3110; http://disney.go.com/disneypictures/el_capitan*), restored by Disney to its original 1926 Art Deco splendour, is where Orson Welles's 1941 *Citizen Kane* premiered.

Hollywood Boulevard Walk of Fame (*Hollywood Blvd, from La Brea Ave to Vine St; Vine St from Yucca St to Sunset Blvd*), a 1960s marketing gimmick to stud the pavements with stars, has turned into an enduring icon. More than 2,400 pink terrazzo stars honour stars of film, stage, television, radio, music and a few odd choices such as the Apollo XI astronauts. Caution: tourists searching for stars can wander off kerbs!

Popular stars include:

Charlie Chaplin	*6751 Hollywood Blvd;*
Cary Grant	*1610 Vine St;*

Hollywood Entertainment District Tel: (323) 463-6767; www.hollywoodbid.org. Has a Visitors Guide and Map.

LA INC.'s Hollywood Los Angeles Visitor Information Center is in the complex. Tel: (323) 467-6412.

Hollywood Bowl Museum 2301 N. Highland Ave; tel: (323) 850-2058; www.hollywoodbowl.com/visit/museum.cfm. Open summer Tue–Sun; rest of year Tue–Fri, call for hours. Free.

The Hollywood Museum $$$ 1660 N. Highland Ave; tel: (323) 464-7776; www.thehollywoodmuseum.com. Open Wed–Sun 1000–1700.

Hollywood Wax Museum $$ 6767 Hollywood Blvd; tel: (323) 462-5991; www.hollywoodwaxmuseum.com/hollywood. Open daily 1000–2400.

Hollywood and Highland 6801 Hollywood Blvd at Highland; tel: (323) 467-6412; www.hollywoodandhighland.com

Alfred Hitchcock	*6506 Hollywood Blvd;*
Anthony Hopkins	*6801 Hollywood Blvd;*
Michael Jackson	*6927 Hollywood Blvd;*
John Lennon	*1750 Vine St;*
Marilyn Monroe	*6774 Hollywood Blvd;*
Mickey Mouse	*6925 Hollywood Blvd;*
Elvis Presley	*6777 Hollywood Blvd;* and
Ringo Starr	*1750 Vine St.*

Hollywood Bowl Museum showcases the music and performing arts in the **Hollywood Bowl** (*www.hollywoodbowl.com*), Tinseltown's quarter-sphere outdoor concert hall, with recordings of performances.

The Hollywood Museum uses the old 1935 Art Deco Max Factor make-up studios building to display costumes, props, posters and film-making equipment illustrating Hollywood eras from silent film to technological wizardry.

Hollywood Forever (Cemetery), adjacent to Paramount Studios, is the resting place for many who never went far away after making it big (*see p61*). LifeStories using touch-screen technology are for visitors dying to know more about those interred recently.

The first venue for the Academy Awards in 1929, **Hollywood Roosevelt Hotel** (*7000 Hollywood Blvd; tel: (323) 466-7000 or (800) 950-7667; www.hollywoodroosevelt.com*) is so rich with Hollywoodiana, it's haunted, allegedly, by Montgomery Clift playing a bugle in Room 928 where he practised when filming *From Here to Eternity*. Refurbishment has again transformed the one-time haunt of Clark Gable, Carole Lombard and Marilyn Monroe into a trendy scene, with poolside cabanas around a David Hockney pool.

The **Hollywood Sign** (*Mount Lee, Griffith Park; www.hollywoodsign.org*), seen from many Hollywood streets, is closed to visits from the public. Real-estate developers created a 'Hollywoodland' sign in 1923 with 4,000 light bulbs to promote a new housing estate; the decrepit sign was restored to its current 50ft height in 1978, having lost the 'land' early on.

Hollywood Heritage Museum $ (*2100 N. Highland Ave, across from the Hollywood Bowl; tel: (323) 874-2276; www.hollywoodheritage.org. Open Wed–Sun 1200–1600*), devoted to the silent film era, is in Hollywood's first major film studio, the Lasky-DeMille Barn.

Hollywood Wax Museum shows how stars like Sean Connery and Johnny Depp, crooners like Elvis and legends like Marilyn would look if eternally preserved in paraffin.

Hollywood and Highland complex hosts the Academy Awards ceremony in the Kodak Theatre. The entertainment complex also includes a hotel, shopping mall, cinema, bowling, restaurants and clubs.

Grauman's Chinese Theater (*6925 Hollywood Blvd; tel: (323) 464-8111*), Hollywood's best-known building, premiered Cecil B De Mille's *King of Kings* when it opened in 1927. The fanciful red and green pagoda tower presides over a courtyard of hands, feet and other

Ripley's Believe It or Not! Hollywood
$$ *6780 Hollywood Blvd;
tel: (323) 466-6335;
http://hollywood.ripleys.com.
Open daily 1000–2400.*

Madame Tussauds Hollywood $$ *6933
Hollywood Blvd;
tel: (323) 798-1670. Open
Mon–Thur 1000–2000,
Fri–Sat 1000–2200.*

body parts (such as Betty Grable's leg) imprinted in cement (see *www.manntheatres.com/chinese/forecourt.htm* for a map of impressions). Original owner Sid Grauman is the target of many inscriptions, some suggestive, a few lewd, most laudatory. The cinema shows first-run films; tours are conducted daily (*tel: (323) 463-9576*).

Pantages Theatre (*6233 Hollywood Blvd near Vine St; tel: (323) 468-1770; www.broadwayla.org*), an ornate 1930 Art Deco film palace, now presents Broadway musicals. A dinosaur and clock mark **Ripley's Believe It or Not! Hollywood** collection of curiosities, including a portrait of John Wayne rendered in laundry lint. **Madame Tussauds Hollywood** wax museum features Denzel Washington, Jennifer Lopez and Uma Thurman, along with classic actors like James Dean and Clark Gable.

Small, 1.9 square-mile **West Hollywood** claims pride of place with Southern California's largest gay/lesbian population, and many services, hotels, eateries and clubs are found on *www.gogaywesthollywood.com*

West Hollywood Marketing and Visitors Bureau *8687 Melrose Ave, Ste M-38, West Hollywood; tel: (800) 368-6020* or *(310) 289-2525; www.visitwesthollywood.com*

Suggested tours

Getting close to the stars and the action is the name of the game. The film industry has increased security for its stars and productions, somewhat curtailing spectators' chances of seeing the magic of filming.

Occasionally, location film shoots will permit visitors to watch; filming may take place on city streets; or another alternative is a film studio tour or tapings of major network TV shows (*see page 50*).

Where is a better spot to attend a film festival but where the industry lives and breathes? Major film festivals include:

Los Angeles, Italia Film, Fashion & Art Fest (*www.losangelesitalia.com*) pays homage to the Italian version of film-making in February–March.
Indian Film Festival in Los Angeles (*tel: (310) 364-4403; www.indianfilmfestival.org*) brings the subcontinent to LA in April.

Below
Universal Studios®, Hollywood

Los Angeles Film Festival (*tel: (866) 345-6337; www.lafilmfest.com*) hosts 85,000 film folk and aficionados in June.
Los Angeles Latino International Film Festival (*tel: (323) 469-9066; www.latinofilm.org*) is on in October.
OUTFEST (Los Angeles Gay and Lesbian Film Festival) (*tel: (213) 480-7088; www.outfest.org*) has its major screenings in July, with year-round events in the area.
Los Angeles International Short Film Festival (LA Shorts Fest) (*tel: (323) 461-4400; http://lashortsfest.com*) has shown films as short as 58 seconds long, in July.
American Film Institute (AFI) **Fest** (*tel: (866) 234-3378; www.afi.com/onscreen/afifest*) has been in a powerhouse venue in November since 1971.

MALIBU

ⓘ Malibu Chamber of Commerce
23805 Stuart Ranch Rd, Suite 100, Malibu; tel: (310) 456-9025; www.malibu.org

Twenty-one miles of coastline, mostly beaches, stars' homes and pricey restaurants along the Pacific Coast Highway (PCH), is flooded every few years. Despite the instability of homes subject to mudslides, stars have flocked here since 1929, when PCH's opening led a developer to create a stars' hideaway. Those $2,600 beach cottages are now worth millions.

Adamson House (*23200 PCH, Malibu Lagoon State Beach; www.adamsonhouse.org*) incorporates locally made, late 1920s decorative tiles. In the Adamson House, the **Malibu Lagoon Museum** covers Native American, Malibu Colony and tile history with guided house tours (*tel: (310) 456-8432. Open Wed–Sat 1100–1400*). Just east near Malibu Pier is **Malibu Surfrider Beach. Leo Carrillo State Park** (*Mulholland Hwy at Hwy 1; tel: (818) 880-0363*) is named after a comic actor who was a conservationist, working to preserve California's parks and open spaces, and a great-grandson of California's last Mexican governor.

Point Dume State Beach (*access via Westward Beach Rd*), with **Paradise Cove** nearby, is a rugged landscape of golden sands and black rock cliffs close to largely concealed stars' homes. A trail climbs 250ft above the beaches for a 32-mile view of Santa Monica Bay to Palos Verdes and California gray whale migration, which lasts from December to March. Just west is the long strand of **Zuma Beach. Broad Beach**, 5 miles north, is celebrity row, well guarded, but accessible on a public footpath at 31346 Broad Beach. (*For more Malibu attractions, see Los Angeles, page 40.*)

MONTECITO

Montecito (Santa Barbara) is where stars, directors and technicians get away from the industry, or retire to semi-tropical foliage, nurseries, oak groves, flowering vines and horse trails. Watch for stars who have become spectators in Santa Barbara at **Center Stage Theater** in **Paseo Nuevo** (*www.centerstagetheater.org*) or the 1931 **Arlington Theatre** (*1317 State St; tel: (805) 963-4408; www.thearlingtontheatre.com*), a film palace decorated as a Mexican village with a ceiling of painted stars that also hosts music concerts and a University of California, Santa Barbara, lecture series.

OJAI

ⓘ Ojai Valley Chamber of Commerce 201 S. Signal St, Ojai; tel: (805) 646-8126; www.ojaichamber.org. Call for hours.

Director Frank Capra saw sunset pink on the Los Padres Mountains around Ojai, and captured it as Shangri-la in the 1937 film *Lost Horizon*. Stars, writers and artists have liked this mountain town, 15 miles and a world away from the Pacific Ocean, as a getaway since the 1920s. **Spa Ojai** at the **Ojai Valley Inn & Spa** (*Country Club Rd; tel: (805) 646-1111 or (888) 697-8780; www.ojairesort.com*) enhances a smart golf resort and mimics the white Spanish architecture so copied by early films.

SUNSET BOULEVARD

Also known as the **Sunset Strip**, this line of clubs and hotspots stretches from 7800 to 9200 Sunset Blvd in West Hollywood. The atmospheric, celebrity-heavy **Viper Room** (*8852 Sunset Blvd; tel: (310) 358-1881; www.viperroom.com*), and **The Roxy** (*9009 Sunset Blvd; tel: (310) 278-9457; http://theroxyonsunset.com*) are well-known over-the-top music joints. Make the scene for the latest in chic slumming or clubbing. **Melrose Ave** (*see Los Angeles, page 45*) is three-quarters of a mile south. In between is the gay/lesbian mecca along Santa Monica Blvd. Posh **Chateau Marmont** (*8221 Sunset Blvd; tel: (323) 656-1010; www.chateaumarmont.com*) has hosted legions of stars, from Monroe and Garbo to Mick Jagger.

WILL ROGERS STATE HISTORIC PARK

Will Rogers State Historic Park (*1501 Will Rogers Park Rd, Pacific Palisades; tel: (310) 454-8212*) shows the good taste, 1924–35 home, stables and polo field of the beloved humorist, broadcaster and actor Will Rogers. Ranch House tours are offered Thursday–Sunday (*tel: (310) 454-8212 ext. 103*), and the Will Rogers Polo Club plays April–October weekends. The heavily used park has easy-to-rugged hiking trails in the Santa Monica Mountains, many with fine views to Downtown Los Angeles and Santa Monica Bay. Will Rogers is also remembered at **Will Rogers State Beach** (*Pacific Palisades/Santa Monica boundary; tel: (310) 305-9503*) and as Beverly Hills' first mayor at **Will Rogers Memorial Park** (*9650 Sunset Blvd across the street from the Beverly Hills Hotel*).

Suggested tour

Total distance: 125 miles.

Time: 4 hours non-stop, but a stop in Ojai is less frantic.

Links: Los Angeles (*see page 40*). At Pacific Palisades, turn south on Hwy 1 to Santa Monica (*see Southern California Beaches, page 68*). Go north at Santa Barbara for **Big Sur and the Central Coast** (*see page 212*).

Route: Take Hollywood Blvd west at Vine St to **La Brea Ave ❶**, turn left two blocks, then right on Sunset Boulevard to Pacific Palisades. Go right on Hwy 1, **Pacific Coast Hwy ❷**, past MALIBU beaches and **celebrity houses ❸** and inland to **Oxnard ❹**. Go west on Hwy 101 at **Montalvo/Ventura ❺**. Take the Hwy 33 exit to OJAI ❻. Return 3 miles west on Hwy 33, then take Hwy 150 past **Lake Casitas ❼**. Continue northwest on Hwy 192, the scenic back road via MONTECITO ❽ to **Santa Barbara ❾**.

Also worth exploring

Mulholland Dr/Mulholland Hwy (with one detour at Encino to Hwy 101 going west; exit Hwy 101 to Topanga Canyon Blvd (south) to rejoin the **Mulholland Scenic Drive**) winds west for 55 miles over the spine of the Santa Monica Mountains from Hwy 101 at Cahuenga Pass (Mulholland Dr exit) to **Leo Carrillo State Beach** in Malibu (*see page 65*). Rugged mountains, ranches, canyons and mansions reflect the area called home by many stars. State and regional parks, along with exclusive houses and the odd golf course, make for an incongruous mix of scenery and recreation.

Several major routes from the coast bisect the long, west–east stretch of Los Angeles's approximation of a national park, the **Santa Monica Mountains National Recreation Area** (**Visitors Center**, *401 W. Hillcrest Dr, Thousand Oaks; tel: (805) 370-2301; www.nps.gov/samo. Open daily 0900–1700*). **Topanga Canyon Blvd, Malibu Canyon Rd/Las Virgenes Rd** and **Kanan-Dume Rd** all offer vistas as they approach their summits before plunging northwards into the San Fernando and Conejo Valleys to Hwy 101.

Paramount Ranch
*2903 Cornell Rd,
Agoura Hills; www.nps.gov/
samo/planyourvisit/
paramountranch.htm*

Paramount Ranch, set up in 1927 as a Western film set, is still used for many television productions. False building façades are boarded up between productions, with each of several blocks having a complete saloon, marshal's office, general store and livery stables, for flexibility.

Southern California Beaches

Ratings

Amusements	●●●●●
Beaches	●●●●●
Children	●●●●○
Scenery	●●●●○
Sport	●●●●○
Food and drink	●●●○○
Wildlife	●●●○○
Museums	●●○○○

In Hollywood mythology, life is a beach, and nowhere on earth has as much beach as Southern California. From the heart-throb days of the Annette Funichello and Frankie Avalon *Gidget* beach films to the feel-good bounce of the Beach Boys, Southern California has been associated with broad sandy crescents, curling waves and a carefree life where problems are as ephemeral as tomorrow's sandcastle.

But Southern California is *not* all beaches. Cliffs intrude, providing spectacular viewpoints to watch the coast, migrating whales and surfers. Piers and harbours break up the coastline, sheltering massive ocean freighters as well as solitary sailing boats. Offshore oil wells and natural oil seeps dribble bits of petroleum that wash up as tar, sticking to feet and bodies.

But for residents as well as visitors, life in Southern California really is a beach. It doesn't matter that beaches can be crowded, the water cold, the parking impossible or the sunburn painful. The sand is waiting, the surf is up and true love could be just over the next crest.

CARLSBAD

ⓘ Carlsbad Convention and Visitors Bureau (CVB) *400 Carlsbad Village Dr; tel: (760) 434-6093 or (800) 227-5722; www.visitcarlsbad.com. Open Mon–Fri 0900–1700, Sat 1000–1600, Sun 1000–1500.*

ⓜ Museum of Making Music $ *5790 Armada Dr; tel: (760) 438-5996 or (877) 551-9976; www.museumofmakingmusic.org. Open Tue–Sun 1000–1700.*

Carlsbad is known mostly for the commercial Flower Fields® at Carlsbad Ranch $$ (*east of 1-5, Palomar, Airport Rd and Paseo del Norte; tel: (760) 431-0352; www.theflowerfields.com. Open Mar–mid-May daily 0900–1800*), which burst into colour when 50 acres of ranunculus flowers are in bloom. One of Carlsbad's major attractions is a theme park, **LEGOLAND® California** and the **adjacent SEA LIFE™ Aquarium** (*see page 57*). The CVB publishes self-guided maps of historical landmark buildings and extensive collections of public art. The **Museum of Making Music** has changing exhibits on the history and making of musical instruments and an assortment of real instruments – many electrified – to test your musical skills.

Surfers and scuba divers congregate off **South Carlsbad State Beach** (*tel: (760) 438-3143*). Watch the action from the bluffs above the beach.

Further south is **Batiquitos Lagoon** (*7380 Gabbiano Ln; tel: (760) 931-0800; www.batiquitosfoundation.org*), an extensive wetlands restoration project. A 1½-mile trail departs from the Nature Center.

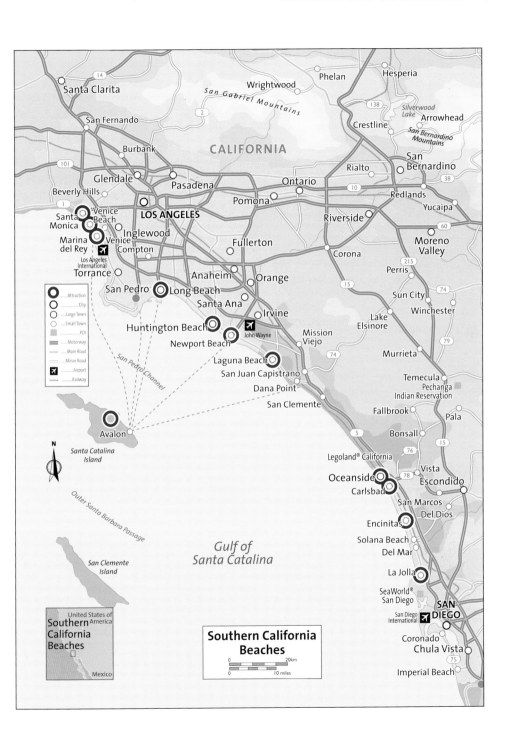

Food in Carlsbad

Carlsbad Mineral Spring Water Spa $ *2802 Carlsbad Blvd; tel: (760) 434-1887; www.carlsbadmineralspa.com.* Offers spa services based on its carbonated mineral water, which comes from a well fed by a 1,700ft-deep aquifer; anyone can bring a bottle and sample the water from vending machines.

Tip Top Meats $ *6118 Paseo Del Norte; tel: (760) 438-2620; www.tiptopmeats.com. Open daily 0600–2000.* A popular local breakfast and lunch stop with good picnic supplies and, of course, meat!

ENCINITAS

ⓘ **Encinitas Chamber of Commerce Visitor Center**
859 2nd St; tel: (760) 753-6041 or (800) 953-6041; www.encinitaschamber.com. Open daily 1000–1600.

ⓜ **Lux Art Institute**
$$ 1550 S. El Camino Real; tel: (760) 436-6611; www.luxartinstitute.org. Open Thur–Fri 1300–1700, Sat 1100–1700.

The town of Encinitas is a flower-growing centre, filled with commercial nurseries and spectacular private gardens. **The Paul Ecke Ranch**, which produces 50 per cent of the world's poinsettias, put Encinitas on the map. **San Diego Botanic Garden** (*230 Quail Gardens Dr; tel: (760) 436-3036; www.sdbgarden.org. Open daily 0900–1700*) is 35 acres planted with exotics from around the world, including some quite local: native plants once used by Kumeyaay indigenous people living in the region.

Encinitas's serenity convinced the **Self-Realisation Fellowship** (*215 K St and 1st Ave; tel: (760) 753-2888; www.yogananda-srf.org*) to set up an ashram, with quiet cliffside **Meditation Gardens** (*216 K St*) just around the corner. The popular surfing beach below, one of eleven in Encinitas, is called 'Swami's'. Scuba divers can explore the East Marine Life Refuge, off Swami's. The **Lux Art Institute**, in the Encinitas hills, hosts one artist-in-residence at a time to display finished work and while working on a commissioned piece for permanent installation at the facility.

HUNTINGTON BEACH

ⓘ **Huntington Beach Marketing and Visitors Bureau**
301 Main St, Ste 208; tel: (714) 969-3492 or (800) 729-6232; www.surfcityusa.com. Open Mon–Fri 0900–1700.

Nicknamed 'Surf City' by 1950s surfers, Huntington Beach is also one of the largest cities in Orange County. The beach stretches 8½ miles, backed by a paved cycling, skating and walking path. Hwy 1, usually called **PCH** (Pacific Coast Highway), is lined with parking meters. The Huntington Beach Pier extends 1,800ft over the Pacific Ocean, a waterfront focal point.

A favourite local surfing spot is just south of the concrete pier. The **International Surfing Museum** (*411 Olive Ave; tel: (714) 960-3483; www.surfingmuseum.org. Open Mon–Fri 1200–1700, Sat–Sun 1100–1800*) is filled with photos and old-time surfing gear. Main St is lined with outdoor cafés and coffee houses. Little Saigon has many Vietnamese restaurants, shops and businesses.

Bolsa Chica (*tours, tel: (714) 840-1575; www.amigosdebolsachica.org*), north of Huntington Beach, is a 1,200-acre salt marsh and home to endangered bird species. There are over 200 species using these restored wetlands.

LA JOLLA

🅘 Promote La Jolla
tel: (858) 454-5718;
www.lajollabythesea.com

La Jolla Visitor Center
7966 Herschel Ave, Ste A;
tel: (619) 236-1212;
www.sandiego.org. Open daily,
call for hours.

🅗 La Jolla Cave Store
$ 1325 Coast Blvd;
tel: (858) 459-0746;
www.cavestore.com. Open
daily 0900–1700.

**Salk Institute for
Biological Studies** 10010
N. Torrey Pines Rd; tel: (858)
453-4100, ext. 1287;
www.salk.edu. Architectural
tours Mon–Fri 1200 by
reservation. Free.

**Museum of
Contemporary Art San
Diego** $$ 700 Prospect St;
tel: (858) 454-3541; www.
mcasd.org. Open Thur–Tue
1100–1700. (MCASD also
has a downtown location,
1100 and 1001 Kettner Blvd,
San Diego.)

Torrey Pines Gliderport
2800 Torrey Pines Scenic Dr;
tel: (858) 452-9858;
www.flytorrey.com

This upmarket San Diego neighbourhood is a mosaic of coves and cliffs battered by the surf. Most of the coastline is protected in public parks and beaches, popular with seals and human visitors. Art galleries cluster along **Prospect St**; new exhibitions usually open on Friday evenings.

La Jolla Cove, just off Prospect St, is popular with snorkellers; **Scripps Park**, beside the cove, attracts sun-worshippers and artists trying to capture views along the cliffs. Just north are seven caves; **Sunny Jim Cave** is accessible through **La Jolla Cave Store**.

The **Salk Institute for Biological Studies** is housed in a spectacular pair of buildings overlooking the Pacific Ocean.

Museum of Contemporary Art San Diego (MCASD La Jolla) was built as the palatial Scripps family home in 1916. The museum specialises in emerging California artists, with an outdoor sculpture garden.

Birch Aquarium at Scripps $$ (*Scripps Institution of Oceanography, 2300 Expedition Way; tel: (858) 534-3474; www.aquarium.ucsd.edu. Open daily 0900–1700*) features ocean life from the entire Pacific Ocean. **Torrey Pines State Natural Reserve** (*N. Torrey Pines Rd; tel: (858) 755-2063; www.torreypine.org. Open daily*) protects the only surviving mainland forest of Torrey pines (*Pinus torreyana*) on an isolated bluff fringed by cliffs popular with paragliders. The **University of California, San Diego** (*9500 Gilman Dr; tel: (858) 534-2117; http://stuartcollection.ucsd.edu*) has the **Stuart Collection of Sculpture** scattered about the campus. Don't miss *Vices and Virtues*, flashing neon around the top of the Charles Lee Powell Structural Systems Laboratory; Niki de Saint Phalle's *Sun God*, a colourful bird opposite Peterson Hall; and Alexis Smith's *Snake Path*, best seen from the **Central Library** upper floors.

LAGUNA BEACH

**🅘 Laguna Beach
Visitors Center** 381
Forest Ave; tel: (949) 497-
9229 or (800) 877-1115;
www.lagunabeachinfo.com.
Open daily 1000–1700.

🅗 Festival of Arts $$
650 Laguna Cyn Rd;
tel: (949) 494-1145 or (800)
487-3378; www.foapom.com

Laguna Beach spawned one of California's first artistic organisations, the Laguna Beach Art Association. There are some 90 galleries and studios, and three annual art festivals. The July–August **Festival of Arts** draws 200,000 visitors, most to see the 'Pageant of the Masters', live tableaux reproducing famous classical paintings.

The coastline is scalloped with beaches separated by rugged cliffs. **Crescent Bay Point Park** (*off Crescent Dr*) offers striking views across the bay. **Heisler Park** (*north of the Art Museum*) is the beginning of a pleasant path to **Main Beach** (*foot of Broadway*), the town's largest beach. The **Laguna Art Museum** $$ (*307 Cliff Dr; tel: (949) 494-8971; http://lagunaartmuseum.org*) specialises in modern art in California.

LONG BEACH

ℹ Long Beach Area Convention and Visitors Bureau
One World Trade Center, Ste 300; tel: (800) 452-7829 or (562) 436-3645; www.visitlongbeach.com. Open Mon–Fri 0800–1700.

Ⓜ The Metro Blue Line (www.metro.net) runs from Los Angeles to Long Beach.

▢ Aquarium of the Pacific $$$
100 Aquarium Way; tel: (562) 590-3100 or (888) 826-7257; www.aquariumofpacific.org. Open daily 0900–1800. A combined same-day ticket package with the Queen Mary is cheaper.

Once a tawdry military town, Long Beach, America's largest container port, has 6 miles of uncluttered sandy beach stretching southeast from Rainbow Harbor. The easiest way to explore the waterfront attractions is by **AquaBus** water taxi, or AquaLink catamaran to Alamitos Bay (*www.lbtransit.com/Services/Aquabus.aspx*). For downtown attractions, hop on the free Passport shuttle.

The incredibly clear tanks of the **Aquarium of the Pacific** re-create local temperate waters, the subarctic Bering Sea and coral lagoons from Micronesia. Don't miss the outdoor touch tanks, Shark Lagoon or the Lorikeet Forest aviary.

Belmont Shore (*along 2nd St, southeast of downtown; www.belmontshore.org*) is a restored 1920s district, with boutiques, galleries, bookshops and restaurants. **Pine Avenue**, Long Beach's restored city centre, lined with early architecture, restaurants and boutiques, is great for people-watching.

The former luxury liner the **Queen Mary $$$** (*1126 Queens Hwy; tel: (877) 342-0738; www.queenmary.com. Open daily 1000–1700*) is moored across Queensway Bay from the Aquarium of the Pacific. It has been fitted out as a hotel, with many of the elegant first-class areas refurbished for tours. A Russian **Foxtrot submarine $$$** (*1126 Queens Hwy; tel: (562) 432-0424; www.russiansublongbeach.com*), next to the Queen Mary, is also open for tours (*1000–1700*).

Shoreline Village (*fronting on Rainbow Harbor; tel: (562) 435-2668; www.shorelinevillage.com*) has waterfront shopping and entertainment.

MARINA DEL REY

ℹ Marina Del Rey Convention and Visitors Bureau Visitors Center 4701 Admiralty Way; tel: (310) 305-9545; www.visitmarinadelrey.com. Open daily.

This immense marina about 5 miles north of LAX is lined with expensive restaurants known mostly for their harbour views. Find day cruises on or near Admiralty Way. Cafés and restaurants line Washington Blvd, near Venice Pier in nearby Venice (*see page 74*).

NEWPORT BEACH

Above
Volleyball on Laguna Beach

Miles of beaches line **Balboa Peninsula**. **Balboa Pavilion** (*400 Main St; tel: (800) 830-7744; www.balboapavilion.com*) was once the terminus for a tourist trolley line from Los Angeles and now has fishing charters, dining, and the *Catalina Flyer* (*tel: (800) 830-7744; www.catalinainfo.com*) to Santa Catalina Island (*see opposite*). The **Balboa Fun Zone** (*600 E. Bay Ave, www.thebalboafunzone.com*) has a Ferris wheel, carousel, shops and restaurants. Have a Balboa Bar, chocolate-dipped square vanilla ice cream on a stick garnished with candy or nuts. The **Newport Harbor Nautical Museum $** (*at the Balboa Fun Zone; tel: (949) 675-8915; www.nhnm.org*.

❶ Newport Beach Conference and Visitors Bureau *1200 Newport Center Drive, Ste 120; tel: (949) 719-6100 or (800) 942-6278; www.visitnewportbeach.com. Open Mon–Fri 0800–1700.*

Open Wed–Sun 1000–1700 or 1800) has a superb collection of ship models and an ocean creature touch tank.

Marinas along Newport Bay boast one of the largest concentrations of pleasure boats in America, while **Upper Newport Bay Ecological Reserve and Nature Preserve** (*tel: (949) 640-6746; www.newportbay.org*) is at the bay's north end. Only very experienced bodysurfers head for the challenging Wedge (beach). Early risers shop at the Newport Pier where Dory fishers sell their fresh catch.

OCEANSIDE

❶ Oceanside Visitor Information Center *928 N. Coast Hwy; tel: (760) 722-1534; www.oceansidechamber. com. Also a California Welcome Center, tel: (800) 350-7873 or (760) 721-1101. Open daily 0900–1700.*

Oceanside hosts several national surfing competitions each year. The free **California Surf Museum** (*312 Pier View Way; tel: (760) 721-6876; www.surfmuseum.org. Open daily 1000–1600)* displays some vintage surfboards, a few blocks from the **Oceanside Pier**, which stretches more than 900ft into the Pacific. The **Buena Vista Audubon Nature Center** (*2202 S. Coast Hwy; tel: (760) 439-2473; www.bvaudubon.org. Call for hours)* explores the mouth of the San Luis Rey River. **Mission San Luis Rey de Francia** (*see page 260*) is 4 miles inland.

SANTA CATALINA ISLAND

❶ Catalina Island Chamber of Commerce *1 Green Pier, Avalon; tel: (310) 510-1520; www.catalina.com or www.visitcatalinaisland. com. Open daily, hours vary.*

❶ Casino *1 Casino Way, Avalon; tel: (310) 510-7400; www.catalina.com or www.visitcatalinaisland.com. Open daily.*

Twenty-one miles off the coast from Long Beach, Catalina Island (as it's usually referred to) is a vision of Southern California before LA. Nearly 90 per cent of the island is undeveloped, a mix of sandy beaches and crumbling cliffs. Organised tours take in the interior, Pacific Ocean views, underwater fish from glass-bottom boats or semi-submersibles, flying fish at night, and the Avalon Casino.

The Art Deco **Casino** overlooking the harbour in Avalon, Catalina's one real town, was a summer escape for Hollywood stars during the 1930s and 1940s; the interior murals are stunning.

Access Catalina by water from Dana Point, Long Beach, Marina del Rey, Newport Beach or San Pedro.

SANTA MONICA

❶ Tide Ride *(www.bigbluebus.com/ miniblue/tide.html) is Santa Monica's inexpensive downtown public transit bus.*

A walking pier, carousel, two upmarket malls, a palm-lined beachfront park and youthful style make Santa Monica an oceanside version of what Hollywood would like to be. **Montana Avenue** (*7th–17th Sts; www.montanaave.com*) is an area of trendy shops and restaurants. **Palisades Park** (*cliff top along Ocean Ave*) provides convenient benches to watch the sunset.

Santa Monica Pier (*end of Colorado Ave; tel: (310) 458-8900; www.santamonicapier.org*) features a carousel, arcades, restaurants, an

ⓘ Santa Monica Visitor Center *1920 Main St, Ste B, Santa Monica; tel: (800) 544-5319 or (310) 393-7593. Open daily 0900–1730.*

Palisades Park Santa Monica Visitor Kiosk *1400 Ocean Ave; tel: (310) 393-0410. Open daily summer 0900–1700; winter 1000–1600.*

Santa Monica Third Street Promenade Visitor Information Cart *Between Arizona Ave and Santa Monica Blvd; www.santamonica.com. Open daily 1100–1600.*

amusement park and the **Santa Monica Pier Aquarium $** (*1600 Ocean Front Walk; tel: (310) 393-6149; www.healthebay.org/smpa*).

Third Street Promenade (*Third St, Wilshire Blvd–Broadway; http://thirdstreetpromenade.org*) is an outdoor pedestrian mall with fountains, dinosaur topiary and cafés. **Santa Monica Place** (*315 Colorado Ave; www.santamonicaplace.com*) is the latest upmarket mall.

Santa Monica has many Farmers' Markets (*www01.smgov.net/farmers_market*); top locations are **Arizona between Second and Third Sts** (*Wed 0830–1330, Sat 0830–1300*), **Virginia Avenue Park** (*Sat 0800–1300*) and **Main St at Ocean Park Blvd** (*Sun 0930–1300*).

The **Ocean Park** area in south Santa Monica by Venice is anchored by the popular galleries, coffee houses and eateries on **Main St. Bergamot Station** (*2525 Michigan Ave; www.bergamotstation.com*) in east Santa Monica is renowned for its galleries and exhibitions, including the **Santa Monica Museum of Art $** (*3100 Airport Ave; tel: (310) 586-6488; www.smmoa.org. Open Tue–Sat 1100–1800*). The **Museum of Flying $** (*tel: (310) 398-2500; http://museumofflying.com*) has more than 20 vintage aircraft not far from LAX.

VENICE

ⓘ LA INC., The Los Angeles Convention and Visitors Bureau (LACVB) *Tel: (213) 624-7300; www.discoverlosangeles.com*

Venice was laid out as a replica of the Italian city. The beach scene revolves around **Venice Boardwalk**, a winding path packed with an ever-changing crowd of exhibitionists, jugglers, fire-eaters, musicians and magicians. **Muscle Beach** (*south of Windward Ave and 19th Ave*) is a legendary outdoor body-building studio. **Abbot Kinney Blvd** (*www.abbotkinneyonline.com*) is a trendy shopping and dining strip.

Suggested tour

Below
Toning up at the Muscle Beach gym in Venice

Total distance: 250 miles.

Time: One long day, or 3–4 days with stops.

Links: San Diego to the south, LA to the north, and Route to the Stars (*see page 60*).

Route: From **LA JOLLA ❶**, follow La Jolla Blvd north to Hwy S21 north of the **Salk Institute ❷** and through **Torrey Pines State Reserve ❸** to **ENCINITAS ❹**, where Hwy S21 becomes Hwy 101, to **CARLSBAD ❺**, **OCEANSIDE ❻** and I-5. Continue north through **Camp Pendleton ❼** to **San Clemente ❽**.

Take the Hwy 1/El Camino Real/Pacific Coast Highway exit from I-5. Drive north through **Orange County ❾** to **LAGUNA BEACH ❿**, **NEWPORT BEACH ⓫** and **HUNTINGTON BEACH ⓬**. Follow Hwy 1 through to **LONG BEACH ⓭** and **Santa Monica Bay ⓮**. Hwy 1 turns inland through **Los Angeles International Airport** (LAX) **⓯** to skirt **MARINA DEL REY ⓰** and **VENICE ⓱**, then goes north to **SANTA MONICA ⓲**.

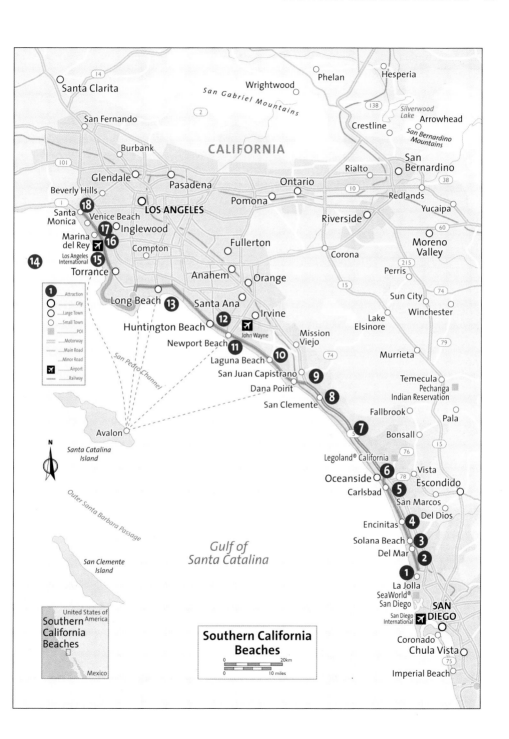

Santa Clarita

San Fernando

Burbank

CALIFORNIA

Glendale
Beverly Hills
Santa
Monica
Pasadena
Venice Beach
Inglewood
Marina
del Rey
Compton
Los Angeles
International
Torrance

LOS ANGELES
Pomona

Anaheim
Orange

Fullerton

Long Beach
Santa Ana
Huntington Beach
Irvine
John Wayne
Newport Beach
Laguna Beach
San Juan Capistrano
Dana Point
San Clemente

Mission
Viejo

Wrightwood
Phelan
Hesperia

San Gabriel Mountains

Silverwood
Lake   Arrowhead
Crestline
San Bernardino
Mountains

Rialto
San
Bernardino

Ontario
Redlands
Yucaipa

Riverside
Corona
Moreno
Valley
Perris

Sun City   Winchester
Lake
Elsinore
Murrieta

Temecula   Pechanga
Indian Reservation
Fallbrook   Pala

Bonsall

Legoland® California
Oceanside   Vista
Carlsbad   Escondido
San Marcos
Del Dios
Encinitas
Solana Beach
Del Mar

La Jolla
SeaWorld®
San Diego
San Diego
International
SAN
DIEGO
Coronado
Chula Vista
Imperial Beach

N

Santa Catalina
Island

Avalon

Outer Santa Barbara Passage

San Pedro Channel

San Clemente
Island

Gulf of
Santa Catalina

1 ......Attraction
O ......City
O ......Large Town
O ......Small Town
   ......POI
   ......Motorway
   ......Main Road
   ......Minor Road
   ......Airport
   ......Railway

United States of
America

Southern
California
Beaches

Mexico

Southern California
Beaches

0   20km
0   10 miles

San Diego

Museums	●●●●●
Architecture	●●●●○
History	●●●●○
Art	●●●○○
Children	●●●○○
Food and drink	●●●○○
Shopping	●●●○○
Beaches	●●○○○

San Diego is as tropical as California gets. Bright sun and ocean breezes combine with the influence of Mexico, 20 miles south, to concoct a casual, easy-going atmosphere in California's second-largest city. Visually, San Diego is uncongested; homes and businesses do not pile above or against one another.

East over the mountains is desert; north along the coast are round, eroded cliffs and golden sand beaches. Coronado Island offers resort dining and shopping a few minutes from Downtown San Diego. Mission Bay has beaches, SeaWorld® San Diego and marinas filled with pleasure boats. Downtown bustles with business, gracefully proportioned high-rises lining the waterfront. Ten inches of annual rainfall encourage alfresco dining most of the year.

While San Diego thrives on tourism and manufacturing, a military presence still defines the city. California's first city was founded in 1769 by soldiers seeking to settle this little-explored area to thwart economic incursions by Russian fur traders – while Spanish Franciscan friars simultaneously Christianised the local native peoples. Mexico ruled from 1821 until 1847, when the United States took over.

Getting there and getting around

ⓘ San Diego Convention and Visitors Bureau (CVB)
2215 India St;
tel: (619) 232-3101;
www.sandiego.org

International Visitor Information Centers
Downtown: 1040 1/3 West Broadway and Harbor Dr, across from the Cruise Ship Terminal; tel: (619) 236-1212. Open daily Jun–Sept 0900–1700; Oct–May 0900–1600. La Jolla: 7966 Herschel Ave at Prospect. Call for hours.

San Diego is 120 miles south of Los Angeles; allow three hours to drive from downtown to downtown, more during rush hour. For information on traffic hotspots tune into a local radio station.

San Diego International Airport, Lindbergh Field (SAN) (tel: (619) 400-2400; www.san.org), is 3 miles north of Downtown. A taxi to downtown is $12. San Diego 511 (for bus, trolley, Coaster tel: 511; www.511sd.com) bus No 992 'The Flyer', runs every 10 minutes, $2.25. Hotel and other shuttles also operate from between Terminals 1 and 2. Pick up car-hire shuttle vans from via a skybridge to ground transport islands outside arriving baggage areas.

Parking
Downtown meters are inexpensive. Horton Plaza offers three hours' free parking with any mall purchase, an alternative to valet parking at trendy 5th Ave restaurants. Seaport Village has two-hour validation.

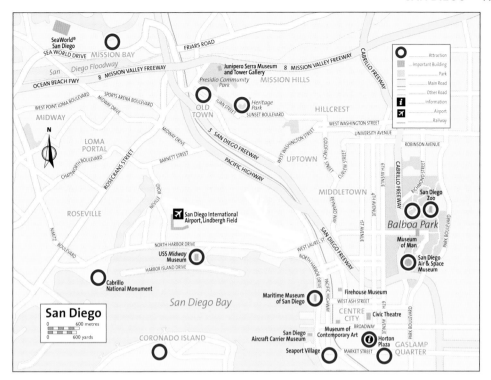

Driving

Freeways can clog abysmally at rush hour. I-5 parallels the coast from Capistrano Beach south to San Diego. Hwy S21 is the much slower scenic route on the coast from Carlsbad to Mission Bay/Mission Beach. I-8 goes east from Old Town, past Mission Valley lodging, to East San Diego County. Around downtown, many streets are one-way; follow directional signs to attractions.

San Diego's public transport is a good alternative to city driving. The **San Diego 511** (*tel: 511; www.511sd.com*) coordinates the **North County Coaster** train (*tel: (800) 262-7837; www.gonctd.com. Operates Mon–Sat*), buses and the **San Diego Trolley**.

Naval San Diego

By 1917, US expansionism dictated a Southern California base for naval operations. San Diego remains an important operations centre for the Pacific Fleet. North Island (Coronado) houses the US Naval Air Station. Aerospace companies thrived from the 1920s until aerospace and naval downsizing shocked the region in the 1970s.

The response? San Diego restored its historic downtown, built a convention centre, accommodated cruise ships, revamped the waterfront, and capitalised on the presence of the hi-tech industry stimulated by La Jolla-based Scripps Institution of Oceanography, Salk Institute for Biological Studies and a large University of California, San Diego campus.

Sights

ⓘ Balboa Park
Visitors Center in the
House of Hospitality,
1549 El Prado, Ste 1;
tel: (619) 239-0512;
www.balboapark.org.
Open daily 0930–1630;
longer in summer.

ⓑ Botanical Building
Look for the Lily Pond.
Open Fri–Wed 1000–1600.
Free.

Marston House $
3525 7th Ave, northwest
corner of Balboa Park; tel:
(619) 298-3142;
http://sohosandiego.org/
marston/index.htm. Open
Fri–Sun, call for hours and
tours.

**Mingei International
Museum $** 1439 El Prado;
tel: (619) 239-0003;
www.mingei.org. Open
Tue–Sun 1000–1600.

Museum of Man $
1350 El Prado;
tel: (619) 239-2001;
www.museumofman.org.
Open daily 1000–1630.

**Reuben H Fleet
Science Center $$**
1875 El Prado; tel: (619)
238-1233; www.rhfleet.org.
Open daily, call for hours.

**San Diego Automotive
Museum $$**
2080 Pan American Plaza;
tel: (619) 231-2886;
www.sdautomuseum.org.
Open daily 1000–1700.

**San Diego Model
Railroad Museum $$**
1649 El Prado, Lower Level;
tel: (619) 696-0199;
www.sdmodelrailroadm.com.
Open Tue–Fri 1100–1600,
Sat–Sun 1100–1700.

Balboa Park

Balboa Park, the 1,200 acres of greenery north of Downtown San Diego, is *the* city park. The collection of plants and trees, California-Spanish Baroque architecture, a collection of museums called the Smithsonian of the West, and the world-renowned **San Diego Zoo** (*see page 83*) have rendered its original 1868 chaparral and cacti desertscape unrecognisable outside the sculptured **Desert Garden** (*Park Blvd, east side*). Many of the Spanish Baroque buildings were installed for the 1915 Panama–California Exposition.

A free **Balboa Park Tram** from the Inspiration Point car park makes a circuit of 11 stops. The 7-day, 14-museum **Passport to Balboa Park** or **Zoo/Passport Combo** provides bargain admission; many museums are free on one Tuesday each month. There is also a one-day **Stay-for-the-Day** pass. The park is full of interesting museums, botanic displays, artists' studios and performing arts venues.

Alcazar Garden, behind the Mingei International Museum, is a formal garden enclosed by arcades with a postcard view of California Tower's tile dome.

The plain name of the **Botanical Building** disguises the beautiful orchids and heliconia which bloom amid exotic palms.

The elegant façade of **Casa del Prado Theater** (*tel: (619) 239-1311; www.juniortheatre.com*) would not be out of place in Spain. Enjoy youth productions of ballet, theatre and dance.

Marston House is a Craftsman-style (*see page 48*) mansion with lovely landscaped English-style gardens.

Mingei International Museum (*House of Charm building*) displays worldwide folk arts.

The **Museum of Man** is an eclectic, fun collection of ethnic artefacts from all over – don't miss the mummies, tortilla-making and Mexican Oaxacan weaving.

The **Museum of Photographic Arts** (MoPA) **$$** (*1649 El Prado, Casa de Balboa; tel: (619) 238-7559; www.mopa.org. Open Tue–Sun 1000–1700, Thur to 2100 in summer*) offers changing exhibitions. It is renowned for the largest photography-oriented bookshop in the US.

The **Old Globe Theatre** (*tel: (619) 234-5623; www.oldglobe.org*), a reproduction of the London original, presents Shakespeare plays and more contemporary works on several stages.

Reuben H Fleet Science Center offers hands-on exhibits and an IMAX® Dome Theater.

San Diego Air & Space Museum (*see page 83*).

San Diego Automotive Museum rotates exhibits of Southern California's *raison d'être* from a fine collection of historic vehicles.

San Diego Model Railroad Museum is heaven for train buffs, where scale-model and mini-gauge trains circle, enhanced by realistic sound effects.

San Diego Museum of Art (SDMA) $$
1450 El Prado, Plaza de Panama; tel: (619) 232-7931; www.sdmart.org. Open Tue–Sat 1000–1700, Sun 1200–1700.

Spanish Village Art Center
Tel: (619) 233-9050; www.spanishvillageart.com. Open daily 1100–1600.

Spreckels Organ Pavilion Tel: (619) 702-8138; www.sosorgan.com. Organ concerts Sun 1400; mid-Jan–Aug Mon 1930.

Timken Museum of Art
1500 El Prado, Plaza de Panama; Tel: (619) 239-5548; www.timkenmuseum.org. Open Tue–Sat 1000–1630, Sun 1330–1630. Free.

San Diego Museum of Art (SDMA) combines contemporary California art with Chinese, Japanese and 15th- to 18th-century European works, supplemented by the outdoor art in the Sculpture Court Café.

Spanish Village Art Center, with its wide, colourful courtyard, offers 37 studios where artists work, display and sell sculpture, jewellery, paintings and other artworks.

Spreckels Organ Pavilion has 4,518 organ pipes which thrill music lovers with free outdoor Sunday afternoon concerts (and Monday evening, mid-June–August).

The European art collections at the **Timken Museum of Art** include magnificent Russian icons.

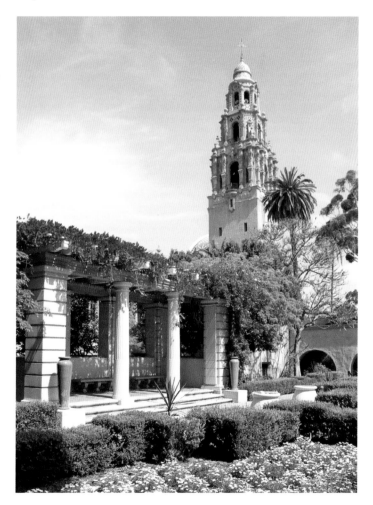

Right
California Tower and the Alcazar Garden

ⓘ Cabrillo National Monument $
Hwy 209–1800 Cabrillo Memorial Dr;
tel: (619) 557-5450;
www.nps.gov/cabr. Open daily 0900–1700.

Visitor centre and Old Point Loma Lighthouse
Open daily 0900–1700.

Cabrillo National Monument

In 1542, three Spanish ships under Portuguese commander Juan Rodríguez Cabrillo found a 'closed and very good port' and Kumeyaay Indians. The explorers landed, claimed 'San Miguel' for the Catholic Majesties, then sailed north to the Channel Islands. The Cabrillo National Monument, atop cliffs at the end of Point Loma peninsula sheltering San Diego Bay, is a majestic, oversized white statue of the explorer flanked by cross, crown and the Spanish coat of arms. Cabrillo's head faces east, above the sweep of the bay channel, Coronado Island and Downtown San Diego to the mountains flanking the border with Mexico. Below the statue, an observation area offers stunning vistas of sailing boat regattas and the to and fro of US naval traffic, comprising vessels of the Pacific Fleet.

Old Point Loma Lighthouse, a 5-minute walk from the monument, sits 422ft above the Pacific. Operational from 1855 to 1891, the light tower sits in the middle of the house, furnished as it was for the last keeper's posting. A 2-mile return **Bayside Trail** passes through a mix of prickly pear and succulents with black sage and chaparral as it descends 300ft. A well-marked path close to the monument entrance gives on to accessible **tide pools**, and the **Whale Overlook** is a prime spot for **California gray whale**-spotting from mid-December to March. Below Point Loma, the eroded **Sunset Cliffs** are a popular rendezvous for photographers and lovers at sundown.

ⓘ Coronado Visitor Center *1100 Orange Ave (lobby, Museum of History and Art);*
tel: (619) 437-8788; www.coronadovisitorcenter.com. Open Mon–Fri 0900–1700, Sat–Sun 1000–1700.

Coronado Island

In the 1880s, the arrival of railways in San Diego cried out for a resort – and the **Hotel del Coronado** (*1500 Orange Ave; tel: (619) 435-6611 or (800) 468-3533; www.hoteldel.com*), just a short ferry ride across the beautiful San Diego Bay, met the need. The white Victorian building with its bright red roof and towers still stands as a luxury landmark.

The **San Diego–Coronado Bay Bridge** arcs gracefully over the bay, a lovely drive except at rush hour. The **San Diego–Coronado Ferry** (*tel: (800) 442-7847; www.sdhe.com/san-diego-bay-ferry.html*) transports passengers and bicycles between Broadway Pier, the Convention Center Marina and Ferry Landing Marketplace. There is a pricey but fast **water taxi** (*tel: (800) 442-7847 or (619) 235-8294; www.sdhe.com/san-diego-water-taxi.html*) service between Coronado, downtown Shelter Island and Harbor Island, and, during baseball season, the water taxi to PETCO Park. Romantics can step aboard a **Venetian gondola $$** (*tel: (619) 429-6317; www.gondolacompany.com*) at Loews Coronado Bay Resort.

Ocean Blvd northwest of the Hotel del Coronado is a superb spot for sunsets. North-side shops and restaurants centre around **Coronado Ferry Landing** (*1201 1st St and B Ave; tel: (619) 234-4111; and Ferry Landing Marketplace; tel: (619) 435-8895; www.coronadoferrylandingshops.com*), which, with its four parks 1½ miles west, has fine views of the afternoon sun glowing on downtown high-rises, while **Orange Ave**, near

Gaslamp Quarter Association 614 5th Ave, Ste E; tel: (619) 233-5227; www.gaslamp.org

Gaslamp Quarter Historical Foundation
William Heath Davis House, 410 Island Ave; tel: (619) 233-4692; www.gaslampquarter.org. Offers district tours Sat 1100. $$.

Heritage Park 2454 Heritage Park Row, Old Town San Diego; tel: (619) 990-1086; www.heritageparksd.com

Horton Plaza Broadway–G St, 1st–4th Aves; tel: (619) 239-8180; www.westfield.com/hortonplaza. Shops open Mon–Sat 1000, Sun 1100.

the Hotel del Coronado, is a trendy area to shop, dine, browse art galleries and people-watch. The **Coronado Museum of History and Art** (1100 Orange Ave; tel: (619) 435-7242 or (619) 437-8788; www.coronadohistory.org) has four galleries, offers Hotel del Coronado, tree, and architectural walking tours, and the Coronado Visitor Center.

Gaslamp Quarter

Opulent late-Victorian architecture and streetlamps grace Downtown San Diego's 16-block Gaslamp Quarter (Broadway and Harbor Dr, 4th and 6th Aves), the trendy shopping, dining and entertainment area. Alone among California's major cities, this civic and business centre has remained visually intact since its beginnings as 'New Town' in 1887, when San Francisco merchant Alonzo E Horton bought up the waterfront and moved the action from Old Town. The 1850s **William Heath Davis House Museum $** (410 Island Ave; tel: (619) 233-4692. Open Tue–Sat 1000–1800, Sun 0900–1500) was an early merchant-developer's residence.

Through the next century, the boom town catered to lawman Wyatt Earp's three gambling halls, bordello patrons, sailors and homeless men, evolving into an infamous 'skid row' as the population and businesses shifted north and east. Some homeless missions remain, but the Gaslamp Quarter's 1970s restoration is cemented by great music clubs, fine dining and a cheerful ambience of rediscovery. **Horton Plaza** (see below), a multilevel shopping mall with excellent fast food, theatres and a cinema, anchors the district on the north side.

Heritage Park

On the edge of Old Town San Diego, Heritage Park (access Heritage Park Row from Juan and Harney Sts) preserves six Victorian mansions and a Jewish synagogue arranged along a pedestrian walk. Some buildings are still in use: look for wedding parties at weekends. The turret marks the 1889 Queen Anne **Christian House**, and there are Victorian-style souvenirs in the 1893 Classic Revival **Burton House**. The 1893 **Temple Beth Israel**'s clean Classic Revival lines appealed to Christian congregations, who used the building before they had permanent sites for their churches.

Horton Plaza

Geometric wedges, odd angles, tilework, the eagle-topped Jessop's 'San Diego Time' Clock and 41 cheerful colours make this chic downtown shopping mall a destination for San Diegans. Horton Plaza, at the north edge of the Gaslamp Quarter, has nearly 130 shops, including Nordstrom and Macy's department stores. The **Lyceum Theatre at Horton Plaza** has comic and classic performances by the San Diego Repertory Theatre (tel: (619) 544-1000; www.sdrep.org). The restored 1924 **Balboa Theatre** (868 4th Ave; tel: (619) 570-1100; www.sandiegotheatres.org) is a performing arts centre.

Mission San Diego de Alcalá $
10818 San Diego Mission Rd; tel: (619) 281-8449; www.missionsandiego.com. Museum open daily 0900–1645.

New Children's Museum $$ *200 W. Island Ave; tel: (619) 233-8792; www.thinkplaycreate.org. Open Mon–Tue & Fri–Sat 1000–1600, Thur 1000–1800, Sun 1200–1600.*

Old Town San Diego Chamber of Commerce *2383 San Diego Ave; tel: (619) 291-4903; www. oldtownsandiego.org*

Old Town San Diego State Historic Park *2645 San Diego Ave; tel: (619) 220-5422; www.parks.ca.gov/default.asp ?page_id=663. Open daily 1000–1700. Free. For a self-guided walking tour, purchase an Old Town San Diego State Historic Park Tour Guide & Brief History, $2 at Seeley Stables, or take a ranger-led tour.*

Mormon Battalion Memorial *2510 Juan St; tel: (619) 298-3317. Open daily 0900–2100. Free.*

Junípero Serra Museum and Tower Gallery $ *2727 Presidio Dr, Presidio Park; tel: (619) 297-3258; www.sandiegohistory.org/ serra_museum.html. Open Sat–Sun 1000–1700.*

Old Town Trolley Tours® $$ *Tel: (800) 213-2474; www.trustedtours.com. Daily 2-hour, 11-stop tours; summer 0900–1800; rest of year 0900–1700.*

Mission Bay

Mission Bay sprang from the imagination when mud dredged from San Diego Harbor created a huge waterside parkland, with beaches on the bay and Pacific Ocean. The best-known attraction is **SeaWorld® San Diego** (*see page 58*). The sheltered bay offers hotels, restaurants, children's playgrounds, jet-skiing, fishing, sailing, boardsailing, jogging, tennis and golf – even camping.

Mission San Diego de Alcalá, California's first mission (*see page 258*), seems strangely isolated 7 miles from the coast or downtown, but its white façade and lush front gardens are exactly the austere and imposing image the Spanish Church and Empire wished to project. A small museum displays vestments and manuscripts written by California missions' founder Fra Junípero Serra.

The **New Children's Museum** skews towards the arts with hands-on creations by young museum visitors and a guest artist in a separate teens' studio space. The museum building is across from a park with playgrounds, not far from the convention center.

Old Town San Diego

Old Town San Diego State Historic Park, northwest of downtown, anchors a larger area of motels, restaurants and shops which serve the tourist trade visiting the city's 19th-century settlement. Three original family adobes, **La Casa de Estudillo, Machado y Stewart** and **Machado y Silvas**, are excellently restored house museums. At weekends, volunteers dressed in mid-19th-century military uniforms are inspected in front of the **Robinson-Rose House Visitor Center**, then drill on the green and parade around the park. A blacksmith demonstrates his skills near **Seeley Stables Museum**; carriages and stagecoaches are on display inside, supplemented by a film on transport in California. The **First San Diego Courthouse**, the first **San Diego Union** (newspaper) building, a school and a dental museum offer insights into daily life, while the **Wells Fargo Museum** in the reconstructed **Colorado House** explains the economics of stagecoaches and the Gold Rush in California. See *www.sandiegohistory.org/links/oldtown.htm*

San Diegans visit Old Town to enjoy margaritas and warm tortillas at good restaurants, including **Casa Guadalajara** (*tel: (619) 295-5111*) along the courtyard of **Bazaar del Mundo's** (*tel: (619) 296-3161; www.bazaardelmundo.com*) hibiscus-entwined shopping arcade, complete with dancers and mariachi bands.

The **Old Town Trolley Tour** begins on Twiggs St. The **Mormon Battalion Memorial**, celebrating the 1847 arrival of Latter Day Saints troops to support American troops in the fight against Mexico, is between Old Town and Heritage Park. North of Old Town, **Presidio Park** was the site of the original 1769 fort and mission. The artefacts and scale models in the **Junípero Serra Museum and Tower Gallery** explain San Diego's pre-American history.

San Diego Air & Space Museum $$
2001 Pan American Plaza, Balboa Park;
tel: (619) 234-8291;
www.aerospacemuseum.org.
Open daily 1000–1630;
1000–1730 Memorial
Day–Labor Day.

USS Midway Museum
$$$ 910 N. Harbor Dr,
alongside Navy Pier 11A; tel:
(619) 544-9600;
www.midway.org.
Open daily 1000–1700.

Maritime Museum of San Diego $$ 1492 N.
Harbor Dr; tel: (619) 234-9153; www.sdmaritime.com.
Open daily summer
0900–2100; rest of year
0900–2000.

San Diego Zoo $$$
2920 Zoo Dr, Balboa Park;
tel: (619) 231-1515;
www.sandiegozoo.org.
Call for hours.

Below
Victorian houses in San
Diego's Heritage Park

San Diego Air & Space Museum
Aviation fans flock to the San Diego Air & Space Museum. The combined influence of naval aviation and the aerospace industry in San Diego makes the aircraft on display in the doughnut-shaped Ford Building one of the best history lessons of airborne flight.

USS *Midway* Museum
San Diego's waterfront has a naval aviation museum on the aircraft carrier that was the Persian Gulf flagship in the 1991 Desert Storm campaign. The *Midway*, as this museum is known, served for 47 years and was the first carrier based in a foreign country, Japan, where it served for 18 years. Restored aircraft are displayed.

Maritime Museum of San Diego
San Diego's embarcadero Maritime Museum is dominated by the majesty of the square rigging of the *Star of India*. One of several ships open for touring, this, the oldest merchant vessel still afloat, has been restored to the condition of her launch from the Isle of Man in 1863. The replica *Californian* is the state's official tall ship, enjoyed on 3-hour sails. The 1898 *Berkeley* ferry boat is the sister ship of the *Eureka*, displayed along the Hyde Park Pier of the National Maritime Museum in San Francisco. Both ferries plied San Francisco Bay. The 1904 steamer *Medea*, a Scots-built luxury yacht, is tied up alongside. The HMS *Surprise* is a replica 18th-century Royal Navy frigate, in dramatic contrast to the B-39 Foxtrot class Soviet attack submarine.

San Diego Zoo
The San Diego Zoo was among the first to pioneer habitats for 4,000 animals and hundreds of birds, freeing them from traditional caged confinement. On several levels of jungle-type vegetation, the zoo wanders through canyons and mesas. Guided (double-decker) bus tours see most of the zoo; **Express Bus Tours** has five drop-off points. **Skyfari® Aerial Tram $** provides a gondola overview with a quick hop to the other side of the park. Queue up early for the **Giant Panda Research Station** for a glimpse of pandas on loan from China. The **Polar Bear Plunge** is happily incongruous in the balmy climate, but gorillas in the **Lost Forest** and the South African klipspringer habitat feel like authentic exotic locales. Rare and endangered species prowl and swing through the Asian and African tropical forests of the Lost Forest habitat, largest at the zoo.

Seaport Village
849 W. Harbor Dr;
tel: (619) 235-4014;
www.seaportvillage.com.
Shops open daily
1000–2100.

Below
The tall-masted *Star of India*
lies at anchor at the Maritime
Museum of San Diego

Seaport Village

Seaport Village has nautical-theme shopping and dining near the San Diego Convention Center. A bayside boardwalk at the south end of the embarcadero offers year-round outdoor music, fashion shows and mimes. Take a spin on the **Looff Carousel**, or try the **Village Café** (*tel: (619) 544-9444*) for a wide assortment of breakfast and other fare for a cheerful wake-up. **Wyland Galleries** (*tel: (619) 544-9995*) has the famous artist's whale paintings and marine art. Like a seaside boardwalk of old, pathways and the bay-front feature entertainers each afternoon, with face painting, artistic balloon creation, or hop on a horse-drawn carriage.

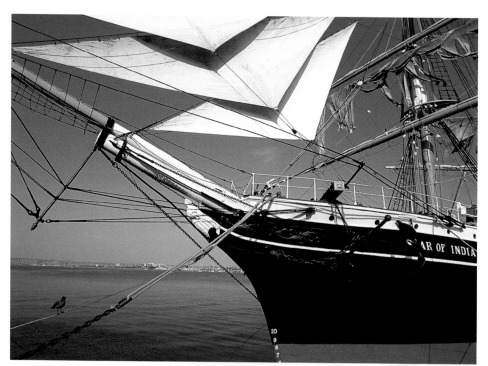

Entertainment

San Diego CVB
offers brochures and online information on arts and cultural offerings in its Art+Sol programme; *www.sandiego.org/nav/ Visitors/WhatToDo/ ArtsCulture*

Local newspapers including the *San Diego Union–Tribune* (*www.signonsandiego.com*) and the free *San Diego Reader* (*www.sdreader.com*) list clubs, nightlife and restaurants. Hopping jazz, blues and rock clubs are attached to Gaslamp Quarter restaurants along 5th Ave, south of Horton Plaza. The **San Diego Performing Arts League** (*www.sdwhatsplaying.com*) has bi-monthly listings in its free *What's Playing in San Diego Guide.*

One of the most venerable companies in the country, the **Old Globe Theatre** (*see page 78*) in Balboa Park fills three theatres with productions every year. ARTS TIX (*northeast corner of Horton Plaza; www.sandiegoperforms.com/ARTSTIX*) offers on-the-spot, half-price tickets for theatre, dance or concert performances on the day. The proximity of UC San Diego draws big-name music groups to the area.

San Diegans love sports: the **Padres** (*http://sandiego.padres.mlb.com*) play baseball April–October at PETCO Park and the **Chargers** (*www.chargers.com*) play NFL American football October–December/January at QUALCOMM Stadium. Good weather encourages outdoor sports with numerous golf courses and tennis courts.

Shopping

Perhaps because of the pleasant climate, it's easy to shop in the San Diego area. **Horton Plaza** (*see page 81*) has restaurants, shops, stores and theatres, and validated parking makes a Gaslamp Quarter exploration a bargain. Shops in the whimsical-coloured shopping hub include the **Sports Fantasy** for genuine US sports team clothing and accessories.

Fashion Valley Mall (*7007 Friars Rd; tel: (619) 688-9113; www.simon.com/mall/?id=765*) in Mission Valley is filled with more than 200 clothing, cosmetic and home-furnishing shops, a food court and a multi-screen cinema. Shop for nautical souvenirs at **Seaport Village**, Mexican at Old Town's **Bazaar del Mundo**, or search for unexpected bargains at **Kobey's Swap Meet** (*3350 Sports Arena Blvd; tel: (619) 226-0650; www.kobeyswap.com. Open Fri–Sun 0700–1500*).

Accommodation and food

San Diego's interest in attracting convention-goers keeps hotel/motel rooms available at reasonable cost almost all the time. Coronado, Mission Bay, coast and downtown hotels are pricey, although prices drop 15–40 per cent from November to March; look for easy freeway access from I-8 in Mission Valley's Hotel Circle, a 15-minute drive to downtown.

The *San Diego CVB Official Visitors Planning Guide* and website (*www.sandiego.org*) lists accommodation by area and makes bookings online or *tel: (800) 350-6205*. **San Diego Visitor Information Center** (*2668 E. Mission Bay Dr; tel: (800) 827-9188; www.infosandiego.com*) can also book accommodation area-wide.

Horton Grand Hotel $$ *311 Island Ave; tel: (800) 542-1886 or (619) 544-1886; www.hortongrand.com*. Combines two restored Victorian-era buildings, furnished with period antiques in the heart of the Gaslamp Quarter.

Bay Club Hotel & Marina $$$ *2131 Shelter Island Dr; tel (800) 672-0800; www.bayclubhotel.com.* One of four hotels on this mini-peninsula that offers a tropical island-atmosphere getaway with a free airport shuttle service.

Britt Scripps Inn $$$ *406 Maple St; tel: (888) 881-1991; www.brittscripps.com.* A nine-room luxury Queen Anne Victorian adjacent to Balboa Park.

Harbor Vacation Club $$$ *1800 Harbor Island Dr, G Dock; tel: (877) 477-7368; www.resortime.com/resorts/profile.asp?resortid=30.* Offers overnight accommodation in a yacht or power cruiser with a veranda or deck for sunset-watching or sunning.

Hotel del Coronado $$$ *1500 Orange Ave, Coronado; tel: (800) 468-3533; www.hoteldel.com.* The grande dame, picture-postcard resort hotel, complete with ghosts.

Omni San Diego Hotel $$$ *675 L Street; tel: (619) 231-6664; www.omnihotels.com.* Near the convention centre, the hotel is connected to PETCO Park by a skybridge.

US Grant $$$ *326 Broadway; tel: (800) 237-5029; www.usgrant.net.* A luxury landmark hotel named after US Civil War hero and later president, Ulysses S Grant.

San Diego's proximity to Mexico makes it easy to find a variety of Mexican food, from bland to chilli-pepper spicy, especially in **Old Town**. San Diego is also getting a reputation for 'fusion cuisines', mixing California's fresh produce with delicate recipes, sauces and presentation from Asia. The **Gaslamp Quarter** has a good choice of restaurants, from moderate to pricey, many with live music in the evening.

Café Coyote $–$$ *2461 San Diego Ave; tel: (619) 291-4695; www.cafecoyoteoldtown.com.* Has margaritas, mariachis and fresh-made tortillas in Old Town.

Anthony's Fish Grotto on the Bay $$ *1360 N. Harbor Dr; tel: (619) 232-5103; www.gofishanthonys.com.* Has been serving seafood for more than six decades.

Café Chloe $$ *791 9th Ave, # 1; tel: (619) 232-3242; www.cafechloe.com.* Serves everything from breakfast and an 'urban tea' to dinner in the style of a French neighbourhood café.

Chopahn $$ *750 6th Ave; tel: (619) 236-9236; www.chopahnrestaurant.com.* Has Afghani specialities with lamb *sabsi challaw* and heavenly *kadu*, sautéed pumpkin with yoghurt and meat sauce.

Croce's $$ *5th Ave and F St; tel: (619) 233-4355; www.croces.com.* Has all-American cuisine with live jazz at **Croce's Jazz Bar**.

Dussini Loft Bar $$ *275 5th Ave; tel: (619) 233-4323; www.dussini.com.* Has small plates that make a meal, with an extensive beverage menu.

The Prado $$ *1549 El Prado; tel: (619) 557-9441; www.cohnrestaurants.com.* Has a Latin and Italian fusion menu in Balboa Park's House of Hospitality.

Sogno DiVino $$ *1607 India St; tel: (619) 531-8887; www.sogno-divino.com.* A wine bar with delicious appetisers.

Bandar Restaurant $$$ *845 4th Ave; tel: (619) 238-0101; www.bandarrestaurant.com.* Serves a wide-ranging menu of Persian classics and vegetarian alternatives in the Gaslamp Quarter.

Island Prime $$$ *880 Harbor Island Dr; tel: (619) 298-6802; www.cohnrestaurants.com.* A steakhouse with superb bay and skyline views.

Stingaree $$$ *454 6th Ave; tel: (619) 544-9500; www.stingsandiego.com.* A three-level nightclub scene with a waterfall near the Gaslamp Quarter.

Suggested tours

Below
San Diego's Old Point Loma Lighthouse

San Diego's **59-Mile Scenic Drive** (*www.sandiego.org/article/visitors/338*) signs have a flying white seagull on a blue and yellow field. The half-day circuit begins at the foot of Broadway near the Santa Fe Depot (AMTRAK/Coaster), and includes La Jolla and Coronado. The orange and green motorised trams of **Old Town Trolley Tours®** (*tel: (800) 213-2474*) can be boarded from Old Town or any of ten other stops for a 2-hour narrated circuit, or reboarded after spending some time in each area.

Have a passport and (for non-US citizens or resident aliens) a multiple-entry visa or visa waiver to hand on the **San Diego Trolley** if you want to make a day trip to the border and walk to **Tijuana** in Mexico.

San Diego Harbor Excursions (*tel: (800) 442-7847; www.sdhe.com*) and **Hornblower Cruises** (*tel: (888) 467-6256; www.hornblower.com*) offer 1- and 2-hour San Diego Bay cruises departing from downtown's Broadway Pier. One-hour Venetian gondola cruises of San Diego Bay depart from Coronado Island with The Gondola Company (*tel: (619) 429-6317*).

Barnstorming Adventures $$$ (*Montgomery Field, 3750 John J Montgomery Dr; tel: (800) 759-5667; www.barnstorming.com*) offers 'flightseeing' from open-cockpit biplanes and other air combat and warplane flights.

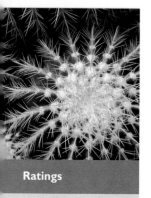

Anza-Borrego Desert State Park

Ratings

Geology	●●●●●
Nature	●●●●●
Outdoor activities	●●●●●
Scenery	●●●●○
Historical sights	●●●○○
History	●●●○○
Children	●○○○○

A short journey east of San Diego or south of Palm Springs is true desert, a desert park surrounding a few golf courses, resort hotels and basic services. Anza-Borrego Desert State Park is rugged, more rocky and mountainous than stereotypical sandy dunes, a place for solitude away from the cities of Southern California. The town of Julian, nestled in forests and apple orchards, is a world in between, a popular and historic getaway for San Diegans. Stop there for an alpine respite before venturing on to Anza-Borrego and an overnight stay in Borrego Springs.

ANZA-BORREGO DESERT STATE PARK

ⓘ Visitor center
1½ miles west of Christmas Circle, Borrego Springs. Open Oct–May daily 0900–1700; Jun–Sept Sat–Sun & holidays, call for hours.
Wildflower Hotline for *Jan–Apr season, tel: (760) 767-4684. Ask at the visitor centre for details of trails.*

ⓜ Anza-Borrego Desert State Park $ *200 Palm Canyon Dr, Borrego Springs; tel: (760) 767-5311; www.parks.ca.gov*

Two-thirds of the 600,000 acres of this largest state park in the contiguous US is wilderness. Thanks to its proximity to the Colorado River, Anza-Borrego Desert State Park (ABDSP) is technically a Colorado Desert section of the Sonoran Desert, with arid, eye-stretching badlands, palm canyons, desert bighorn sheep camouflaged by raw mountain scarps, temperature- and saline-adaptable pupfish, seas of spring wild flowers and fossils of mammoth elephants and sabre-toothed cats.

In a few places, such as the 3-mile return **Borrego Palm Canyon Trail**, native California fan palm trees, North America's largest palms, offer shade against blistering temperatures from June to September, even as the *borrego* (desert bighorn sheep) move down to water at palm-lined waterholes. Elsewhere, the panoramas and vistas are worth a well-provisioned hike into a sere desert – follow established trails, or risk being caught in a rare but potentially fatal flash-flood downpour. Brilliant expanses of **wild flowers**, between late-January and March/April, are legendary.

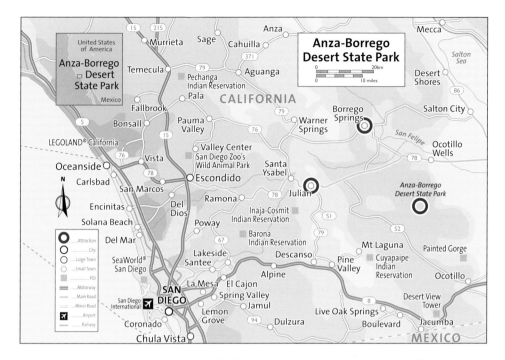

Accommodation in Anza-Borrego Desert State Park

Reserve camp pitches for **Borrego Palm Canyon** and **Tamarisk Grove** (*tel: (800) 444-7275; www.reserveamerica.com*). **Bow Willow Camp** has 16 pitches; **Borrego Springs** has standard accommodation.

BORREGO SPRINGS

❶ Borrego Springs Chamber of Commerce *786 Palm Canyon Dr; tel: (800) 559-5524 or (760) 767-5555; www.borregospringschamber.com*

Anza-Borrego Desert Natural History Association Borrego Desert Nature Center *652 Palm Canyon Dr; tel: (760) 767-3098; www.california-desert.org*

Surrounded by Anza-Borrego Desert State Park, and a service point for park visitors, Borrego Springs holds its own as a desert resort centre and citrus fruit producer for worldwide export. Red grapefruit is the best-known local product, though oranges, lemons and limes also grow in north-side groves, now impinged by real-estate development.

Accommodation and food in Borrego Springs

Cooler weather between October and May draws a million tourists a year – book in advance. Accommodation includes ABDSP camping, RV parks, Bed & Breakfast, motels and resort hotels. Prices can drop dramatically in summer.

The Palms Hotel: Krazy Coyote Restaurant $$–$$$ 2220 Hoberg Rd; tel: (760) 767-7788; www.thepalmsatindianhead.com. On-site where 1950s film stars went for a ranch getaway, with a zen garden.

Borrego Springs Resort $$–$$$ 1112 Tilting T Dr; tel: (888) 826-7734 or (760) 767-5700; borregospringsresort.com. Has a green, 18-hole Championship golf course in the midst of rugged desert.

Palm Canyon Resort $$–$$$ 221 Palm Canyon Dr; tel: (760) 767-5341 or (800) 242-0044; www.palmcanyonresort.com. Has a Western theme and is close to the park. There is also an RV park.

JULIAN

Julian Chamber of Commerce 2129 Main St; tel: (760) 765-1857; www.julianca.com. Open daily 1000–1600.

The Eagle and High Peak Mine $ End of C St; tel: (760) 765-0036. Open year-round, weather permitting, for 1-hour guided mine tours and gold panning. Call for hours.

California Wolf Center $ Tel: (619) 234-9653 or (760) 765-0030 (reservations); www.californiawolfcenter.org. Call for tour days and times. Reservations required.

Cuyamaca Rancho State Park $ 12551 Hwy 79, Descanso; tel: (760) 765-0755; www.parks.ca.gov

Julian's wooden shopfronts and horse-drawn carriage riders evoke the 1869 Gold Rush, which created the town. **The Eagle and High Peak Mine** has guided tours. The town also attracts visitors for its alpine climate, delicious apples served in pies or quaffed as juice, several wineries, art galleries and llama trekking. The **California Wolf Center** conducts tours, including observation of an Alaskan gray wolf pack as education to encourage wolf conservation. **Cuyamaca Rancho State Park**, 17 miles south on Hwy 79, is a good introduction to the region's pine, cedar and oak forests.

Accommodation and food in Julian

The Chamber of Commerce has an accommodation list. The **Julian Bed and Breakfast Guild** (tel: (760) 765-1555; www.julianbnbguild.com) represents about a dozen Bed & Breakfast lodgings. Apple pie is easy to find on menus!

Dudley's Bakery Hwys 78 and 79, northwest of Julian; tel: (760) 765-0488; www.dudleysbakery.com. Open Mon 0900–1300, Thur–Sun 0800–1700. Famous for its jalapeño pepper and potato breads.

**Observer's Inn $$$** 3535 Hwy 89; tel: (760) 765-0088; www.observersinn.com. Adds guided astronomy tours ($) with a powerful telescope to traditional Bed & Breakfast.

Suggested tour

Total distance: 90 miles.

Time: 3 hours' driving.

Links: From the Erosion Road Auto Tour, Hwy S22, east of Borrego Springs, continue east. Turn left at Hwy 86, the Salton Sea, going 32 miles north to Hwy 111 at Indio at the eastern side of the Coachella Valley to join the Palm Springs Route (see page 92). To include San Diego Zoo's Wild Animal Park (see page 57), continue west of Julian on Hwy 79 to the Hwy 78 junction, and go southwest for 25 miles on Hwy 78 through Ramona and San Pasqual.

Palomar
Observatory
Northwest of Julian and
Santa Ysabel Mission, via
Hwy 76, right on Hwy S7,
then right on Hwy S6;
tel: (760) 742-2119;
www.astro.caltech.edu/
observatories/palomar.
Open daily Apr–Oct
0900–1600; Nov–Mar
0900–1500. One-hour
facility tours Apr–Oct
Sat–Sun.

Route: North of Downtown **San Diego ❶**, take I-8 east for 38 miles. Turn left (north) on Hwy 79 to **Cuyamaca Rancho State Park ❷** and **JULIAN ❸**. For the most direct route from Julian to **ANZA-BORREGO DESERT STATE PARK ❹/BORREGO SPRINGS ❺**, take Hwy 78 18 miles east, veer left on to Hwy S3 (Yaqui Pass Rd) for 7 miles, then follow Borrego Springs Rd to town.

Detour: An alternative route to ABDSP continues 18 miles northwest of Julian on Hwy 79 passing **Santa Ysabel Mission ❻** (*tel: (760) 765-0810*), a reconstructed chapel and museum which served as a satellite of Mission San Diego (*see page 258*). Turn east on to Hwy S2/S22 24 miles to **Borrego Springs ❺** .

Also worth exploring

Palomar Observatory ❼ has a museum and video explaining astronomical phenomena sighted using the huge 200in Hale Telescope. The white-domed research facility does not offer night visits, but a special platform allows visitors to view the apparatus's works.

The mountains in the **Cleveland National Forest ❽** are rocky, stark and impressive. Close by the observatory is **Palomar Mountain State Park ❾** (*2 miles west of the Hwys S6/S7 junction; tel: (760) 742-3462*), with high meadows rivalling the Sierra Nevada Mountains for scenic beauty.

Palm Springs

Ratings

Golf	●●●●●
Scenery	●●●●●
Shopping	●●●●●
Nightlife	●●●●○
Food and drink	●●●○○
Historical sights	●●●○○
Museums	●●●○○

Surrounded by thousands of square miles of stark desert beauty, Palm Springs is an artificial oasis overrun with the rich, the famous and the star-struck, all joined in the common pursuit of golf, eternal youth and the perfect suntan. It's California's desert destination for those who *don't* want to get away from it all.

Palm Springs was originally an isolated hot springs among the desert palms, known only to the Agua Caliente band of the Cahuilla Indians and a few health fanatics. In the 1930s, Hollywood discovered the joys of distant desert getaways, with real-estate developers and golf-course designers in close pursuit. Three generations later, the town created for luxury and leisure has become a string of eight resort cities strung along Hwy 111 through the Coachella Valley. The area is noted for being gay and lesbian friendly. The Valley remains one of America's richest agricultural areas, though fields and orchards are now disappearing beneath a jigsaw puzzle of interlocking golf courses and malls.

Getting there and getting around

❶ Palm Springs Bureau of Tourism *777 N. Palm Canyon Dr, Ste 201; tel: (760) 778-8415; www.visitpalmsprings.com*

City of Palm Springs Visitor Center *2901 N. Palm Canyon Dr (at Hwy 111); tel: (800) 347-7746 or (760) 778-8418. Open daily 0900–1700.*

Palm Springs is 110 miles from Los Angeles (about 2½ hours) off I-10 on Hwy 111, which becomes North Palm Canyon Dr. From San Diego, follow I-15 north to Hwy 215, then to Hwy 60 and I-10. From Anaheim/Orange County, take Hwy 55 north to Hwy 91. Go east on Hwy to I-10.

Palm Springs International Airport (PSP) *3400 E. Tahquitz Canyon Way, Palm Springs; tel: (760) 318-3800; www.palmspringsairport.com.* A taxi to Palm Springs is about $12, to Rancho Mirage, $40. Most hotels offer a free or reduced-rate shuttle service.

Traffic can be slow on Palm Canyon Dr near major shopping malls and in central Palm Springs. There is plenty of parking, almost always free, but watch for golf carts – drivers occasionally swerve without warning or signal as though they were still on the course. Palm Springs is busiest during the winter months, and traffic is heaviest in the evening when crowds come out to shop and drive.

Cities and sights

ⓘ Palm Springs Desert Resort Communities CVA
70–100 Hwy 111, Rancho Mirage; tel: (800) 967-3767 or (760) 770-9000; www.palmspringsusa.com **Visitor Center** *Open Mon–Fri 0830–1700.*

The eight cities that make up the Palm Springs resort area tend to blur into each other, especially along Palm Canyon Dr (Hwy 111), an endless strip of low-rise development.

Cathedral City was named after the rocky spires that are all but hidden behind new sporting complexes and other higher-rise development. The city is family oriented during the day, but has a bustling gay scene at night, second only to Palm Springs itself.

Desert Hot Springs is noted for the underground wells that supply most of the area's spas and swimming pools. Located north of Palm Springs, it's a convenient location for day-trippers to Joshua Tree National Park (*see page 105*) and other desert sights.

Indian Wells became famous as a golf venue thanks to US President Eisenhower's frequent golf holidays here in the 1950s. The town has the valley's largest concentration of grand resorts and private courses.

Indio is the low-key agricultural heart of the Coachella Valley, as well as the commercial, gambling and polo centre.

Palm Desert is mostly a place to shop, relax, play golf and watch wildlife at **The Living Desert** (*see page 95*). The best time to visit is

◆ Fabulous Palm Springs Follies $$$
Plaza Theater, 128 S. Palm Canyon Dr; tel: (760) 327-0225; www.psfollies.com. Performances Nov–May.

◆ Indian Canyons $
End of S. Palm Canyon Dr; tel: (760) 323-6018; www.indian-canyons.com. Open Oct–Jul daily 0800–1700; rest of year Fri–Sun 0800–1700.

October, when the growing golfing population stages America's first (and possibly only) golf cart parade.

Palm Springs is where it all began with a primitive mineral hot springs in the 1890s. Most of the city's hotels remain small, inherited from earlier days.

La Quinta is named after the area's first exclusive resort, which opened in 1927. Hollywood director Frank Capra wrote the script for his Academy Award-winning *It Happened One Night* at the resort and kept coming back with stars such as Clark Gable and Greta Garbo in tow.

Rancho Mirage, the Valley's high-profile neighbourhood, attracts presidents, kings and stars to its golf courses. Golf links share centre stage and newspaper headlines with the Betty Ford Center, California's celebrity health clinic.

Desert tours
The only way to appreciate the desert is to see it up close and off the main roads. **Desert Adventures Jeep Tours $$$** *(tel: (760) 340-2345 or (888) 440-5337; www.red-jeep.com)* offers a variety of off-road jeep tours through local canyons, over the San Andreas Fault and into nearby mountains with experienced naturalist guides. **Elite Land Tours $$$** *(tel: (800) 514-4866 or (760) 318-1200; www.elitelandtours.com)* does it in a Hummer H2 all-terrain vehicle with an array of outings to the desert at night, Joshua Tree National Park, the Salton Sea, Indian Canyons, and safaris to see wolves or tigers.

Fabulous Palm Springs Follies
The best introduction to Palm Springs' image of itself, this feathers-and-sequins tribute to 1930s and 1940s musicals gives veteran showgirls and gents a chance to strut their stuff – all are over the age of 55. So is the historic **Plaza Theater**, where they perform each winter.

Indian Canyons
The Agua Caliente band of Cahuilla Indians was forced to give up half of the Coachella Valley in the 1890s, but they retained picturesque canyons in the lower slopes of the San Jacinto Mountains south of Palm Springs. Four canyons contain extensive groves of California fan palms (*Washingtonia filifera*), California's only native palm, nourished by year-round streams. Pleasant hiking and equestrian trails climb the canyons from the car park at the head of Palm Canyon. Horses can be hired from **Smoke Tree Stables** *(tel: (800) 787-3922; www.smoketreeranch.com/smoketreestables.html)* for individual or guided rides – Western style only.
Tahquitz Canyon Visitor Center $$$ *(500 W. Mesquite, Palm Springs; tel: (760) 416-7044; www.tahquitzcanyon.com. Open Oct–Jul daily 0730–1700; rest of year Fri–Sun 0730–1700)* has a canyon observation deck, cultural presentations, tribal artefacts, and ranger-led tours of rock art, a 60ft waterfall, flora and fauna.

The Living Desert
*$$ 47900 Portola Ave,
Palm Desert/Indian Wells;
tel: (760) 346-5694;
www.livingdesert.org. Open
daily Oct–May 0900–1700;
Jun–Sept 0800–1330.*

Palm Canyon shelters about 3,000 palms. Most grow in groves that extend 2 miles up the canyon from below the car park, with shady walking paths through the sandy flats. The trail becomes more difficult and rockier higher in the canyon. **Andreas Canyon** is smaller and equally lush, but an initial section of trail clambers over boulders that have fallen from the canyon rim above.

The trail into **Murray Canyon** passes through a mile of low, unshaded brush before dropping into a shady grove of palms in the stream bed. It's a pleasant walk in winter, but beware the sun in summer.

The Living Desert

The Living Desert is a 1,200-acre botanic garden with rare plants and animals from arid climes around the world. The core of the reserve represents the main deserts of North America, including the Upper Colorado. Animals include bighorn sheep, Arabian oryx, gazelles, javelinas, chuckwallas and giraffes, many of them endangered or already extinct in the wild. **Village WaTuTu** is a 3-acre African trading village area. There are model trains on a railway track to perfect scale.

Below
Tahquitz Canyon

ⓜ Moorten Botanical Garden $ *1701 S. Palm Canyon Dr; tel: (760) 327-6555; www. moortengarden.com. Open Mon–Tue & Thur–Sat, 0900–1630, Sun 1000–1600.*

ⓘ Santa Rosa and San Jacinto Mountains National Monument Visitors Center *51–500 Hwy 74, Palm Desert; tel: (760) 862-9984; www.blm.gov/ca/st/en/fo/palmsprings/santarosa.html. Open daily 0900–1600. Free.*

Moorten Botanical Garden

This private garden and plant store displays more than 3,000 varieties of desert plants from around the world, often in whimsical, seemingly haphazard displays. Though technically a nursery, few specimens are actually for sale.

Mount San Jacinto

Fifty-four miles of trails at the crest of Mount San Jacinto (pronounced 'ha-seen-toe') are Palm Springs' escape from itself. In summer, altitude tempers the blazing desert temperatures while conifer forests provide welcome shade. The endangered Peninsular bighorn sheep makes its home here, but is hard to spot. The national monument website lists springtime wild flower viewing locations.

Agua Caliente

US government survey reports originally dismissed the Coachella Valley as 'an immense waste of uninhabited country', but it was neither waste nor uninhabited to the Agua Caliente band of Cahuilla Indians. The band hunted and harvested the Valley floor in winter and retreated up the canyons to cooler country as summer temperatures climbed towards 120°F (49°C).

Early white settlers appropriated what land and water sources they pleased with little regard to traditional Agua Caliente uses. In the 1890s, railway developers took half the Valley for real-estate development, forcing the band to accept a chequerboard pattern of alternative square-mile blocks. The Agua Caliente lost control of their land, but, financially at least, they got the last laugh.

Rather than evicting settlers, the band began charging rent. The group owns 6,700 acres, nearly 10¼sq miles, of Palm Springs itself, plus similar sections across the Valley. The Agua Caliente have long been among the most prosperous Native American groups in the country. With legal changes that effectively open Native lands to unrestricted gambling and casino operations, with two casinos and downtown Palm Springs development, the Agua Caliente have been the biggest winners in Palm Springs' steady explosion in popularity.

Palm Springs Aerial Tramway $$$ One Tramway Rd; tel: (760) 325-1391 or (888) 515-8726; www.pstramway.com. Open Mon–Fri 1000–2145, Sat–Sun 0800–2145.

Palm Springs Aerial Tramway

The Palm Springs Aerial Tramway rotating tramcars float 2½ miles from the Valley floor to San Jacinto Mountain (8,516ft) in 10 minutes. The views up (or down) are breathtaking, stretching from the San Jacinto Mountains east to the highlands of **Joshua Tree National Park** (see page 105). Be prepared for a 40°F (22°C)-plus temperature change between top and bottom, including deep snow in winter.

Palm Springs Air Museum $$ 745 N. Gene Autry Trail; tel: (760) 778-6262; www.air-museum.org. Open daily 1000–1700.

Palm Springs Air Museum

World War II is the focus for the Air Museum. Ageing air buffs (and occasionally their grandchildren) slaver over 30 restored aircraft, including a Curtiss P-40 Warhawk, a P-51 Mustang and a Boeing B-17 Flying Fortress.

Palm Springs Art Museum $$ 101 Museum Dr; tel: (760) 322-4800; www.psmuseum.org. Open Tue–Wed & Fri–Sun 1000–1700, Thur 1200–2000.

Palm Springs Art Museum

The museum art collection focuses on the 20th century and California artists, and there are also Native American and Mesoamerican collections.

Village Green Heritage Center $ 221 S. Palm Canyon Dr; tel: (760) 323-8297; http://palmsprings.com/history. Open mid-Oct–May Wed & Sun 1200–1500, Thur–Sat 1000–1600.

Village Green Heritage Center

The **Village Green Heritage Center** contains Palm Springs's first two permanent buildings, a hotel and adobe home, both now used as museums by the Palm Springs Historical Society.

Wind farms

It's impossible to miss the ranks of windmills off I-10 at the San Gorgonio Pass just before Palm Springs. Look for the spreading groves of more than 4,000 wind turbines, their steel blades glinting in the desert sun. Steady breezes blow through the pass nearly every day of

Opposite
Wind turbines near Palm Springs

ⓘ Palm Springs Windmill Tour $$
Tel: (760) 320-1365; www.thebestofthebesttours.com/tour3.html. Tours daily 0900, 1130, 1400.

ⓖ Golf
The Coachella Valley boasts 115 golf courses, some with up to 54 holes. Most of the world's best-known course designers have at least one Palm Springs course to their credit. But regardless of the designer, nearly every Palm Springs course incorporates the almost jarring juxtaposition of rolling emerald green fairways with dusky cacti and stark rock formations leading to mountain heights. The scenery can be as hazardous as any sand trap or hidden lake.

Most courses are open for public play, but tee times can be difficult to obtain on short notice, especially the much-sought-after early morning slots in winter. Major resorts can arrange tee times to match guest hotel bookings, but public courses generally only accept tee reservations between one and seven days in advance. Several local companies guarantee tee times up to six months in advance, but demand full prepayment of course fees. Decorated golf carts create a carnival atmosphere in Palm Desert each Oct; tel: (760) 346-6111; www.golfcartparade.com

the year (carrying Los Angeles smog into the desert in the process), generating enough electricity to power a small city. The way to see the turbines up close is with a 2-hour **windmill tour**, driving among the whirling generators in a small passenger bus.

Shopping

Shopping in Palm Springs has become entertainment, a way to see, be seen and confirm one's place in the world of conspicuous consumption. Most shops and boutiques open by mid-morning, but serious shoppers restrain themselves until after lunch. That's when the crowds begin to trawl the pavements along north **Palm Canyon Drive** in Palm Springs.

All of the famous brand names are represented, usually at full price, as well as the requisite number of T-shirt shops, souvenir stands and Southwestern art that ranges from the exquisite to exquisitely painful. Best bet is the Thursday evening **Villagefest street fair** (www.palmspringsvillagefest.com), which features a collection of stands hawking anything from tawdry souvenirs to artful jewellery.

Serious shoppers make a pilgrimage to **Palm Desert**, just down Hwy 111, and El Paseo, a 2-mile strip of trendy boutiques that can match anything on offer along LA's Rodeo Drive. The slightly younger set heads for the nearby **Gardens on El Paseo**, which bills itself as Palm Springs's first development for shoppers in their 20s, 30s and 40s, touting prices more in line with Los Angeles than Beverly Hills.

Accommodation and food

Palm Springs was built for the rich and famous. Luxury resorts abound, especially in Indian Wells, La Quinta and Rancho Mirage. Rates can be exorbitant in winter, but look for summer discounts of up to 70 per cent at major resorts and 20–30 per cent at smaller hotels. The Palm Springs Desert Resort Communities CVA has information on accommodation, golf and other activities.

La Quinta Resort & Club $$$ 49499 Eisenhower Dr, La Quinta; tel: (760) 564-4111 or (800) 598-3828; www.laquintaresort.com. La Quinta is 'Old Palm Springs', the Coachella Valley's original 1920s resort. It's still one of Palm Springs's most attractive, a collection of flower-bedecked casitas at the foot of the Santa Rosa Mountains, surrounded by three PGA West® Courses and two others.

Spa Resort Casino $$$ 401 E. Amado Rd, Palm Springs; tel: (888) 999-1995; www.sparesortcasino.com. The spa is built around mineral hot springs long used by the Agua Caliente band for healing; the elegant buildings, hotel and casino are more recent (and more profitable) additions.

The Coachella Valley made its first fortune on farming, watered by an immense Ice Age aquifer that lies beneath the sands. Early immigrants who saw the physical and climatic resemblance to North Africa and the Middle East planted groves of date trees. A number of growers remain, most notably **Shields Date Garden** *80225 Hwy 111, Indio; tel: (760) 347-7768; http://shieldsdategarden.com.* Built in the 1920s, Shields produces the best date milk-shakes in the Valley, the perfect accompaniment to its tongue-in-cheek film, *The Romance and Sex Life of the Date.* Free entry.

Two Bunch Palms Resort and Spa \$\$\$ *67-425 Two Bunch Palms Trail; Desert Hot Springs; tel: (760) 329-8791* or *(800) 472-4334; www.twobunchpalms.com.* Two Bunch was the area's original resort escape, a favourite with gangster Al Capone as well as Hollywood celebs of the 1930s. It's still Palm Springs's most sybaritic, private and star-ridden resort – and no sightseers allowed.

All of the major resorts have much-advertised restaurants, most offering Californian or Southwestern fusion cuisine at top prices. Other Palm Springs possibilities:

Las Casuelas Terraza \$\$ *222 S. Palm Canyon Dr; tel: (760) 325-2794; www.lascasuelasterraza.com.* The original of a string of family-owned Mexican restaurants (and most popular with locals).

Kaiser Grille \$\$ *205 S. Palm Canyon Dr; tel: (760) 323-1003; www.restaurantsofpalmsprings.com/kaiser.php.* A local favourite in the heart of Palm Springs serves seafood, steaks and pasta.

Sherman's Deli & Bakery \$\$ *401 E. Tahquitz Canyon Way; tel: (760) 325-1199; www.shermansdeli.com.* Palm Springs's only kosher deli and bakery.

Below
La Quinta Resort & Club

Desert Parks

Ratings

Scenery	●●●●●
Children	●●●●○
Geology	●●●●○
History	●●●●○
Outdoor activities	●●●○○
Food and drink	●●○○○
Museums	●●○○○
Architecture	●○○○○

California's desert parks include the lowest and the hottest corners of the Western hemisphere. To the uninitiated, desert is dry and dangerous, at best an empty quarter to be skirted or transited as quickly as possible. On closer look, it's a delicate balance of extremes between too hot and too cold, too dry and too wet, stark, twisted and irresistibly alluring.

The harsh midday sun seems to bleach all colour and texture from desert landscapes, leaving neither shade nor relief from the ceaseless glare. But the softer light of morning and afternoon reveals a rugged grace, a palette of colours and shapes that change almost by the second. Far from the crowds, the pollution and the enveloping vegetation of the coast, the desert is California in its finest and most unabashed grandeur.

DEATH VALLEY JUNCTION

 Amargosa Opera House & Hotel $
PO Box 88; tel: (760) 852-4441; www. amargosa-opera-house.com

Once a railway junction town, Death Valley Junction is little more than the **Amargosa Opera House**. Owner Marta Becket produces and performs mime-ballets on winter Saturdays; call for schedule and required advance bookings. The opera house also has 16 air-conditioned rooms.

DEATH VALLEY NATIONAL PARK

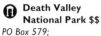 **Death Valley National Park $$**
PO Box 579; tel: (760) 786-3200; www.nps.gov/deva

Roughly 140 miles long and 10 miles across, Death Valley offers the nation's most dramatically desolate scenery. America's hottest temperature, 134°F (56°C), was recorded in Death Valley in 1913; average summer days hit 116°F (47°C). The national park protects vast stretches of mountain and desert surrounding the basin.

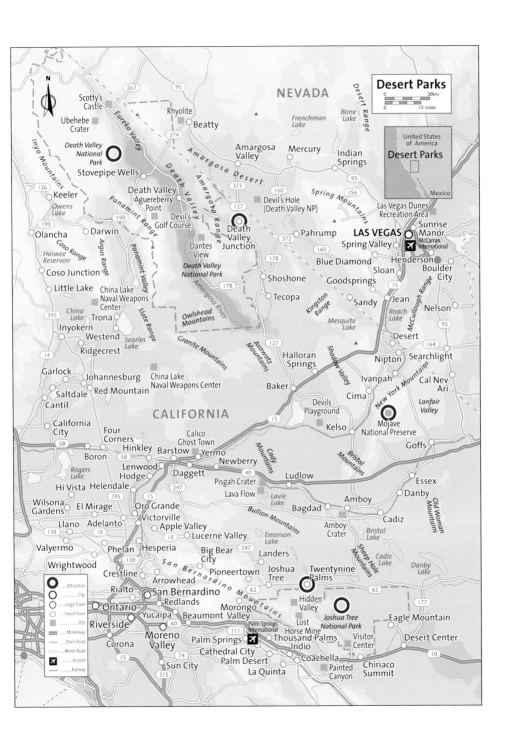

ℹ️ Death Valley Chamber of Commerce
118 Hwy 127, PO Box 157, Shoshone; tel: (760) 852-4524; www.deathvalleychamber.org. Open daily 1000–1600.

Death Valley was formed as the basin floor subsided, leaving precipitous mountains on all sides. The Sierra Nevada blocks nearly all rainfall; Furnace Creek averages barely 1½in of rain yearly. Climatic changes turned an enormous lake 600ft deep into desert pans cracked into hexagons and piled high with salt crystals. Softer sediments have eroded into vast badlands stained every colour of the rainbow.

Despite its name, Death Valley is anything but dead. Conifers grow on the cooler, wetter heights of the Panamint Mountains. The lower slopes are generally too dry and too salty for cacti, but creosote and other coarse bushes thrive. Even the valley bottom, 282ft *below* sea level, sports unique plants and animals in hot, salty marshes.

Errant immigrants gave Death Valley its name and reputation. Hoping to avoid snowy Sierra Nevada Mountain passes to the north, two bands of gold prospectors stumbled into the valley in 1849. Nearly all survived but were impressed enough by the harsh terrain to call it Death Valley.

There were several abortive mining booms in the 19th century, but only a late-century borax boom brought much permanent change. Millennia of evaporation concentrated boron salts into fluffy

Below
Badwater – nearly as low as you can get in North America

ℹ Furnace Creek Visitor Center and Museum *Tel: (760) 786-3200. Open daily 0900–1700. Visitor centres at* **Scotty's Castle Visitor Center** *Tel: (760) 786-2392. Open daily winter 0830–1730; summer 0900–1630.*

Since 1983, the **Furnace Creek 508 Bicycle Race** (www.the508.com) has tested endurance from Santa Clarita north of Los Angeles, 508 miles through the desert and Death Valley, to Twentynine Palms. The race is held in early October. For sheer difficulty, it is matched in July's heat by the **Badwater Ultramarathon 135 Mile Running Race** (www.badwater.com) from Death Valley to Mount Whitney.

'cottonball' crystals. Workers collected the cottonballs, which were processed into borax and used to make fine jewellery, glass and washing powder.

Twenty-mule teams hauled wagons from **Harmony Borax Works** 165 miles to the railway at Mojave. In 1907, a railway (now abandoned) began hauling borax to **Death Valley Junction**. Hoping to stimulate tourism and boost revenues, railway owners built the **Furnace Creek Inn** in 1927. As the inn prospered, less expensive cabins were added at **Furnace Creek Ranch**. Death Valley became a national monument in 1933 and a national park in 1994.

Paved roads are passable all year, but most of Death Valley's gravel roads are meant for 4WD. Always check with park rangers before venturing off-road.

Artists Drive (*south of Furnace Creek, off Badwater Rd, vehicles over 25ft prohibited*) is a 9-mile, one-way loop through brightly coloured badlands and alluvial fans. **Artists Palette**, halfway through the drive, displays a startling patchwork of intense red, yellow, orange, green, violet, brown and black tones – most vivid in late afternoon.

Badwater (*south of Furnace Creek*), 279ft below sea level, was long accepted as the nadir of North America. More accurate surveys have found two lower spots, both 282ft below sea level, a few miles away and unmarked. The highly mineralised water isn't poisonous, just a very effective laxative.

Dantes View (*off Hwy 190 east of Furnace Creek*) is one of the most stunning vistas in Death Valley. Located 1 mile directly above Badwater, the view stretches across the basin to **Telescope Peak** (11,049ft) and beyond to **Mount Whitney** (14,494ft), the tallest peak in the continental US. Colours and views are best in early morning.

Devil's Golf Course (*south of Furnace Creek*) is more than 200 square miles of crystalline salt towers sculpted by wind and rain. The salt cracks and groans audibly with temperature changes.

Furnace Creek is an oasis that has become Death Valley's centre for accommodation (Furnace Creek Inn and Ranch) and activities (park visitor centre). The natural spring that watered hayfields in the last century now keeps the world's lowest golf course green. The **Borax Museum** (*Furnace Creek Resort; tel: (760) 786-2345; open daily 0900–1600*) was originally the office and bunkhouse for 20-mule team borax trains. Museum collections include borax mining equipment as well a 20-mule wagon. The Timbisha Shoshone Tribe has land in this area.

Harmony Borax Works (*north of Furnace Creek*) commemorates the 1880s borax boom. A short path passes the refinery ruins and outlying buildings; a 3-mile trail leads to the borax 'cottonballs' labourers collected.

🅖 **Goldwell Open Air Museum** *in the desert near Rhyolite; tel: (702) 870-9946; www.goldwellmuseum.org. A free Amargosa Desert large sculptures installation.*

Rhyolite (*35 miles northeast of Furnace Creek, near Beatty, Nevada; www.nps.gov/deva/historyculture/rhyolite-ghost-town.htm*) is a stark, imposing collection of stone and concrete ruins from a 1904 boom town. The ruins are haunting at sunset.

Salt Creek (*north of Furnace Creek*) shows the resilience of the inch-long pupfish (genus *Cyprinodon*) which has adapted to the heat, salinity and periodic drought of Death Valley. Related species are found in **Anza-Borrego Desert State Park** (*see page 88*) and other desert watercourses.

Scotty's Castle $$ (*north of Furnace Creek; tel: (760) 786-2392; www.nps.gov/deva/historyculture/scottys-castle.htm. Open daily winter 0830–1730; summer 0900–1630*) represents the extravagant marriage of money (Chicago insurance magnate Albert Johnson) and myth (local cowboy, occasional miner and full-time prevaricator Walter 'Scotty' Scott). 'Scotty' convinced Johnson to build the Spanish-Moorish mansion in 1924 as a restful retreat. Grounds surrounding the $2.4 million extravaganza were never completed, but the interior is elegantly finished with tiles, handcrafted furniture, leather and textiles. The house interior is open by guided tour only ($$) – expect long queues in winter. An Underground (technology) tour is offered daily, November–April. The Gas House Museum has castle artefacts.

Stovepipe Wells (*23 miles northwest of Furnace Creek*) was Death Valley's original settlement; stovepipes driven into the sand to create wells gave it its name. Visitor facilities at Stovepipe Wells Village are a few miles south of the original well, across an immense field of **sand dunes**. The dunes are at their sensuous best in the long shadows near dawn and sunset.

Ubehebe Crater (*west of Scotty's Castle*), 600ft deep and 2,600ft wide, was created by an immense volcanic explosion in the last few thousand years. The sides of the cauldron are layered with tones of orange and grey.

Zabriskie Point (*south of Furnace Creek*) overlooks the Golden Canyon badlands from the east. The heavily eroded landscape glows pink in the first few minutes after dawn.

Accommodation and food in Death Valley

Panamint Springs Resort $$ *Hwy 190, 31 miles west of Stovepipe Wells; tel: (775) 482-7680; www.deathvalley.com*. Has a motel, restaurant, campsite and RV park.

Stovepipe Wells Village $$ *Stovepipe Wells; tel: (760) 786-2387; www.stovepipewells.com*. Offers accommodation, supplies, a restaurant, saloon, RV park and information for the northern end of Death Valley.

Furnace Creek Ranch $$–$$$ *Furnace Creek; tel: (760) 786-2345 or (800) 236-7916; www.furnacecreekresort.com.* The inn's motel-like alternative, open year-round with rooms, cabins and three restaurants.

Furnace Creek Inn $$$ *Furnace Creek; tel: (760) 786-2345 or (800) 236-7916; www.furnacecreekresort.com. Open mid-Oct–mid-May.* Built in the 1920s as a vaguely Moorish resort, is still among the poshest accommodation in an American desert park.

All four accommodation locations have restaurants and general stores. Picnic supplies are more reasonable outside the park.

JOSHUA TREE NATIONAL PARK

ⓘ Joshua Tree Visitor Center *Park Blvd, one block south of Hwy 62, Joshua Tree Village. Open daily 0800–1700.*

ⓟ Joshua Tree National Park $$ *74485 National Park Dr, Twentynine Palms; tel: (760) 367-5500; www.nps.gov/jotr*

Named after wildly gesticulating trees that are actually lilies, Joshua Tree is an anomaly among national parks. There are no IMAX® theatres, no grand lodges, no biggest-smallest-best-tallest-only-on-earth attractions. In fact, there isn't much of *anything* here except nature – more than 800,000 acres, nearly all of it wilderness.

The park is an eerie, almost mystical landscape. Early and late in the day, long shadows and reddish sunlight seem to animate the bizarre landforms and even stranger plants. Jumbled piles of rounded golden boulders rise from the surface, immense mounds of monzogranite that have been cracked, broken, stacked and eroded into shapes reminiscent of twisted Henry Moore sculptures. Climbers from around the world revere the sheer faces of Wonderland Rocks and 4,500 routes.

Namesake Joshua trees (*Yucca brevifolia*) seem to march across the rolling hills, a vast army of stick figures with multiple arms raised to the heavens as though pointing the way to unseen oases fringed with palm trees and willows. Fuzzy cacti that glow like soft velvet in the sun are actually covered with microscopic spines that are nearly impossible to remove.

In spring, the arid hills and canyons disappear beneath carpets of wild flowers. Just weeks later, the same hillsides have become a blazing midday furnace, parched by the sun. In summer, stick to the Joshua tree forests where temperatures top out around 100°F (38°C), a good 25°F (13°C) cooler than the lowlands. In winter, the lowland canyons are a comfortable 75°F (24°C) as the highlands shiver in snow.

The two temperature zones are actually two different deserts, the Mojave and the Colorado. There are few sharp distinctions between the two, no boundary signs to mark the amorphous transition. It's a matter of altitude and, even more, of rainfall variations.

The lower, hotter and drier Colorado Desert is marked by spindly ocotillo bushes, thorny green sticks dripping scarlet blossoms in spring and practically leafless most of the year. With an average of 3in of rain yearly, double the moisture of Death Valley, the Colorado Desert also supports a varied cactus community. The most common is the

**ⓘ Cottonwood
Visitor Center**
*Cottonwood Spring entrance.
Open daily 0900–1500.*

**Black Rock Nature
Center** *Black Rock
Campsite. Open Oct–May
Sat–Thur 0800–1600, Fri
1200–2000.*

jumping cholla (pronounced 'choi-yuh'), named after its proclivity to hook into unwary passers-by.

Life is easier in the higher and moister Mojave Desert. Lying above 3,000ft, the Mojave gets nearly 6in of rain annually, enough to support vast groves of Joshua trees. Though they grow up to 60ft tall, Joshua trees aren't proper trees, but yuccas, lilies with woody stems. Clumps of spindly leaves at the end of the branches give the appearance of arms waving wildly against the sky. The trees were named by Mormon immigrants who likened the trees to the biblical prophet Joshua, pointing the way across the desert with raised arms.

One main road bisects the park, from **Cottonwood** in the south, near I-10, to **Twentynine Palms** and Hwy 62 in the north. Another major road runs from the town of **Joshua Tree** south into the park to meet Pinto Basin Rd. Most of the dirt tracks are passable only by 4WD vehicles; check for current conditions at ranger stations before venturing off the hard surface in passenger vehicles. Trailers and RVs are generally not recommended on dirt roads.

Cholla Cactus Garden (*near Pinto Basin Rd*) provides an easy opportunity to see (but *not* to touch) the most common indicator plant of the Colorado Desert. A short, easy trail winds through an especially dense stand of cholla cacti (*Opuntia bigelovii*). Also called 'teddybear cholla' for their soft, fuzzy appearance, 'jumping cholla' is more painfully accurate. Chunks of cactus seem to leap out, propelled by microscopic spines which snag skin, clothing and almost anything else that brushes past. The large piles of dead cholla are nests built by packrats, which use the prickly pads to protect their dwellings, usually built at the base of a creosote bush.

Just south along Pinto Basin Rd is the **Ocotillo Patch**, the park's most accessible ocotillo thicket. This spiny shrub, noted for its brilliant crimson flowers, is the Colorado Desert's other indicator plant. It's also called Jacob's staff, candlewood, coachwhip and vine cactus, a testament to the thorns along the limber, nearly leafless branches.

Cottonwood Spring (*south entrance, off I-10*) is a pleasant oasis 1 mile east of the visitor centre. The springs are natural, the palms a human addition much used by birds and other wildlife.

Desert Queen Mine (*off a dirt road running north opposite Geology Tour Rd*) lies ¾ mile along an easy trail, a collection of rusting mine machinery. The mine shafts and tunnels are extremely dangerous. A more strenuous half-day walk leads to the **Lost Horse Mine** and the remains of a ten-stamp mill (stamps are blocks for crushing ore).

Fortynine Palms Oasis (*off Canyon Rd, 4 miles west of Twentynine Palms*) is the best area for spring wild flowers. Desert annuals carpet the ground, barrel cacti explode with blooms and the canyon pool is rimmed with native fan palms. The 3-mile return hike is moderately

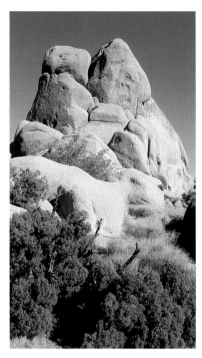

Above
Eroded boulders in Joshua
Tree National Park

strenuous; the trail may be closed during late summer
against fire danger.

General Patton Memorial Museum, outside the park,
contains World War II memorabilia, with special
displays of tanks and artillery used by Patton's training
camps in Joshua Tree and ten other southwestern desert
camps. A West Coast Vietnam Veterans' Wall here
honours veterans.

Geology Tour Road (*from Queen Valley, check road
conditions at the visitor centre before setting out*) is an 18-
mile gravel loop (*sometimes* passable by passenger cars)
through some of the park's most spectacular geological
features. Great alluvial fans spill towards the road and
massive monzogranite heaps tower over the Joshua trees
surrounding a desert playa, or dry lake bed. Visitor
centres sell an excellent road guide.

Keys Ranch (*open by guided walking tour only, tel: (760)
367-5555, $, Oct–May Tue, Thur & Sat–Sun 1000, 1300;
living history and other tours occasionally scheduled*) is a
one-family ghost town that died in 1969. The ranch
includes an adobe barn from the 1880s, a schoolhouse,
junked cars, a windmill, antique mining equipment
and ranch fittings crafted from Joshua tree wood.

Keys View (*20 miles south of Joshua Tree town, via Quail Springs and
Keys View Rds*) offers the most spectacular panoramas in the park, from
atop the San Bernardino Mountains (5,185ft) across the Coachella
Valley to the San Jacinto Range and south to the Salton Sea.

Oasis of Mara (*Oasis Visitor Center, Twentynine Palms*) was the original
oasis of 29 palms first recorded in an 1855 survey. The name *mara*
means 'little water' in the language of the Chemehuevi people, who
occupied the area before white prospectors and settlers arrived. The
oasis once held an open pool of water, but years of overdrafting have
lowered the water table. An easy ½-mile trail leads from the visitor
centre to the oasis.

Queen Valley (*Pinto Valley Rd, centre of the park*) has the park's largest
and healthiest stands of Joshua trees, thousands of them marching
towards the horizon in every direction. **Jumbo Rocks Campground**
offers fine vistas with Joshua trees set against soaring monzogranite
towers and spires.

ⓘ **Oasis Visitor
Center** *Utah Trail
and National Park Dr,
Twentynine Palms; tel: (760)
367-5500. Open daily
0800–1700.*

ⓖ **General Patton
Memorial Museum**
$ *Off I-10, 4½ miles east of
Cottonwood Spring Rd,
62-510 Chiriaco Rd, Chiriaco
Summit; tel: (760) 227-
3483;
www.generalpattonmuseum.
com. Open daily
0930–1630.*

Accommodation and food in Joshua Tree National Park

There are a number of campsites in the park, but no accommodation or
restaurants. The Palm Springs area (*see page 92*) has the best variety near
the park, although Twentynine Palms (*see page 110*) is the closest centre.

MOJAVE NATIONAL PRESERVE

Above
Joshua trees thrive even in the hot, dry desert

ℹ️ **Mojave National Preserve**
(headquarters) 2701 Barstow Rd, Barstow; tel: (760) 252-6100; www.nps.gov/moja. Open Mon–Fri 0800–1630.

Hole-in-the-Wall Information Center *Essex and Black Canyon Rds, 20 miles north of I-40; tel: (760) 928-2572. Open Oct–Apr 0900–1600; May–Sept Fri–Sun 0900–1600.*

Kelso Depot Visitor Center *35 miles south of Baker or 22 miles north of I-40 on Kelbaker Rd; tel: (760) 252-6108. Open daily 0900–1700.*

This 'Lonesome Triangle' of Mojave Desert between I-40, I-15 and the Nevada border is more mountain than sand and combines Great Basin, Sonora and Mojave desert ecosystems. The vast expanse (1.6 million acres) is accented by cinder cones, sand dunes, caverns, precipitous mountains and lava mesas. Joshua tree forests thrive in the upper elevations; the lower slopes are threadbare beneath a sparse carpet of creosote brush.

Though desolate in human terms, this rugged triangle is home to 700 species of plants and 300 different kinds of animals. It's also a historic thoroughfare. Native Americans have been traversing the region for at least 10,000 years, trading Coastal California goods as far east as central Mexico. Spanish explorers followed in the 1770s, then American explorers, ranchers, railway lines and highways.

But except for scattered ranches and mines, there has been little permanent settlement. The eastern Mojave has been a land where anything goes and no one much minded so long as it was safely out of sight. Growing recreational use has changed the government's traditional hands-off policies. The area became a National Preserve in 1994 over fierce local opposition. Ranchers, miners, off-road vehicle users and landowners still object to stricter controls over what many see as *their* land, by right of use if not of ownership.

Signs of human use are never far away, from abandoned mine sites to shot-out Preserve signs, rusted railway tracks and decrepit buildings, but the desert has managed to preserve its expansive emptiness. Without 4WD, stick to the main roads. Rutted sidetracks often disappear into fields of sand or boulders bounded by steep cliffs.

The tiny town of **Amboy** (*www.rt66roys.com*), south of Mojave National Preserve, was once an important stop for the transcontinental railway service and auto traffic on Route 66, America's first transcontinental highway. More modern routes have since bypassed Amboy, and its volcanic cone, the **Amboy Crater Natural National Monument** (*www.blm.gov/ca/st/en/fo/needles/amboy.html*).

Cima Dome (*off Cima Rd, south of Valley Wells*) is best seen from a distance. The almost perfectly formed white batholith (molten magma that solidified before reaching the surface) rises 1,500ft above the surrounding plain, but the gentle rise is difficult to see up close. The 75-sq-mile dome is cloaked in Joshua trees. The tiny town of **Cima** originated as a railway siding.

Cinder Cones Natural National Landmark (*off Kelbaker Rd, north of Kelso*) is a collection of young (1,000–10 million-year-old) cinder cones.

**California
Welcome Center**
2796 Tanger Way, Ste 100
(Tanger® Outlets), Barstow;
tel: (760) 253-4782.
Open daily.

**Mitchell Caverns
Natural Reserve,
Providence Mountains
State Recreation Area**
Box 1, Essex;
tel: (760) 928-2586;
www.parks.ca.gov/default.asp
?page_id=615. Caverns open
by tour ($), daily. Call in
advance for reservation
forms.

Hole-in-the-Wall Campground (*Essex Rd, off I-40*) is named after the wall of rhyolite lava, filled with holes like rocky Swiss cheese.

Kelso Depot The main Preserve visitor center was a railway stop for the Los Angeles and Salt Lake Railroad from 1924 to 1962. After many years of neglect, the restored depot, at a convenient stopping point at Preserve crossroads, has exhibits, information, a fine art gallery, bookshop and lunch counter.

Kelso Dunes (*near Kelso, centre of the Preserve*) are among the tallest sand dunes in California, 600–700ft at the crest fanning out across 45 square miles. The golden rose quartz sand has blown in from the Mojave Sink, to the northwest. Allow about 2 hours to walk to the dune crest and back, plus time to play. The dunes 'sing' as sand slides from the crest, reverberations that sound like a whispering Tibetan gong. Best times to visit are early or late in the day, preferably sunrise/sunset, when long shadows highlight the undulating dune ridges.

Mitchell Caverns Natural Reserve (*Essex Rd off I-40*) are the only caves in Southern California developed for tourism. Water-borne deposits have created a wonderland of limestone curtains, stalactites, stalagmites and other rocky formations, all accessible by stairs and walkways. The cave is open for guided tours only. The easy **Mary Beal Nature Trail** offers a scenic introduction to the surrounding **Providence Mountains State Recreation Area**.

Shoshone is a small supply town for Death Valley at the junction of Hwy 178 (the route from Pahrump and Las Vegas, Nevada) and Hwy 127 from Baker.

Zzyzx (*Zzyzx Rd, off I-10 west of Baker*) is the remains of a 60-room spa, hotel, church, castle and radio station built in the 1940s by self-proclaimed minister/healer Curtis Springer. Springer invented the name (pronounced 'zye-zix', to rhyme with 'size six') to be the last entry in the telephone book. The spa was closed in 1974 when Springer was convicted on tax, health and drug charges; the facility is now a California State University Desert Studies Center.

Researchers are usually more than happy to be interrupted. If the station is unstaffed (as it usually is), noticeboards describe local natural history and the endangered Mojave chub (a desert fish). On a shoreside walk, the old bathhouse offers good views of Soda Dry Lake and the picturesque mountains beyond.

Accommodation and food in Mojave National Preserve

There is camping, but no accommodation, within the Preserve. Fuel and very limited picnic supplies are available in Cima and Nipton. Pick up supplies before entering the Preserve, or have lunch at the Kelso Depot Visitor Center at the restored 1924 Beanery.

TWENTYNINE PALMS

ℹ Twentynine Palms Chamber of Commerce *73491 29 Palms Hwy; tel: (760) 367-3445; www.29chamber.org. Open Mon–Fri 0900–1700, Sat–Sun 1000–1600.*

ℹ Hi-Desert Nature Museum $ *Community Center Complex, 57090 29 Palms Hwy, Yucca Valley; tel: (760) 369-7212; www.hidesertnaturemuseum. org. Open Tue–Sun 1000–1700.*

Twentynine Palms Murals *www.oasisofmurals.org/ murals.html*

🍴 Edchada's $ *73502 29 Palms Hwy; tel: (760) 367-2131. Open for lunch and dinner; serves good Mexican dishes and margaritas.*

Named after the palm trees surrounding Mara Oasis (Joshua Tree National Park headquarters), Twentynine Palms has become a busy desert town as headquarters for the Marine Corps Air Ground Combat Center (the US Marine Corps' largest base) and **Joshua Tree National Park** (*see page 105*). Almost two dozen public murals depict area history. **Hi-Desert Nature Museum** covers Southern California flora, fauna and natural history.

Accommodation and food in Twentynine Palms

Sunnyvale Garden Suites Hotel $$ *73843 Sunnyvale Dr; tel: (760) 361-3939 or (877) 411-3939; www.sunnyvalesuites.com.* Close to the national park, with full kitchens and desert landscaping.

The 29 Palms Inn $$–$$$ *73950 Inn Ave, close to the Visitor Center; tel: (760) 367-3505; www.29Palmsinn.com.* The closest accommodation to the park. The inn also has the best restaurant ($$) in the area, with steaks, seafood and chicken.

Suggested tour

Total distance: 260 miles.

Time: One gruelling driving day, Palm Springs to Death Valley National Park; 3–5 days' touring with overnight stops in Twentynine Palms and Baker.

Links: Palm Springs to the west, Las Vegas to the east, Anza-Borrego Desert State Park to the south.

Route: From **Palm Springs ❶** take I-10 southeast to **Indio ❷**. Continue east 24 miles on I-10 to Cottonwood Spring Rd and **JOSHUA TREE NATIONAL PARK ❸**. Drive north through the park to **TWENTYNINE PALMS ❹**, then east and north to **Amboy ❺** and the **MOJAVE NATIONAL PRESERVE ❻**. Follow Kelbaker Rd through the Preserve to **Kelso ❼**, then continue northwest to **BAKER ❽** (at I-15). Take Hwy 127 north to **DEATH VALLEY JUNCTION ❾**, then enter **DEATH VALLEY NATIONAL PARK ❿** on Hwy 190.

Also worth exploring

Shimmering **Salton Sea** (*www.saltonsea.ca.gov*), south of Palm Springs, was created when a Colorado River aqueduct ruptured in 1905. Measuring 35 miles by 15 miles, it's one of the world's largest inland bodies of salt water, a state recreation area, and excellent for birdwatching at the Salton Sea National Wildlife Refuge.

Spine of the Sierra

Ratings

Geology	●●●●
Outdoor activities	●●●●
Scenery	●●●●
Children	●●●○○
History	●●●○○
Wildlife	●●●○○
Food and drink	●●○○○

The eastern slope of the Sierra Nevada is steeper and more dramatic than the gentle foothills leading up from the Central Valley, a mix of serrated peaks, blistering desert, alkaline lakes and rushing streams squeezed into a narrow corridor between snow-capped summits and the Great American Desert in Nevada. It's also an area almost devoid of people – no Interstate Highways and no rush hour. Hwy 395 provides easy north–south travel, but heavy snow can close east–west mountain passes south of Hwy 88 from November to May.

BIG PINE

🏛 **Ancient Bristlecone Pine Forest** *Off Hwy 168 east of Big Pine. For information: US Forest Service White Mountain Ranger District, 798 N. Main St, Bishop; tel: (760) 873-2500. Open May–Oct daily; Nov–Apr Mon–Fri.*

The town of Big Pine is little more than a collection of petrol stations and motels, but it is the gateway to two of the region's top attractions, the **Ancient Bristlecone Pine Forest** (*off Hwy 168; tel: (760) 873-2500*) and **Palisade Glacier** (*Glacier Lodge Rd, west*).

Bristlecone pines (*Pinus longaeva*) are the oldest living things on earth, usually clinging to inaccessible mountain slopes. The world's only drive-up stand of bristlecones is 10,000ft up the White Mountains, east of Big Pine. Bristlecones have been growing on these mountains for at least 4,500 years, gnarled branches bleached blonde by centuries of blasting wind, snow and sand beneath a burning sun. The twisted trunks grow only an inch in diameter each century, dead as any chunk of driftwood except for an occasional ribbon of bark leading to a splash of needles and cones on some remote branch.

Schulman Grove $, named after the researcher who first dated the trees in the 1950s, lies at the end of a twisting paved road at 10,000ft.

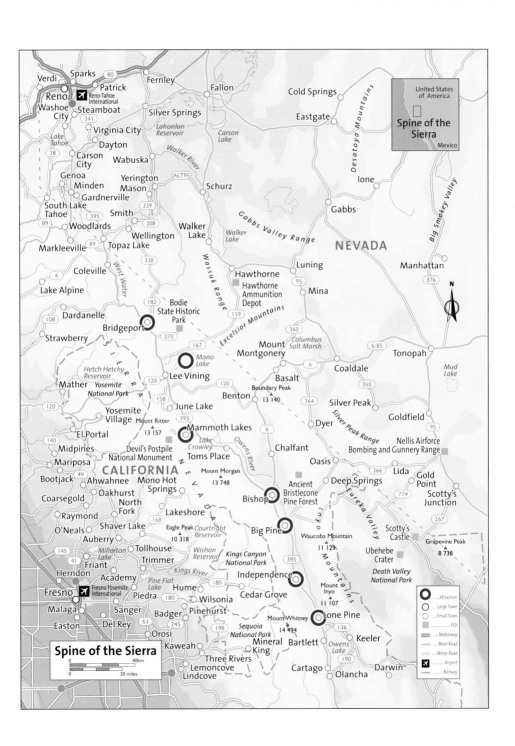

Spine of the Sierra

United States of America

Spine of the Sierra

Mexico

NEVADA

CALIFORNIA

Spine of the Sierra

0 _____ 40km
0 _____ 20 miles

O .....Attraction
O .....Large Town
O .....Small Town
■ .....POI
━━ .....Motorway
━━ .....Main Road
─── .....Minor Road
✈ .....Airport
──── .....Railway

Look for two self-guiding trails, the 1-mile **Discovery Trail** and the slightly longer **Methuselah Trail**, which passes the 4,700-year-old Methuselah Tree and the **Visitor Center**. **Patriarch Grove**, 12 miles beyond on a gravel road at 11,320ft, offers spectacular views of the Sierra, the Great Basin in Nevada, and the Patriarch Tree, the largest bristlecone. **Palisade** is the southernmost glacier in the US, looming above Big Pine Canyon west of town at the end of Glacier Lodge Rd, 11 miles west from Hwy 395.

BISHOP

Bishop Chamber of Commerce and Visitors Bureau *690 N. Main St; tel: (760) 873-8405 or (888) 395-3952; www.bishopvisitor.com*

Bureau of Land Management (BLM) *351 Pacu Lane, Ste 100; tel: (760) 872-5000; www.ca.blm.gov/ bishop/index.html. Open Mon–Fri 0800–1630.*

Public Lands Information Center *798 N. Main St; tel: (760) 873-2503. Call for hours.*

Mountain Light Gallery *106 S. Main St; tel: (760) 873-7700; www.mountainlight.com. Open daily 1000–1800.*

Red Rock Canyon Petroglyphs *Off Hwy 6. Stop at the BLM office for free permit and maps.*

Bishop is the largest town in the Owens Valley, one of the few to survive Los Angeles's insatiable thirst. In 1910, about 4,500 people lived between Bishop and Owens Lake, just south of Lone Pine. The valley floor was once a maze of orchards, vineyards and fields of corn, wheat and potatoes, while a steamship plied the waters of **Owens Lake** (now dry).

But Los Angeles, one of California's fastest-growing cities, needed more water. The **Owens Valley** had the bad luck to be the nearest source. LA's Department of Water and Power (DWP) chief engineer William Mulholland and his cronies bought up most of the valley, through either sham corporations or questionable legal tactics. Local officials were bribed or intimidated with the sort of semi-legal real-estate schemes depicted in the 1974 Jack Nicholson film *Chinatown*.

When the Owens Valley Aqueduct opened in 1913, nearly all of the water that once ran through the Owens Valley was diverted to Los Angeles. Steely blue Owens Lake became a pinkish salt flat, and fields and orchards gave way to dunes as the population drifted away.

Bishop, at the head of the valley, survived to become a burst of civilisation surrounded by mountain wilderness that lures anglers (fantastic fly fishing), hikers, mountain climbers and other outdoor lovers. **Mountain Light Gallery** features photography by the late nature and adventure photographer Galen Rowell, including images of the nearby High and Eastern Sierras. The most visible signs of Native American history are the **petroglyphs** scattered about the valley. The meaning of the figures pecked into rocks is long lost, but the best place to see them is the **Red Rock Canyon Petroglyphs** (*off Hwy 6*). Most of the images are found at places where water used to be, nearly all of them now dry, courtesy of Los Angeles.

Food in Bishop

Erick Schat's Bakkerÿ $ (*763 N. Main St; tel: (760) 873-7156*) has good espresso, light meals and Dutch-style baked goods. **Jack's Restaurant and Bakery $** (*437 N. Main St; tel: (760) 872-7971*) is an institution. **Whiskey Creek $$** (*524 N. Main St; tel: (760) 873-7174; www. whiskeycreekbishop.com*) offers American cuisine and Bishop's liveliest bar.

BRIDGEPORT

Bridgeport Chamber of Commerce *PO Box 541;* tel: *(760) 932-7500;* www.bridgeportcalifornia.com

Film buffs might recognise Bridgeport as the village that gave fugitive Robert Mitchum a new start in the 1947 film *Out of the Past.* Mitchum's Mono Motor Service petrol station has disappeared, but the tiny town with its 1880 Mono County Courthouse is otherwise little changed. Those not addicted to the film noir genre might look out for the turn-off to **Bodie** (*see page 118*), 6 miles south.

INDEPENDENCE

Independence Chamber of Commerce *145 N. Edwards (Hwy 395);* tel: *(760) 878-0084;* www.independence-ca.com. *Open Mon–Tue 0900–1700, Fri–Sat 0800–1600.*

Manzanar National Historic Site Tel: *(760) 878-2194;* www.nps.gov/manz. *Site open daily dawn–dusk. Free.*

Eastern California Museum *155 N. Grant St;* tel: *(760) 878-0258;* www.countyofinyo.org/ecmuseum. *Open daily 1000–1700. Admission by donation.*

The small town was named after Fort Independence, established in 1862 to protect white settlers from Paiutes angry at the usurpation of their lands. It is better known for the **Manzanar Relocation Camp**, 6 miles south.

Manzanar (the name means 'apple orchard' in Spanish) was a thriving apple- and pear-growing town around the turn of the 20th century that died when Los Angeles diverted its water south. It was reborn during World War II as a desolate internment camp for 10,000 mostly California-born Americans of Japanese ancestry. Considered a threat by military officials, Japanese-Americans were imprisoned until 1944 and their property confiscated.

Most of the internees had owned businesses and homes in coastal California; Manzanar gave them 500sq ft per family in flimsy, paper-covered wooden barracks behind barbed-wire fences, buffeted by freezing winter winds and sweltering summer heat. It took the US government more than 40 years to settle compensation claims and apologise.

All that remains are foundations visible amid the sagebrush, a pair of ornamental gates, a garage and a cemetery obelisk marking the National Historic Site, and the visitors centre in a rebuilt former high-school auditorium originally constructed by internees. Rangers lead guided tours, or you can drive the 3¼-mile self-guided auto tour around the site.

The **Eastern California Museum** details the impact of Manzanar on the many children who grew up behind the barbed wire. Other displays cover Owens Valley environments, Paiute and settler artefacts, farming implements and mining equipment.

Just north of town is **Mount Whitney State Fish Hatchery** (*Fish Hatchery Rd; tel: (760) 878-2272*), a stone monastery-style building with a Tudor tower and the ruins of Fort Independence, abandoned in 1877.

LONE PINE

This is a convenient base for exploring the nearby mountains, including 14,494ft **Mount Whitney** and desert areas. It's also the first touch of civilisation west from Death Valley. The best stop is the

Lone Pine Chamber of Commerce 120 S. Main St, Lone Pine, CA 93545; tel: (760) 876-4444; www.lonepinechamber.org. Open Mon–Fri 0830–1630.

Beverly & Jim Rogers Museum of Lone Pine Film History $ Hwy 395, S. Main St; tel: (760) 876-9909; www. lonepinefilmhistorymuseum.org. Open Mon–Wed 1000–1800, Thur–Sat 1000–1900, Sun 1000–1600.

Lone Pine Film Festival (www.lonepinefilmfestival.org) is in October.

Eastern Sierra Interagency Visitor Center (*Hwy 395/136 junction; tel: (760) 876-6222; www.fs.fed.us/r5/inyo. Open daily winter 0800–1700; longer in summer*), which has complete information on Owens Valley attractions as well as routes into Death Valley and a front-porch view of Mount Whitney.

If the scenery seems familiar, it probably is. Cowboys, Indians (Native Americans), outlaws, Bengal lancers and space aliens have been parading before cinema cameras in the **Alabama Hills** (*www.ca.blm.gov/pdfs/bishop_pdfs/suv/route2.pdf*) since the early 1920s. Six-mile **Movie Flat Rd** (*Hwy 395 to Whitney Portal Rd*) remains a favourite with film-makers. The gravel road is easily passable by cars and RVs, but unsigned side roads can be rough. Having driven Movie Flat Rd, visit the **Indian Trading Post** (*137 S. Main St*). The souvenir stock is standard, but the front door frame was signed by Gary Cooper, Errol Flynn, John Wayne and other film stars.

The **Beverly & Jim Rogers Museum of Lone Pine Film History** is a private effort to preserve the Eastern Sierra's film history with posters, photographs and other artefacts of the West and its (film) landscape. The October **Lone Pine Film Festival** screens films from the Westerns' heyday and gives film location tours.

MAMMOTH LAKES

Mammoth Lakes Visitors Bureau Tel: (760) 934-2712 or (888) 466-2666; www.visitmammoth.com

Mammoth Ranger Station and Welcome Center (*Inyo National Forest; www.fs.fed.us/r5/inyo*) Hwy 203; tel: (760) 924-5500. Open daily 0800–1700. The centre dispenses outdoor recreation and camping information, backcountry permits, and directions to the shuttle to Devil's Postpile National Monument, mid-Jun–Sept.

Originally a short-lived Gold Rush town, Mammoth is California's second-most popular mountain resort after Lake Tahoe. A major ski centre in winter, more than 50 miles of skiing trails become mountain-bike runs in summer. Either season, the gondola to the top of Mammoth Mountain provides stunning **views** north to Mono Lake. The top of the Sierra Interpretive Center provides an informative preview. **Mammoth Lakes Basin**, just south, is a glacial depression with six scenic lakes as alluring to winter alpine skiers as to summer hikers. **June Lake**, just north, is a quieter alternative with similar scenery.

The Mammoth area's most unusual sight is **Devil's Postpile National Monument**, a wall of basalt columns 60ft tall, rising above the middle fork of the San Joaquin River. The pile was formed about 100,000 years ago as a basalt flow from Mammoth Mountain cooled and cracked into hexagonal and octagonal posts. A glacier cut through the area about 10,000 years ago, exposing the formation.

Right
Tufa formations at Mono Lake echo the peaks of the Sierra Nevada Mountains

Devil's Postpile National Monument ($ for road access, not shuttle) Tel: (760) 934-2289; www.nps.gov/depo. Open Jun–Oct. In summer, day visitors (but not campers) must take shuttle transport from the Forest Service Adventure Center adjacent to the Mammoth Mountain Inn.

Mammoth Ski Museum $ 100 College Parkway; tel: (760) 934-6592; www. mammothskimuseum.org. Open Wed–Sun.

The pile is less than a ½-mile by trail from monument headquarters; a second trail leads to the top of the pile, which resembles a tiled floor. The main trail continues 2 miles to **Rainbow Falls**, a 101ft waterfall renowned for rainbows refracted in the spray around midday. A shorter trail leads to the Falls from **Reds Meadow**.

Mammoth is famous for its **hot springs**, which may be the legacy of North America's most destructive volcanic eruption (about 760,000 years ago) or the forerunner of eruptions yet to come. **Hot Creek Geothermal Area** (*Airport/Hot Creek Fish Hatchery Rd, off Hwy 395*) is an icy mountain stream that mixes with near-boiling water from natural vents creating blue pools beautiful to contemplate, but closed as too dangerous for soaking. Don't expect solitude and don't settle too close to heat sources – bathers have been scalded to death by unexpected blasts of superheated water. Skiers search out the Beekley International Collection of Skiing Art and Literature at **Mammoth Ski Museum** to see how the Mammoth resort began and admire skiing pioneers' stories.

Accommodation and food in Mammoth Lakes

Beware of winter weekends, when Los Angeles skiers pour into Mammoth, and summer weekends, nearly as popular with mountain bikers and climbers. Midweek is more reasonable.

The Stove $ *644 Old Mammoth Rd; tel: (760) 934-2821.* A long-time favourite especially at breakfast for gargantuan portions of American specialities.

Whiskey Creek $$ *Main St and Minaret Rd; tel: (760) 934-2555.* One of Mammoth's liveliest restaurants and bars and has its own good microbrews.

Mammoth Mountain Inn $$$ *Tel: (800) 626-6684; www. mammothmountain.com. The* place to sleep, at the base of the ski lifts, next to the bike park and overlooking the climbing rock.

MONO LAKE

Mono Basin National Forest Scenic Area Visitor Center Hwy 395, 1 mile north of Lee Vining; tel: (760) 647-3044; www.fs.fed.us/r5/inyo/ recreation/rec-reports/ mono.shtml. Call for hours.

This other-worldly lake, rimmed by salt flats, twisted mineral towers and newborn mountains, may be the oldest lake in North America. It is also the nesting ground for 85 per cent of all California gulls, which feed on the trillions of shrimp and flies that hatch in the salty, alkaline shallows. The towers are made of tufa, limestone deposited underwater when mineral-laden springs bubbled into the alkaline lake. A new aqueduct to Los Angeles that opened in 1941 dropped water levels by more than 40ft, exposing the bizarre towers and nearly destroying the lake. Twenty years of environmental battles forced

ℹ Mono Lake Committee Information Center/Lee Vining Chamber of Commerce
Hwy 395 and 3rd St, Lee Vining; tel: (760) 647-6595; www.monolake.org. Open daily winter 0900–1700; later in summer.

Mono County Tourism has Motor Touring in the Eastern Sierra-Mono County, a booklet with suggested tours: tel: (800) 845-7922; www.monocounty.org/backroads/index.html

Inyo County Tourism provides suggested tours in Motor Touring in the Eastern Sierra and Death Valley: www.inyocounty.us/InyoMarketing/index.php?page=trip-planning

ℹ Mono Lake Tufa State Nature Reserve $
Tel: (760) 647-6331; www.parks.ca.gov/default.asp?page_id=514

Mono Basin Bird Chautauqua $ (www.birdchautauqua.org) in a fun birding area hosts a natural history event near the summer solstice. The leading experts on fauna and flora of the Sierra Nevada present hikes, walking tours and talks.

Bodie State Historic Park $ Hwy 270 (last 3 miles gravel); tel: (760) 647-6445; www.parks.ca.gov/default.asp?page_id=509. Park open all year, but the road may be closed in winter.

Opposite
Bodie

LA to cut its water usage and agree to restore Mono Lake to historical levels.

The best place to see the tufa towers is **Mono Lake Tufa State Reserve**, on the south shore. The volcanic cones to the south are the **Mono Craters**, explosion pits, cinder cones and lava flows from California's youngest mountains. A short trail leads up to the rim of **Panum Crater**, about 650 years old. **Lee Vining**, just north, sits next to Hwy 120 east of **Tioga Pass** (summer only) and **Yosemite National Park** (see page 232).

Suggested tour

From **Reno**, follow Hwy 395 south to **Carson City**, the twin towns of **Minden** and **Gardnerville** and back into California. The scenic highway continues south over **Devil's Gate Summit** (7,519ft) and down to **Bridgeport**, starting point for a detour to **Bodie State Historic Park**. Hwy 395 climbs up over **Conway Summit** (8,138ft) before dropping down to **Mono Lake** and **Lee Vining**, then climbing past **June Lake** to **Deadman Summit** (8,041ft) and down past **Mammoth Lakes** into the **Owens Valley**, a desert corpse sucked dry to keep Los Angeles green. **Bishop** is the starting point for a side trip to **Laws**. Continue south on Hwy 395 through **Big Pine** and **Independence** to **Lone Pine** and **Mount Whitney**. Take Hwy 136 southeast to **Panamint Springs**, over **Towne Pass** (4,956ft) and down into **Death Valley National Park**.

Also worth exploring

Bodie State Historic Park

'Goodbye, God, we are going to Bodie' is how one girl faced the prospect of moving to Bodie in the 19th century. In its Gold Rush glory during the 1880s, Bodie boasted the widest streets, the meanest men and the most disgusting whisky in the West. A local preacher called the booming town of 10,000 'a sea of sin lashed by tempests of lust and passion'. He probably understated the daily tally of murder and mayhem that wracked California's most remote and lawless outpost. When the gold disappeared, so did the town, along with the churches, saloons, shops, brothels, schools and newspapers. Most people left possessions behind as though they expected to return.

About 170 buildings remain, all in a state of 'arrested decay'. Dusty shop windows are still loaded with merchandise; bedrooms still have tattered lace curtains and sagging mattresses. Pick up a self-guiding brochure for California's official Gold Rush ghost town at the former **Miners' Union Hall**.

🔵 **Laws Railroad
    Museum and
Historical Site** (operated
by the Bishop Museum
and Historical Society)
*From Bishop, take Hwy 395
to Hwy 6, drive 4 miles north
and east to Silver Canyon Rd.
Laws is ½ mile east.
Tel: (760) 873-5950;
www.lawsmuseum.org.
Open daily 1000–1600.
Donation.*

Laws
The **Laws Railroad Museum and Historical Site** was once a major
stop on the narrow-gauge Carson and Colorado Railroad between
Carson City, Nevada and Owens Lake. The 11-acre open-air museum
preserves the old station, the *Slim Princess*, the last steam locomotive
engine to work the line, and other rolling stock. Buildings include a
frontier physician's office and dispensary, the station agent's home,
Wells Fargo office, library and post office, all furnished with period
antiques. The drover's cottage across the road was built for the 1966
Steve McQueen film *Nevada Smith*.

Lake Tahoe and Reno

Ratings

History	●●●●●
Gambling	●●●●○
Scenery	●●●●○
Sport	●●●●○
Children	●●●○○
Food and drink	●●●○○
Lake cruises	●●●○○
Architecture	●○○○○

Lake Tahoe is California Mountain Country at its best, a 12-mile sapphire oval, 6,227ft above sea level, more than 1,600ft deep and surrounded by snow-capped Sierra peaks laced with hiking, cycling and skiing trails. Although the California–Nevada border divides Lake Tahoe east–west, the real division is north–south. South Shore revolves around Stateline, a miniature Las Vegas just inside Nevada, and the urban clutter of South Lake Tahoe on the California side of the border. North Shore sports a sprinkling of casinos, but the focus is firmly fixed on outdoor activities, from hiking and waterskiing in summer to snowshoeing and snowskiing in winter.

Hwys 28, 50 and 89 link to circle Tahoe, a scenic 72-mile drive that can take 2 hours midweek or most of the day at weekends. The towns of Virginia City, Carson City and Reno, in the historic heart of Nevada, lie just east.

The US National Park Service has *A National Register of Historic Places Travel Itinerary* online for Three Historic Nevada Cities: Carson City, Reno and Virginia City: *www.nps.gov/nrl travel/nevada/nev.htm*

CARSON CITY, NEVADA

ℹ Carson City Convention and Visitors Bureau *1900 S. Carson St, Ste 100; tel: (775) 687-7410 or (800) 638-2321; www.visitcarsoncity.com. Open Mon–Fri 0800–1700.*

♜ Mormon Station State Historic Park *$ Foothill Rd, Genoa; tel: (775) 782-2590; www.parks.nv.gov/ms.htm. Open mid-May–Sept daily 1000–1630.*

Nevada State Capitol *101 N. Carson St. Open during business hours. Free.*

Ask the Convention and Visitors Bureau for their free self-guided 2½-mile walking and driving map or podcast to the **Kit Carson Trail** historic district, west of Carson St. The tours include a home used as a set in John Wayne's final film, *The Shootist* (1976).

Nevada settlement began in 1851 at **Mormon Station State Historic Park**. When silver was discovered beneath what became **Virginia City** (*see page 130*), the Territorial Legislature moved the capitol to **Carson City**, nearer the mines.

The silver-domed **Nevada State Capitol** is open to the public, including the old legislative chambers. **Nevada State Museum** occupies the US Mint where Virginia City silver was turned into legal tender. Exhibits include a mine reproduction, a ghost town, minerals, a mint-mark coin collection, guns and a mammoth.

The **Nevada State Railroad Museum $** (*2180 S. Carson St; tel: (775) 687-6953; www.nsrm-friends.org. Open Fri–Mon 0830–1630, call to confirm departures for 'steam up' rides*) has more than 60 pieces of

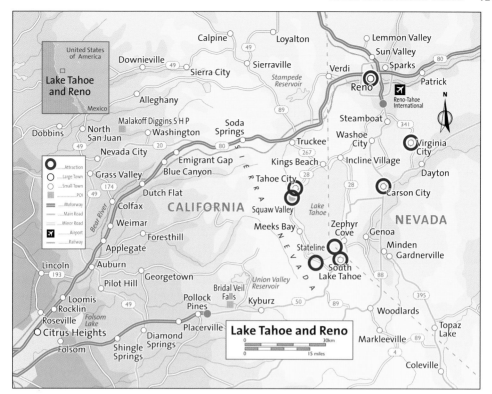

Nevada State Museum $ 600 N. Carson St; tel: (775) 687-4810; http://museums. nevadaculture.org. Open Wed–Sat 0830–1630.

rolling stock from the Virginia and Truckee Railroad, which ran from Virginia City to Carson City. Historic steam trains and motor cars make short trips in summer.

LAKE TAHOE CIRCUIT

Lake Tahoe Visitors Authority 169 Hwy 50, Stateline NV 89449; tel: (775) 588-5900 or (800) 288-2463; www.bluelaketahoe.com. Open daily 0900–1700.

Most drivers circle Lake Tahoe in a clockwise direction to avoid left turns into car parks. Allow at least a full day for the drive. Must-sees include **Emerald Bay** and **Inspiration Point**, on the southwest shore, and **Cave Rock Tunnel**, **Sand Harbor State Park** and **Zephyr Cove** on the Nevada side. You can request a tailor-made free Visitor Packet from AroundLakeTahoe.com (*www.aroundlaketahoe.com*) from the Lake Tahoe South Shore Chamber of Commerce to give you as much information as you like about Tahoe before travelling.

Tahoe's greatest concentration of hiking trails is on the southwest shore around **Fallen Leaf Lake**. The **Tahoe Rim Trail** circles the lake in 150 ridge-top miles, although parts of the route make pleasant day hikes. The **US Forest Service Taylor Creek Visitor Center** (*3 miles north of South Lake Tahoe on Hwy 89; tel: (530) 543-2674. Open Memorial Day–Oct, call for hours*) offers good recommendations, maps and

D L Bliss State Park $ Hwy 89, South Shore; tel: (530) 525-7277; www.parks.ca.gov. Campsites open May–Sept.

Emerald Bay State Park $ Hwy 89, South Shore; tel: (530) 541-3030; www.parks.ca.gov. Open daily.

Vikingsholm $ www.vikingsholm.com. Open Memorial Day–Sept daily for tours every half-hour 1000–1600.

Ed Z'berg-Sugar Pine Point State Park $ 10 miles south of Tahoe City on Hwy 89; tel: (530) 525-7982; www.parks.ca.gov/default.asp?page_id=510. *Hellman-Ehrman Mansion $* Open Memorial Day–Sept daily for tours 1000–1500.

brochures for everything from easy strolls to high-altitude leg burners. For information, ask at the **Lake Tahoe Basin Management Unit Forest Supervisor's Office** (35 College Dr, South Lake Tahoe; tel: (530) 543-2600; http://fs.usda.gov/ltbmu. Open Mon–Fri 0800–1630). South Shore is dominated by America's only bi-state ski resort, **Heavenly**, with 15 lifts in each state. North Shore has California's greatest concentration of ski resorts. Most ski mountains are open in summer for sightseeing, hiking and mountain biking.

D L Bliss State Park (South Shore) has one of Tahoe's most scenic beaches, though the water is icy and the car park fills up early. **Balancing Rock Nature Trail** is a ½-mile loop to a 128-ton boulder that appears balanced precariously on a granite slab. The **Rubicon Trail** is 4½ miles of spectacular lake views from **Rubicon Point** south to **Emerald Bay**.

Emerald Bay State Park (South Shore) surrounds **Emerald Bay**, a shallow, glacier-carved inlet named after its colour. The bay is best viewed from **Inspiration Point** on Hwy 89. A steep trail (2 miles return) leads from a car park at the north side of the bay down to **Vikingsholm**, a 1929 summer residence built to resemble a 9th-century Nordic castle. Just offshore is **Fanette Island**, with a ruined

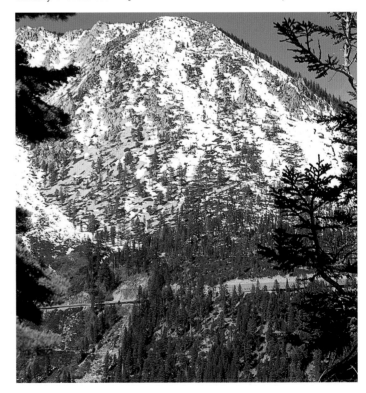

Right
Snowy peaks rise from
Emerald Bay

ⓘ Incline Village/ Crystal Bay Visitors Bureau 969 Tahoe Blvd, Incline Village; tel: (775) 832-1606 or (800) 468-2463.

North Lake Tahoe Visitors & Convention Bureau Tahoe City; tel: (800) 462-5196 or (530) 581-8703; www.gotahoenorth.com

Lake Tahoe-Nevada State Park Incline Village; tel: (775) 831-0494; http://parks.nv.gov/lt.htm

Nevada Commission on Tourism has a specialised website for ski resorts, especially those in Reno and Tahoe, with winter season information: http://ski.travelnevada.com

ⓘ Tahoe Rim Trail (TRT) 948 Incline Way, Incline Village; tel: (775) 298-0012; www.tahoerimtrail.org

tea house. Scuba divers can explore boats and barges in **Emerald Bay State Underwater Park**.

Ed Z'berg-Sugar Pine Point State Park (north of Emerald Bay along the west side of Lake Tahoe) is Lake Tahoe's largest state park. Sugar Pine Point holds several of Tahoe's oldest buildings. **Phipps Cabin** was built in 1872 by early resident William Phipps. The 1903 **Hellman-Ehrman Mansion**, known as the Ehrman (pronounced 'ermine'), made of local wood and granite quarried from nearby Meeks Bay, is furnished in mid-1930s style. The expansive grounds and the turreted mansion with large sitting porch were used as the opulent Lake Tahoe mansion setting in Godfather II.

Incline Village (North Shore) is the largest town on Tahoe's Nevada shore, with the closest casinos to Tahoe City and other North Shore hideaways. **Hyatt Regency Lake Tahoe Resort, Spa & Casino** $$$ (Lakeshore & 111 Country Club Dr, Incline Village; tel: (775) 832-1234 or (800) 233-1234; www.laketahoehyatt.com) is North Shore's most luxurious lakeside hotel and biggest casino.

Lake Tahoe-Nevada State Park, a largely undeveloped forest and lakeshore, is dotted with house-sized boulders and occasional patches of sandy beach. **Sand Harbor**, the largest beach, has a small boat dock. Hwy 28 joins Hwy 50 just south of the park to continue around the lake or east towards Carson City.

The 165-mile free **Tahoe Rim Trail** circles Lake Tahoe, offering stunning views of the lake and surrounding countryside. Allow a week to hike the entire trail or spend a few hours walking a short segment. The Tahoe Rim Trail Association arranges shuttle service ($) between several of the more popular trailheads in summer so visitors can walk one way, then get a ride back to their cars.

Hikers, mountain bikers and horses share the trail that was more than 20 years in the making. The trail is narrow – 2ft wide – with varied terrain, track obscured by snow in winter, no predictable source of fresh water and predators like mountain lions (cougars) in their element. Winter hikers and snowshoers carry GPS and quad maps. The TRT's official summer season begins when snow has melted, in most years from mid-July to late October.

RENO, NEVADA

ⓘ Reno/Sparks Convention & Visitors Authority (RSCVA) 4001 S. Virginia St; tel: (775) 827-7600 or (800) 367-7366; www.visitrenotahoe.com. Open Mon–Fri 0800–1700.

Reno's slogan, 'The Biggest Little City in the World', blazes from a neon arch (N. Virginia St and Commercial Row) in the downtown casino district. Reno is also a burgeoning commercial city with a relatively mild winter climate and desert summers made bearable by air conditioning. Spreading suburbs blend imperceptibly into the town of **Sparks**, which has its own set of casinos along I-80, just east of Reno.

The **National Automobile Museum** is one of America's finest auto collections. Galleries trace the automobile from the 'horseless carriage' of the 1890s to modern and experimental models.

RTC Sierra Spirit
Tel: (775) 348-7433;
www.rtcwashoe.com/public-
transportation-11; runs daily
0700–1900 every 10 minutes
and provides a free yellow bus
with stops from the University
of Nevada campus to
downtown.

National Automobile Museum $$ *10 S. Lake St;*
tel: (775) 333-9300;
www.automuseum.org.
Open Mon–Sat 0930–1730,
Sun 1000–1600.

Nevada Historical Society Museum $
1650 N. Virginia St;
tel: (775) 688-1190; http://
museums.nevadaculture.org/
*index.php?option=com_*
content&view=article&id=
446&Itemid=437. Open
Wed–Sun 1000–1700.

Nevada Museum of Art $$
160 W. Liberty St;
tel: (775) 329-3333;
www.nevadaart.org.
Open Wed–Sun 1000–1700,
Thur 1000–2000.

Wilbur D May Center
Rancho San Rafael Regional
Park, 1595 N. Sierra St;
tel: (775) 785-5961; www.
washoecounty.us/parks/

The **Nevada Historical Society Museum** is Nevada's oldest museum. Displays include Native American artefacts, pioneer relics, antique furniture, guns and minerals.

The **Nevada Museum of Art** (NMA) features touring exhibitions as well as permanent collections of Nevada art and artists. The most striking element in the four-storey museum is the stark black exterior inspired by the nearby Black Rock Desert. A Truckee River **Arts District** around the NMA has galleries, coffee houses and restaurants and a **River Walk** along the Truckee River.

Pyramid Lake, 30 miles long by 9 miles wide (*36 miles north on Hwy 445*), is the remnant of a prehistoric lake that once covered central Nevada. The sparkling lake, named after a pyramid-shaped formation, is surrounded by sagebrush and brown sandstone mountains, but has some of Nevada's finest trout fishing.

Truckee River Whitewater Park (*Truckee River, Lake St–Idlewild Park*) is a shady riverside park for downtown office workers and casino habitués surrounding a ½-mile river kayak course with Class II and III rapids, 11 drop-pools for manoeuvres, and gates for timed races. Park and course are deserted in winter and thronged on summer weekends.

The **Wilbur D May Center** includes the **Wilbur May Museum** and the **Arboretum and Botanical Garden**. The museum is a hodgepodge of tourist trinkets and *objets d'art* collected by department store heir Wilbur D May. The botanic garden re-creates a dozen different eastern Sierra Nevada plant habitats.

Accommodation and food in Reno

Downtown casinos offer good-value accommodation midweek, but prices jump dramatically at the weekend. For special offers, contact the RSCVA.

The local speciality is Basque, thanks to generations of Basque shepherds who have settled across Nevada. The best is **Louis' Basque Corner $$** (*301 E. 4th St; tel: (775) 323-7203. Open daily for lunch and dinner*).

Casino buffets (breakfast, lunch or dinner) are barely more expensive than fast food. The best restaurant in town is **La Strada $$$** (*Eldorado Hotel & Casino; tel: (800) 879-8879; www.eldoradoreno.com. Open daily for dinner*). Northern Italian dishes are from the owners of the Ferrari-Carrano Winery in California's Dry Creek Valley (*see page 164*).

SOUTH LAKE TAHOE

South Lake Tahoe (*South Shore*) is a collection of hotels, motels, restaurants and businesses sprawling from **The Y**, the junction of Hwys 50 and 89. South Lake Tahoe has the bulk of Tahoe's accommodation, restaurants and other tourist services, and casinos are a free shuttle ride away just across the border in Stateline, Nevada.

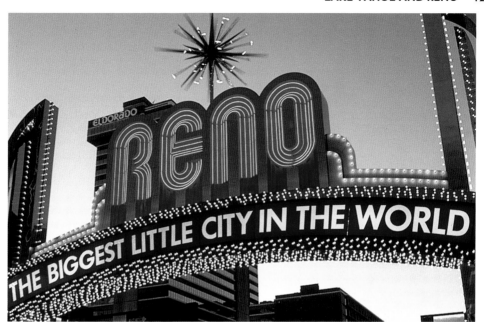

Above
Glittering lights welcome
visitors to Reno

ℹ **Lake Tahoe South
Shore Chamber
of Commerce/
Lake Tahoe Visitors
Authority (LTVA)/
North Blue Lake Tahoe**
Tel: (775) 588-5900 or
(800) 288-2463;
www.tahoesouth.com. Visitor
information centers: 3066
Lake Tahoe Blvd and 169
Hwy 50. Open daily
0900–1700.

🏛 **Tallac Historic Site**
Hwy 89, 3 miles north
of The Y; tel: (530) 541-
5227; www.fs.fed.us/r5/
ltbmu/recreation/tallac.
Grounds open daily.
Museum $ Open Memorial
Day–Sept daily1000–1600.

Tallac Historic Site is Tahoe's original resort area. The site contains several late 19th- and early 20th-century mansions, when Tahoe was the elegant escape of choice for upper-crust Californians. The grounds are open all year; buildings are open in summer.

Pope-Tevis Estate is the most lavish of the mansions with tours and living history programmes late June to September. **Valhalla** features wide verandas and walk-in fireplaces; the interior is open during the summer festival, special events and cultural performances (*www.valhallatahoe.com*).

The **US Forest Service Visitor Center** is the best source of information on outdoor activities around Lake Tahoe. Rangers lead nature walks and campfire programmes daily in summer; there are also a number of self-guiding hikes.

Inside the Visitor Center, **Taylor Creek Stream Profile Chamber** offers a glimpse beneath a genuine mountain stream. Bright-red kokanee salmon make their way from Lake Tahoe past the chamber in October to spawning beds further upstream.

South Lake Tahoe also has a series of fine beaches, though the icy water keeps most people on the sand even in midsummer. The best people-watching is at **Jamison Beach** (*Camp Richardson, 2½ miles north of The Y*), **Nevada Beach** (*Elk Point Rd, 1 mile east of Stateline*) and **El Dorado Beach**, in the centre of town.

The **Heavenly Gondola** provides the best views across Lake Tahoe from the mid-station observation deck, perched 9,123ft high on the slopes of Monument Peak. The gondola makes the 2½-mile run from the base village near Lake Tahoe and the Stateline casinos in 12 minutes. The Carson Valley spreads to the east and the Desolation Wilderness to

ℹ️ **US Forest Service**
Lake Tahoe Basin Management Unit, 35 College Dr; tel: (530) 543-2600; www. fs.fed.us/r5/ltbmu/contact. Open Mon–Fri 0800–1630.

Taylor Creek US Forest Service Visitor Center *3 miles north of South Lake Tahoe, on the lake side of Hwy 89; tel: (530) 543-2674; www. fs.fed.us/r5/ltbmu/contact. Open Memorial Day–Oct daily.*

🔘 **Heavenly Gondola** *$$ Hwy 50; tel: (775) 586-7000; www.skiheavenly.com. Open ski season–mid-Oct daily.*

Lake Tahoe Visitors Authority *Tel: (800) 288-2463; www.bluelaketahoe.com, handles bookings for the South Shore.*

the west, with the entire expanse of Lake Tahoe directly below. In winter, the gondola provides access to the largest ski resort in California; in summer it provides a lift to miles of scenic hiking trails.

For superb lake photography, visit **The Jon Paul Gallery** (*4000 Lake Tahoe Blvd, Ste C-18; tel: (530) 544-4269; www.jonpaulgallery.com*).

Accommodation and food in South Lake Tahoe

Sprouts Natural Foods Café $ *3123 Harrison Ave; tel: (530) 541-6969. Open daily.* An easy stop for picnic ingredients and vegetarian friendly.

Marriott's Timber Lodge® $$ *4100 Lake Tahoe Blvd; tel: (530) 542-6600; www.marriott.com/hotels/travel/rnotl-marriotts-timber-lodge.* Next to Heavenly Gondola base.

Scusa! on Ski Run $$ *1142 Ski Run Blvd; tel: (530) 542-0100. Open daily.* Tahoe's top Italian restaurant despite the casino-like lighting.

Embassy Suites Lake Tahoe Resort & Ski $$$ *4130 Lake Tahoe Blvd; tel: (530) 544-5400 or (877) 497-8483; www.embassytahoe.com.* Next to Stateline.

Evan's American Gourmet Café $$$ *536 Emerald Bay Rd; tel: (530) 542-1990; www.evanstahoe.com. Open daily.* Offers a mix of Italian, Caribbean, Asian and Southwestern dishes and a large wine list.

Marriott Grand Residence Club $$$ *1001 Heavenly Village Way; tel: (530) 542-8400; www.marriott.com/hotels/travel/rnogr-grand-residences-by-marriott–tahoe.* The luxury resort in South Lake Tahoe.

SQUAW VALLEY

 Squaw Valley USA Cable Car $$
Tel: (530) 583-6985 or (800) 403-0206; www.squaw.com.
Open daily, call or check website for hours.

Aerial trams make it easy to explore the near-vertical mountains that lured the 1960 Olympic Winter Games to Squaw Valley. The **Squaw Valley USA Cable Car** climbs 2,000ft to **High Camp Bath & Tennis Club**, with ice-skating, swimming, a climbing wall, restaurants and killer views. Skiing, hiking and mountain biking are among Tahoe's best. Down below, golf courses and hotels have taken over what was one of Tahoe's most tranquil corners.

Accommodation and food in Squaw Valley

River Ranch Lodge $$–$$$ (*Hwy 89 and Alpine Meadows Rd; tel: (530) 583-4264 or (866) 991-9912; www.riverranchlodge.com*) is an old-fashioned inn on the Truckee River, midway between Squaw Valley and Alpine Meadows ski areas. **River Ranch Lodge Restaurant $$$** (*open daily for dinner*) is a long-time local favourite overlooking the Truckee.

PlumpJack Squaw Valley Inn $$$ (*1920 Squaw Valley Rd; tel: (530) 583-1576 or (800) 323-7666; www.plumpjack.com*) has a sophisticated restaurant, **PlumpJack Café $$$** (*www.plumpjackcafe.com*).

The **Resort at Squaw Creek $$$** (*400 Squaw Creek Rd; tel: (530) 583-6300 or (800) 327-3353; www.squawcreek.com*) is Tahoe's most luxurious resort, complete with adult toys like a private golf course and ski lift.

STATELINE, NEVADA

Stateline is the Nevada side of South Lake Tahoe, dominated by the jangling slot machines and flashing neon of **MontBleu Resort Casino & Spa** (*tel: (775) 588-3515 or (888) 829-7630; www.montbleuresort.com*), **Harrah's** (*tel: (800) 427-7247; www.harrahslaketahoe.com*), **Harvey's** (*tel: (800) 427-8397; www.harveystahoe.com*), **Horizon** (*tel: (800) 648-3322; www.horizoncasino.com*) and a handful of smaller casinos.

Casino accommodation packages can be good value midweek and the buffets are always popular with teenagers and others with gargantuan appetites. Lounges and showrooms offer scaled-down versions of Las Vegas spectacles and the gambling is non-stop. Most restaurants and other services are in South Lake Tahoe.

Opposite
Pioneer transport

TAHOE CITY

North Lake Tahoe Resort Association
Tel: (888) 434-1262 or (530) 583-3494;
www.gotahoenorth.com

North Lake Tahoe Visitors Information Center 380 N. Lake Blvd; tel: (530) 581-6900; www.gotahoenorth.com. Open daily 0900–1700.

Road conditions Tel: (800) 427-7623 (California only); www.dot.ca.gov/cgi-bin/roads.cgi. For Nevada highways: tel: 511 or from outside Nevada: (877) 687-6237; www.safetravelusa.com/nv

Tahoe City (*North Shore*) is the hub of North Shore. Hwy 89 meets Hwy 28 at the western edge of town and **Fanny Bridge**, named after the view pedestrians present as they peer down at the enormous trout in the Truckee River, which flows from lakeshore gates to Pyramid Lake, in the desert near Reno.

The gates were once opened and closed by a gatekeeper who lived at **Gatekeeper's Museum**, a reconstruction of the original 1910 lodgepole pine cabin. The museum covers pioneer and Native American settlement in the area, with the extensive Marion Steinbach Indian Basket Museum collection.

One of the most popular summer pastimes is rafting the Truckee River from Tahoe City to River Ranch Lodge. White-water enthusiasts need not apply – the placid 4-mile, 3-hour trip is more suited to inner tubes and air mattresses than crash helmets. Operators provide raft, life jacket, paddle and a lift back to Tahoe City, but arrive before 1100 to avoid the worst of the crowds. Lunch or drinks at the River Ranch Lodge Restaurant is the traditional float finale. The **Truckee River Bike Trail** offers similar scenery from land.

Watson Cabin (*560 N. Lake Blvd; tel: (530) 583-1762; www.northtahoemuseums.org/watson.aspx*), built in 1908, is the oldest North Shore building still in its original location and is now the Gatekeeper's Museum satellite store.

Opposite
Lake Tahoe

Lake Cruises

Traffic and heavy lakeshore development can make the drive around Lake Tahoe disappointing. A more scenic way to tour Tahoe is from the lake itself. Commercial boats ply the lake with breakfast cruises, several trips during the day and sunset/dinner cruises. Some boats also ferry skiers in winter, and you can parasail above the lake in summer, from Zephyr Cove. Advance bookings are required all year.

MS Dixie II $$ 760 Hwy 50, Zephyr Cove; tel: (888) 896-3830; www.zephyrcove.com. A replica paddlewheeler sails from Zephyr Cove to Emerald Bay all year.

Tahoe Gal $$ Lighthouse Marina, 850 N. Lake Blvd, Tahoe City; tel: (800) 218-2464; www.tahoegal.com. Breakfast, scenic and dinner/dance cruises on the North Shore, mid-Jun–Oct.

Tahoe Queen $$ Zephyr Cove; tel: (888) 896-3830; www.zephyrcove.com. This sternwheeler once hauled cotton on the Mississippi River, and departs for Emerald Bay from Ski Run Marina, South Lake Tahoe.

Woodwind Sailing Cruises $$ Camp Richardson and Tahoe Keys Marina; tel: (888) 867-6394; www.sailwoodwind.com. Yacht and powerboat sailing cruises.

Accommodation and food in Tahoe City

Gatekeeper's Museum $ *130 W. Lake Blvd, William B Layton Park; tel: (530) 583-1762; www.northtahoemuseums.org. Open year-round, call to confirm hours.*

Bridgetender Tavern and Grill $ *65 W. Lake Blvd, Fanny Bridge; tel: (530) 583-3342. Lunch and dinner daily.* Tahoe City's busiest tavern, with fine burgers.

Fire Sign Café $$ *1785 W. Lake Blvd; tel: (530) 583-0871. Open daily for breakfast and lunch.* A long-time local breakfast favourite, with house-smoked salmon.

Christy Hill $$$ *115 Grove St; tel: (530) 583-8551; www.christyhill.com. Open Tue–Sun for dinner, call for reservations.* One of Tahoe's best restaurants with traditional California combinations and sunset views over the lake.

VIRGINIA CITY, NEVADA

Virginia City Convention & Tourism Authority *86 S. C St; tel: (775) 847-4386 or (800) 718-7587; www.visitvirginiacitynv.com. Open daily 1000–1700.*

Liberty Engine Company No 1, The Comstock Firemen's Museum *117 S. C St; tel: (775) 847-0717; www.comstockfiremuseum.com. Open Memorial Day–Labor Day daily 1000–1700.*

Julia Bulette Red Light Museum $ *5 N. C St, downstairs from Mandarin Gardens Chinese Restaurant; tel: (775) 847-9288. Open daily 1100–1900.*

Ponderosa Saloon Mine Tour $ *106 S. C St; tel: (775) 847-0757. Open daily.*

Piper's Opera House $ *B and Union Sts; tel: (775) 847-0433. Tours May–Oct daily, call to verify hours.*

The **North Lake Tahoe Resort Association** (*tel: (888) 434-1262; www.gotahoenorth.com*) has accommodation information and lists special discounts for the North Shore. Last-minute accommodation *may* be available north of Tahoe City towards the towns of **Tahoe Vista** and **Kings Beach**, but advance bookings are advisable all year and necessary at weekends, holidays and June–August.

Home to 30,000 residents and 110 saloons during the 1860s–80s Comstock Lode silver-mining boom years, Virginia City nearly died when the mines played out around the turn of the 20th century. Slopes above, beneath and around the town are riddled with hundreds of miles of unmapped mine shafts.

The almost-ghost town resurrected itself as a tourist destination after World War II, building on a reputation laid by former residents Mark Twain and Bret Harte. Twain's novel *Roughing It* recounts his days as a sometime miner, sometime journalist in Virginia City.

Comstock Firemen's Museum displays antique fire wagons and fire-fighting equipment in the original volunteer fire hall. **Julia Bulette Red Light Museum** is all that remains of what was once the biggest and busiest red-light district between Chicago and San Francisco.

Piper's Opera House was the cultural centre of the entire West during the 1880s. Highlights include original 19th-century scenery and furnishings and a floor built on ore cart springs to dampen dynamite blasts in the tunnels deep below. Most of those old tunnels have flooded or collapsed, but the fully operational **Ponderosa Saloon** offers tours of a small section of mine below the building.

The **Storey County Courthouse** (*B St near Union St*) acknowledges the legal realities of the profitable boom years through the 1880s – the statue of Justice that adorns the building façade shows her without her traditional blindfold.

Virginia and Truckee Railroad $
Washington and F Sts; tel: (775) 847-0380; www.virginiatruckee.com. Open late May–Oct daily 1030–1650.

Virginia and Truckee Railroad trains travel part of the railway's original line to Carson City. The V&TR runs through countryside just as rugged, just as dry and just as starkly beautiful as it was when Mark Twain worked the same hills. Regular service runs to the town of Gold Hill. Summertime express steam trains run on Saturdays from Virginia City to Carson City, but check for return arrangements.

September visitors should be prepared for the crowds and zaniness of the **Virginia City International Camel Races** (*tel: (775) 847-4386*).

Suggested tour

Circle **LAKE TAHOE ①** on Hwys 28, 50 and 89 and continue northeast to **CARSON CITY ②** on Hwy 50, with awesome desert views snaking down the eastern side of the Sierra Nevada. Take Hwy 395 north to **RENO ③**, or, for a more scenic route, follow Hwy 50 east to Hwy 341/342 and **VIRGINIA CITY ④** before looping north to Reno **③**.

Lake Tahoe and Reno

San Francisco

Ratings

Food and drink	●●●●○
Nightlife	●●●●○
Shopping	●●●●○
Architecture	●●●○○
Art	●●●○○
Children	●●●○○
Museums	●●●○○
Parks	●●●○○

For those who live here, San Francisco is *never* 'Frisco'; it's *The City*, a refuge of civilisation in an otherwise Wild West. It was, after all, The City the world encountered on the way to Gold Rush riches and The City where the successful few returned to splurge on real estate along the Barbary Coast. After The City was destroyed by an earthquake in 1906, it rebuilt itself to host the 1915 Panama-Pacific Exposition, then rebuilt reality.

The beatniks of the 1950s shook American society, political demonstrations in the 1960s shook government, the 1967 Summer of Love shook the world and in 2004 Mayor Gavin Newsom shook up the status quo by mandating same-sex unions. Los Angeles may be California's cultural capital, but San Francisco remains its fractious soul, an aggregation of minorities who dislike each other but still manage to live together. Precipitous hills, a sparkling bay, bridges, cable cars, 3,000 restaurants and benign tolerance for almost anything short of mayhem are eternal touchstones.

Getting there and getting around

San Francisco Convention & Visitors Bureau (SFCVB) *Visitor Information Center, 900 Market St, Hallidie Plaza, Lower Level, Powell and Market Sts;* tel: *(415) 391-2000 or (800) 637-5196;* www.onlyinsanfrancisco.com. *Open May–Oct Mon–Fri 0900–1700, Sat–Sun 0900–1500; Nov–Apr Mon–Fri 0900–1700, Sat 0900–1500.* 24-hour recorded event information: *(415) 391-2001.*

San Francisco International Airport (SFO) (*tel: (800) 435-9736 or (650) 821-8211; www.flysfo.com*) is 14 miles south on Hwy 101. A taxi to downtown is $37. Door-to-door van service is $14–$17 single. There are free shuttles to car-hire locations and airport hotels.

Bay Area Rapid Transit (BART) (*www.bart.gov*) offers inexpensive public transport to Downtown San Francisco, the East Bay and SFO. For area-wide transport, *tel: 511; www.511.org*

Parking

Public parking is scarce downtown. Fees range from $2–$20 per hour. Best bets are city-operated garages: **Sutter Stockton Garage** *444 Stockton St, near Union Square*; **Fifth & Mission Garage** *833 Mission St, between Union Square and Yerba Buena Gardens*; **Vallejo Street Garage** *766 Vallejo St*; **Portsmouth Square Garage** *733 Kearny St*. Charges are exorbitant at **Fisherman's Wharf** and **Pier 39**.

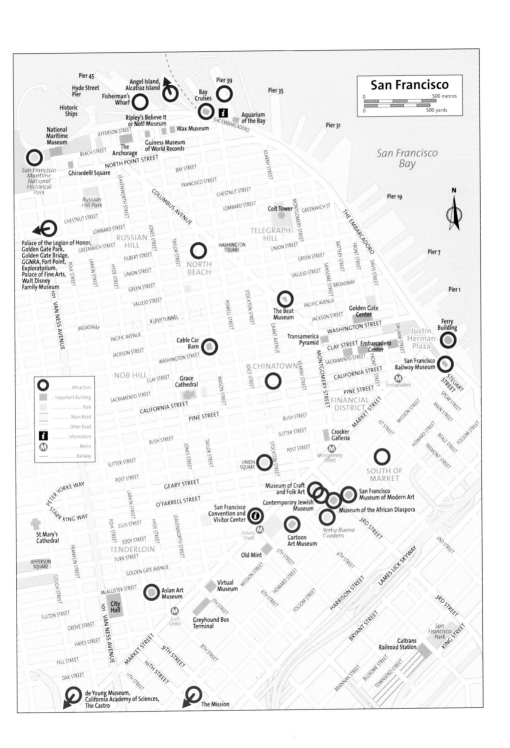

San Francisco

0   500 metres

0   500 yards

Pier 45
Hyde Street Pier
Historic Ships
National Maritime Museum
San Francisco Maritime National Historical Park
Ghirardelli Square

Angel Island, Alcatraz Island
Fisherman's Wharf
Ripley's Believe It or Not! Museum
The Anchorage
Guiness Museum of World Records

Pier 39
Bay Cruises
Wax Museum
Aquarium of the Bay

Pier 35

Pier 31

San Francisco Bay

Pier 19

N

JEFFERSON STREET
BEACH STREET
NORTH POINT STREET
BAY STREET
FRANCISCO STREET
CHESTNUT STREET
LOMBARD STREET

Russian Hill Park
CHESTNUT STREET
LOMBARD STREET

Palace of the Legion of Honor, Golden Gate Park, Golden Gate Bridge, GGNRA, Fort Point, Exploratorium, Palace of Fine Arts, Walt Disney Family Museum

GREENWICH STREET
FILBERT STREET
UNION STREET
GREEN STREET
VALLEJO STREET

RUSSIAN HILL

COLUMBUS AVENUE

Coit Tower
GREENWICH ST
TELEGRAPH HILL
WASHINGTON SQUARE
UNION STREET
GREEN STREET
VALLEJO STREET
BROADWAY
PACIFIC AVENUE

NORTH BEACH

Pier 7

Pier 1

THE EMBARCADERO

BROADWAY
PACIFIC AVENUE
JACKSON STREET
WASHINGTON STREET

R LEVY TUNNEL

The Beat Museum
Cable Car Barn

NOB HILL
Grace Cathedral

Golden Gate Center
Transamerica Pyramid
WASHINGTON STREET
CLAY STREET
Embarcadero Center
SACRAMENTO STREET
CALIFORNIA STREET

CHINATOWN

Justin Herman Plaza
Ferry Building
San Francisco Railway Museum

SACRAMENTO STREET
CALIFORNIA STREET
PINE STREET

PINE STREET
BUSH STREET
SUTTER STREET
POST STREET

FINANCIAL DISTRICT

Embarcadero

STEUART STREET
SPEAR STREET
MAIN STREET
BEALE STREET
FOLSOM STREET
FREMONT STREET
1ST STREET
MISSION STREET
HOWARD STREET

Crocker Galleria
Montgomery Street

BUSH STREET
SUTTER STREET
POST STREET
GEARY STREET
O'FARRELL STREET

PETER YORKE WAY
STARR KING WAY

UNION SQUARE

SOUTH OF MARKET

Museum of Craft and Folk Art
Contemporary Jewish Museum
San Francisco Convention and Visitor Center

San Francisco Museum of Modern Art
Museum of the African Diaspora

Powell Street

Cartoon Art Museum
Yerba Buena Gardens

St Mary's Cathedral
JEFFERSON SQUARE

TENDERLOIN
TURK STREET
GOLDEN GATE AVENUE

Old Mint

Virtual Museum

MISSION STREET
HOWARD STREET
FOLSOM STREET
HARRISON STREET
BRYANT STREET
BRANNAN STREET
TOWNSEND STREET

JAMES LICK SKYWAY

ELLIS STREET
EDDY STREET

McALLISTER STREET
City Hall
FULTON STREET
GROVE STREET
HAYES STREET
FELL STREET
OAK STREET

Asian Art Museum

Civic Center
Greyhound Bus Terminal

101 VAN NESS AVENUE
FRANKLIN STREET
GOUGH STREET
POLK STREET
LARKIN STREET
HYDE STREET
LEAVENWORTH STREET
JONES STREET
TAYLOR STREET
MASON STREET
POWELL STREET
STOCKTON STREET
GRANT AVENUE
KEARNY STREET
MONTGOMERY STREET
SANSOME STREET
BATTERY STREET
FRONT STREET
DAVIS STREET
DRUMM STREET

MARKET STREET
9TH STREET
10TH STREET
11TH STREET
8TH STREET
7TH STREET
6TH STREET
5TH STREET
4TH STREET
3RD STREET
2ND STREET
1ST STREET
KING STREET

de Young Museum, California Academy of Sciences, The Castro

The Mission

Caltrans Railroad Station
San Francisco Park

Attraction
Important Building
Park
Main Road
Other Road
Information
Metro
Railway

511 *tel: 511;*
www.511.org. Provides
area travel and transit
information, fares, weather
reports and highway
construction alerts.

Street parking is nearly impossible in Chinatown, North Beach, Fisherman's Wharf and Union Square, scarce elsewhere. Parking meters accept quarters, dimes and nickels, good for 15–60 minutes. Try to park and explore on foot rather than driving, or use the Municipal Railway (MUNI) transport when possible.

Driving

One-way streets, steep hills and lack of parking turn driving into a challenge. Coloured signs point the way to key areas: a green outline of Italy for **North Beach**; a red Chinese lantern for **Chinatown**; an orange crab for **Fisherman's Wharf**; a blue Victorian house for **Union St** and a white female statue for **Union Square**.

Public transport

The San Francisco Municipal Transportation Agency (MUNI; *tel: 311* or *(415) 701-2311 outside San Francisco; www.sfmta.com/cms/home/ sfmta.php*) reaches most major tourist attractions, but schedules can be erratic. **Buses** follow numbered routes on city streets. **Metro, light rail and streetcars** follow lettered routes underground in the city centre and on the surface in outlying districts. Historic streetcars ply the F-Line along Market St and The Embarcadero to Fisherman's Wharf. Trolleys are powered by overhead wires. **Cable cars** serve Nob Hill, Fisherman's Wharf, the Aquatic Park and California St. **MUNI Passport** (*www.sfmta.com/cms/mfares/passports.htm*) offers one-, three- or seven-day discounts. BART, the Bay Area Rapid Transit (*tel: (415) 989-2278; www.bart.gov*), provides service from SFO and San Francisco beneath the Bay to Oakland and other East Bay cities. Fares vary by distance. **San Francisco CityPass $$** (*www.citypass.com*) offers seven days of MUNI and cable-car transit, a Bay cruise and admission to four museums.

Below
Golden Gate Bridge

Ferries

Blue & Gold Fleet (*tel: (415) 705-8200; www.blueandgoldfleet.com*) departs from Pier 39/41 and the Ferry Building (*foot of Market St*) for AT&T Park (in Giants' baseball season, *Apr–Sept/Oct*), the East Bay, Sausalito, Angel Island, Tiburon, Six Flags Discovery Kingdom (*Vallejo*) and sightseeing cruises. **Red and White Fleet** (*tel: (415) 673-2900; www.redandwhite.com*) has around-the-bay cruises from Pier 43½. **Alcatraz Cruises** (*tel: (415) 981-7625; www.alcatrazcruises.com*) operates from Pier 33 to Alcatraz Island. **Golden Gate Transit** (*tel: (415) 451-4650; http://goldengateferry.org*) serves Sausalito and Larkspur (Marin County, north of San Francisco) from the Ferry Building and AT&T Park (during the Giants' baseball season).

Sights

Alcatraz Island $$
www.nps.gov/alcatraz.
For tours, tel: (415) 981-
7625; www.alcatrazcruises.
com. Departs from Pier 33.

Angel Island State Park
Tel: (415) 435-5390;
www.parks.ca.gov/
default.asp?page-id=468 or
www.angelisland.org

Asian Art Museum $$$
200 Larkin St, Civic Center
Plaza; tel: (415) 581-3500;
www.asianart.org. Open
Tue–Wed & Fri–Sun
1000–1700, Thur
1000–2100. Free first Sun
of the month.

Bay Quackers $$
Ellis and Powell Sts,
Union Square area; tel: (415)
431-3825;
www.bayquackers.com

**Ride the Ducks-San
Francisco $$** Jefferson
and Taylor Sts,
Fisherman's Wharf area;
tel: (800) 452-4386;
www.sanfranciscoducks.com

Alcatraz Island

The list of prisoners incarcerated in the infamous federal penitentiary reads like a *Who's Who* of Hollywood celebrity criminals. Al 'Scarface' Capone, Robert 'Bird Man of Alcatraz' Stroud and George 'Machine Gun' Kelly were among the 1,554 convicts who spent an average of eight years within sight of San Francisco, yet completely out of touch.

The tiny island is 1½ miles offshore, accessible only by boat. Alcatraz Cruises, with the National Park Service, operates daily self-guided and guided tours of what was once touted as America's only 'escape-proof' prison, as well as a refurbished wardens' wives' garden, and night tours.

Visitors may wander freely through the former cell blocks, including the 'dark holes' or solitary confinement cells used to punish prisoners. To appreciate fully the dank, depressing atmosphere of Alcatraz, listen to an **audio tour** narrated by former prison guards and inmates. An evening tour is eerie and evocative. The pervasive security apparently worked. Only 36 prisoners tried to escape: 10 were killed in the attempt; 21 captured; and 5 were never found.

Angel Island

Once the main port of entry from Asia, this was the West Coast equivalent of Ellis Island Immigration Station. The largest island in San Francisco Bay is a rural state park with stunning views of San Francisco, Alcatraz and the Bay Area. Facilities include restored **Angel Island Immigration Station**, with its depiction of the suffering of Chinese immigrants under exclusion laws, picnic grounds, a campsite, hiking and cycling trails and a narrated tram ride (*tel: (415) 897-0715*) around the island. Access is by private boat or ferry service.

Asian Art Museum

Some of the West's best and most prestigious Asian art collections are in San Francisco's Civic Center. Architect Gae Aulenti, designer of Paris's Musée d'Orsay, took an existing Beaux Arts main library building and revamped the interior with skylights and modern galleries. Of the museum's 13,000 artefacts, 2,500 are on permanent display, emphasising Buddhism, trade and regional crafts from most of Asia.

Bay cruises

The budget version is a commuter ferry ride. Bigger spenders can choose from the official Red and White Fleet tour that circles beneath the **Golden Gate Bridge** and the **San Francisco–Oakland Bay Bridge** with views of **Alcatraz, Angel Island, Treasure Island** and the **San Francisco waterfront**, as well as luxury yacht cruises and overnight escapes (*see Ferries, opposite*). **Bay Quackers'** bright-yellow and **Ride the Ducks-San Francisco** white World War II amphibious vehicle tour drives

The Beat Museum
540 Broadway and
Columbus Ave, North Beach;
tel: (800) 537-6822 or
(831) 372-4911;
www.thebeatmuseum.org.
Open daily 1000–1900.

**Cable Car Barn and
Museum** 1201 Mason and
Washington Sts;
tel: (415) 474-1887;
www.cablecarmuseum.org.
Open daily Apr–Sept
1000–1800; Oct–Mar
1000–1700. Free.

**California Academy of
Sciences $$** 55 Music
Concourse Dr, Golden Gate
Park; tel: (415) 379-8000;
www.calacademy.org.
Open Mon–Sat 0930–1700,
Sun 1100–1700.

Cartoon Art Museum $
655 Mission St; tel: (415)
227-8666;
www.cartoonart.org. Open
Tue–Sun 1100–1700. First
Tue of month is 'Pay What
You Wish Day'.

**Cruisin' the
Castro $$** Tel: (415)
225-1821;
www.cruisinthecastro.com.
The Castro District's
must-do tour. Mon–Tue &
Thur–Sat 1000–1200.
Reservations required.

from Fisherman's Wharf or Union Square to AT&T Park, then launches into San Francisco Bay where game passengers can pilot the 'boat'.

The Beat Museum
Beat artefacts are lovingly displayed in North Beach, Ground Zero for the 1950s beatniks, with correspondence, photographs, books and other personal items that bring the era to life.

Cable Car Barn
San Francisco's original mechanised transport still climbs halfway to the stars up **Nob Hill** between the Bay and the turnaround at **Hallidie Plaza** (*Powell and Market Sts*) and along California St. The **Hyde Street Line** runs to **Aquatic Park** (*Beach St between Hyde St and Van Ness Ave*) for easy access to **Fisherman's Wharf**, the historic ships at **Hyde Street Pier** in **San Francisco Maritime National Historical Park** and **Ghirardelli Square**, a former bayside chocolate factory.

Queue up (sometimes for hours) to board at the end of each cable-car line or follow the locals who walk a couple of blocks up the street to climb aboard without waiting. To see how the system works, visit the **Cable Car Barn**. Don't miss the gallery overlooking the 14ft pulleys that haul miles of steel cable beneath city streets to power the cable cars at a constant 9mph. The **Cable Car Museum** in one corner of the Barn displays the history of the system.

California Academy of Sciences
The oldest scientific institution in the Western US (1874) has returned to Golden Gate Park in a new complex with a grass and wild-flower-landscaped roof, aquarium, planetarium, natural history exhibits and a domed rainforest. Use your mobile phone for a free exhibits' tour.

Cartoon Art Museum
A museum devoted to cartoon art, with 6,000 original works and cheerful enthusiasm. Look for comic books, editorial cartoons, cartoon strips, animations, advertisements, greeting cards and the odd video.

Castro District
For a quarter of a century, The Castro as it's known (neighbourhood centres around Castro and Market Sts, look for the huge Rainbow Flag at that intersection) has been a mecca for the gay (and lesbian and transgender) lifestyle, with restaurants, clubs, stores and services sensitively serving a community that has lovingly preserved some of the most beautiful Victorian residences in the city.

Chinatown
What began as a shanty town of Chinese miners expelled from the goldfields around 1850 has become the largest Chinese community outside Asia (*Pine St to North Beach between Kearny and Powell Sts*).

Above
San Francisco Conservatory of Flowers

Dr Sun Yat-sen planned the revolution that became the Chinese Nationalist Republic from a tiny building on Spofford Alley. More recently, Chinatown's Waverly Pl has featured prominently in San Franciscan Amy Tan's bestselling novel *The Joy Luck Club*. Place names used in the book are as real as the slap of mah-jong tiles that can still be heard through neighbourhood doorways.

Grant Ave, Chinatown's official high street, is a tourist trap. Stockton St, one block west, is piled high with vegetables, live fish, smoked duck and other necessities. Dim sum (filled dumplings), noodles and Chinese bakeries are a sure bet for delicious local colour.

Contemporary Jewish Museum
(CJM) $$ *736 Mission St, SOMA; tel: (415) 655-7800; www.thecjm.org. Open Fri–Tue 1100–1700, Thur 1300–2000.*

Contemporary Jewish Museum

The shimmering blue block in the Yerba Buena Arts District, a section of a refurbished power substation, changes colour with the sky as planned by designer Daniel Libeskind to house exhibitions of commissioned and other work reflecting Jewish culture.

de Young Museum $$
50 Hagiwara Tea Garden Dr; tel: (415) 750-3600; www.famsf.org/deyoung. Open Tue–Sun 0930–1715, Fri 1700–2245 for free multicultural performances. Free first Tue of the month.

de Young Museum

The copper-clad museum and free (cityscape) observatory tower in Golden Gate Park has 17th- to 20th-century American art, collections from the Americas, the Pacific and Africa, and important textile collections.

Exploratorium $$ *Palace of Fine Arts, 3601 Lyon St and Marina Blvd; tel: (415) 561-0360 (recorded information); www.exploratorium.edu. Open Tue–Sun 1000–1700. Tactile Dome charges additional admission.*

Exploratorium and Palace of Fine Arts

This museum of science, art and perception is designed for children, but adults are just as eager to get their hands on 500 do-it-yourself exhibits. The highlight is the **Tactile Dome**, moving by touch through a maze of shapes and textures in pitch blackness. The Exploratorium adjoins the beautiful Palace of Fine Arts, built to resemble a classical ruin for the 1915 **Panama-Pacific Exposition**.

Ferry Building *The Embarcadero at the foot of Market St; tel: (415) 983-8000; www. ferrybuildingmarketplace.com*

Ferry Building

Say 'Farmers' Market' in this food-loving city and this is the one everyone thinks of – crowded with shoppers, foodies and chefs on Tuesday, Thursday and Saturday mornings. Inside the Ferry Building, restored to 1898 glory, is a food-hall corridor marketplace of 30-odd individual local purveyors of crafted foods. Restaurants offer a spot to dine on Vietnamese (at **The Slanted Door**), and **Book Passage** stocks a selection to browse through while waiting until a ferry is ready to depart to the East Bay.

Ferry Plaza Farmers' Market
Tel: (415) 291-3276; www. ferryplazafarmersmarket.com. Tue & Thur 1000–1400, Sat 0800–1400.

🔋 Fisherman's Wharf
Jefferson and Taylor Sts; take a cable car or historic F-Line streetcar. Open daily. Free.

USS *Pampanito* $$ *East side of Pier 45, Fisherman's Wharf; tel: (415) 775-1943; www.maritime.org/pamphome.htm. Open daily.*

Fort Point National Historic Site *Golden Gate National Recreation Area (GGNRA); tel: (415) 556-1693; www.nps.gov/fopo. Open Fri–Sun 1000–1700. Free.*

Golden Gate Bridge
Hwy 101 between San Francisco and Marin County. $6 auto toll southbound; pedestrians and cyclists free.

Golden Gate National Recreation Area
Tel: (415) 561-4700; www.nps.gov/goga. Call for hours and location of specific areas of GGNRA. Free.

Golden Gate Park
Stanyan St to the Pacific Ocean between Fulton St and Lincoln Ave.

Japanese Tea Garden $
Hagiwara Tea Garden Drive.

San Francisco Botanical Garden at Strybing Arboretum
9th Ave and Lincoln Way, Golden Gate Park; tel: (415) 661-1316; www.sfbotanicalgarden.org. Open Mon–Fri 0800–1630, Sat–Sun 1000–1700. Free guided walks daily at 1330. Free.

Conservatory of Flowers $ *JFK Dr, Golden Gate Park; tel: (415) 831-2090; www.conservatoryofflowers.org. Open Tue–Sun 0900–1630.*

Fisherman's Wharf

This one-time home to San Francisco's commercial fishing fleet now has more T-shirt and souvenir shops than fishing boats. The USS *Pampanito* submarine is open for tours. Explore on foot between **Pier 39**, **Fisherman's Wharf, Aquatic Park** and the **San Francisco Maritime National Historical Park, Ghirardelli Square, The Cannery** and **Fort Mason**.

Fort Point National Historic Site

The red-brick fort beneath the Golden Gate Bridge was built to defend San Francisco during America's Civil War, 1861–5. Costumed guides re-create life inside the fort with cannon-loading demonstrations, while waves sweeping through the **Golden Gate** blast spray 30ft into the air.

Golden Gate Bridge

The bridge opened in 1937, linking the gap above the tides churning through the Golden Gate, the narrow passage into San Francisco Bay. 'Golden' refers to the Golden Horn in Istanbul, after which adventurer-explorer John Frémont named the entrance in 1846. The bridge is painted orange for better visibility in heavy fog. Park at the San Francisco end to walk or cycle across; drive to the vista point just beyond the north end of the bridge to look back towards San Francisco.

Golden Gate National Recreation Area (GGNRA)

A string of former military bases and coastal defences has become the world's largest urban park, stretching west from **Aquatic Park** and **Fort Mason** along the Bay to the **Presidio**, then south along the Pacific beyond San Francisco. Also included are **Alcatraz** and **Angel Islands**, the **Marin Headlands, Muir Woods National Monument, Mount Tamalpais** and much of **Tomales Bay** shoreline. Best views can be had from **Crissy Field**, the Golden Gate Bridge to Downtown San Francisco; from the **Golden Gate Promenade; Baker Beach**, facing the Golden Gate Bridge from the ocean; **Lands End** with the city's most natural landscape and best sunsets; and **upper Fort Mason** for Bay vistas.

Golden Gate Park

America's second great urban park (after Central Park in New York), Golden Gate Park is 1,000 acres of drifting sand dunes transformed into shady forests, winding drives, lakes surrounded by open glades and museums. Don't miss jasmine tea and fortune cookies in the **Japanese Tea Garden**.

The park is also home to **San Francisco Botanical Garden at Strybing Arboretum**, 8,000 plant species arranged in 25 distinct garden habitats and the restored white glass Victorian **Conservatory of Flowers**, with five galleries crammed with tropical plants, including a centenarian *Philodendron* twisting skywards.

San Francisco Railway Museum
77 Steuart St, at the Steuart St F-Line stop; tel: (415) 974-1948; www.streetcar.org. Open Tue–Sun 1000–1800.

Museum of the African Diaspora $$ 685 Mission and 3rd Sts; tel: (415) 358-7200; www.moadsf.org. Open Wed–Sat 1100–1800.

Museum of Craft and Folk Art $ 51 Yerba Buena Lane; tel: (415) 227-4888; www.mocfa.org. Open Mon–Tue & Fri 1100–1800, Sat–Sun 1100–1700. Free first Tue of the month.

Coit Tower $
1 Telegraph Hill Blvd; tel: (415) 362-0808. Open daily 1000–1800. Parking is extremely limited; walk up or take bus 39. The hilltop view is free.

North Beach Chamber of Commerce Tel: (415) 989-2220; www.sfnorthbeach.org

Palace of the Legion of Honor $$ 34th Ave and Clement St, Lincoln Park; tel: (415) 750-3600; www.famsf.org/legion. Open Tue–Sun 0930–1715. Free first Tue of the month.

Market Street Railway: San Francisco Railway Museum

Seen the historic streetcars from all over the world trundling along Market St and along The Embarcadero? A stop signal marks a collection of lore, history and artefacts gathered by private streetcar restorers, including a transfer that expired several minutes before the 1906 earthquake.

The Mission (District)

Named after **Mission Dolores** (*17th and Dolores Sts, page 258*), founded in 1776, The Mission is Central and South America come north. Look for brilliant murals blazing messages of equality, ethnic pride and hope, a wide range of Mexican and other Hispanic restaurants, innovative cuisine and lively streets.

Museum of the African Diaspora

The art, music, food, rituals, clothing, photographs, slave history and freedom struggles of people of African origins are catalogued in well-captioned galleries.

Museum of Craft and Folk Art

Sandwiched between the Four Seasons Hotel and Moscone Convention Center, this tiny museum hosts four superb exhibits each year. Shop at its alley-front store for craft art from around the world.

North Beach

Once a northern beach on San Francisco Bay, North Beach (*blocks surrounding Broadway and Columbus Ave*) was settled by Portuguese and Italians. The area has been an entertainment and nightlife district for more than a century. The topless and nude dancing clubs that have spread across America began at **The Condor** (*300 Columbus Ave/560 Broadway; tel: (415) 781-8222*) in the 1960s. Sourdough bread is still baked in North Beach.

The beatnik era survives at poet Lawrence Ferlinghetti's **City Lights Bookstore** (*261 Columbus Ave; tel: (415) 362-8193; www.citylights.com*) and **Vesuvio Café** (*255 Columbus Ave; tel: (415) 362-3370; www.vesuvio.com*). **The Beat Museum** (*see page 136*) is up the block. It's a short, if steep, walk from the coffee houses to the high point of North Beach, tiny **Telegraph Hill**, topped by 212ft **Coit Tower**. The nozzle-shaped tower was built by Lillie Coit, an early city socialite with a notorious fondness for burly firemen. The interior features splendid Depression-era murals.

Palace of the Legion of Honor

This copy of Napoleon's Hôtel de Salm in Paris, usually called the Legion of Honor, displays ancient and European art from 2500 BC to the 20th century, and a large collection of graphic and print artworks. Check for major touring exhibitions and the Rodin sculpture collection.

Above
Nature in the city's midst –
basking sea lions at San
Francisco's Pier 39

**ⓘ San Francisco
Maritime National
Historical Park $**
Beach St between Hyde St
and Van Ness Ave; tel: (415)
447-5000; www.nps.gov/safr.
Open daily. **Visitor center,**
Hyde and Jefferson Sts in the
Argonaut Hotel complex.
Open daily winter
0930–1900; later in summer.

**San Francisco Museum
of Modern Art
(SFMOMA) $$** 151 3rd
St, SOMA; tel: (415) 357-
4000; www.sfmoma.org.
Open Thur 1100–2045,
Fri–Tue 1100–1745;
Memorial Day–Labor Day
Thur 1000–2045, Fri–Tue
1000–1745.

**Walt Disney Family
Museum $$$** 104
Montgomery St, the Presidio;
tel: (415) 345-6800; http://
disney.go.com/disneyatoz/
familymuseum/index.html.
Open Wed–Mon
1000–1800.

Pier 39

One of the state's most popular tourist attractions is an abandoned pier converted to more than 110 retail shops, entertainment and restaurants with fine views of Alcatraz and the Bay (*The Embarcadero at Beach St; tel: (415) 981-7437; www.pier39.com. Open daily*). The Pier's most famous residents are the barking **sea lions** that have taken over the north side marina. Most Blue & Gold Fleet ferries leave from Pier 41, just west. A **California Welcome Center** (*tel: (415) 981-1280*) is on the second floor.

San Francisco Maritime National Historical Park

The nation's only floating national park includes the **Maritime Museum** housed in a gleaming white Art Deco streamline modern building in Aquatic Park and historic ships docked at the **Hyde Street Pier $** (*Open 0930–1700, longer in summer*). The square rigger *Balclutha* and the *Eureka*, a former San Francisco Bay ferry, are among the ships open for tours.

San Francisco Museum of Modern Art (SFMOMA)

Northern California's largest collection of modern art is noted for its distinctive architectural design by Mario Botta and the popular Caffé Museo, and is the city's most visited museum.

SOMA

The South of Market (Street) Area (SOMA) was once an industrial haven filled with brick buildings and dark alleyways, but has metamorphosed into a trendy residential, entertainment, art and museum district. Clubs suit every taste from Springsteen to Grunge. **AT&T Park** (*www.mlb.com/sf/ballpark*), at SOMA's south end, is the waterfront baseball park home of the **San Francisco Giants**.

Union Square

The heart of the shopping and theatre district (*Powell, Post, Stockton and Geary Sts*), with a café and people-watching.

Walt Disney Family Museum

Mickey Mouse's creator's life progresses through ten galleries in this renovated red-brick military building in the Presidio. Personal mementos on the walls frame numerous animation artefacts, innovative filming equipment and sound and visual integration techniques that the Disney empire's creator invented.

Yerba Buena Gardens

A former SOMA slum, Yerba Buena (*north of Moscone Convention Center between 4th, Mission, 3rd and Howard Sts*) has become a lively nexus with SFMOMA, a Performing Arts Center (Yerba Buena Center for the Arts; *tel: (415) 978-2700; www.ybca.org*), ice-skating rink, Moscone Convention Center, cinemas, shopping, entertainment, hotels, restaurants, a carousel and gardens.

Entertainment

TIX Bay Area Half-price tickets for theatre, dance and music events on performance day (*Powell St side of Union Square; www.tixbayarea.com*). Full-price advance tickets to area performance events are also sold. *Open Tue–Fri 1100–1800, Sat 1000–1800, Sun 1000–1500.*

San Francisco has taken entertainment seriously since admiring miners tossed bouquets of roses to touring opera stars and pouches of gold dust to dance-hall girls. The *San Francisco Chronicle* Thursday 96 *Hours* section and the *Datebook* section in the *San Francisco Sunday Chronicle* (*www.sfgate.com*) hold the most complete listings; the *SF Bay Guardian* (*www.sfbg.com*) and *SF Weekly* (*www.sfweekly.com*) list more avant-garde offerings.

Most clubs are in SOMA, catering to every taste from old-line jazz to the latest electronic creations.

The Cannery (*2801 Leavenworth St; tel: (415) 771-3112*), **Del Monte Square Courtyard, Pier 39** and other centres offer stages for buskers. Pier 39's Crystal Geyser Alpine Spring Water Center Stage has a whole street performer schedule.

Stern Grove Festival *Sigmund Stern Grove, 19th Ave and Sloat Blvd; tel: (415) 252-6252; www.sterngrove.org. Summer Sun afternoons mid-Jun–mid-Aug.* Free outdoor classical, opera, popular and jazz music.

Audium $$ *1616 Bush St; tel: (415) 771-1616; www.audium.org. Fri–Sat.* Sound sculptures from 136 speakers surround the audience, sitting in a darkened theatre.

Beach Blanket Babylon $$ *Club Fugazi, 678 Beach Blanket Babylon Blvd (Green St, North Beach); tel: (415) 421-4222; www.beachblanketbabylon.com. Open Wed–Sun, adults only except Sun afternoon.* Zany cabaret-style musical spoof of popular culture, updated regularly to reflect current and local events.

Grace Cathedral Concerts $$ *1100 California St; tel: (415) 749-6355; www.gracecathedral.org.* Concerts and organ recitals in California's finest Gothic cathedral, and a walkable labyrinth.

Old First Concerts $$ *Old First Church, Van Ness Ave and 1751 Sacramento St; tel: (415) 474-1608; www.oldfirstconcerts.org. Year-round.* Solo, chamber, choral, jazz and world music concerts.

San Francisco Blues Festival $$ *Great Meadow, Fort Mason; tel: (415) 979-5588; www.sfblues.com. Late Sept.* The oldest blues festival in the nation.

San Francisco Jazz Festival $$ *Many venues in San Francisco; tel: (415) 788-7353; www.sfjazz.org. Oct–Nov.* For more than two decades the City by the Bay has attracted the best jazz musicians in the world.

American Conservatory Theater (ACT) $$$ *415 Geary St, Union Square; tel: (415) 749-2228; www.act-sf.org.* San Francisco's leading repertory theatre company.

Below
Carousel at San Francisco's Yerba Buena Gardens

San Francisco Ballet $$$ *455 Franklin St; tel: (415) 865-2000; www. sfballet.org.* Annual dance season late January–early May in the War Memorial Opera House; annual *Nutcracker* performances in December.

San Francisco Opera $$$ *War Memorial Opera House, Van Ness Ave and McAllister St; tel: (415) 864-3330; www.sfopera.com. Sept–Dec & Jun.* A world-famous company in an opera palace.

San Francisco Symphony $$$ *Davies Symphony Hall, Van Ness Ave and Grove St; tel: (415) 864-6000; www.sfsymphony.org.* Year-round symphony, summer Pops and holiday programmes.

Shopping

San Francisco is a shopper's dream regardless of budget. The hip, or those who wish to be, gravitate to **Haight St**. The Haight's latest reincarnation is a trendier-than-thou mix of fashion, food and body piercing. **Union Square** is shopping central with Nike, Saks Fifth Avenue and Tiffany. The **Westfield San Francisco Centre** (*865 Market and 5th Sts; tel: (415) 512-6776; http://westfield.com/sanfrancisco*) is anchored by Nordstrom and Bloomingdale's. **Union St** caters to the stylishly trendy, offering jewellery, marbled paper, clothing, antiques, furnishings and bric-a-brac from around the world.

Accommodation and food

San Francisco has been famous for high prices since Gold Rush days. It's one of America's most visited cities, which keeps hotels and restaurants busy all year. *Always* book ahead. The SFCVB (*tel: (800) 637-5196; www.onlyinsanfrancisco.com*) helps with your bookings. **San Francisco Reservations** (*tel: (800) 677-1570; www.hotelres.com*) makes free bookings for more than 225 local hotels. **Union Square** is the best location if you don't have a car, near the main shopping and theatre areas, most major tourist sights and public transport routes. Add $20–$25 per day for parking. Motels along **Lombard St** and **Van Ness Ave** generally offer free parking; ask for a room at the back to minimise street noise. **Fisherman's Wharf** is group-tour territory. Nob Hill is a posh address.

The **Galleria Park Hotel $$$** (*191 Sutter St; tel: (800) 792-9639; www.galleriapark.com*) is a refurbished boutique hotel with a rooftop garden near Union Square and Chinatown. The ultra-trendy **Hotel Triton $$$** (*342 Grant Ave; tel: (800) 800-1299; www.hoteltriton. com*) is filled with irregular shapes, wavy lines and corners that appear not to meet. The **Palace Hotel $$$** (*2 New Montgomery St; tel: (415) 512-1111; www.sfpalace.com*) is one of the oldest, most historic hotels in San Francisco – and one of the few major buildings to survive the 1906 earthquake. The **Garden Court $$$** is a palm-filled restaurant beneath a restored stained-glass dome over the original carriage entrance.

to keep them out, leading to the indefinite detention of many would-be immigrants at the Angel Island Immigration Station in San Francisco Bay. Local laws banned Chinese (and other Asians) from most occupations; sporadic anti-Chinese riots encouraged them to band together for self-protection. Los Angeles, Sacramento, San Francisco and isolated Delta towns such as Locke gained significant Chinatowns and other Asian neighbourhoods.

Discrimination began to ease after World War II, when the US and China found themselves allied. Immigration opened for refugees fleeing the Chinese Communist government after 1949. By the time quotas were raised again in the 1960s, San Francisco had the largest Chinese population outside Asia – and the Golden Dragon continues an annual New Year Parade dance down Chinatown's Grant Ave that began in the 1860s.

With 3,000 eateries, from ultra-luxe to ethnic hole-in-the-wall, San Francisco calls itself the food capital of America, a title justly contested by Los Angeles, New York and New Orleans. The website *www. sfgate.com* offers a selection of current reviews.

Boudin at the Wharf $ (*160 Jefferson St; tel: (415) 928-1849; www.boudinbakery.com/at-the-wharf*) has the best Fisherman's Wharf sandwiches, a demonstration bakery and a sourdough bread museum.

Beach Chalet $$ (*1000 Great Highway (Golden Gate Park); tel: (415) 386-8439; www.beachchalet.com*), with its **Park Chalet Garden Restaurant**, is a brewery, restaurant and visitor centre with murals from 1936.

Yoshi's Jazz Club & Restaurant $$ (*1330 Fillmore St; tel: (415) 655-5600; www.yoshis.com/sanfrancisco*) is revitalising the Fillmore Jazz District – a musical hotbed after World War II.

Aqua $$$ (*252 California St; tel: (415) 956-9662; www.aqua-sf.com*) serves great seafood.

Boulevard $$$ (*1 Mission St; tel: (415) 543-6084; www.boulevard restaurant.com*) is revered for its French-inspired dishes.

McCormick & Kuleto's Seafood Restaurant $$$ (*900 North Point (Ghirardelli Square); tel: (415) 929-1730; www.mccormickandschmicks.com*) has food to equal the views across Aquatic Park and the Bay.

Suggested tours

49-Mile Drive
Allow at least a half-day and avoid downtown during rush hours. The drive was created for the 1939 Golden Gate International Exposition. Blue and white seagull signs still mark an outstanding driving circuit. The route is marked on the SFCVB's 49-Mile Scenic Drive map (*www.onlyinsanfrancisco.com/maps/49miledrive.asp*).

Walking tours
San Francisco is best seen on foot. Top guided walking tours: **City Guides** (*tel: (415) 557-4266; www.sfcityguides.org; free*) for culture, history and architecture; **Local Tastes of the City Tours** (*tel: (888) 358-8687 or (415) 665-0480; www.localtastesofthecitytours.com*) has tours of North Beach, Chinatown or both on a night tour; **Cruisin' The Castro** (*tel: (415) 255-1821; www.cruisinthecastro.com*) for The City's gay subculture from 1849 to the present; **Wok Wiz Chinatown Tours** (*tel: (650) 355-9657; www.wokwiz.com*) for Chinatown with chef and author Shirley Fong-Torres; **Victorian Home Walk** (*tel: (415) 252-9485; www. victorianwalk.com*) for SF's Victorian architecture, lifestyle and history.

Do-it-yourselfers can follow plaques on the 3¾-mile **Barbary Coast Trail** (*www.sfhistory.org/bct*) from the Old Mint (SOMA) via Chinatown, Nob Hill and North Beach, to Fisherman's Wharf.

San Francisco Bay Area

Ratings

Art	●●●●○
Food and drink	●●●●○
Scenery	●●●●○
Architecture	●●●○○
Children	●●●○○
History	●●●○○
Nature	●●●○○
Museums	●●○○○

San Francisco has given its name to the Bay Area, but it's hardly the dominant force in a region filled with vibrant cities, each with its own distinctive look and feel. The Bay unites a montage of soaring bridges, windswept islands, distant skylines piercing the fog, sailing boats and boardsailers weaving past lumbering cargo vessels, Nobel Prize-winners and world-renowned chefs. It's possible to breeze through the entire Bay Area in a day, but more productive to spread the sights over several days. Bridges and freeways can become stop-and-go car parks during rush hours.

BERKELEY

ⓘ Berkeley Convention and Visitors Bureau Visitor Information Center
2015 Center St; tel: (800) 847-4823 or (510) 549-7040; www.visitberkeley.com. Open Mon–Fri 0900–1700.

University of California Berkeley Campus Visitor Center
101 Sproul Hall, Telegraph Ave and Bancroft Way; tel: (510) 642-5215; www.berkeley.edu/visitors. Open Mon–Fri 0830–1630. Walking, podcast or mobile phone campus tours are free.

It's hard to separate Berkeley from the **University of California, Berkeley**. The campus, usually called Cal, lends a schizophrenic air to a town already known as 'Berserkely' for its benign loonies and strident politics. It also usually has America's greatest concentration of Nobel laureates.

About 35,000 students make Cal the physical heart and soul of Berkeley. **Sather Tower**, aka **The Campanile**, towers 307ft above them all, slightly shorter than the original in St Mark's Square, Venice. From an observation platform below the 61-bell carillon, views span the Bay. On the ground, **Sproul Plaza** (*north of Telegraph Ave and Bancroft Way*) is a non-stop circus, dominated by the student union in **Sproul Hall**.

Campus collections worth seeing are: the **Phoebe A Hearst Museum of Anthropology** (*102 Kroeber Hall; tel: (510) 642-3682; http://hearstmuseum.berkeley.edu. Open Wed–Sat 1000–1630, Sun 1200–1600. Free*), with artefacts used by 'Ishi', last survivor of

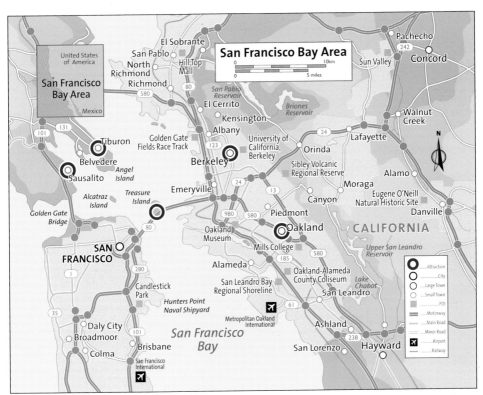

California's Stone Age Yahi aboriginals; modern and contemporary· art at the **UC Berkeley Art Museum $$** (*2626 Bancroft Way; tel: (510) 642-0808; www.bampfa.berkeley.edu. Open Wed–Sun 1100–1700*); the **Pacific Film Archive** (*2575 Bancroft Way; tel: (510) 642-1124*), which screens popular, foreign, independent and avant-garde films; the **Lawrence Hall of Science**, a popular participatory museum with a fine Bay view from the Berkeley Hills; and a few foyer exhibits from the enormous fossil collection at the **Museum of Paleontology**.

The **UC Botanical Garden $** (*200 Centennial Dr; tel: (510) 643-2755; botanicalgarden.berkeley.edu. Open daily 0900–1700. Free first Thur of the month*) has over 12,000 species from around the world, neatly labelled and divided into regional habitat zones. The rhododendron collection is stunning during the spring bloom. Cacti, a Chinese medicinal herb garden and California native plants are major collections, and views of San Francisco Bay are eye-catching.

Off-campus Berkeley swirls around **Telegraph Ave**, an ever-changing collection of coffee houses, booksellers, street musicians, panhandlers, students and homeless people. The **Judah L Magnes Museum**, the first Jewish museum in the Western US, collects fine art, ceremonial objects and rare books, and will relocate on-campus soon.

Lawrence Hall of Science $$
Centennial Dr; tel: (510) 642-5132; www.lhs.berkeley.org. Open daily 1000–1700.

Museum of Paleontology
Near Oxford St/University Ave, 1101 Valley Life Sciences Building; tel: (510) 642-1821; www.ucmp.berkeley.edu. Call for hours. Free.

Judah L Magnes Museum $ 2911 Russell St; tel: (510) 549-6950; www.magnes.org. Call for current location (expected to move to the UC Berkeley campus in early 2011) and hours.

Food in Berkeley

Cheese Board Collective *1504 Shattuck Ave; tel: (510) 549-3183.*

The Cheese Board Pizza Collective *1512 Shattuck Ave; tel: (510) 549-3055; shared website: cheeseboardcollective.coop*

Below
Modelled on St Mark's Campanile in Venice, The Campanile at the Berkeley campus of the University of California

Berkeley takes everything seriously, including food. California cuisine got its start here, the idea that fresh ingredients, cultivated on small plots by happy farmers, are absolutely vital to health, taste, prosperity and peace on earth. To see the raw ingredients, tiny 'baby' vegetables and exotically coloured produce, visit the **Monterey Market** (*1550 Hopkins St; tel: (510) 526-6042; www.montereymarket.com. Open Mon–Fri 0900–1900, Sat 0830–1800*) and **Berkeley Bowl** (*920 Heinz Ave; tel: (510) 898-9555; www.berkeleybowl.com. Open Mon–Sat 0900–2000, Sun 1000–1800*).

High temple to the Cult of Cuisine is **Chez Panisse $$$** (*1517 Shattuck Ave; tel: (510) 548-5525; www.chezpanisse.com*), whose reputation exceeds its execution, but upstairs **The Café** (*tel: (510) 548-5049*) offers better value. Both restaurants book tables exactly one month in advance.

The area around Chez Panisse, Shattuck Ave near Cedar and Vine Sts is called **Gourmet Ghetto** for the enormous concentration of fine restaurants. Chez Panisse neighbours include the employee-owned **Cheese Board Collective** with cheeses and on-premises baked goods and its independent adjunct, **The Cheese Board Pizza Collective**, for late-afternoon and dinner pizza pies. Nearby, **Café Gratitude $$** (*1730 Shattuck Ave; tel: (510) 725-4418; www.cafegratitude.com*) offers a vegetarian menu based on affirmative phrases.

People-watchers head for **Bette's Oceanview Diner $$** (*1807 4th St; tel: (510) 644-3230; www.worldpantry. com/bettes/home.html*), a casual breakfast and lunch-only diner with some of the area's tastiest American traditions: pancakes, French toast, blintzes (thin rolled pancakes filled with cheese or fruit and then baked or fried), sandwiches, soup, meatloaf and to-die-for milkshakes. It is in the bustling **Fourth Street Shopping District**, a former warehouse area that has become a lively artistic, shopping, dining and entertainment district.

OAKLAND

ⓘ Oakland Convention & Visitors Bureau (OCVB) 463 11th St; tel: (510) 839-9000; http://oaklandcvb.com. Open Mon–Fri 0900–1700.

ⓩ Oakland Int'l Airport (OAK) Tel: (510) 563-3300; www.oaklandairport.com

ⓝ Oakland Public Library Oakland History Room 125 14th St, 2nd floor; tel: (510) 238-3222; www.oaklandlibrary. org. Open Mon, Tue & Sat 1000–1730, Wed–Thur 1200–2000, Fri 1200–1730, Sun 1300–1700.

Pardee Home Museum $ 672 11th St; tel: (510) 444-2187; www.pardeehome.org. Call for tours.

Oakland Museum of California $$ 1000 Oak St; tel: (510) 238-2200; www.museumca.org. Open Wed & Sat–Sun 1100–1700, Thur–Fri 1100–2000, second Fri of the month 1100–2100. First Sun of the month free.

Chabot Space & Science Center $$ 10000 Skyline Blvd; tel: (510) 336-7300; www.chabotspace. org. Hours change seasonally.

Lake Merritt Boating Center $$ Tel: (510) 238-2196. Open daily except rainy days, call for hours.

Oakland traditionally doesn't get much respect. Yet it is a sunny, diverse city with a long cultural, musical and artistic heritage. Jack London, Oakland's first literary light, has his name plastered along the waterfront where he once stole oysters and lobsters for a living. **Jack London Square** (*west of downtown; tel: (510) 645-9292; www.jacklondonsquare.com*) is a modern complex of shops, restaurants and museums. The **Oakland Public Library Oakland History Room** and **Jack London State Historic Park** (*see page 172*) have better London collections. The square's only genuine Londoniana is **Heinold's First and Last Chance Saloon** (*48 Webster St; tel: (510) 839-6761; www.heinoldsfirstandlastchance.com*), where London drank. The **USS Potomac** (*540 Water St; tel: (510) 627-1215; www.usspotomac.org*), FDR's one-time American presidential yacht, is *open Wed, Fri & Sun* for dockside tours $$, and *May–early Nov Thur & Sat* for Bay cruises $$$.

The square's other highlights are a **ferry terminal** with hourly connections to San Francisco, and **Yoshi's Oakland** (*510 Embarcadero West; tel: (510) 238-9200; www.yoshis.com*), a Japanese restaurant that is the East Bay's top jazz club. Stalls at **Jack London Market** offer produce, cheese and other locally produced edibles in a permanent space.

The best place to see early Oakland is **Preservation Park** (*Martin Luther King Jr Way and 13th St; tel: (510) 874-7580; www. preservationpark.com*), a re-created neighbourhood with restored buildings from 19th-century Victorian to early 20th-century Craftsman. Most are private offices, but **Pardee Home Museum** is open for guided tours. **Old Oakland** (*Broadway, Clay, 8th and 10th Sts; http://oldoakland.org*) is the former commercial district, largely restored as an official historic district. **Chinatown** (*Broadway, Fallon, 6th and 8th Sts*), more Pan-Asian than Chinese, has shops, restaurants and bakeries that are as busy – and far less touristy – than San Francisco, and Oakland Chinatown Streetfest in August (*www.oaklandchinatownstreetfest.com*).

Many of Oakland's grand buildings from the early 20th century survive in the downtown city centre, including **City Hall** (*14th St*) and the **Tribune Tower** (*Franklin St*), former home of the *Oakland Tribune* newspaper. A restored 1920s film palace, the **Paramount Theatre** (*2025 Broadway; tel: (510) 465-6400; www.paramounttheatre.com*), shows Hollywood classics as well as stage productions and Oakland Symphony performances.

The stunning **Oakland Museum of California**, reopened in 2010 after renovations, is California's de facto state museum. **Lake Merritt**, the nation's oldest wildlife refuge, has Venetian gondola rides (*Gondola Servizio; tel: (866) 737-8494; www.gondolaservizio.com*). The **Chabot Space & Science Center**, in Oakland's hills, has interactive exhibits, a dome theatre and planetarium, and offers one of the best spots for year-round public telescope perusal of the heavens on clear Friday and Saturday evenings. **Camron-Stanford House** is the last of the elegant Victorian

Children's Fairyland $ *Grand and Bellevue Aves; tel: (510) 238-6876; www.fairyland.org. Hours vary by season, closed rainy days.*

USS Hornet Museum $$ *Pier 3, Alameda Point, Alameda; tel: (510) 521-8448; www.uss-hornet.org. Self-guided and guided tours daily 1000–1700.*

Old Oakland Farmers' Market *Broadway and 9th St; tel: (510) 745-7100; www.urbanvillageonline.com/ markets/oldOakland.php. Fri 0800–1400.*

mansions that once lined the lake. Canoes, paddle boats, kayaks and sailing boats can be hired from the **Lake Merritt Boating Center**. **Children's Fairyland** was reputedly the model for Fantasyland in Walt Disney's original Disneyland®.

The **USS Hornet Museum** preserves a ship in fit-for-duty state that saw service in World War II Pacific combat, Vietnam, and recovered the first two lunar modules, Apollo 11 and Apollo 12. Painted footsteps on Hangar Bay 2 deck are where Neil Armstrong walked after returning from the first moon walk.

Accommodation and food in Oakland

The white gleam against the hills is the **Claremont Resort & Spa** $$$ *Ashby and Domingo Aves; tel: (510) 843-3000 or (800) 551-7266; www.claremontresort.com*

Oakland is filled with colourful eateries, from a rainbow of Asian flavours in Chinatown to Oakland's own Gourmet Ghetto, **Rockridge** (*College Ave between 63rd and Alcatraz Sts*).

Zachary's Pizza $$ *5801 College Ave; tel: (510) 665-6385; www.zacharys.com.* Has won awards since 1983 for several-inch-thick pies with layers of ingredients. Prepare to wait in long queues ordering to go or stake out a feast spot at a table. There are also locations in Berkeley and San Ramon.

Bay Wolf $$$ *3853 Piedmont Ave; tel: (510) 655-6004; www.baywolf.com.* Avoids Berkeley-like flights of fancy for restrained Mediterranean-California dishes.

Citron $$$ *5484 College Ave; tel: (510) 653-5484; www.citronrestaurant.com.* Shows distinct French and Italian touches.

SAUSALITO

Sausalito Chamber of Commerce *10 Liberty Ship Way, Bay 2, Ste 250; tel: (415) 332-0505 or (415) 331-7262; www.sausalito.org. Visitor Center, 780 Bridgeway. Open Tue–Sun 1130–1600.*

Blue & Gold Fleet (ferry) *Pier 39, San Francisco; tel: (415) 705-8200; www.blueandgoldfleet.com*

Golden Gate Transit (ferry) *Ferry Building, San Francisco; tel: 511 or (415) 451-4650; http://goldengateferry.org*

A small 19th-century summer resort and fishing town expanded as a shipbuilding centre during World War II, then sank into obscurity as a haven for 1950s artists, poets and beatniks. A free-thinking reputation was assured when Sally Stanford, one of San Francisco's infamous bordello madams, retired here, opened a restaurant and became mayor.

Sausalito marinas and houseboats orient the town to the bayfront. Shopping complexes wind and twist like rabbit warrens. Much of the town centre is a National Historic Landmark District, including the **Plaza de Viña del Mar**, with its Spanish-style fountain and elephants from the 1915 Panama-Pacific Exposition. At the north end of Sausalito is the **San Francisco Bay Model**, used to test the impact of development, dredging and clean-up efforts. The best way to see the Bay is a 3-hour guided sea kayak tour from **Sea Trek Ocean Kayaking Center**, a 30-minute **ferry ride** from San Francisco.

San Francisco Bay Model *2100 Bridgeway; tel: (415) 332-3871; www.spn.usace. army.mil/bmvc. Call for hours and tours. Free.*

Bay Area Discovery Museum $$ *557 McReynolds Rd, East Fort Baker; tel: (415) 339-3900; www.baykidsmuseum. org. Open Tue–Fri 0900–1600, Sat–Sun 1000–1700.*

 Sea Trek Ocean Kayaking Center $$ *Tel: (415) 488-1000; www.seatrek.com. Open daily; advance booking required.*

To go back to Sausalito's roots, stop and watch craftspeople and students at the **Arques School of Traditional Wooden Boatbuilding** *(Spaulding Wooden Boat Center, foot of Gate 5 Rd; arqueschl@sbcglobal.net; www.arqueschl.org. Open Tue–Sat 1200–1300 for visits).*

Getting out of the car in Sausalito

Sausalito's best Bay vistas are from Bridgeway, walking south to Second St, Alexander Ave and Fort Baker Rd to the former military base. It's a 2-mile walk with unexpected views of the **Golden Gate Bridge** to reach the **Bay Area Discovery Museum**, with lively science, art and media exhibits geared to children aged 1 to 10.

Accommodation and food in Sausalito

Casa Madrona Hotel and Spa $$$ *801 Bridgeway; tel: (800) 288-0502 or (415) 332-0502; www.casamadrona.com.* A collection of cottage rooms, modern spaces and a posh spa stretching up the hillside from Bridgeway to a Victorian mansion.

Cavallo Point – the Lodge at the Golden Gate $$$ *601 Murray Circle, Fort Baker; tel: (415) 339-4700 or (888) 651-2003; www.cavallopoint.com.* A posh inside-a-national-park remake of historical army officer quarters within sight of the Golden Gate Bridge.

Inn Above Tide $$$ *30 El Portal; tel: (800) 893-8433 or (415) 332-9535; www.innabovetide.com.* The only hotel built *over* San Francisco Bay.

Scoma's $$$ *588 Bridgeway; tel: (415) 332-9551; www.scomassausalito. com.* Has Bay views with seafood.

Spinnaker Restaurant $$$ *100 Spinnaker Ave; tel: (415) 332-1500; www.thespinnaker.com.* Has on-the-water views.

TIBURON

Tiburon Peninsula Chamber of Commerce *96B Main St; tel: (415) 435-5633; http:// tiburonchamber.wildapricot. org. Call for hours.*

Originally called Punta de Tiburón (Shark Point) by Mexican fishermen, today's town was born in 1884 as the terminus for the San Francisco and North Pacific Railroad ferry to San Francisco. Sweeping Bay views, and daily ferries, helped turn Tiburon and neighbouring **Belvedere** into exclusive dormitory communities for San Francisco.

Tiburon's tiny and almost always sunny **waterfront** has become a trendy San Francisco getaway. Restaurants with outdoor decks surround the ferry landing. A long park offers space to run and enjoy views of San Francisco shimmering beyond Angel Island, a few hundred yards offshore. Central Tiburon was once a lagoon dotted with houseboats, or arks, that were eventually placed on pilings. **Ark**

Row has become a popular dining and shopping area. Other sites include **Old St Hilary's**, a restored Carpenter Gothic church overlooking the town; **Tiburon Uplands Nature Preserve's** 0.7-mile loop trail; and the **Richardson Bay Audubon Center and Sanctuary**.

Food in Tiburon

Frequent ferry connections make Tiburon an easy restaurant excursion from San Francisco.

Above
Going to Angel Island from Tiburon

🚻 **Richardson Bay Audubon Center and Sanctuary $**
376 Greenwood Beach Rd;
tel: (415) 388-2524;
www.tiburonaudubon.org.
Open Mon–Sat 0900–1700.

Sam's Anchor Cafe $$ (*27 Main St; tel: (415) 435-4527; www.samscafe.com*) is noisy, hospitable, busy and worth the wait for simply prepared seafood and burgers. Arrive about an hour early, leave your name with the maître d' and go explore.

Guaymas $$$ (*5 Main St; tel: (415) 435-6300; www.guaymasrestaurant. com*), Mexican, and **Servino's Ristorante $$$** (*9 Main St; tel: (415) 435-2676; www.servino.com*), Italian seafood, have similar views and require reservations.

TREASURE ISLAND

ℹ️ **Treasure Island**
Tel: (415) 274-0660;
www.sftreasureisland.org

⛵ **Treasure Island Sailing Center $$**
Tel: (415) 421-2225;
www.tisailing.org. Conducts reasonably priced sailing classes at all experience levels.

The tabletop expanse of Treasure Island was created for the 1939 Golden Gate International Exposition, with access via the **San Francisco–Oakland Bay Bridge**. The large Art Moderne building facing San Francisco was originally the control tower and terminal building for Pan American Airways' flying boat service to Asia.

The island became a naval base during World War II and reverted to the city of San Francisco 50 years later. Some of the former Navy buildings are now studios and sound stages for cinema and television productions. Part of the island has become a small marina and public park with seldom-seen views of the **San Francisco waterfront**. Best vistas are in the morning and at sunset.

Suggested tour

From San Francisco, follow I-80 east on the **San Francisco–Oakland Bay Bridge ❶** to TREASURE ISLAND ❷, then continue through the toll plaza area. Follow I-580 southbound to OAKLAND ❸. From Oakland, return northbound on I-580 to I-80 eastbound. Take the **University Ave ❹** exit into BERKELEY ❺ towards the **University of California, Berkeley ❻**.

Return to I-80 westbound along San Francisco Bay to the **Richmond–San Rafael Bridge ❼** to **Marin County ❽**. The golden structure just south of the Marin County end of the bridge is **San Quentin Federal Prison ❾**. Take Hwy 101 south to Paradise Dr and the **Tiburon Peninsula ❿**. The road becomes narrow, winding and steep, but passengers can expect good Bay views.

Continue around the peninsula to **TIBURON ⓫** and **Belvedere ⓬**. Follow Tiburon Blvd along the shores of **Richardson Bay ⓭** to Hwy 101 and turn south to **SAUSALITO ⓮**. Cross the **Golden Gate Bridge ⓯** into San Francisco or, for pleasant afternoon views of the bridge, take the last exit before the bridge on to the **Marin Headlands ⓰** and drive uphill to any of several car parks.

Also worth exploring

Belvedere ⓬ is Tiburon's smaller and wealthier neighbour. The name means 'beautiful view' in Italian, an assessment of the panorama west towards Sausalito and south across San Francisco Bay. The **SS China Cabin** (*54 Beach Rd; tel: (415) 435-1853; www.landmarks-society.org/landmarks/china_cabin.php; call for tour hours*) is an elegantly restored Victorian social saloon salvaged from the 1867 steamship SS *China*. The floor is made of oak and walnut; cut-glass floral window panes provide light; and the cabin is trimmed in 22-carat gold.

Napa Valley Wine Country

Ratings

Food and drink	●●●●●
Wine	●●●●●
Outdoor activities	●●●○○
Scenery	●●●○○
Shopping	●●●○○
Walking	●●○○○
Wildlife	●●○○○
Children	●○○○○

This 30-mile strip of valley covered with lush vineyards and more than 400 wineries could be a theme-park version of Southern France. Some of America's finest wines and extraordinary promotional skills have made Napa the self-proclaimed Capital of California Wine – and turned Hwy 29 into one long traffic jam during the summer and every weekend. The best time to visit is midweek during the spring and autumn. If you must visit in summer, traffic is less congested on the Silverado Trail, which runs along the eastern side of the valley. The **Napa Valley Destination Council** (*1310 Napa Town Center, Napa; tel: (707) 226-5813; www.legendarynapavalley. com*) represents towns and communities in the area.

CALISTOGA

ⓘ Calistoga Chamber of Commerce/Calistoga Visitors Center *1133 Washington St; tel: (707) 942-6333 or (866) 306-5588; www.calistogavisitors.com. Open daily 0900–1700.*

ⓜ Sharpsteen Museum $ *1311 Washington St; tel: (707) 942-5911; www.sharpsteen-museum.org. Open daily 1100–1600.*

The town's mud baths and hot springs are better known than its wineries, thanks to Sam Brannan, the entrepreneur who quietly bought up San Francisco's entire supply of picks and shovels before shouting news of James Marshall's gold discovery on the streets of San Francisco in 1848. In 1860, Brannan founded a town he intended to promote as the 'Saratoga of California' after a famed resort town in New York state. What purportedly emerged was the 'Calistoga of Sarifornia'. Brannan's other historic contributions survive at the **Sharpsteen Museum**.

Hot springs, volcanic mud and a relatively low-key atmosphere have come together in California's most relaxed spa town. Treatments run the gamut from simple soaks in hot mineral water to wallows in volcanic mud, herbal wraps and deep tissue massage. **Dr Wilkinson's Hot Springs Resort** caters to the famous and the film stars. **Lavender Hill Spa** caters to couples and is known for its 'unthick' mud baths of volcanic ash mixed with kelp. Ordinary people flock to the down-to-

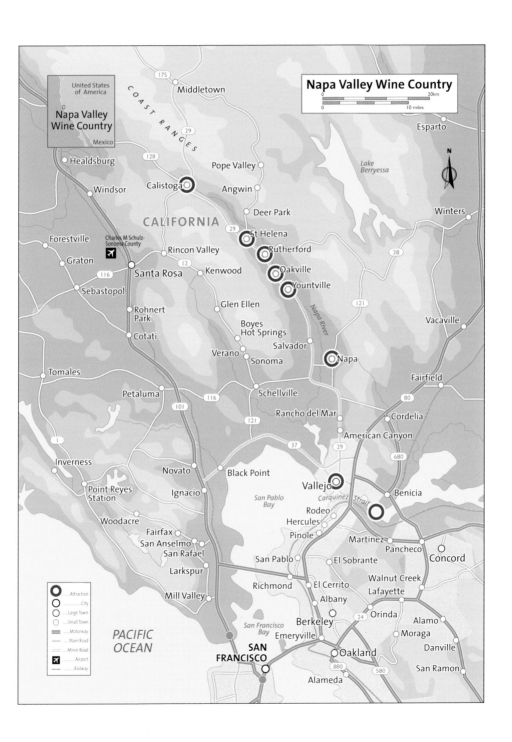

Napa Valley Wine Country

United States
of America

Napa Valley
Wine Country

Mexico

Middletown

175

COAST RANGES

29

128

Healdsburg

Windsor   Calistoga

CALIFORNIA

Forestville   Charles M Schulz-
                   Sonoma County

Graton   Rincon Valley

116   Santa Rosa   Kenwood

Sebastopol

                   Rohnert
                   Park

                   Cotati

Tomales

                   Petaluma   116

101

1

Inverness   Novato   Black Point

Point Reyes   Ignacio
Station

Woodacre   Fairfax
                   San Anselmo
                   San Rafael

                   Larkspur

                   Mill Valley

Attraction
City
Large Town
Small Town
Motorway
Main Road
Minor Road
Airport
Railway

PACIFIC
OCEAN

Pope Valley

Angwin

Deer Park

29   St Helena
                   Rutherford
                   Oakville
                   Yountville

Glen Ellen

Boyes
Hot Springs   Salvador

Verano   Sonoma

Schellville

Rancho del Mar

121

37   29

San Pablo
Bay

Vallejo

Rodeo

Hercules

Pinole

San Pablo   El Sobrante

Richmond   El Cerrito

                   Albany

San Francisco   Berkeley
Bay   Emeryville

SAN
FRANCISCO

Alameda

Esparto

Lake
Berryessa

N

Winters

28

Napa River

121   Vacaville

Napa

Fairfield

80

Cordelia

American Canyon

680

Benicia

Carquinez Strait

Martinez   Pancheco   Concord

Walnut Creek
Lafayette

24   Orinda   Alamo

                   Moraga

                   Danville

Oakland   San Ramon

880   580

Ⓓ Dr Wilkinson's Hot Springs Resort
$$ 1507 Lincoln Ave; tel: (707) 942-4102; www. drwilkinson.com. Open daily.

Lavender Hill Spa $$
1015 Foothill Blvd; tel: (707) 942-4495 or (800) 528-4772; www.lavenderhillspa. com. Open daily 0900–2100.

Indian Springs $$
1712 Lincoln Ave; tel: (707) 942-4913; www.indianspringscalistoga. com. Open daily 0900–2000.

Old Faithful Geyser $
1299 Tubbs Ln; tel: (707) 942-6463; www.oldfaithfulgeyser.com. Open daily summer 0900–1800; winter 0900–1700.

Petrified Forest $
4100 Petrified Forest Rd; tel: (707) 942-6667; www. petrifiedforest.org. Open daily summer 0900–1900; winter 0900–1700.

Schramsberg $$$
1400 Schramsberg Rd; tel: (800) 877-3623 or (707) 942-4558; www.schramsberg.com. Tours and tastings daily by appointment.

Chateau Montelena Winery $$$ 1429 Tubbs Ln; tel: (707) 942-5105; www.montelena.com. Open daily 0930–1600, most tours by appointment.

Cuvaison $$ 4550 Silverado Trail; tel: (707) 942-2468; www.cuvaison. com. Open daily 1000–1700.

Sterling Vineyards® $$
1111 Dunaweal Ln; tel: (800) 726-6136; www.sterlingvineyards.com. Open Mon–Fri 1030–1700, Sat–Sun 1000–1700.

earth spas along Lincoln Ave. **Indian Springs** is one of the more popular, with a sunbathing pool with a hot spring (geyser water).

Napa's hot underground springs also surface at **Old Faithful Geyser**, which spits boiling water and steam every half-hour or so. The geyser was born when an exploratory oil rig drilled into a geothermal source in the 1920s. After numerous failed attempts to cap the regular eruptions, landowners turned the inevitable into a tourist attraction. The source is part of the volcanic plumbing system that gave rise to eruptions at nearby **Mount St Helena** (4,344ft) and turned a lush grove of redwood trees into the **Petrified Forest** about three million years ago.

The mountain is protected within **Robert Louis Stevenson State Park** (7 miles north on Hwy 29; tel: (707) 942-4575). A 2½-mile trail leads to the top of the Napa Valley, with spectacular views stretching north to **Mount Shasta** on clear days. The park is named after the Scottish novelist Robert Louis Stevenson, who honeymooned in an abandoned miner's cabin on Mount St Helena in 1880. The cabin is long gone, but a trailside plaque marks the site. The highlight of his stay, Stevenson wrote in *Silverado Squatters*, was sampling 18 different champagnes from wine baron Jacob Schram's nearby **Schramsberg Vineyards**.

Don't miss winery visits around Calistoga. **Chateau Montelena Winery** has a formal Chinese garden with a traditional pagoda-pavilion overlooking a lake with a half-sunken junk. The French château-like architecture is also worth the drive, as is the Cabernet Sauvignon. **Cuvaison** is a winery on the Silverado Trail on the Valley's east side, with a picnic area beneath oak trees. **Sterling Vineyards®** sits atop a small hill, an extravagant white Greek island-style mansion accessible by aerial tram. The bells of London's St Dunstan Church (destroyed in World War II) ring every half-hour.

Accommodation and food in Calistoga

Rooms in all categories are snapped up quickly at peak periods, so book in advance all year. Some spas, including **Dr Wilkinson's Hot Springs Resort** and **Indian Springs**, offer accommodation.

All Seasons $$ *1400 Lincoln Ave; tel: (707) 942-9111; www. allseasonsnapavalley.net.* Gets raves for its gnocchi and lobster bisque.

Bosko's Ristorante $$ *1364 Lincoln Ave; tel: (707) 942-9088; www.boskos.com. Open daily 1130–2130.* Calistoga's best Italian choice.

Wine Way Inn $$ *1019 Foothill Blvd; tel: (707) 942-0680 or (800) 572-0679; www.winewayinn.com.* A historical Craftsman-style inn.

Mount View Hotel & Spa $$$ *1457 Lincoln Ave; tel: (707) 942-6877 or (800) 816-6877; www.mountviewhotel.com.* One of Calistoga's oldest spas.

CARQUINEZ STRAIT

ℹ Benicia Chamber of Commerce & Visitors Center *601 First St, Ste 100, Benicia; tel: (800) 559-7377 or (707) 745-2120; www.beniciachamber.com. Call for hours.*

🏛 Benicia Capitol State Historic Park $ *115 W. G St; tel: (707) 745-3385; www.parks.ca.gov. Open Thur–Sun 1000–1700.*

Below
Sterling Vineyards

This narrow channel is the sole outflow for Central Valley rivers draining the Sierra Nevada. The tiny port town of **Crockett** is cut into the hills along the south side of the Strait, dominated by the gigantic C&H Sugar refinery. **Carquinez Strait Scenic Drive** leads 2 miles to the former ferry town of **Port Costa**, which lost its *raison d'être* when the recently rebuilt **Carquinez Bridge** originally was built at Crockett. The town is still a good spot to watch huge freighters sailing to the inland ports of **Sacramento** and **Stockton**.

On the north side of the Strait is **Benicia**, a one-time rival to San Francisco and the state capital for 13 months. **Benicia Capitol State Historic Park** preserves the 1852 Greek Revival capitol building, as well as the **Fischer-Hanlon House** (*137 W. G St*), a renovated Gold Rush-era hotel. The capitol is furnished in the legislative style of the era, complete with polished spittoons. The Chamber of Commerce publishes a free self-guided walking tour map of this Victorian town, which is still largely intact. An arts community includes several well-known art-glass artists (*www.beniciachamber.com/guide/arts.html*).

NAPA

Napa Valley Destination Council/Napa Valley Visitor Information Center *1310 Napa Town Center off 1st St; tel: (707) 226-5813; www.legendarynapavalley.com. Call for hours.*

Oxbow Public Market *610 1st St; tel: (707) 226-6529; www. oxbowpublicmarket.com. Open daily.*

Napa Valley Opera House $$ *1030 Main St; tel: (707) 226-7372; www. napavalleyoperahouse.org*

Napa Valley Wine Train $$ *1275 McKinstry St; tel: (707) 253-2111 or (800) 427-4124; www.winetrain. com. Excursions daily.*

Domaine Carneros $$ *1240 Duhig Rd, off Hwy 12/121; tel: (800) 716-2788; www.domaine.com. Open daily 1000–1800; call for tour times.*

The Hess Collection $ *4411 Redwood Rd; tel: (707) 255-1144; www.hesscollection.com. Open daily 1000–1730, art collection 1000–1715.*

di Rosa Preserve $ *5200 Sonoma Hwy; tel: (707) 226-5991; www.dirosaart.org. Open Wed–Sat, tours by reservation, call for hours.*

Napa River Adventures $$ *Tel: (707) 224-9080; www.napariveradventures. com*

Napa, the town, is the economic heart of Napa, the Valley. The town centre, west of the Napa River, remains a scenic reminder of a less hurried past, filled with Victorian homes, spreading trees and quiet pavements. Napa also has the majority of the Valley's hotels, restaurants and tourist facilities. The **Oxbow Public Market** has locally grown fruit and vegetable purveyors, restaurants, wine tasting and sales, a bakery and enough to make a 'sustainable' picnic. The restored **Napa Valley Opera House**, built in 1879, has a wide range of famous-name music, plays, musical theatre, opera and dance productions in the Margrit Biever Mondavi Theatre.

To see (but not to visit more than one of) the greatest number of wineries in the shortest possible time, ride the **Napa Valley Wine Train**, an elegantly restored passenger train that makes 3-hour, 25-mile lunch and dinner runs up and down the Valley between Napa and St Helena.

Not far away on the highway to Sonoma is **Domaine Carneros**, Taittinger's Napa Valley sparkling winery modelled on the French champagne maker's 18th-century Château de la Marquetterie.

Art lovers should make time to visit at least two collections: **The Hess Collection**, a restored early 20th-century winery and eclectic modern art collection neighbouring a calm Franciscan retreat centre, and the **di Rosa Preserve** with hundreds of contemporary Bay Area artists' work, amassed over 40 years, displayed amid vineyards and olive trees – look for the cow on the lake!

Napa River Adventures offers narrated cruises, or active holidaymakers can hire a kayak or canoe to navigate the tidal river.

Accommodation and food in Napa

The best way to absorb wine country is to spend a night or two in an inn or Bed & Breakfast (usually pricey). Contact **Bed and Breakfast.com**® (*www.bedandbreakfast.com/napa-california.html; www.napavalley.com/lodging*) or **Napa Valley Reservations** (*www. napavalleyreservations.com*).

Alexis Baking Company $ *1517 3rd St; tel: (707) 258-1827; www.alexisbakingcompany.com. Open Mon–Fri 0700–1500, Sat 0730–1500, Sun 0800–1400.* Has breakfast and picnic supplies.

Downtown Joe's Brewery & Restaurant $$ *902 Main St; tel: (707) 258-2337; www.downtownjoes.com. Open daily 1000–2200.* Great for beers, ales and Napa River views.

ZuZu $$ *829 Main St; tel: (707) 224-8555; www.zuzunapa.com.* Has tapas and Latin background music, for small tastes of Spain, Portugal, South America and organic California.

Napa River Inn $$$ *500 Main St; tel: (877) 251-8500; www.napariverinn.com.* Combines three buildings, one with views overlooking the Napa River in a historical mill complex. Look for artist Alan Shepp's Napa River mural, *Ars Longa Vita Brevis,* rendered on a mosaic fountain.

Ubuntu $$$ *1140 Main St; tel: (707) 251-5656; www.ubuntunapa.com.* Earnt a Michelin star for 2010 for its 'vegetable' cuisine, a.k.a. vegetarian based on biodynamic agriculture, and offers yoga classes $$.

RUTHERFORD/OAKVILLE

Robert Mondavi Winery $-$$
7801 St Helena Hwy, Oakville; tel: (888) 766-6328; www.robertmondaviwinery. com. Open daily 0900–1700.

Mumm Napa $$ *8445 Silverado Trail, Rutherford; tel: (707) 967-7700 or (800) 686-6272; http://mummnapa.com. Open daily 1000–1700, call for tour times.*

Rubicon Estate $$$
1991 St Helena Hwy, Rutherford; tel: (800) 782-4266 or (707) 968-1161; www.rubiconestate.com. Open daily 1000–1700 only for those purchasing wine or touring.

Rutherford Hill Winery $ *200 Rutherford Hill Rd, Rutherford; tel: (707) 963-1871; www.rutherfordhill. com. Open daily 1000–1700. Tours at 1130, 1330, 1530.*

St Supéry Winery $
8440 St Helena Hwy, Rutherford; tel: (707) 963-4507 or (800) 942-0809; www.stsupery.com. Open daily 1000–1700.

The tiny hamlets of Rutherford and Oakville, along Hwy 29, are ground zero in the continuing explosion of Napa wineries. **Robert Mondavi Winery** is the standard-bearer for the Napa Valley, named after the first American winemaker in modern times to commit to the French heresy that wine tastes better if made in small barrels rather than in 40,000-litre vats and that Cabernet Sauvignon demands different vinification from Cabernet Franc or Sauvignon Blanc. Mondavi's tours are among the most informative and the best suited to wine beginners. The downside is that the winery is so well known it attracts enormous crowds. Make tour bookings five days in advance in summer and at holiday weekends. There are a number of other good tours on offer.

Mumm Napa offers sweeping views of the Valley, sparkling wine and fine art photography galleries.

Rubicon Estate is a historical château (formerly the Inglenook Estate Winery, now Rubicon Winery) with a tasting room and Centennial Museum (cinema memorabilia) owned by director Francis Ford Coppola. Book in advance for château and vineyard tours.

Rutherford Hill Winery has an excellent cave tour as well as shady picnic grounds.

St Supéry Winery has the Valley's best interactive exhibit, with a 3-D Valley map, samples of the varied aromas – 'SmellaVision' – found in fine wines and enormous windows overlooking winery operations.

Food in Rutherford/Oakville

Above
The late Robert Mondavi, pioneer standard-bearer for Napa Valley wineries

The **Oakville Grocery** *7856 St Helena Hwy, Oakville; tel: (707) 944-8802; www.oakvillegrocery.com. Open Mon–Thur 0700–1700, Fri–Sat*

0700–1800, Sun 0800–1700 has been selling oil, vinegar and barbed wire since 1881, but the Valley's oldest mercantile has grown into a gourmet haven. The store is packed with food, wine and – at lunchtime – people queuing for sandwiches. Have lunch or watch the sun set over olive trees and vineyards on the balcony at the **Auberge du Soleil Restaurant** *180 Rutherford Rd; tel: (800) 348-5406; www. aubergedusoleil.com*

St Helena

St Helena Chamber of Commerce *1010 Main St (Hwy 29), Ste A; tel: (707) 963-4456 or (800) 799-6456; www.sthelena.com. Call for hours.*

Robert Louis Stevenson/ Silverado Museum *1490 Library Ln; tel: (707) 963-3757; www. silveradomuseum.org. Open Wed–Sun 1200–1600. Free.*

St Helena's attractive and lively town centre has the Valley's finest collection of historical buildings. The literati should visit the **Robert Louis Stevenson/Silverado Museum**, with more than 8,000 items related to Stevenson. The other half of the former library building is occupied by the **Napa Valley Wine Library**, a collection of photographs and newspaper cuttings related to local viticulture. **Ambrose Bierce House** (*1515 Main St; tel: (707) 963-3003; www.ambrosebiercehouse.com*), where the misanthropic author lived for 15 years before disappearing into the Mexican Revolution, is a Bed & Breakfast with a small collection of Bierce memorabilia.

The town also has two of the Valley's better outdoor attractions. **Bale Grist Mill State Historic Park** (*3 miles north on Hwy 29; tel: (707) 942-4575; www.parks.ca.gov*) surrounds an 1846 grist mill. Hiking trails lead to the mill pond and **Bothe-Napa Valley State Park** (*4 miles north on Hwy 29; tel: (707) 942-4575; www.parks.ca.gov*), once home to the Wappo Indians. The park has several fine hiking trails, a swimming pool, camping, and spots to dine on wine, cheese and your own picnic.

Below
Vines in St Helena

Californian Wine

Rules about drinking white wine with fish and red wine with meats seemed sensible enough when both food and wine were predictable. But today's recipes incorporate a wider range of ingredients and flavours – and not just in California. It's more useful to find out what a wine actually tastes like than to look to the colour for guidance, especially as winemakers are now experimenting with lesser-known varietals. Here are the major California grapes and wines, with an important caveat: every wine develops a different taste, depending on where and how the grapes were grown and how they were vinified, or made into wine. No two wines taste precisely the same and no two drinkers experience precisely the same taste from the same bottle. If it doesn't taste good to *you*, it doesn't taste good, no matter how long or loudly the 'experts' declaim. Most California wineries sell their own wine by the bottle or the case. Case purchases usually bring a 10–20 per cent discount off the list price, but it's often cheaper to buy wine at a local supermarket or discount store than at the winery or a wine shop. The disadvantage: smaller wineries have limited distribution, so their wines may be available only at the winery. If in doubt, ask at the winery.

Blanc de Blancs Literally 'white from whites', wine made from white grapes, usually Chardonnay.

Blanc de Noirs 'White from blacks', sparkling white wine made from red grapes, usually Pinot Noir. The skins, which contain most of the colour, are separated from the juice immediately after pressing to preserve the light colour. Blanc de Noirs normally has a richer, fruitier taste than Blanc de Blancs. Both are quite dry in California.

Blush Pink wines, usually white Zinfandels, are somewhere between almost-white and almost-red. The longer the juice is left with the skins after crushing, the darker the colour and the more intense the flavour. Most blush wines are light, sweet and meant to be drunk as young as possible.

Cabernet Sauvignon California 'Cabs' are normally dry, medium to full-bodied, and can be tannic, a less direct way to say astringent. The dominant flavours are berries and cherries.

Chardonnay The white wine of choice for many people. Pick your style: light, with simple flavours like apples, citrus and flowers; rich, with oak, butter and nuts; or steely, with very little taste at all.

Gewürztraminer California winemakers usually opt for a slightly sweet German style, but Gewürz can also be made dry, in the Alsatian style, or as an almost too-rich dessert wine. All three styles taste of spice, flowers and fruit.

Merlot This red is softer than Cabernet, i.e. it is less astringent and more 'fruity'. Winemakers traditionally blend Merlot with Cabernet to create a softer, more drinkable wine that requires less ageing.

Petit Sirah A delicate red that is less common in California. Look for it as Syrah in French blends or Shiraz in Australia.

Pinot Noir Usually a silky-smooth light red that leaves a lingering freshness rather than the heaviness more typical of Cabernet and Merlot.

Riesling Germany's other white grape is the classic for sweet dessert wines, but can also be made as a delicate dry wine filled with flower and fruit flavours.

Sauvignon Blanc or **Fumé Blanc** By either name, wines made from this white grape are normally lighter and less pronounced in flavour than Chardonnay.

Sparkling wine California's way around Champagne's legal lock on the name champagne. Look for *méthode champenoise* or 'fermented in this bottle' for top quality. 'Charmant' is plonk produced in bulk. Most of the major French champagne houses also produce sparkling wine in California.

Viognier Emerging as a staple on Californian wine lists, this dry white varietal is also known for hints of stone fruits and is recommended for hearty dishes or with cream sauces.

Zinfandel This rich red is usually spicy, with a strong hint of berries.

**Ⓑ Beringer
Vineyards $–$$**
*2000 Main St;
tel: (707) 967-4412;
www.beringer.com. Open
daily Jun–Oct 1000–1800;
Nov–May 1000–1700.
Tel: (707) 963-8989,
ext. 2222 for tours.*

At **Beringer Vineyards, Beringer Vineyards' Rhine House** is the Valley's most-photographed building, modelled after an ancestral Gothic German homestead. The winery can be crowded, but it's worth seeing the rich, wood-panelled interior and regal tasting room.

Accommodation and food in St Helena

Cindy's Backstreet Kitchen $$–$$$ (*1327 Railroad Ave; tel: (707) 963-1200; www.cindysbackstreetkitchen.com*) is famed chef Cindy Pawlcyn's relatively informal eatery, with her favourite, spice-rubbed quails on the menu, along with meatloaf, pork chops and other locally sourced plates.

Auberge du Soleil $$$ (*180 Rutherford Hill Rd, Rutherford; tel: (707) 963-1211 or (800) 348-5406; www.aubergedusoleil.com*) is a Mediterranean-inspired retreat surrounded by olive groves and Valley vistas.

Go Fish $$$ (*641 Main St; tel: (707) 963-0700; www.gofishrestaurant.net*) is another Pawlcyn eatery with seafood on the menu.

Meadowood Resort $$$ (*900 Meadowood Ln, St Helena; tel: (707) 963-3646 or (800) 458-8080; www.meadowood.com*) off the Silverado Trail, surrounds a private croquet lawn and golf course.

Tra Vigne $$$ (*1050 Charter Oak Ave; tel: (707) 963-4444; www.travignerestaurant.com*) specialises in Italian-laced California cuisine, with a separate brick-oven pizzeria and wine bar.

The **Wine Spectator Greystone Restaurant $$$** (*2555 Main St; tel: (707) 967-1010; www.ciachef.edu/restaurants/wsgr*), part of the Culinary Institute of America's nearby campus at the former Christian Brothers Winery, has California versions of Mediterranean staples. The **Flavor Bar** at the **Spice Islands Marketplace** offers themed tastings of products such as chocolate, olive oil, and sweet and sour food flavours, by reservation (*$; tel: (707) 967-2320*).

Woodhouse Chocolate $$$ (*1367 Main St; tel: (800) 966-3468 or (707) 963-8413; www.woodhousechocolate.com*) is worth a stop for heavenly by-the-piece house-made confections.

VALLEJO

**ⓘ Vallejo Convention
and Visitors
Bureau** *Vallejo Ferry
Terminal, 289 Mare Island
Way; tel: (707) 642-3653
or (800) 482-5535;
www.visitvallejo.com. Open
Mon–Fri 0830–1700,
Sat–Sun 0830–1300.*

Vallejo was California's first state capital, named after General Mariano Vallejo, one of California's few Mexican leaders who became a successful American politician. Vallejo was also home to a major US Navy repair facility and mothball fleet, the **Mare Island Naval Shipyard**, which closed in 1996. The rusting hulks that once lined the mouth of the Napa River are gone and the **Mare Island Historic Park Foundation** (*tel: (707) 644-4746; www.mareislandhpf.org*) offers tours ($) of Officers' Row mansions, a Tiffany stained-glass-window base chapel and (call in advance) the Mare Island Artifact Museum.

Vallejo Naval and Historical Museum
$ 734 Marin St;
tel: (707) 643-0077;
www.vallejomuseum.org.
Open Wed–Sat 1200–1600.

Local history is recounted in the **Vallejo Naval and Historical Museum** in the old city hall building. Many of Vallejo's graceful Victorian buildings were replaced or altered beyond recognition during the frantic growth and shipbuilding of World War II. Enough historical structures survived to create a small **Architectural Heritage District**, between Georgia, Sutter, Carolina, Monterey and York Sts.

Vallejo's theme park is **Six Flags Discovery Kingdom** (*www.sixflags.com/discoveryKingdom/index.aspx*). The most scenic way to visit is aboard a Blue & Gold Fleet (*www.blueandgoldfleet.com*) high-speed catamaran ferry from San Francisco's Pier 39 (*see page 140*).

YOUNTVILLE

Yountville Chamber of Commerce
6484 Washington St, Ste F;
tel: (707) 944-0904;
http://yountville.com.
Open daily 1000–1500.

Napa Valley Museum $
55 Presidents Circle;
tel: (707) 944-0500;
http://napavalleymuseum.org.
Open Wed–Mon 1000–1700.

This is the culinary heart of the Napa Valley and the beginning of serious, shoulder-to-shoulder wineries. Art lovers head for the **Napa Valley Museum**, an art gallery, wine museum and cultural centre. **V Marketplace** (*6525 Washington St; tel: (707) 944-2451; www.vmarketplace.com*) is a one-time winery turned boutique shopping mall.

Domaine Chandon has the Valley's most informative sparkling winery tour. Hot-air balloons frequently take off from the winery grounds or nearby.

Food in Yountville

Yountville is Napa's answer to Berkeley's Gourmet Ghetto, with prices to match. Make bookings as far in advance as possible. (*All are open daily; hours change with the economy.*)

Californian Wine History

California has been producing wine since mission friars first planted *Criolla* grapes for sacramental use. In 1857, Hungarian immigrant Agoston Haraszthy planted European *Vinifera* grapes in Sonoma. His successful **Buena Vista Winery** soon attracted competitors **Gundlach-Bundschu** (1858), **Charles Krug** (1861), **Schramsberg** (1862) and a host of other familiar names. By the 1890s, California wines were winning gold medals in every major European competition.

The 1906 San Francisco earthquake and subsequent fire destroyed enormous stocks of wine ageing in San Francisco warehouses as well as wineries up and down Wine Country. By the time the industry was back on its feet, America was plunging into Prohibition. From 1919 to 1933, it was illegal to make or consume wine (or any other alcoholic beverage) except for sacramental, medicinal or family purposes.

A few vineyards hung on, but most switched to fruit trees and other crops or went bankrupt. Robert Mondavi and the few other 1940s and 1950s winemakers who dreamt of re-establishing the glory days were dismissed as dreamers. Today, they're worshipped as saints.

Their dogged vision, plus research from the University of California at Davis, near Sacramento, and technological improvements from bulk winemakers such as Gallo, gave California vintners more control over the art of turning grape juice into wine than any winemakers in the world. When **Stag's Leap** bested Mouton Rothschild in a Paris competition in 1976, the California wine rush was on.

Domaine Chandon $$$ | *California Dr; tel: (888) 242-6366; www.chandon.com. Open daily 1000–1700, call for tour times.*

Above the Wine Country Ballooning *Tel: (800) 759-5638 or (707) 538-7359; www.balloontours.com*

Balloons Above the Valley *Tel: (707) 253-2222 or (800) 464-6824; www.balloonrides.com*

Napa Valley Balloons *Tel: (707) 994-0228 or (800) 253-2224; www.napavalleyballoons.com*

Chef Thomas Keller's **The French Laundry $$$** (*6640 Washington St; tel: (707) 944-2380; www.frenchlaundry.com*) is one of the Valley's original name eateries with nine-course tasting menus, followed by **Mustards Grill $$$** (*7399 St Helena Hwy; tel: (707) 944-2424; www. mustardsgrill.com*), **Bistro Jeanty $$** (*6510 Washington St; tel: (707) 944-0103; www.bistrojeanty.com*) and a constantly changing constellation of would-be stars.

Wine Country from the air

Right
Ballooning over the vineyards
of the Napa Valley

One of the most common sounds on a Napa morning is the gentle roar of propane burners from hot-air balloons drifting above the vineyards. Balloon tours nearly always lift off near dawn, when breezes are light, just as the night mists burn away to reveal rank upon rank of trellised vines sweeping across Valley contours. Plan on landing 90 minutes later to a champagne breakfast.

It's not cheap – about $225 per person – but it's worth the experience. Advance booking is required.

Suggested tour

Take the **San Francisco–Oakland Bay Bridge ❶** to I-80 eastbound. Cross the **Carquinez Bridge ❷**. Detour through VALLEJO ❸ or continue on I-80 to Hwy 37 then to Hwy 29. Follow Hwy 29 north through NAPA ❹, YOUNTVILLE ❺, OAKVILLE ❻, RUTHERFORD ❼, ST HELENA ❽ and CALISTOGA ❾.

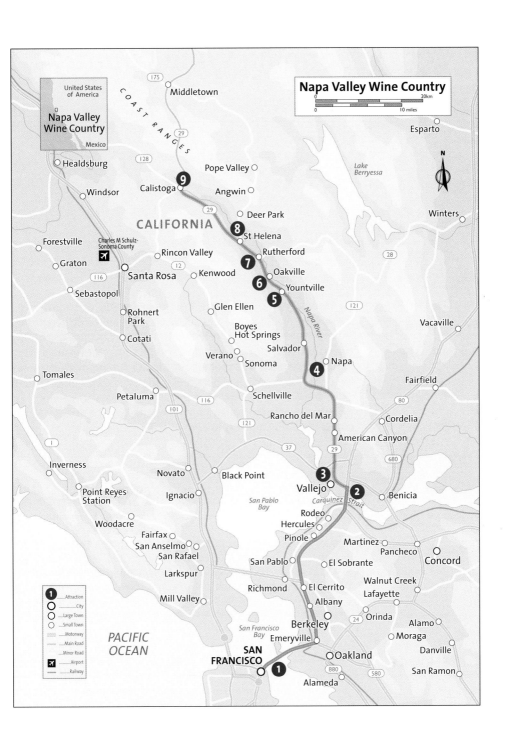

Napa Valley Wine Country

0 ___ 20km
0 ___ 10 miles

United States
of America

Napa Valley
Wine Country

Mexico

Middletown

Esparto

COAST RANGES

Healdsburg

128

Pope Valley

Lake
Berryessa

Windsor

Calistoga

Angwin

Winters

CALIFORNIA

Deer Park

St Helena

Forestville

Charles M Schulz-
Sonoma County

Rincon Valley

Rutherford

28

Graton

12

Kenwood

Oakville

Santa Rosa

116

Yountville

Sebastopol

Glen Ellen

121

Rohnert
Park

Boyes
Hot Springs

Vacaville

Cotati

Verano

Salvador

Sonoma

Napa

Napa River

Tomales

Schellville

Fairfield

Petaluma

101

116

Rancho del Mar

80

121

Cordelia

37

American Canyon

29

680

Inverness

Novato

Black Point

Point Reyes
Station

Ignacio

Vallejo

Benicia

San Pablo
Bay

Carquinez Strait

Rodeo

Woodacre

Hercules

Fairfax

Pinole

Martinez

Pancheco

Concord

San Anselmo

San Rafael

El Sobrante

Larkspur

San Pablo

Walnut Creek

Richmond

El Cerrito

Lafayette

Mill Valley

Albany

Berkeley

24

Orinda

Alamo

San Francisco
Bay

Emeryville

Moraga

PACIFIC
OCEAN

SAN
FRANCISCO

Oakland

Danville

Alameda

880

580

San Ramon

1 ....Attraction
○ ....City
○ ....Large Town
○ ....Small Town
........Motorway
........Main Road
........Minor Road
✈ ....Airport
........Railway

Sonoma Wine Country

Ratings

Food and drink	●●●●●
Scenery	●●●●●
Wine	●●●●●
Architecture	●●●○○
History	●●●○○
Children	●●○○○
Museums	●●○○○
Wildlife	●●○○○

Sonoma Wine Country is an agglomeration of several wine valleys, one of which is actually called Sonoma. The geographic variety makes Sonoma slower to drive through than neighbouring Napa, but far more rustic and interesting. California's wine industry was born in Sonoma, but despite having more than 300 wineries, the region has been less aggressive in promoting itself than Napa. For visitors, that makes Sonoma a somewhat less crowded and far more pleasurable experience – and Sonoma wines win at least as many medals as their Napa counterparts.

DRY CREEK VALLEY

 Sonoma County Tourism Bureau
Tel: (800) 576-6662; www.sonomacounty.com

Dry Creek, a twisting valley running north from Healdsburg to **Lake Sonoma**, was one of Sonoma's first official wine appellations. **Dry Creek Vineyard** (*3770 Lambert Bridge Rd; tel: (800) 864-9463; www. drycreekvineyard.com. Open daily 1030–1630*) is one of its first and most-awarded wineries. **Preston of Dry Creek Winery and Vineyards** (*9282 W. Dry Creek Rd; tel: (800) 305-9707 or (707) 433-3372; www. prestonvineyards.com. Open daily 1100–1630*) offers picnic tables and home-made bread to go with rich red wines. **Ferrari-Carano Vineyards & Winery** (*8761 Dry Creek Rd; tel: (707) 433-6700; www.ferrari-carano.com. Open daily 1000–1700*) is an architectural masterpiece with delicious Chardonnay.

GEYSERVILLE

The famous film director has begun transformation of a château-inspired winery into **Francis Ford Coppola Winery**. Continue

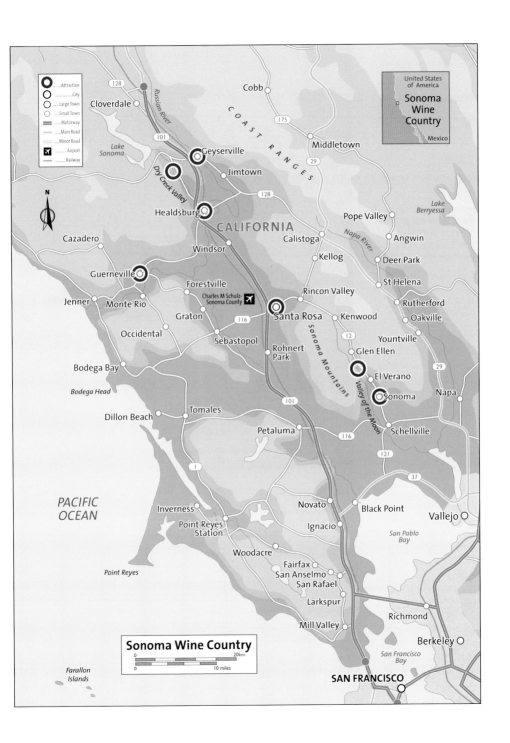

ⓘ Geyserville Chamber of Commerce *Tel: (707) 857-3745; www.geyservillecc.com*

ⓘ Francis Ford Coppola Winery *300 Via Archimedes; tel: (877) 767-7624 or (707) 857-1462; www. franciscoppolawinery.com. Call for hours.*

Pedroncelli Winery *1220 Canyon Rd; tel: (707) 857-3531 or (800) 836-3894; www.pedroncelli.com. Open daily 1000–1630.*

Trentadue Winery *$–$$ 19170 Geyserville Ave; tel: (707) 433-3104 or (888) 332-3032; www.trentadue.com. Open daily 1000–1700.*

Right
Francis Ford Coppola Winery, in Geyserville

exploring the Alexander Valley at **Pedroncelli Winery**, one of the area's last family-owned wineries, and Tuscan-inspired **Trentadue Winery**, which espouses sustainable agricultural practices.

Accommodation in Geyserville

Victoriana lovers may swoon at **Hope-Merrill House $$** (*21253 Geyserville Ave; tel: (800) 825-4233 or (707) 857-3356; www.hope-inns.com*). A three-storey Bed & Breakfast jewel with symmetrical landscaping, extravagant silk-screened wallpaper, carved armchairs and velvet-covered divans.

Hope-Bosworth House $$ (*across the street at 21238 Geyserville Ave; tel: (800) 825-4233 or (707) 857-3356; www.hope-inns.com*) is a more cheerful, less formal and less expensive Queen Anne restoration.

GUERNEVILLE

ⓘ Russian River Chamber of Commerce and Visitors Center
16209 1st St; tel: (877) 644-9001 or (707) 869-9000; www.russianriver.com. Call for hours.

Korbel Visitor Center
13250 River Rd (in Railroad Station). The Visitor Centers carry an excellent Russian River Wine Road map listing all the wineries along the river. Unlike their more formal counterparts in the Napa and Sonoma Valleys, Russian River and nearby wineries seldom charge, or charge less, for tasting.

ⓗ Armstrong Redwoods State Natural Reserve $
2 miles north of Guerneville, 17000 Armstrong Woods Rd; tel: (707) 869-2015. Open daily 0800–1 hour after dusk. Visitor Center tel: (707) 869-2958; www.parks.ca.gov. Open daily 1100–1500.

Korbel Champagne Cellars *13250 River Rd; tel: (707) 824-7000; www.korbel.com. Open daily for wine tasting 1000–1700. Call for hours for winery and rose garden tours.*

Russian River Vineyards *5700 Gravenstein Hwy N., Forestville; tel: (707) 887-3344; www.russianrivervineyards.com. Open daily 1100–1700.*

Pronounced 'gurnvil', the biggest settlement in the Russian River Valley began as a logging town in the 1880s, blossomed as a San Francisco summer resort and slipped into the hippy era. Wealthy city escapees have since filtered into the valley, creating an appealing mix of counter-culture, urban sophisticates, gay holidaymakers and local winemakers, none of them in a rush to get anywhere.

Wine touring and lazing about the Russian River are the main activities in Guerneville. **Johnson's Beach**, a placid strand in the centre of town, offers sand, canoes, paddle boats and rubber rafts in summer. The beach is also the main stage for the wildly popular **Russian River Jazz & Blues Festival** (*www.russianriverfestivals.com*), held each September. The river is less benign in winter, when heavy rains produce periodic floods. Many river-front homes and businesses have been raised to the first floor to escape the high waters.

Guerneville's most often ignored asset is **Armstrong Redwoods State Natural Reserve**, 750 acres of virgin coast redwood groves, hiking trails and primitive camping. Don't stray off the trails as it's easy to get lost in the tangled thickets in the centre of the park. **Armstrong Woods Pack Station** (*tel: (707) 887-2939; www.redwoodhorses.com*) offers half-day tours and overnight forest expeditions on horseback (advance booking required).

The Russian River is lined with vineyards and wineries, most of them upstream (east) from Guerneville. One must-see, even if you are not doing the wineries, is **Korbel Champagne Cellars**, which makes beer, wine, brandy and yes, champagne-style sparkling wines. The red-brick buildings are swathed in ivy and surrounded by hundreds of varieties of roses with plenty of shaded picnic tables.

Russian River Vineyards produces reds and is one of the river's friendliest wineries in a pleasant forest retreat.

Accommodation and food in Guerneville

The Stumptown Brewery $ (*15045 River Rd; tel: (707) 869-0705; www.stumptown.com/brews*) has beer, a sense of humour about itself, and ribs, smoked chicken and meat at its **Stumptown Grill** restaurant (*open Wed–Sun*).

The **Russian River Resort $–$$** (*16390 4th St; tel: (800) 417-3767 or (707) 869-0691; www.russianriverresort.com*) has a pool and fine downtown location, popular with gay and lesbian holidaymakers.

Applewood Inn & Restaurant $$$ (*13555 Hwy 116; tel: (800) 555-8509; www.applewoodinn.com*) is the Russian River's most luxurious inn and best gourmet restaurant (*www.dineatapplewood.com*) with its own kitchen garden.

HEALDSBURG

ⓘ Healdsburg Chamber of Commerce and Visitors Bureau *217 Healdsburg Ave; tel: (707) 433-6935; www.healdsburg.org. Open Mon–Fri 0900–1700, Sat 0900–1500, Sun 1000–1400.*

ⓦ Gallo Family Vineyards Tasting Room *320 Center St; tel: (707) 433-2458; www.gallosonoma.com. Open daily 1000–1800.*

Kendall-Jackson Healdsburg Tasting Room *$ 337 Healdsburg Ave; tel: (707) 433-7102; www.kj.com/visit/healdsburg-tasting-room. Open daily 1000–1700.*

Healdsburg Museum *221 Matheson St; tel: (707) 431-3325; www.healdsburgmuseum.org. Open Wed–Sun 1100–1600. Free.*

Hand Fan Museum *$ 219 Healdsburg Ave (H₂ Hotel); tel: (707) 431-2500; www.handfanmuseum.com*

This is one of the few Wine Country towns that may have more grape growers and farm workers than tourists. Founded in 1857 by a migrant farmer turned merchant, the tranquil town remains focused on its tree-lined **central Healdsburg Plaza**. Healdsburg straddles an invisible border between the Russian River, Dry Creek and Alexander Valleys, which makes it a popular starting point for wine tours.

If time is short, half a dozen wineries have tasting rooms on or near the plaza, including **Gallo Family Vineyards** and **Kendall-Jackson**. More than 20 wineries are within easy cycling distance of the Bed & Breakfasts that have sprung up all over town, and dozens lie within a quick drive. And when wine touring gets too much, try **Veterans Memorial Beach Park** *(tel: (707) 433-1625)* on the Russian River, a mile south of the plaza. Canoes and rubber rafts can be hired for a cooling float downstream; the hire company provides the return trip.

The **Healdsburg Museum**, in the 1910 Carnegie Library building, has a collection of Pomo Indian baskets and artefacts from California's Mexican period. Extensive displays explain local history, assisted by one of the area's largest photographic archives. The **Hand Fan Museum** shows off 2,500 fans, in a new H₂ Hotel space.

Accommodation and food in Healdsburg

Downtown Bakery & Creamery *$ 308A Center St; tel: (707) 431-2719; www.downtownbakery.net. Open Mon–Fri 0600–1730, Sat 0700–1730, Sun 0700–1600* and **Flying Goat Coffee Roastery and Cafe** *$ 324 Center St; tel: (707) 433-3599; www.flyinggoatcoffee.com. Open daily 0700–1900.* Two favourite local breakfast stops.

Belle de Jour Inn *$$ 16276 Healdsburg Ave; tel: (707) 431-9777; www.belledejourinn.com.* A luxurious collection of refreshingly simple cottages and carriage house.

Bistro Ralph *$$ 109 Plaza St; tel: (707) 433-1380. Open Mon–Sat.* An intimate bistro and long-term survivor in a turbulent restaurant scene.

Healdsburg Inn on the Plaza *$$$ 112 Matheson St; tel: (707) 433-6991 or (800) 431-8663; www.healdsburginn.com.* The best town-centre choice.

Madrona Manor *$$$ 1001 Westside Rd and Dry Creek Rd; tel: (707) 433-4231 or (800) 258-4003; www.madronamanor.com.* A rambling manor house surrounded by exotic gardens and a citrus orchard amid the vineyards.

Madrona Manor Restaurant *$$$ 1001 Westside Rd; tel: (707) 433-4231; www.madronamanor.com.* One of the most sought-after tables in Healdsburg, known for its ambience, presentation, fresh garden ingredients and one Michelin star.

SANTA ROSA

**ⓘ Santa Rosa
Convention and
Visitors Bureau**
9 4th St; tel: (707) 577-
8674 or (800) 404-7673;
www.visitsantarosa.com.
Open daily 0900–1700. The
North Coast California
Welcome Center is in the
same location, in Railroad
Square.

Santa Rosa is ringed with shopping malls and plagued by traffic jams. It also has splendid residential neighbourhoods and more than its fair share of quirky museums, gardens and other attractions.

One of the quirkiest is the **Church of One Tree** (*Juilliard Park*), built in 1872 of wood milled from a single redwood tree with objects and papers from the life of native son Robert Ripley, of Ripley's Believe It or Not! fame. The **Charles M. Schulz Museum**, named after the late creator of the 'Peanuts' comic strip, has exhibits devoted to his illustration, as well as other comic illustrators. Most novel are the full-scale SNOOPY™ Labyrinth, named after the beloved beagle of the strip, and the 3,588 four-panel 'Peanuts' strips which compose a huge Peanuts Tile Mural. Another attraction is the **Luther Burbank Home & Gardens**, the long-time home and gardens planted by the horticulturist who created more than 800 new varieties of commercial fruits, flowers, vegetables and other plants.

There are several other traditional museums worth visiting. The **Sonoma County Museum**, in a restored 1909 post office and federal building, spans the eras from Native American habitation to the

Above
Grapes ripening in the
Californian autumn sun

Ⓖ Charles M. Schulz Museum $$
2301 Hardies Ln;
tel: (707) 579-4452;
www.schulzmuseum.org.
Open summer Mon–Fri
1100–1700, Sat–Sun
1000–1700; autumn–spring
Mon & Wed–Fri
1100–1700, Sat–Sun
1000–1700.

Luther Burbank Home & Gardens $
Santa Rosa and Sonoma
Aves; tel: (707) 524-5445;
http://ci.santa-rosa.ca.us/
departments/
recreationandparks/parks/
lbhg/Pages/default.aspx.
Gardens open daily
0800–dusk; building tours
Apr–Oct Tue–Sun
1000–1530.

Sonoma County Museum $ 425 7th St;
tel: (707) 579-1500; www.
sonomacountymuseum.org.
Open Tue–Sun 1100–1700.

Jesse Peter Native American Art Museum
Bussman Hall, Santa Rosa
Junior College, 1501
Mendocino Ave; tel: (707)
527-4479; www.santarosa.
edu/museum. Open mid-Aug–
mid-May, call for hours. Free.

Kendall-Jackson Wine Center $ 5007 Fulton Rd;
tel: (866) 287-9818 or
(707) 571-8100;
www.kj.com/visit. Open daily
1000–1700, garden tours
1100, 1300, 1500.

Safari West Wildlife Preserve and African Tent Camp $$$ 3115
Porter Creek Rd; tel: (800)
616-2695 or (707) 579-
2551; www.safariwest.com.
Open year-round, call for
hours, tour and overnight
safari tent accommodation.

Victorian era. **Jesse Peter Native American Art Museum** displays Native American arts and crafts from across the continent and beyond.

Grapes are only one of many products that have made Sonoma County famous; the area is at least as well known for apples, escargot, berries, salad greens, lamb, goat's milk cheese, duck and other comestibles. The best guide to local farms, seasonal produce and agricultural tours is **Sonoma County Farm Trails** (*tel: (800) 207-9464; www.farmtrails.org*), a free self-guiding tour map available at most wineries and visitor centres and online.

The **Kendall-Jackson Wine Center** has wine tasting, but its wine-sensory and culinary gardens – designed for visitor tasting – are the stunning highlights of this 120-acre winery between Santa Rosa and Healdsburg. Have a craving for Africa in Wine Country? **Safari West** is a 400-acre Wildlife Preserve with as many animals as acres. It's an eclectic combination of safari tours, winter walking tours, day visits, overnight stays, and occasional educational fund-raisers on an enclave amid vineyards and ranches, but the stars are endangered species of African animals and birds and two conserved species of extinct-in-the-wild Saharan antelope. Visitor sightings and encounters may take in ostriches, cheetahs, lemurs, giraffes, Cape buffalo and zebras.

Accommodation and food in Santa Rosa

Hotel La Rose $$$ (*308 Wilson St; tel: (707) 579-3200 or (800) 527-6738; www.hotellarose.com*) occupies a historic landmark building. **John Ash & Co $$$** (*4350 Barnes Rd; tel: (707) 527-7687; www.vintnersinn.com/dining.asp. Open daily*) blends Asian, French, Italian and Southwestern American flavours. **Kenwood Restaurant and Bar $$$** (*9900 Hwy 12, Kenwood; tel: (707) 833-6326; www.kenwoodrestaurant.com. Open Wed–Sun*) is a Wine Country favourite east of Santa Rosa.

SONOMA

 Sonoma Valley Visitors Bureau
453 1st St E.; tel: (707) 996-1090 or (866) 996-1090; www. sonomavalley.com. Open Mon–Sat 0900–1700, Sun 0900–1000. The other visitor centre is in 23750 Arnold Dr at Cornerstone Gardens, Hwy 121, south of Sonoma. Open daily.

Sonoma State Historic Park $
363 3rd St W.; tel: (707) 938-9560; www.parks.ca.gov. Open Fri–Wed 1000–1700.

Buena Vista Winery $
18000 Old Winery Rd; tel: (800) 926-1266; http:// buenavistacarneros.com. Open daily 1000–1700.

Gundlach-Bundschu Winery $ 2000 Denmark St; tel: (707) 938-5277 or (707) 939-3015; www.gunbun.com. Open daily 1100–1630.

Sebastiani Vineyards & Winery $ 389 4th St E.; tel: (800) 888-5532; www.sebastiani.com. Open daily 1000–1700.

 Viansa Winery & Italian Marketplace $$ 25200 Arnold Dr, Hwy 121; tel: (800) 995-4740; www.viansa.com. Open daily 1000–1700.

Cornerstone Gardens $ 23570 Hwy 121; tel: (707) 933-3010; www.cornerstoneplace.com. Open daily 1000–1600.

Opposite
Preston of Dry Creek Winery and Vineyards

Sonoma town retains much of its original Mexican flavour despite years of Wine Country gentrification, thanks in large part to the 8-acre **plaza** designed by General Mariano Vallejo in 1835. The Bear Flag Revolt of 1846 that catapulted California into America began in Sonoma. The revolt, which looms large in California history books, involved about three dozen American settlers who seized control of the unused and unguarded presidio at Sonoma. Their chief prisoner was General Vallejo, a long-time supporter of American annexation for California. Both the revolt and the California Republic dissolved a month later when the US Navy sailed into Monterey Bay.

A monument to the revolt sits in the middle of the shady plaza, across from **Sonoma State Historic Park**, which includes **Mission San Francisco Solano de Sonoma** (*tel: (707) 938-9560; tours Fri–Sun 1100, 1200, 1300, 1400*), **Vallejo's Home** (*tel: (707) 938-9559; tours Sat–Sun 1300, 1400, 1500*) and the **Sonoma Barracks** (*tel: (707) 939-9420*), once occupied by a handful of Mexican soldiers. A dozen or so mission-era buildings surround the plaza, most of them now used as restaurants, shops or boutiques. One of the more interesting is the 1850 **Swiss Hotel** (*18 W. Spain St; tel: (707) 938-2884; www.swisshotelsonoma.com*), a good restaurant and small hotel.

California's modern wine industry was born at **Buena Vista Winery**, a large estate with a stone winery, hillside tunnels, an art gallery and picnic area. **Gundlach-Bundschu Winery** is nearly as scenic with rich, up-to-date vintages. **Sebastiani Vineyards & Winery** has embarked on a second century. Look for the hand-carved casks. **Viansa Winery & Italian Marketplace** has one of Sonoma's best winery shops and a picnic area overlooking a wildlife refuge. Not far down Hwy 121 is **Cornerstone Gardens**, an eclectic collection of changing garden sculpture, salvaged items as fine arts, galleries and a café.

Accommodation and food in Sonoma

Cafe La Haye $$ *140 E. Napa St; tel: (707) 935-5994; http:// cafelahaye.com. Open Tue–Sun for dinner.* A fine American-style choice.

Della Santina's $$$ *133 E. Napa St; tel: (707) 935-0576; www. dellasantinas.com. Open daily 1100–1500, 1700–2130.* Does Italian.

The Fairmont Sonoma Mission Inn & Spa $$$ *100 Boyes Blvd at 18140 Sonoma Hwy; tel: (707) 938-9000 or (866) 540-4499; www.fairmont.com/sonoma.* The most elegant and most expensive spa in Sonoma County. The luxurious spa is the main draw, but the inn is a traditional favourite for visiting Hollywood types.

The Swiss Hotel $$$ *18 W. Spain St; tel: (707) 938-2884; www. swisshotelsonoma.com. Open daily 1130–1430 and from 1700.* Concentrates on modern California cuisine, pizza and pasta.

VALLEY OF THE MOON

Jack London State Historic Park $
2400 Jack London Ranch Rd, Glen Ellen; tel: (707) 938-5216; www.parks.ca.gov. Museum and park open daily.

Triple Creek Horse Outfit $$
Tel: (707) 887-8700; www.triplecreekhorseoutfit. com

Wine Country Chocolates $$
14301 Arnold Dr (Jack London Village); tel: (707) 996-1010; www. winecountrychocolates.com. Has a free tasting bar for heavenly home-made chocolates. Open daily 1000–1700. A Sonoma tasting room 414 1st Street E. is on Sonoma Plaza.

This is the capital of the Jack London cult. The author of *Call of the Wild* and numerous other stories that celebrate nature, manhood and the nobility of suffering in the Great Outdoors named the valley between Santa Rosa and Sonoma after the way the moon seems to appear and disappear behind the surrounding mountain peaks. London and his wife settled at the well-named **Beauty Ranch**, 800 acres that have become **Jack London State Historic Park**. London was the highest-paid writer of his era, which makes more intriguing the collection of rejection letters displayed in his house, now the park museum. A series of trails leads to the ruins of **Wolf House**, built for the couple in 1913 and destroyed by arson just before they moved in. Both are buried on a hilltop above Wolf House. **Triple Creek Horse Outfit** offers guided horseback rides through the state historic park from spring to autumn.

Accommodation and food in Valley of the Moon

Glen Ellen Inn Restaurant $$ *13670 Arnold Dr; tel: (707) 996-6409; www. glenelleninn.com. Call for opening hours.* Specialises in local ingredients.

Saffron $$ *13648 Arnold Dr; tel: (707) 938-4844; www. saffronrestaurant.com. Open Tue–Sat 1700–2100.* Serves California cuisine with ingredients from local farms.

Beltane Ranch $$$ *11775 Sonoma Hwy (Hwy 12); tel: (707) 996-6501; www.beltaneranch.com.* A buttercup-yellow ranch bunkhouse B&B.

Gaige House Inn $$$ *13540 Arnold Dr; tel: (707) 935-0237 or (800) 935-0237; www.gaige.com.* A Victorian house, very modern inside with an eclectic collection of modern art.

Suggested tour

Follow Hwy 101 north from San Francisco across the **Golden Gate Bridge ❶** through Marin County to **Rohnert Park ❷**, SANTA ROSA **❸** and HEALDSBURG **❹**. Take Healdsburg Ave and Alexander Valley Rd north, then east to **Jimtown ❺** and Hwy 128. Turn south to **Kellog ❻** and Franz Valley Rd to Porter Creek Rd and follow Calistoga Rd to Hwy 12 and **Kenwood ❼**. Take Warm Springs Rd south to **Glen Ellen ❽**. Continue south to **El Verano ❾** and turn east to SONOMA **❿**. Return to San Francisco via the Carneros Hwy and the Napa Valley or take Hwy 121 to Hwy 37 and back to Hwy 101.

Detour: From Healdsburg **❹**, take Dry Creek Rd through the **DRY CREEK VALLEY ⓫** to Canyon Rd, then turn east on Canyon Rd to Hwy 101. Either follow Hwy 101 south to Alexander Valley Rd or take Hwy 128 to GEYSERVILLE ⓬ and Jimtown **❺**.

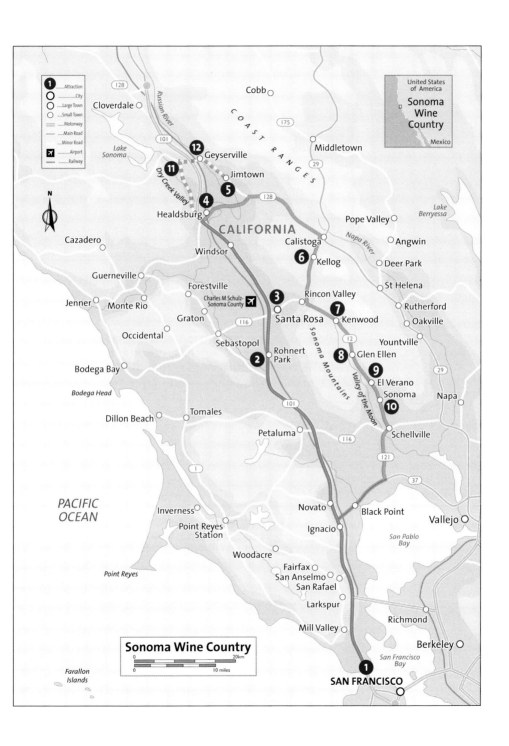

Sonoma Wine Country

United States of America

Sonoma Wine Country

Mexico

1 Attraction
City
Large Town
Small Town
Motorway
Main Road
Minor Road
Airport
Railway

Cobb

Cloverdale

Russian River

COAST RANGES

Lake Sonoma

Middletown

Geyserville

Jimtown

Dry Creek Valley

Healdsburg

CALIFORNIA

Lake Berryessa

Pope Valley

Angwin

Cazadero

Windsor

Calistoga

Napa River

Kellog

Deer Park

Guerneville

St Helena

Forestville

Rincon Valley

Jenner

Monte Rio

Charles M Schulz-Sonoma County

Santa Rosa

Rutherford

Graton

Kenwood

Oakville

Occidental

Sebastopol

Sonoma Mountains

Yountville

Rohnert Park

Glen Ellen

Bodega Bay

Valley of the Moon

El Verano

Bodega Head

Sonoma

Napa

Dillon Beach

Tomales

Schellville

Petaluma

PACIFIC OCEAN

Inverness

Novato

Black Point

Vallejo

Point Reyes Station

Ignacio

San Pablo Bay

Woodacre

Fairfax

San Anselmo

San Rafael

Point Reyes

Larkspur

Richmond

Mill Valley

Berkeley

Sonoma Wine Country

0   20km
0   10 miles

Farallon Islands

San Francisco Bay

SAN FRANCISCO

N

Lake Sonoma

Marin Coast

Ratings

Nature	●●●●●
Scenery	●●●●○
Children	●●●○○
Coastal villages	●●●○○
Wildlife	●●●○○
Beaches	●●○○○
Food	●●○○○
Museums	●●○○○

The western edge of Marin County (pronounced 'mah-rinn') offers the most civilised, most accessible and most crowded stretch of Northern California coast. The possibilities run from fine beaches with frigid water to shady, almost dank redwood groves, open pastures, sheer cliffs, windy picnic sites and elegant hideaways.

Marin's scenic bounty is natural, albeit highly modified by early loggers and farmers who stripped the forests from miles of coastal hills. But the style in which the coast is enjoyed, the roads, the parks, the restaurants and country inns, are imports from East Marin, the San Francisco Bay side of the county.

The Bay side of Marin is a striving, style-conscious enclave whose tone has largely been set by 1960s Flower Power survivors. Most have long since traded psychedelic trips for more prosaic journeys by BMW, Mercedes and top-of-the-line mountain bikes, but personal gratification remains central to life in Marin – thousands swarm across the open hillsides, beaches and trails of West Marin and a section of Sonoma County coast just north at weekends to keep bodies and auras well exercised.

BODEGA BAY

ℹ Marin Convention and Visitors Bureau *1 Mitchell Blvd, Ste B, San Rafael; tel: (866) 925-2060 or (415) 925-2060; www.visitmarin.org. Open Mon–Fri 0900–1700.*

Sonoma Coast Visitors Center *850 Hwy 1, Bodega Bay; tel: (707) 875-3866; www.bodegabay.com. Open Mon–Thur & Sat 0900–1700, Fri 0900–1800, Sun 1000–1700.*

Pomo and Miwok bands lived along the sheltered curve of Bodega Bay when Juan Francisco de la Bodega y Quadra Mollineda stopped by on his way north to British Columbia in 1775. The Native Americans were long gone by the time Alfred Hitchcock portrayed the fishing village as a town under siege from the air in *The Birds* (1963). Squawking hordes of seagulls and other birds still haunt the harbour, but they're far more interested in stealing scraps from fishermen than in dive-bombing tourists and schoolchildren.

Bodega was failing fast as commercial fishing declined in the 1970s, but holidaymakers discovered the town and turned the economic tide. The best walks are over **Bodega Head**, one of the first California sites where local opposition successfully derailed utility schemes to build nuclear power stations along the coast. The **University of California Davis Bodega Marine Laboratory** offers public tours.

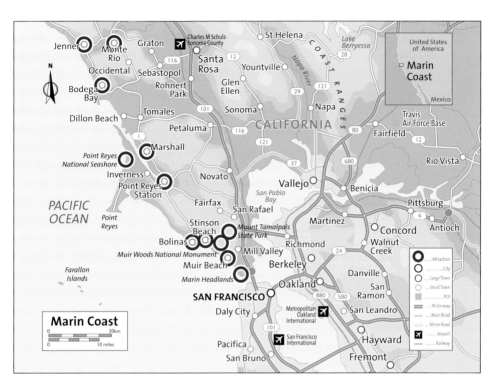

University of California Davis Bodega Marine Laboratory *2099 Westside Rd, Bodega Head; tel: (707) 875-2211; www.bml.ucdavis.edu. Open Fri 1400–1600. Free.*

Sonoma Coast State Park *Beaches along 17 miles from Bodega Head to 4 miles north of Jenner; tel: (707) 875-3483; www.parks.ca.gov*

Sonoma Coast State Park is multiple beaches separated by headlands and bluffs overlooking craggy cliffs and small coves. Views are magnificent, swimming is treacherous, and there is environmental protection of western snowy plover breeding grounds.

Accommodation and food in Bodega Bay

Bookings are essential in summer; at weekends all year.

Lucas Wharf Restaurant $$ *595 Hwy 1; tel: (707) 875-3522; www.suncompsvc.com/lucas.* Concentrates on more traditional seafood. **Lucas Wharf Deli and Fishmarket**, next door, is the best source for picnic supplies.

Bay View Restaurant $$$ *The Inn at the Tides, 800 Hwy 1; tel: (800) 541-7788 or (707) 875-2751; www.innatthetides.com.* Offers monthly five-course winemaker dinners and continental cuisine Wednesday to Sunday.

Bodega Bay Lodge & Spa $$$ *103 Hwy 1 (Doran Beach Rd); tel: (888) 875-2250 or (707) 875-3525; www.woodsidehotels.com/bodega.* A posh resort.

Bodega Coast Inn & Suites $$$ *521 Hwy 1; tel: (707) 875-2217 or (800) 346-6999; www.bodegacoastinn.com.* Has large view rooms.

BOLINAS

🄸 **Audubon Canyon
Ranch Bolinas
Lagoon Preserve** *4900
Hwy 1, 2 miles north of
Stinson Beach; tel: (415)
868-9244; www.egret.org.
Open mid-Mar–mid-Jul
Sat–Sun 1000–1600.*

Just north of Stinson Beach along Hwy 1 is **Bolinas Lagoon**, a usually
sunny resting spot for seabirds and harbour seals that haul out on
sandbars. Off the eastern side of the lagoon is **Audubon Canyon
Ranch Bolinas Lagoon Preserve**, the premier place on the entire
West Coast to observe majestic great blue herons and great and snowy
egrets as well as dozens of other species.

Bolinas is an anti-outsider, though not unfriendly, surfer and beach
town west of Bolinas Lagoon. It's worth the short drive off Hwy 1
(look for the unmarked paved road beyond the lagoon, as there's a
long tradition of locals removing signs to discourage visitors) to get
picnic supplies from **The People's Store $** (*end of the gravel drive, next
to Bolinas Bakery; tel: (415) 868-1433*), a cooperative famous for locally
grown produce and sublime service. To find the real Bolinas and
denizens, check out the bar and live music at weekends at **Smiley's
Schooner Saloon and Hotel $** (*41 Wharf Rd; tel: (415) 868-1311;
www.coastalpost.com/smileys*), operating since 1851.

Duxbury Reef Nature Reserve (*end of Elm Rd*) is a rocky shelf with
wonderful tide pooling. Keep an eye on the water, especially on a
rising tide. Birdwatchers usually opt for the **PRBO Palomarin Field
Station and Visitor Center** (*999 Mesa Rd; tel: (415) 868-0655, ext. 395;
www.prbo.org. Days and hours vary seasonally*), which has a self-guided
visitor centre and nature trail at one of America's few full-time
ornithological research stations.

JENNER

Below
Arcadian countryside around
Jenner

The tiny village marks both the mouth of the Russian River and the end
of Hwy 116, which follows the river inland to dozens of wineries. The
'logs' on the sand at the mouth of the river are most likely seals
warming themselves. Beaches north of Jenner are wild, windy and
fabulously popular for hiking, beachcombing and enjoying the scenery.

Accommodation in Jenner

Jenner Inn & Cottages $$$ *Hwy 1; tel: (707)
865-2377 or (800) 732-2377; www.jennerinn.
com.* A collection of several houses and Bed
& Breakfast establishments, with 20 rooms
'where the river and ocean meet'.

Timber Cove Inn $$$ *21780 N. Hwy 1; tel:
(800) 997-8319 or (707) 847-3231; www.
timbercoveinn.com.* Has ocean-front lodging.

MARIN HEADLANDS

ℹ Marin Headlands Visitor Center
3 miles west of Alexander exit from Hwy 101 in the former Fort Barry Chapel; tel: (415) 331-1540; www.nps.gov/goga. Open daily 0930–1630.

🏛 Golden Gate National Recreation Area *Tel: (415) 561-4700; www.nps.gov/goga*

Nike Missile Site SF-88
Tel: (415) 331-1453; www.nps.gov/goga/nike-missile-site.htm. Open Wed–Fri 1230–1530 & the first Sat of the month. Free.

Marine Mammal Center *2000 Bunker Hill Rd, Fort Cronkhite; tel: (415) 289-7325; www.tmmc.org. Open daily 1000–1700. Free, donations welcome.*

☾ Marin Headlands Hostel $ *Fort Barry; tel: (888) 464-4872 or (415) 331-2777; www.norcalhostels.org*

The windswept, nearly naked headlands directly north of the Golden Gate Bridge are the least-changed hillsides in Marin. They have been a military preserve since the US Civil War, when artillery batteries were installed to repel an invasion that never happened. Slopes facing the Pacific Ocean and the Golden Gate were honeycombed with batteries, observation posts and supply bunkers during World War II; anti-aircraft and Nike missile batteries were added during the Cold War years. The demilitarised Headlands is now part of the **Golden Gate National Recreation Area** (*see page 138*).

Most of the old batteries survive as scenic vantage points. Among the best is **Battery Wallace** (*above the southwestern tip*), with nicely framed views of the Pacific and the Golden Gate Bridge. The last surviving **Nike Missile Site SF-88** is complete with decommissioned missiles. **Point Bonita Lighthouse** (*western tip of the Headlands*) is open for visits via a steep hike and a tunnel (*Sat–Mon 1230–1530*).

Most Headlands activities begin around the point from the lighthouse turn-off at the **Marin Headlands Visitor Center**. A wide, sandy beach separates the cold Pacific surf from the warmer waters of **Rodeo Lagoon** (no swimming, to protect nesting birds). Nearby is **Marine Mammal Center**, a rescue and rehabilitation centre for injured and sick marine mammals. The centre is open daily for tours, volunteer staff and workload permitting. Officers' quarters at the former **Fort Barry**, just inland, have been converted into a spacious youth hostel.

MARSHALL

🏛 Tomales Bay Oyster Company
15479 Hwy 1, just south of Marshall; tel: (415) 663-1242; www.tomalesbayoysters.com. Open daily 0800–1800.

Hog Island Oyster Co
20215 Hwy 1; tel: (415) 663-9218; www.hogislandoysters.com. Open daily 0900–1700.

Marin Agricultural Land Trust (MALT) $–$$$ (tours)
Tel: (415) 663-1158; www.malt.org/programs/index.php

Marshall was once a major oyster and fishing port for San Francisco. The fishing is long gone, but the oysters are back, courtesy of the **Tomales Bay Oyster Company** and **Hog Island Oyster Co**, which sell oysters fresh from the water. Another reason to stop is **Tony's Seafood Restaurant $** (*18863 Hwy 1; tel: (415) 663-1107*), which has specialised in oysters for half a century. Barbecue is the preferred preparation.

Since it became the first certified organic dairy west of the Mississippi River in the 1960s, the **Straus Family Creamery** (*www.strausmilk.com*) has been a leader in preserving West Marin County agricultural lands while making superb, flavourful milk, butter, yoghurt and other dairy products, including award-winning ice cream, all found in local markets.

MONTE RIO

Monte Rio Chamber of Commerce
Tel: (707) 865-2304;
www.monterio.org

This Russian River resort town 3 miles south of Guerneville (*see page 167*) is filled with gracefully crumbling Victorian houses and a few more modern resorts. The town is best known as the entrance to the **Bohemian Grove**, a private camp that lets out San Francisco's Bohemian Club for an annual camp-out for the world's biggest boys – former heads of state, bank presidents, media moguls, military leaders, politicos and the like, with neither women nor cameras allowed.

Accommodation and food in Monte Rio

Village Inn & Restaurant $$–$$$ *20822 River Blvd; tel: (707) 865-2304; www.villageinn-ca.com.* Has ten rooms in a refurbished, century-old building that was the location for several scenes in the 1942 film *Holiday Inn*. The restaurant serves dinner Wednesday to Sunday.

Rio Villa Beach Resort $$$ *20292 Hwy 116; tel: (877) 746-8455 or (707) 865-1143; www.riovilla.com.* Has pleasant views of the Russian River and a private river-front beach.

MOUNT TAMALPAIS STATE PARK

Mount Tamalpais State Park $
801 Panoramic Hwy, Mill Valley; tel: (415) 388-2070; www.parks.ca.gov. Open daily 0700–dusk.

Mountain Home Inn $$$ *lodging $$ restaurant, 810 Panoramic Hwy, Mill Valley; tel: (415) 381-9000; www.mtnhomeinn.com*

Mount Tamalpais (Mount Tam to locals) dominates the Marin skyline. Ridges leading up to the 2,571ft peak neatly divide the county into wild western slopes leading to the Pacific Ocean and suburbanised slopes leading to San Francisco Bay. More than 50 miles of hiking and biking trails wind through the park to connect with another 200 miles in surrounding recreation areas. If fog and smog permit, panoramic views stretch from the Farallon Islands (*26 miles west*) to the Sierra Nevada (*150 miles east*). The Panoramic Hwy is the most direct route from Hwy 1 to Muir Woods, but traffic on the winding road can be extremely slow.

MUIR BEACH

Just down the road from **Muir Woods National Monument** (*see opposite*), Muir Beach is one of Marin's prettiest beaches, a deep crescent of sand behind a semicircular cove. It is seldom crowded during the week, but can turn into a zoo (with almost no parking) at weekends and holidays during fine weather. Swimming is not recommended on account of ferocious rip tides.

Accommodation and food in Muir Beach

The **Pelican Inn** $$$ (*10 Pacific Way; tel: (415) 383-6000; www.pelicaninn.com*) is the creation of a homesick British expatriate, who conjured up a dark and inviting 16th-century Tudor inn. Book as early as possible – the inn is even more popular for its food, drink and boarding than its romantic atmosphere.

MUIR WOODS NATIONAL MONUMENT

Muir Woods National Monument $
Mill Valley;
tel: (415) 388-2595;
www.nps.gov/muwo.
Open daily 0800–dusk.

Right
A hundred shades of green:
Muir Woods National
Monument

This 560-acre virgin grove of coastal redwoods is all that remains of the vast redwood forests that once cloaked Mount Tam and most of the rest of coastal Marin, Sonoma and Mendocino Counties – Mill Valley, just over the flank of Mount Tam, was named after the many lumber mills the town once supported. The next significant stand of easily accessible redwoods, in **Redwood National and State Parks** (*see page 201*), is towards the Oregon border.

Muir Woods sits in a steep canyon that was uneconomical for early lumbermen to log. Today, it's a calm and majestic place, with tatters of fog and beams of sunlight filtering through 250ft-tall redwoods to the valley floor carpeted with ferns and laurel.

Paved, self-guided trails circle the flat canyon floor. Unpaved trails climb the canyon walls to connect with Mount Tam and Pacific Ocean routes. The monument was named after pioneer conservationist John Muir in 1908.

Easy access also makes Muir Woods impossibly popular. The small car park fills up early at weekends and holidays and sightseeing coaches from San Francisco clog the road every day. Crowds are smallest midweek and in winter, which is also when salmon and steelhead trout migrate up **Redwood Creek** to spawn. (*For salmon viewing updates during the Nov–Mar season, tel: (415) 388-2595.*)

POINT REYES NATIONAL SEASHORE

Point Reyes National Seashore
Point Reyes Station; tel:
(415) 464-5100;
www.nps.gov/pore

Point Reyes is a patch of semi-wilderness surrounded by the Pacific Ocean and Tomales Bay. This wing-shaped peninsula of rolling hills, sheer cliffs and drifting fog is a mecca for hikers, cyclists, bird-watchers, backpackers, mountain bikers, sea kayakers, wild-flower enthusiasts and just about anyone else who enjoys outdoor activities.

ⓘ Bear Valley Visitor Center *Off Hwy 1 from Olema; tel: (415) 464-5100. Open Mon–Fri 0900–1700, Sat–Sun 0800–1700.*

Kenneth C Patrick Visitor Center *Drakes Beach; tel: (415) 669-1250. Open Sat–Sun 1000–1700.*

Lighthouse Visitor Center *Above the lighthouse; tel: (415) 669-1534. Visitor Center open Thur–Mon 1000–1630, lighthouse stairs and exhibits open 1000–1630, lens room open as staffing permits.*
    In late Dec–mid-Apr, a weekend and holiday **shuttle bus $** (www.nps.gov/pore/ planyourvisit/shuttlemap.htm) from the Kenneth C Patrick Visitor Center is mandatory to visit the lighthouse and Chimney Rock.

ⓓ Drakes Bay Oyster Farm *17171 Sir Francis Drake Blvd; tel: (415) 669-1149; www. drakesbayfamilyfarms.com. Open daily 0830–1630.*

Northern elephant seals (*Mirounga angustirostris*) have returned to the Point Reyes headlands after a century's absence. Volunteers provide tours of the colony of up to 1,800 5,000lb animals during the December–March pupping and breeding season; for schedule, *tel: (415) 464-5134.* Best spots for viewing are the lighthouse car park overlooking South Beach, and a viewing area about ¼ mile from the Chimney Rock car park.

It is also the most itinerant piece of California. Five million years ago, Point Reyes was south of San Francisco Bay, about where Monterey now stands. A hundred million or so years earlier, it was part of the Tehachapi Mountains in Southern California. Presuming it hasn't been swamped by erosion and global warming, the whole peninsula will eventually end up in the Gulf of Alaska.

Point Reyes is drifting northwestwards along the San Andreas Fault, which produced California's most famous earthquake. The 1906 quake that destroyed San Francisco was centred beneath Point Reyes; the entire peninsula jumped 16ft to the north in the blink of an eye. The only damage was to a few fences, which can be seen along the easy Earthquake Trail from the Bear Valley Visitor Center.

The park, which is adjacent to, but not part of, the Golden Gate National Recreation Area, has several distinct areas.

Bear Valley Visitor Center is the main visitor centre. The huge, barn-shaped building houses exhibits covering local history and ecosystems.

The easy 1-mile **Earthquake Trail** displays some of the more notable effects of the 1906 San Francisco earthquake, which was far stronger at largely uninhabited Point Reyes than it was in San Francisco. Behind the visitor centre stands the **Morgan Horse Ranch**, a working ranch for the Morgan horses that used to patrol seashore wilderness areas. **Kule Loklo** is a re-created Miwok village that offers a glimpse of local life before European contact. An easy ½-mile walk with self-guiding exhibits leads from the visitor centre to the village.

Several popular hikes leave from the Bear Valley centre, including an 8-mile return walk to **Arch Rock** on the coast. Check with rangers before setting out; the coast can be dramatically wetter, colder and windier than this protected valley.

Drakes Beach (*off Sir Francis Drake Blvd*) is a calm strand backed by white sandstone cliffs behind the crook of Point Reyes. The beach and **Drakes Estero**, a shallow estuary, designated as a wilderness area that shelters harbour seals and many bird species, are generally accepted as the place Sir Francis Drake careened the *Golden Hinde* in 1579 during his round-the-world pursuit of Spanish booty. Exhibits in the **Kenneth C Patrick Visitor Center** focus on 16th-century maritime explorations as well as the local marine environment. Contemporary accounts have Drake remarking upon the white cliffs behind his makeshift shipyard and their resemblance to the white cliffs of Dover. A weathered copper plaque claiming *Nova Albion* for Queen Elizabeth I was discovered in the 1930s, but it is widely regarded as a forgery. Harder to dismiss are English coins of the era found in Native American encampments as far inland as **Olompali State Historic Park**, off Hwy 101 between **Novato** and Petaluma. As Drake's logbook was burnt in an Admiralty fire, the truth may never be known.

Also on the estero is **Drakes Bay Oyster Farm**, one of several oyster producers in the area selling the bivalves for about half the price of area restaurants.

Sir Francis Drake

Francis Drake was the first English tourist to California, a sometime-pirate, sometime-privateer who found fame, fortune and Point Reyes in the course of 'annoying' King Philip of Spain. Drake was so successful that his tiny *Golden Hinde* was splitting at the seams from the Spanish treasure his crew had captured during 18 months in the Caribbean and the Pacific. In 1579, he put ashore in a place whose physical description matches Drakes Bay for five weeks of rest and repair, then posted a brass plate claiming *Nova Albion* for Queen Elizabeth I before sailing west for Plymouth.

In 1937, University of California archaeologists announced that they had found Drake's plate; x-ray diffraction tests in the 1970s revealed that the plate was made in the 20th century, not the 16th. Silver sixpenny coins found in local Native American encampments support Drakes Bay as Drake's landing place, but this has never been confirmed. Drake's three-year round-the-world voyage earnt him a knighthood, but England never tried to capitalise on his claim to *Nova Albion*.

Great Beach (*off Sir Francis Drake Blvd*), sometimes called 'Point Reyes Beach', is more than 10 miles of undeveloped beach, backed by untrammelled dunes and beach grasses. The beach is open to the full force of the Pacific, which makes swimming dangerous (and cold), but the wave action inspires awe, particularly during the winter storm season. Snowy plovers, a threatened and protected species, nest north of the north entrance May to October.

Limantur Beach (*end of Limantur Rd*) is one of the best swimming beaches in the area, protected from the full force of the Pacific by the Point Reyes headland. The nearby estuary is a good spot for birdwatching.

Mount Vision Overlook (*Mt Vision Rd, off Sir Francis Drake Blvd*), at 1,282ft, provides the best panoramic view of the entire Point Reyes peninsula, especially for colourful sunsets.

One of the oldest and most successful of the many dairy ranches established on Point Reyes in the 19th century is **Pierce Point Ranch** (*Pierce Point Rd, Tomales*). A short self-guided trail guides visitors through the historical complex.

Point Reyes Light Station (*end of Sir Francis Drake Blvd; tel: (415) 669-1534*) stands 300 weather-whipped steps below the visitor centre at the tip of Point Reyes. Panoramas are stunning on clear days, but the winter whale migration is visible even on many foggy days. The visitor centre is ¼ mile from the car park; on weekends and holidays during winter whale-watching, board a free shuttle. Dress warmly, even on sunny days, as temperatures can drop as precipitously as the cliffs surrounding the lighthouse.

Tomales Point (*off Pierce Point Rd*), the northern end of Point Reyes, protects Tomales Bay, immediately to the east. Herds of dairy cattle and tule elk wander the windy moors.

Tule Elk Reserve (*end of Pierce Point Rd*) protects reintroduced tule elk which once ranged over coastal grasslands throughout Northern and Central California.

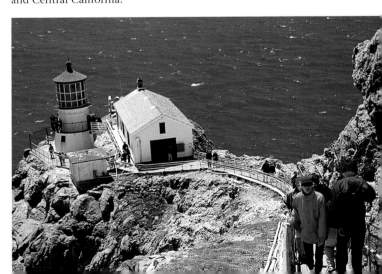

Right
The Point Reyes Light Station

POINT REYES STATION

 West Marin Chamber of Commerce *60 4th St; tel: (415) 663-9232; www.pointreyes.org. Open Sat–Sun 1100–1700.*

 Old Point Reyes Schoolhouse $$$ *11559 Hwy 1; tel: (415) 663-1166; www.oldpointreyesschoolhouse. com.* A compound of hand-restored cottages and the historical schoolhouse, with peaceful gardens.

Cowgirl Creamery *80 4th St; tel: (415) 663-9335; www.cowgirlcreamery.com. Open Wed–Sun 1000–1800. Tours ($), called classes, Wed 1500, Fri 1130.*

This former ranching town is turning from milking dairy cows to milking tourists, yet **Cowgirl Creamery** has wide renown for the quality and variety of the artisan cheeses made in Point Reyes Station. Visitors can watch cheese making and sample the best of the best.

Accommodation and food in Point Reyes Station and Olema

West Marin accommodation is booked out early, especially at weekends and in summer. For help, try the **Inns of Marin** *(tel: (415) 663-2000 or (800) 887-2880; www.innsofmarin.com)*, or **Point Reyes Lodging Association** *(www.ptreyes.com)*.

Bovine Bakery $ *11315 Hwy 1, Point Reyes Station; tel: (415) 663-9420.* Has heavenly muffins and pastries. Cash only.

Point Reyes Farmers Market $ *In front of Toby's Feed Barn, Hwy 1, Point Reyes Station. Open Sat 0900–1300.* A super place to sample the locally grown organic produce that attracted Prince Charles and the Duchess of Cornwall in late 2005.

Farm House Restaurant Bar & Deli $$ *10021 Hwy 1, Olema; tel: (800) 404-5634; www.pointreyesseashore.com/farmhouse_deli.htm.* Serves local seafood, burgers and local beer in an 1865 building.

STINSON BEACH

 West Marin Chamber of Commerce *Tel: (415) 663-9232; www. pointreyes.org/stinson_beach _marin_county.html*

Stinson is where Marin teenagers (adults, too) head when they need a taste of sand, Southern California beer-and-bikini-style. Swimming is allowed (there are lifeguards on duty in summer), but the bone-numbing water tends to discourage more than perfunctory dips. For recorded weather and surf conditions, *tel: (415) 868-1922.*

Food in Stinson Beach

The Parkside Café $$ *43 Arenal Ave; tel: (415) 868-1272; www. parksidecafe.com.* A popular neighbourhood café for breakfast and lunch with more complex offerings at dinner. Outdoor tables.

Sand Dollar Restaurant $$ *3458 Shoreline Hwy; tel: (415) 868-0434; www.stinsonbeachrestaurant.com.* Has live music at weekends.

Suggested tour

Total distance: 60 miles.

Time: Half to full day.

Links: San Francisco south, Mendocino Coast north, Sonoma Wine Country east.

Route: From San Francisco, follow Hwy 101 north over the **Golden Gate Bridge ❶** to the Hwy 1 exit at the south end of **Sausalito ❷**. Take Hwy 1 to the Panoramic Hwy; follow Panoramic Hwy through **MOUNT TAMALPAIS STATE PARK ❸** to **MUIR WOODS NATIONAL MONUMENT ❹** and back to Hwy 1 at **MUIR BEACH ❺**. Turn north past **STINSON BEACH ❻** and **BOLINAS LAGOON ❼** along the **POINT REYES NATIONAL SEASHORE ❽** to **Olema ❾** and **POINT REYES STATION ❿**. If time allows, follow Sir Francis Drake Blvd west through Point Reyes National Seashore to the **Point Reyes Light Station ⓫**. Otherwise, continue north on Hwy 1 along **Tomales Bay ⓬**, then inland to **Valley Ford ⓭** and to **BODEGA BAY ⓮** and on to **JENNER ⓯**.

Detour: Tired of ocean? From Valley Ford ⓭, take Valley Ford Rd north to the Bodega Hwy. Turn east to the Bohemian Hwy, then go north through **Camp Meeker ⓰** to the **Russian River ⓱** at **MONTE RIO ⓲** and Hwy 116. Take Hwy 116 west along the Russian River to Hwy 1 and rejoin the main route at Jenner ⓯.

Mendocino Coast

Ratings

Birdwatching ● ● ● ● ○

Nature ● ● ● ● ●

Scenery ● ● ● ● ●

Food ● ● ● ● ○

Art and craft ● ● ● ○ ○

Beaches ● ● ● ○ ○

History ● ● ● ○ ○

Outdoor activities ● ● ● ○ ○

The Mendocino Coast, once a fishing and redwood lumbering centre, has become one of the most sought-after and most pleasant tourist destinations in the United States. This 100-mile stretch of Pacific Coast is legendary for its dramatic cliffs and coves, quaint but artistic towns and varied flora.

It also has a hidden secret which confounds visitors expecting Southern California's sunny strands: thick fog which rolls in year-round, treacherous for fishing boats entering the narrow coves and adding a drippy nip to a climate where forests, rhododendrons, roses and heathers thrive. The fog can be invigorating, inviting exploration of the half-hidden scenery just around the next bend of Hwy 1.

FORT BRAGG

ⓘ **Visit Mendocino County** *120 S. Franklin St; tel: (866) 466-3636 or (707) 462-7417; www.visitmendocino.com*

Mendocino Coast Chamber of Commerce *217 S. Main St; tel: (800) 726-2780 or (707) 961-6300; www.mendocinocoast.com. Open Mon–Fri 0900–1700, Sat 0900–1500.*

City of Fort Bragg *www.fortbragg.com*

Fort Bragg is the pragmatic commercial centre between San Francisco and Eureka. Eight miles north of Mendocino, Fort Bragg has a historic railway excursion, a tidy downtown, a commercial fishing harbour and economical accommodation and dining.

Pomo and Coast Yuki Native Americans, permanent residents when Russians settled Fort Ross in 1812, became otter pelt suppliers. By 1855, with the Russians and fur trade gone, the tribes were confined to a reservation, pushed out by Western US settlement. An army base on reservation land marked Fort Bragg's founding in 1857.

Local coast redwoods provided strong, fire-resistant lumber for San Francisco's Gold Rush-era construction; by 1869, mills on headlands above every cove were rendering lumber for shipment south. Noyo Harbor, south of the main section of Fort Bragg, was the largest port for over 100 miles, and Fort Bragg's mills were among the largest.

A railway east to Willits was begun to enable shipment of lumber south. Most of Fort Bragg was rebuilt after the 1906 San Francisco

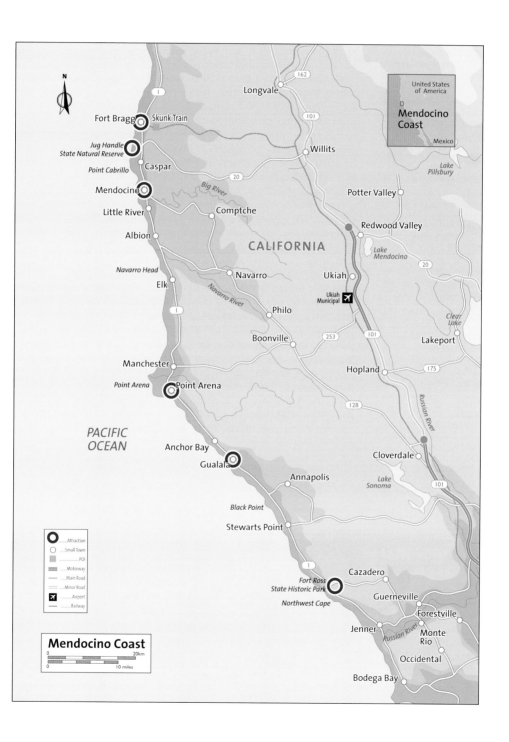

N

Longvale

162

101

United States
of America

Mendocino
Coast

Mexico

Fort Bragg ◎ Skunk Train

Jug Handle ◎
State Natural Reserve

Point Cabrillo   Caspar

Willits

Lake
Pillsbury

Big River

20

Potter Valley

Mendocino ◎

Little River

Comptche

Redwood Valley

Albion

CALIFORNIA

Lake
Mendocino

20

Navarro Head

Elk

Navarro

Navarro River

Ukiah

Ukiah
Municipal ✈

Clear
Lake

Philo

Boonville

253

101

Lakeport

Manchester

Hopland

175

Point Arena ◎ Point Arena

128

Russian River

PACIFIC
OCEAN

Anchor Bay

Gualala ◎

Annapolis

Lake
Sonoma

Cloverdale

101

Black Point

Stewarts Point

◎ ......Attraction
◯ ...Small Town
▪ ....POI
▬ ....Motorway
— ....Main Road
— ....Minor Road
✈ ....Airport
— ....Railway

Cazadero

Fort Ross ◎
State Historic Park

Northwest Cape

Guerneville

Forestville

Jenner

Russian River

Monte
Rio

Mendocino Coast

0   20km
0   10 miles

Occidental

Bodega Bay

⊓ Mendocino Coast Botanical Gardens
$ 18220 N. Hwy 1;
tel: (707) 964-4352;
www.gardenbythesea.org.
Open daily Mar–Oct
0900–1700; Nov–Feb
0900–1600.

⊛ Skunk Train $$$
Foot of Laurel St;
tel: (866) 457-5865;
www.skunktrain.com. Check
in advance for schedule.

⊓ Pacific Star Winery $$
33000 N. Hwy 1, 12 miles
north of Fort Bragg;
tel: (707) 964-1155;
www.pacificstarwinery.com.
Open daily 1100–1700.

Below
Getting ready to ride the
Skunk Train through the
redwood forests

earthquake levelled it and 1950s redevelopment removed most, but not all, architectural distinctiveness.

Mendocino Coast Botanical Gardens is 47 acres of plants, flowers, landscaping and eroded ocean bluffs where coastal fog and surprisingly mild winter temperatures permit an astounding variety of flora in formal plantings, fern canyons, wetlands and a pioneer cemetery. A nursery sells the gardens' signature rhododendrons and heathers. Bloom schedules include rhododendrons (*Feb–May*), camellias, flowering plums and Pacific Coast irises (*Feb–Mar*), wild flowers, heritage roses and cacti (*May–Jul*), dahlias, fuschias and heathers (*Aug–Oct*) and winter heathers and mushrooms (*Nov–Jan*).

Gray whales migrate December to April, and butterflies swarm in summer. The gardens and Mendocino Coast Audubon Society bird list covers 100 resident species, including hummingbirds, ospreys, pelagic cormorants and black oystercatchers.

California Western Railroad's wonderfully named **Skunk Train** hauls 65,000 holidaymakers a year on a 40-mile route through the redwoods from Fort Bragg to Willits. The all-day return excursion, named Skunk for 1920s cars which had an unbearable stench, crosses 31 bridges and manoeuvres 381 curves and two tunnels in a 1,740ft rising journey east. The railway offers fair-weather open cars and closed passenger carriages pulled by diesel locomotive engines, or by No 45, a classic 1924 Baldwin Steam Engine. The loud steaming up whenever No 45 is rolled out is an attraction in its own right, worth arriving 45 minutes before scheduled departure to see the spectacle.

Pacific Star Winery, California's westernmost winery, sits just above the crashing surf. In addition to winery tours, coastal walks explore caves and bluffs, with fine views of migrating whales in autumn and late winter.

Accommodation and food in Fort Bragg

Chain and independent motels abound and Fort Bragg has its share of Bed & Breakfast inns. Book summer and holiday weekends in advance as reasonable prices will make accommodation so close to Mendocino very popular. Restaurants use fresh, locally grown ingredients and freshly caught fish.

Harvest Market $ *Hwys 1 and 20, 171 Boatyard Dr, Boatyard Shopping Center; tel: (707) 964-7000; www.harvestmarket.com. Open daily*

0500–2300. Stocked with a huge assortment of picnic provisions, preserves, fresh produce and local fare.

North Coast Brewing Co $$ *455 N. Main St; tel: (707) 964-2739; northcoastbrewing.com,* **Tap Room and Grill** restaurant, *open daily from 1130.* Relaxed atmosphere, with tasty salads, appetisers and entrées, seafood, fine beer and cheerful service.

The Atrium $$–$$$ *700 N. Main St; tel: (800) 287-8392 or (707) 964-9440; www.atriumbnb.com.* Known for the friendly greeting from owner and dog.

FORT ROSS STATE HISTORIC PARK

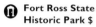 **Fort Ross State Historic Park** $
Hwy 1, 12 miles north of Jenner; tel: (707) 847-3286; www.fortrossstatepark.org. Call for opening times.

Fort Ross's reconstructed wooden stockade beneath rugged hills encompasses two blockhouses, officials' quarters, two houses, a well and a chapel. Russian Orthodox services are conducted on Memorial Day and Fourth of July weekends. Visitors can take part in occasional 'Living History Day' events, when the daily life and dances of California's Russian settlement are re-enacted throughout the year. You get an idea of life as it was here in the early 19th century, the formal contact between Russians and Mexicans – who succeeded the Spanish in California – and soldiers and colonists.

GUALALA

ⓘ Redwood Coast Chamber of Commerce *Tel: (800) 778-5252 or (707) 884-1080 takes enquiries for Hwy 1 communities between Fort Ross and Gualala; www.redwoodcoastchamber.com. Open Thur–Sat 1100–1700, Sun 1100–1400.*

'Water-coming-down place' residents can spot visitors to their town, 100 miles north of San Francisco, by how they say the name. 'Wah-la-la', once a lumber centre, now has posh inns, fine restaurants, a pleasant rock-sheltered coast, artists, film stars, musicians and a few metaphysical devotees left from the 1960s.

Accommodation and food in Gualala

Gualala is blessed with accommodation good enough to be destinations in their own right.

St Orres $$$ *36601 Hwy 1; tel: (707) 884-3303; www.saintorres.com.* Stops traffic with the inn's weathered old redwood and Douglas-fir dome turrets *à la Russe.* Succulent game specialities include wild boar, venison, quail and pheasant. The chef gathers wild mushrooms for the vegetarian tart selection herself.

Whale Watch Inn $$$ *35100 Hwy 1, 5 miles north of Gualala; tel: (800) 942-5342; www.whale-watch.com.* Has large rooms and a golden strand of private beach below.

JUG HANDLE STATE NATURAL RESERVE

**ⓝ Jug Handle State
Natural Reserve**
*Hwy 1, 5 miles north of
Mendocino; tel: (707) 937-
5804; www.parks.ca.gov.
Free.*

Looking at wave action against rocks and cliffs along the Mendocino
Coast gives little hint of geological formation at Jug Handle State
Natural Reserve. The 2½-mile **Ecological Staircase** takes a path
upwards through five successive and distinctive land/vegetation areas,
each one 100ft and 100,000 years older than the one before.

A combination of earth crust uplift, repeated cycles of rising seas
when retreating glaciers melted and thawed, and layering of gravel and
sand upon the terraces that formed has created a natural west-to-east
staircase. The path, within a 1-mile-wide strip, crosses Hwy 1. The
forests become more dwarfed with each higher terrace, gnarled pygmy
forests of Mendocino cypresses, rare Bolander pines and dwarf Fort
Bragg manzanita growing in rock-hard soil which has been leeched of
nutrients by wind and rain over the ages.

MENDOCINO

**ⓘ Mendocino Coast
Chamber of
Commerce**
*217 S. Main St, Fort Bragg;
tel: (800) 726-2780 or
(707) 961-6300;
www.mendocinocoast.com.
Open Mon–Fri 0900–1700,
Sat 0900–1500. Covers
Point Arena–Westport.*

**ⓝ Ford House
Museum** *735 Main
St; tel: (707) 937-5397;
www.mendoparks.org/
Mendocino-Headlands/
the_mendocino_headlands_
ford_h.html. Open daily
1100–1600. Free.
Incorporates Mendocino
Headlands State Park
Visitor Center.*

Kelley House Museum
*45007 Albion St;
tel: (707) 937-5791;
www.mendocinohistory.org.
Open Jun–Sept Thur–Tue
1100–1500; Oct–May
Fri–Mon 1100–1500.*

Views of the sea in three directions, artists and galleries galore,
Victorian buildings, inns, restaurants, saloons, occasional solitude and
the ever-mysterious fog make the town of Mendocino (and its almost
indistinguishable southern neighbour, Little River) a mecca for all who
can take the time to drive there and can afford it. It's a free-spirited
place, where the neat grid of blocks disappears close to the ocean, dogs
abound, hikers are determined to get somewhere, seals mimic surfers
waiting for waves in the bay, canoeists paddle rivers and
honeymooners walk hand-in-hand. Mendocino is also a ready-made
film set, often used to represent quaint New England seaside towns, as
it did for Angela Lansbury's television series *Murder, She Wrote*.

Ford House Museum is the **Mendocino Headlands State Park
Visitor Center,** with a fine museum explaining lumbering, 'doghole
port' (*see Point Cabrillo Light Station, opposite*) and schooner history.
The restored 1854 home originally had a basement kitchen and dining
room, requiring 23-year-old newlywed Martha Hayes Ford to
illuminate her house with candles even on sunny days. Rangers
maintain a fine herb garden outside, resembling the one cultivated
around Mendocino's second house in the 1880s.

Owner Jerome Ford stopped in Mendocino while searching for
the valuable Asian cargo carried in the hold of the *Frolic*. What he
found were redwoods, a discovery followed by his establishing
lumbering operations to supply the heavy demand of newly rich
San Franciscans.

Kelley House Museum shows a family home constructed from local
redwood which was built by a couple from Prince Edward Island,
Canada, in 1861. Restored period rooms display photographs of early
coastal shipping and artefacts from the family whose patriarch,

Mendocino Headlands State Park *North, west and south of Mendocino town; tel: (707) 937-5804; www.parks.ca.gov*

Point Cabrillo Light Station *At the north side of Russian Gulch State Park, ¾ mile west on foot; tel: (707) 937-6122; www.pointcabrillo.org*

Lightkeeper's Home & Museum *Open daily 1100–1600.*

Van Damme State Park *Hwy 1 at Little River, 3 miles south of Mendocino; tel: (707) 937-5804; www.parks.ca.gov. Visitors Center open daily in summer; call for winter hours.*

Below
The scenic coast of Mendocino

William Henry Kelly, once owned most of the Mendocino Headlands, sawmills and lumbering operations for miles around.

Mendocino Headlands State Park combines the beach and surf at the mouth of the Big River, favoured by surfers and aquatic mammals, grassy headlands, eroded cliffs, nestled coves, bluffs, carpets of wild flowers and prime gray whale-spotting November to April. The fog rolls over the western headland as a blanket, with nothing to define the horizon; just as suddenly, it retreats.

Point Cabrillo Light Station is a small, well-proportioned 1908 lighthouse with several keeper houses nearby. The walk from the car park to the shore traverses the Point Cabrillo Reserve meadows with grasses and wild blackberries lining the route. Guides conduct exterior tours with winter whale-watch weekends.

Craggy coast broken by narrow, rocky coves offered little protection from shipwreck and weather. These 'dogholes' (inlets only large enough, it was said, to permit a dog to go in, turn around and depart) became ports for lumber schooners plying to San Francisco. Specially designed wharves, chutes and cables from the tops of cliffs transported goods and people back and forth over the water. The invention of a steam engine attached to windjammer-style doghole schooners made for swifter shipping of milled redwood lumber south.

Van Damme State Park is popular for camping. The 1864 lumber mill site on the Little River is now the park recreation hall. The park and **Fern Canyon Trail** extend 5 miles east of the ocean to the **Pygmy Forest. Kayak Mendocino $$** *(tel: (707) 964-7480; www.kayakmendocino.com)* departs from the beach for sea-cave tours.

Head Lightkeeper's House at Point Cabrillo $$$ *Tel: (707) 937-5033 or (800) 262-7801; www. mendocinovacations.com*

It's easier to drive than hike to the **Pygmy Forest** (*3½ miles east of Hwy 101 on Little River Airport Rd*), a segment of the dwarf species forest formed by the terracing of the ecological staircase along the Mendocino Coast (*see Jug Handle State Natural Reserve, page 188*). Periodic signs for the 10-minute circuit around a boardwalk indicate California huckleberries, Bolander pines, Mendocino cypresses, bordering Bishop pines and red-pink California Rose Bay rhododendrons, five times smaller than relatives in the redwood forest.

Shopping in Mendocino

Mendocino could be the only tourist town in California that boasts more art galleries than T-shirt emporia. The **Mendocino Art Center** (*45200 Little Lake St; tel: (707) 937-5818 or (800) 653-3328; www. mendocinoartcenter.org. Open daily*) offers art and craft classes with resident artists, exhibitions, and a retail shop with reasonably priced visual art and sculpture by local artists. Visit the artist-owned **Artists' Cooperative of Mendocino** (*45270 Main St; tel: (707) 937-2217; www. artgallerymendocino.com*). Ask at the Chamber of Commerce, galleries or museums for the *Mendocino Gallery Guide*. **Arts Council of Mendocino County** (*www.artsmendocino.org*) lists event details on its website. There are openings and artists' receptions (*second Sat of the month 1700–2000*).

William Zimmer Gallery (*Lansing and Ukiah Sts; tel: (707) 937-5121; www.williamzimmergallery.com*) has an upper-crust attitude with one-of-a-kind *objets d'art*, including glass, wooden furniture and jewellery. **Highlight Gallery** (*45052 Main St; tel: (707) 937-3132; www. thehighlightgallery.com*) joins clothing shops, wine tasting and real-estate brokers on Main St. **Lark in the Morning** (*45011 Ukiah St; tel: (707) 937-5275; http://larkinthemorning.com*) sells unique musical instruments.

Accommodation and food in Mendocino

Mendocino's attractions and ambience drive prices high and accommodation availability low, especially in summer, at weekends and during holidays. Camping in state parks (*tel: (800) 444-7275*) can be an alternative, but pitches fill quickly. Enough restaurants are deliberately vegetarian to make a full meat, fowl and fish menu a surprise – and most post menus outside. Call ahead to reserve dining and arrive early to ensure a seat.

Cafe Beaujolais $$ *961 Ukiah St; tel: (707) 937-5614; www. cafebeaujolais.com. Open daily for dinner 1730.* Known for its fresh ingredients. Gardens offer brick-oven-baked breads (*1100–1500*).

Dennen's Victorian Farmhouse $$$ *Little River, 2 miles south of Mendocino; tel: (800) 264-4723 or (707) 937-0697; www.victorianfarmhouse. com.* Has a quiet country atmosphere and a pet-free, no-barking zone.

illI'll

MacCallum House Inn & Restaurant $$$ *45020 Albion St; tel: (800) 609-0492 or (707) 937-0289; www.maccallumhouse.com.* The restaurant is an 1882 mansion surrounded by flower gardens.

Stanford Inn by the Sea $$$ *Hwy 1 and Comptche-Ukiah Rd, south of Big River; tel: (707) 937-5615 or (800) 331-8884; www.stanfordinn.com.* The owners have created a luxury inn on the south side of the Big River, and, with their resident cats, dogs, llamas and other animals, welcome pets, from dogs and cats to iguanas. An extensive organic produce and herb garden supplies the vegetarian- and vegan-accommodating **Ravens' Restaurant** $$$ (*www.ravensrestaurant.com*); ferns decorate an indoor pool and spa area. The inn offers **Catch a Canoe & Bicycles, Too!** (*tel: (707) 937-0273*), for recreation around the area.

POINT ARENA

Russians in California

Europe was at war over Napoleon when the Russians built Fort Ross in 1812. Distant turmoil mandated extension of Russian imperialism, a direct challenge to the Spanish, whose northernmost California outpost was at San Francisco. The lucrative fur trade with China was the impetus to send soldiers and colonists south from the Russian settlement at Sitka, Alaska, to hunt and grow crops. With the Russians came Aleuts from Alaska, adept with kayaks.

Russian officials had not counted on the coastal fog, which limited productivity, nor on the colonists' lack of interest in farming, or the virtual extinction of the fur seals, harbor seals and river otters within three decades. In 1841, the Russians sold the fort to John Sutter (of subsequent Gold Rush fame), and it became a ranch. The 1906 earthquake destroyed most traces of the Russian era.

Point Arena Cove (*½ mile west of Point Arena*) is a lovely cove with a fish-packing plant, several restaurants and an inn. It was once a late 19th-century whaling station and lumber boom town.

Point Arena Lighthouse and Museum (*Lighthouse Rd, 2 miles north of Point Arena (town); tel: (877) 725-4448 or (707) 882-2777; www.pointarenalighthouse.com*), a 115ft white beacon, is visible for miles south. The light station property is fenced to discourage after-hour visitors. There is a 145-step circular climb to the first-level Fresnel lens. (*The lighthouse museum and tower ($) are open daily 1000–1530.*) **Vacation rental cottages** $$$ (*Point Arena Lighthouse Keepers, Inc; tel: (707) 882-2777 or (877) 725-4448*) are on-site. **Coast Guard House Historic Inn** $$$ (*695 Arena Cove; tel: (707) 882-2442; www.coastguardhouse.com*) offers Arts and Crafts movement décor in a former life-saving station.

Russian Gulch State Park (*Hwy 1, 2 miles north of Mendocino; tel: (707) 937-5804*) offers beautiful views from every angle: the Hwy 1 arch bridge over the gulch near a blowhole, the gulch beach popular with abalone and urchin divers and sea kayakers, the canyon trail with redwoods and Douglas fir, and inland to a waterfall and pygmy forest.

Salt Point State Park (*Hwy 1, 20 miles north of Jenner in Sonoma County; tel: (707) 847-3221; www.parks.ca.gov*) is supplemented by **Kruse Rhododendron State Natural Reserve**, and **Gerstle Cove Marine Reserve** with scuba diving. Damage from a 1993 campfire is obvious, but attractions include the spring wild flowers, abalone diving, ocean fishing and the only state park permitting mushroom hunting for king boletes and chanterelles.

The Sea Ranch's (*29 miles north of Jenner*) unique, skylit, weathered wooden homes were developed in the 1960s to harmonise with landscape and vegetation. Widely copied, these homes along 10 miles of Hwy 1 are exclusive and gated or landscaped away from public areas. An 18-hole golf course provides fine views to the Pacific. Real-estate companies handle rentals (*tel: (888) 732-7262; http://searanchescape.com*),

ⓘ Anderson Valley Chamber of Commerce *Boonville; tel: (707) 895-2379; www.andersonvalleychamber.com*

Anderson Valley Winegrowers Association *Box 63, Philo; tel: (707) 895-9463; www.avwines.com*

ⓑ Navarro River Redwoods State Park *11 miles west from Hwy 1 on Hwy 128; tel: (707) 937-5804; www.parks.ca.gov. Free.*

Anderson Valley Brewing Company $ *17700 Hwy 253, Boonville; tel: (800) 207-2337 or (707) 895-2337 for brewery tours; www.avbc.com*

ⓒ Boonville Hotel $$$ *14050 Hwy 128 and Lambert Ln; tel: (707) 895-2210; www.boonvillehotel.com. Ten bright, simply furnished rooms and a family-style, prix fixe restaurant.*

Highland Guest Ranch $$$ *Philo; tel: (707) 895-3600; www.highlandranch.com. All-inclusive, with cabins, meals, horse riding, hiking, swimming, tennis and occasional yoga retreats.*

or stay at **Sea Ranch Lodge $$$** (*60 Shore Walk Dr; tel: (707) 785-2371 or (800) 732-7262; www.searanchlodge.com*). **Twofish Baking Company $$** (*35590 Verdant View, Sea Ranch; tel: (707) 785-2443. Open Thur–Sun*) is renowned for artisan-baked breakfast pastries, fresh coffee and lunches.

Suggested tour

Total distance: 100 miles.

Time: 3 hours' driving; speed limits are slow, traffic congested, lanes narrow. There are few restaurants or services between Jenner and Albion except in Gualala. Picnicking overlooking the Pacific Ocean is a local tradition. The 8-mile stretch north from Albion to Mendocino (town) has some of the most popular inns and Bed & Breakfasts in California.

Links: From Jenner at the beginning of this route, join the Marin Coast Route (*see page 174*). To continue north, for redwoods, Victorian homes and more coastline, join the Coast Redwoods Route (*see page 194*) from Point Bragg. For a Wine Country experience, follow the Anderson Valley Detour from Hwy 1 (via Hwy 128) to Hwy 101, 1 mile north of Cloverdale. Take Hwy 101 south 10 miles, then turn left at Canyon Rd on to the continuation of Hwy 128 to Jimtown and Calistoga (*see Sonoma Wine Country, page 164, and Napa Valley Wine Country, page 152*).

Route: From **Jenner ①**, at the mouth of the **Russian River ②**, follow Hwy 1 north to **MENDOCINO ③** and **FORT BRAGG ④**.

Also worth exploring

The **Anderson Valley ⑤** along Hwy 128 between Hwy 1 and Hwy 101 at Cloverdale offers magnificent coast redwoods at **Navarro River Redwoods State Park ⑥**, fine wines and sparkling wines around **Navarro ⑦**, apples at **Philo ⑧**, and **Boonville ⑨**, one of the state's quaintest towns. *Boontling*, a locally invented dialect (*www.avbc.com/visit/boontling*), has faded with the influx of tourists, but Bucky Walters remain (phone booths named after the cost of early calls – a nickel, or 'bucky').

Right
The coastline at Point Arena

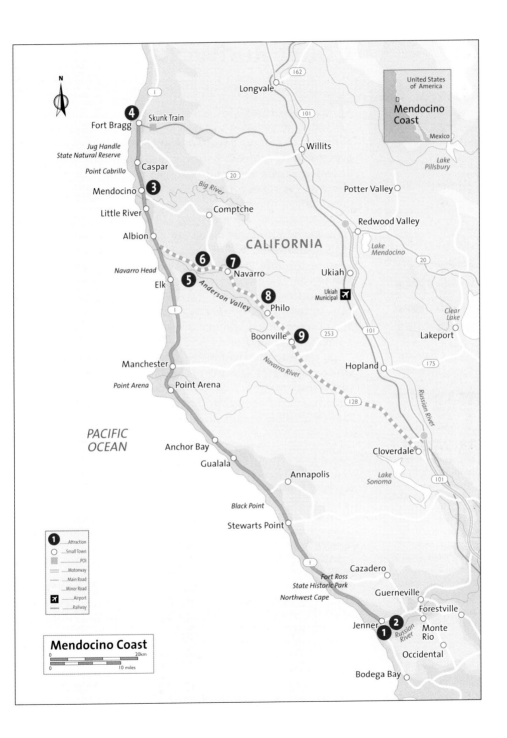

N

162
Longvale
1
101

4 Skunk Train
Fort Bragg

Willits

Jug Handle
State Natural Reserve
20

Point Cabrillo Caspar

Big River

3
Mendocino

Potter Valley

Little River Comptche
Redwood Valley

Albion
CALIFORNIA
Lake
Mendocino
20

Navarro Head **6** **7**
Elk **5** Navarro
Ukiah
Anderson Valley
Ukiah
Municipal

8
Philo

Boonville **9**
253
Lakeport
101

Manchester
Navarro River
Hopland
175
Point Arena Point Arena

Clear
Lake

PACIFIC
OCEAN
Anchor Bay
128
Russian River

Gualala
Cloverdale

Annapolis
Lake
Sonoma
101

Black Point
Stewarts Point

Cazadero

1 ....Attraction
○ ....Small Town
▪ ....POI
....Motorway
....Main Road
....Minor Road
✈ ....Airport
....Railway

Fort Ross
State Historic Park
Northwest Cape
Guerneville
Forestville

Jenner **2**
1 *Russian* Monte
River Rio

Mendocino Coast
0   20km
0   10 miles

Occidental

Bodega Bay

United States
of America

▫
Mendocino
Coast

Mexico

Lake
Pillsbury

Coast Redwoods

Ratings

Birdwatching ●●●●●

Nature ●●●●●

Scenery ●●●●●

Architecture ●●● ○○

Children ●●● ○○

History ●●● ○○

Outdoor activities ●●● ○○

Walking ●●● ○○

Towering forests of coast redwoods, pastoral dairies, historical Victorian towns, lighthouses, sea stacks and rocky bluffs isolate this northwesternmost section of California, while preserving its regional personality. Timber and fishing were Redwood Empire economic mainstays, and much of the region has not recovered financially or emotionally from the diminishment of both.

Coast redwoods are preserved in the Redwood National and State Parks, a series of mixed-use parks and groves along Hwy 101 some of which are located a few miles south of Garberville. Despite the late President Ronald Reagan's comment that, having seen one redwood, you've seen them all, the clumps and groves differ in character. Second growth allows much more light to penetrate the canopy, but the size and magnitude of one or more old-growth giants, the world's tallest living things, is simply astounding.

Fog clings to this coast much of the year with a mild coolness which stimulates vibrant green ferns, redwood sorrel and surprising numbers of wild flowers twined with mint underneath the redwoods. Roosevelt elk and birds, and even foot-long yellow banana slugs, thrive.

ARCATA

ℹ Arcata Chamber of Commerce/ California Welcome Center *1635 Heindon Rd; tel: (707) 822-3619; www. arcatachamber.com. Open daily 0900–1700.* Ask for information on the excellent Victorian Building/Architectural Homes walking tour.

Youth, counterculture, environmentalism, organic produce and vegetarianism are bywords in this youthful enclave by Humboldt State University. Sand dunes and marshy wetlands are within a mile of an urban forest sheltering magnificent redwoods along trails. Bicycles are common, especially by the marshes and estuaries of the Mad River between Arcata Bay and McKinleyville.

Arcata Community Forest/Redwood Park (*east on 14th to Redwood Park Dr; tel: (707) 822-8184; www.cityofarcata.org/departments/ environmental-services/city-forests/trail-map*) is this town's answer to timber clear-cutting: the preservation of 622 acres on a slope east of Hwy 101 near Humboldt State University, with 10 miles of trails.

Arcata Marsh and Wildlife Sanctuary (*G–I Sts; tel: (707) 826-2359; www.cityofarcata.com/departments/environmental-services/water-wastewater/wildlife-sanctuary. Visitor Center, 669 S. G St*) is a birdwatcher's paradise year-round with marsh tours (*Sat 0830*). River otters and 200 species of birds are visible from trails and blinds on a flat track by grassy uplands. There is also a freshwater marsh, a tidal slough, a brackish lake

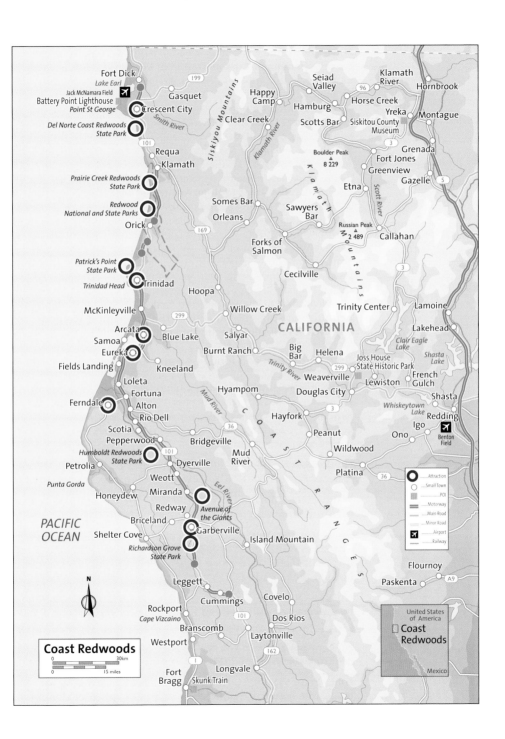

Coast Redwoods

PACIFIC OCEAN

CALIFORNIA

Fort Dick
Lake Earl
Jack McNamara Field
Battery Point Lighthouse
Point St George
Crescent City
Del Norte Coast Redwoods State Park
Gasquet
Smith River
Requa
Klamath
Prairie Creek Redwoods State Park
Redwood National and State Parks
Orick
Patrick's Point State Park
Trinidad Head
Trinidad
Hoopa
McKinleyville
Arcata
Samoa
Eureka
Fields Landing
Loleta
Fortuna
Ferndale
Alton
Rio Dell
Scotia
Pepperwood
Humboldt Redwoods State Park
Petrolia
Punta Gorda
Honeydew
Weott
Miranda
Redway
Briceland
Shelter Cove
Richardson Grove State Park
Garberville
Leggett
Rockport
Cape Vizcaino
Branscomb
Westport
Fort Bragg
Skunk Train
Longvale

Siskiyou Mountains
Happy Camp
Clear Creek
Klamath River
Somes Bar
Orleans
Forks of Salmon
Cecilville
Willow Creek
Salyar
Blue Lake
Burnt Ranch
Big Bar
Trinity River
Kneeland
Hyampom
Mud River
Hayfork
Bridgeville
Dyerville
Mud River
Eel River
Avenue of the Giants
Cummings
Covelo
Dos Rios
Island Mountain
Laytonville

Seiad Valley
Hamburg
Scotts Bar
Boulder Peak
8 229
Etna
Sawyers Bar
Russian Peak
2 489
Trinity Center

Klamath River
Horse Creek
Yreka
Siskitou County Museum
Grenada
Fort Jones
Greenview
Gazelle
Callahan
Lamoine
Lakehead
Clair Eagle Lake
Helena
Joss House State Historic Park
Weaverville
Douglas City
Lewiston
Whiskeytown Lake
Peanut
Wildwood
Ono
Platina
Flournoy
Paskenta

Hornbrook
Montague

Shasta Lake
French Gulch
Shasta
Redding
Igo
Benton Field

United States of America

Coast Redwoods

Mexico

N

Coast Redwoods
0   30km
0   15 miles

	Attraction
	Small Town
	POI
	Motorway
	Main Road
	Minor Road
	Airport
	Railway

and mudflats, and a system designed to purify waste water naturally. A 5½-mile **Hammond Coastal Trail** from Mad River Beach in Arcata to Clam Beach near Trinidad (*see page 201*) is a locals' place to hike, bike or jog.

Arcata Plaza (*8th–9th and G–H Sts*) is the town square set aside by original lumber company owners as a park and meeting place. Among well-restored buildings near the plaza are the 1857 **Jacoby's Storehouse** (*8th and H Sts*) with 2ft-thick stone walls sheltering three restaurants; the 1914 **Minor Theatre** (*10th and H Sts; tel: (707) 822-3456*), the oldest operating cinema in the US, enhanced by isinglass door panels; and the 1915 **Hotel Arcata** (*9th and G Sts*).

The **Kinetic Grand Championship** (*Kinetic Universe; tel: (707) 499-0643; www.kineticgrandchampionship.com*), Memorial Day weekend in May, begins at Arcata Plaza, and takes three days for contestants to navigate the 38 or so miles to Ferndale. Whimsical people-powered contraptions, the essence of clever design, ornamentation and wackiness, are in keeping with Arcata's nickname, Ecotopia, and race founder Hobart Brown's belief in a 'New Race, conceived in insanity, and dedicated to the proposition that all mechanical nightmares definitely are not created equal'. The mechanical sculptures are displayed in **Ferndale's Kinetic Museum** (*see page 199*).

Accommodation and food in Arcata

Chain motels cluster around E. Guintoli Ln. Closer to downtown, a smattering of Bed & Breakfasts offer Victoriana. Book in advance for **Kinetic Grand Championship** weekend in May. Vegetarian and vegan is easy to find in this organic-conscious town, but freshness of ingredients is what counts.

North Coast Co-Op $ *811 I St; tel: (707) 822-5947; www.northcoastco-op.com. Open daily 0600–2100.* Socialism applied to food, groceries to all.

Wildberries Marketplace $ *747 13th St; tel: (707) 822-0095; www.wildberries.com. Open daily 0700–2400.* A newer, hipper rival to the Co-Op.

Abruzzi $$ *791 8th St in Jacoby's Storehouse; tel: (707) 826-2345; www.abruzziarcata.com.* Offers Italian dinners nightly in a historical building on Arcata Plaza.

Golden Harvest Cafe $$ *1062 G St; tel: (707) 822-8962; www.goldenharvestcafe.com.* Has a wide range of vegetarian and meat-eater dishes two blocks north of Arcata Plaza.

Hotel Arcata $$ *708 9th St; tel: (800) 344-1221 or (707) 826-0217; www.hotelarcata.com.* A cheerful 1915 former hunting lodge on Arcata Plaza.

Folie Douce $$$ *1551 G St; tel: (707) 822-1042; www.holyfolie.com.* Fine dining with organic and sustainable deeply incorporated into the menu.

AVENUE OF THE GIANTS

ⓘ Avenue of the Giants Association
PO Box 1957; 3493
Briceland Rd, Redway; tel:
(707) 923-3727;
www.avenueofthegiants.net

Just north of Garberville, coast redwood groves extend for a narrow 31-mile strip along both sides of Hwy 101 from Phillipsville to Pepperwood, cutting left and right over the south fork of the Eel River. Most of the groves are named in tribute to the group of people who, in the early 20th century, worked to save a small number of redwoods before they disappeared. **Humboldt Redwoods State Park** (*www.humboldtredwoods.org*) (*see page 200*) surrounds and helps interpret the long lifespan and predator-resistant coastal species. Most of the groves have a lay-by to park in so that you can explore the forest.

CRESCENT CITY

ⓘ Crescent City/Del Norte County Chamber of Commerce 1001 Front
St; tel: (800) 343-8300;
http://exploredelnorte.com.
Call for hours.

ⓑ Battery Point Lighthouse West
end of Front St; tel: (707)
464-3089; www.cr.nps.gov/
maritime/light/battery.htm.
Tours Apr–Sept (tide
permitting).

As elsewhere on the north coast, Crescent City, 18 miles south of the Oregon border, was dependent upon fishing and timber. It is also a crossroads for over-the-border traffic and eastward routes to more redwood parks and the Hwy 199 Smith River Wild and Scenic River drive to the Rogue River Region in Oregon.

The city is named after the shape of its bay. A tsunami tidal wave caused by a major Alaskan earthquake in 1964 wiped out the harbour and downtown; a Japanese earthquake in November 2006 caused a tsunami that wiped out docks and caused other waterfront damage. Local activities include fishing, cycling, scuba diving and surfing in frigid waters.

Battery Point Lighthouse, perched since 1856 on well-eroded golden rock, has lovely proportions from any angle and at any time of the day or night when it is illuminated around the outside. Check in advance about walking from the beach to a causeway at low tide.

North from Battery Point Lighthouse, scenic **North Pebble Beach Drive** looks west to sea stacks and **Castle Rock National Wildlife Refuge** (*tel: (707) 733-5406; www.fws.gov/refuges/profiles/index. cfm?id=81647*), home to huge numbers of seabirds and noisy sea lions. Go left on Washington Blvd to **Point St George** where there are vistas, beaches and trails, with its namesake lighthouse 6 miles offshore.

Below
Battery Point Lighthouse

Accommodation and food in Crescent City

Proximity to Oregon (where prices are lower and there's no state sales tax) keep prices at Crescent City motels to bargain levels. Hwy 101 divides into north (*M St*) and south (*L St*) throughways between Front and 9th Sts; most motels are found here. Others are near the harbour at Anchor Rd.

Dining is basic, but seafood is an excellent choice. Ask for the fresh-caught special of the day.

In June–October the town turns out at the Del Norte County Fairgrounds for the **Crescent City Certified Farmers Market** fresh produce (*3rd and K Sts. Sat 0900–1300*).

DEL NORTE COAST REDWOODS STATE PARK

One of the Redwood National and State Parks (*7 miles south of Crescent City; tel: (707) 465-2146; www.parks.ca.gov*), Del Norte Coast Redwoods State Park has old-growth forest which includes redwoods with spectacular rocky coast and uncrowded Damnation Creek and Footsteps Rock Trails.

EUREKA

❶ Humboldt County Convention & Visitors Bureau
1034 2nd St; tel: (707) 443-5097 or (800) 346-3482; www.redwoods.info. Open Mon–Fri 0830–1700.

No building in far Northern California is more recognisable than the green Victorian **Carson Mansion**, built in 1885 by a lumber baron's employees to fill time. Now a private club, this centrepiece of Eureka's Historic Old Town (*B–I Sts, Waterfront–7th St*) shows the 19th-century value of a good fishing harbour with access to lumber. Galleries, stores, restaurants and Bed & Breakfasts are found in this area. **Arts Alive! Eureka** (*tel: (707) 442-9054. Open first Sat of the month 1800–2100*), Old Town's art walk, shows an art scene comparable to San Francisco or Seattle. Salmon and Dungeness crab are still menu staples, though fisheries are restricted. Catch the **MAKADET $** (*foot of F St; tel: (707) 445-1910; www.humboldtbaymaritimemuseum.com/makadetcruises.html. Operates mid-May–Sept*), one of seven Humboldt Bay ferries, for a narrated harbour cruise.

Food in Eureka

The **Lost Coast Brewery $** *617 4th St; tel: (707) 445-4480; www.lostcoast.com. Open daily 1100*. With eight brews, this is the liveliest place in town, beyond a giant string spider guarding its 1892 door.

Samoa Cookhouse $ *Samoa Peninsula in Humboldt Bay; tel: (707) 442-1659; www.samoacookhouse.net. Open daily winter 0700–2200; later in summer*. Serves large, family-style portions of stick-to-the-ribs lumberjack fare in keeping with its status as the last-surviving lumber camp cookhouse in the West. Prices are low. There is a free logging museum and the **Humboldt Bay Maritime Museum $** (*tel: (707) 444-9440; www.humboldtbaymaritimemuseum.com*) is next door.

Café Waterfront $$ *102 F St; tel: (707) 443-9190. Open daily 0900–2130*. Has seafood, salads, sandwiches, a long wooden bar, a stained-glass window, and, most remarkable in the landmark Old Town Eureka building, wall paintings of flowers and natural scenes. Two Victorian-style flats can be rented upstairs.

Below
Carson Mansion, centrepiece of Eureka's Old Town

FERNDALE

 Ferndale Chamber of Commerce *PO Box 325; tel: (707) 786-4477; www.victorianferndale.com*

Ferndale Art & Culture Building Merchants *(580 Main St)* have maps and brochures.

Ferndale has trademarked its moniker, 'The Victorian Village', and the entire village is a California Historical Landmark. Settled in 1852, the town's low-lying, lush pastures were perfect for dairy cattle. Prosperity arrived, and by the 1890s dairymen in Cream City were building heavily embellished Victorian mansions called 'Butterfat Palaces'. Two subsequent earthquakes wreaked havoc, but the homes, mansions, churches and Main St shopfronts were repaired and repainted.

Ferndale is a walker's paradise. **Main St** is the place for shops, galleries, restaurants, bakeries, a meat market, a pioneer museum and the **Kinetic Museum** (*part of the Ferndale Art & Culture Building, 580 Main St; see also Arcata, page 194*).

Ferndale's de facto image is the **Gingerbread Mansion Inn** (*400 Berding St*), an 1899 turreted and gabled froth of Victorian style, with magnificent English formal garden landscaping and a perfect and perfectly incongruous palm tree.

Accommodation in Ferndale

Ferndale is about 5 miles southwest of Hwy 101 from the Fernbridge/Ferndale exit. Five Bed & Breakfast inns, motels, cottages and a county fairground camping area should be booked in advance, as Ferndale is popular with local tourists from San Francisco and Los Angeles.

The Victorian Inn $$–$$$ *400 Ocean Ave; tel: (888) 589-1808 or (707) 786-4949; www.victorianvillageinn.com*. Offers Bed & Breakfast in 1880 Victorian splendour.

Gingerbread Mansion Inn $$$ *400 Berding St; tel: (800) 952-4136 or (707) 786-4000; www.gingerbread-mansion.com*

GARBERVILLE

Garberville Redway Chamber of Commerce *782 Redwood Dr; tel: (800) 923-2613; www.garberville.org. Call for hours.*

Garberville serves as a hub for forestry, for holidaymakers seeking the redwoods, a base for exploring the **Avenue of the Giants** (*see page 197*) and a convenient stopping point for travellers taking Hwy 101 between San Francisco and Eureka/Crescent City. The friction between environment protection and lumbering is notable, while musicians and young counterculture types hang out for the atmosphere.

Accommodation and food in Garberville

As a service hub, Garberville is well supplied with motels.

Sicilitos $ *445 Conger St; tel: (707) 923-2814; www.asis.com/sicilitos*. With old advertising and sports memorabilia around the walls, it serves tasty Mexican food and Italian-American fare, made from scratch.

Benbow Inn $$$ *445 Lake Benbow Dr, 1 mile south of Garberville; tel: (707) 923-2124 or (800) 355-3301; www.benbowinn.com.* A stunning redwoods version of Tudor style, with lovely flower gardens outside and a high-ceilinged lobby and dining room.

HUMBOLDT REDWOODS STATE PARK

ⓘ Humboldt Redwoods State Park $ *Tel: (707) 946-2409; www.parks.ca.gov.* **Visitor Center** *2 miles north of Weott on Avenue of the Giants; tel: (707) 946-2263. Open daily Apr–Oct 0900–1700; Nov–Mar 1000–1600. Find more park information at www.humboldtredwoods.org*

Most visitors encounter Humboldt Redwoods State Park as the **Avenue of the Giants** (*see page 197*), but its 52,000 acres include the awesome trees of **Rockefeller Forest**, estimated to constitute 10 per cent of remaining old-growth redwoods. Stop at the convenient and informative **Visitor Center** (*2 miles north of Weott on Avenue of the Giants*); a short path outside gives a rare opportunity to see all three redwood species side by side: dawn (*Metasequoia glyptostroboides*), coast (*Sequoia sempervirens*) and giant (*Sequoiadendron giganteum*).

PATRICK'S POINT STATE PARK

ⓟ Patrick's Point State Park $ *West of Hwy 101, 4150 Patrick's Point Dr, 5 miles north of Trinidad; tel: (707) 677-3570; www.parks.ca.gov*

Patrick's Point State Park has superb views offshore to whale migrations, northwards to Agate Beach and Big Lagoon and south to Trinidad Head, a bluff-top **Rim Trail** and a **Yurok** (Native American) **Sumêg Village**, with wooden houses, a sweat house, a dance pit still reserved for use by tribal members, and a Native American Plant Garden.

PRAIRIE CREEK REDWOODS STATE PARK

ⓟ Prairie Creek Redwoods State Park $ *West of Hwy 101, 50 miles north of Eureka; tel: (707) 465-7354, (707) 465-7347 or (707) 464-6101, ext. 5300; www.parks.ca.gov. Visitor Center open daily.*

ⓒ Elk Meadow Cabins $$$ *2 miles north of Orick; tel: (866) 733-9637; www.redwoodadventures.com.* Offers interpretive tours in the park, including the tall redwoods. **Redwood National Park Eco-Lodge** (*www. redwoodparkslodge.com*) should be open in 2012.

Prairie Creek is best known for the Roosevelt elk which roam around three areas from August to October: **Davidson Rd, Elk Prairie** and **Gold Bluffs** (remote). These huge animals can cause traffic jams on Hwy 101.

Prairie Creek is rich in redwoods, with connecting trails circling through the major groves. Try **Newton B Drury Scenic Parkway exit** from Hwy 101. The most dramatic redwoods, however, are near the south exit where Elk Prairie and the **Prairie Creek Visitor Center** offer previews of what's ahead. Stop and hike to **Big Tree**, 304ft high and 216in in diameter, and to the twined trunks of the **Corkscrew Tree**.

REDWOOD NATIONAL AND STATE PARKS

ⓘ **Thomas H Kuchel Visitor Center** *Hwy 101, west of Orick; tel: (707) 465-7765; www.nps.gov/redw. Open daily Mar–Oct 0900–1800; Nov–Feb 0900–1600.*

Redwood National and State Parks Information Center *1111 2nd St, Crescent City; tel: (707) 465-7835; www.nps.gov/redw. Open daily Mar–Oct 0900–1800; Nov–Feb 0900–1600.*

The jointly managed park, with three state parks: **Prairie Creek Redwoods** (*visitor centre 8 miles north of Orick on Hwy 101. Open daily*), **Del Norte Coast Redwoods** and **Jedediah Smith Redwoods** (*east of Crescent City*) protect old-growth (250 years or more) coast redwoods, among the tallest, biggest and oldest natural objects on the planet. The parks are a **World Heritage Site** and an **International Biosphere Reserve**, accessible by vehicle, but much better enjoyed on foot, by bicycle or on a horse (trails are well marked). Dress for frequent fog and rain. While coast redwoods and elk are the focus, the parks conserve coastline, tide pools, waterfalls, oak woodlands and prairies. As tame as the stately trees look, it's a wild world out there full of ticks, banana slugs, cougars (mountain lions), bears and elk.

RICHARDSON GROVE STATE PARK

Richardson Grove (*tel: (707) 247-3318*), 7 miles south of Garberville, provides services and an early glimpse of stands of coast redwoods on the Hwy 101 route north. Families can swim in the Eel River south fork in summer, while anglers fish for steelhead later in the year.

TRINIDAD

ⓘ **Greater Trinidad Chamber of Commerce** *PO Box 356; tel: (707) 677-1610; http://discovertrinidadca.com*

Below
Some of the world's oldest and largest trees

Trinidad qualifies as a hamlet, just south of Patrick's Point State Park (*see opposite*), with more than its share of Bed & Breakfast inns and a fishing fleet. Its symbol is the red-roofed, white replica of an 1871 **Memorial Lighthouse**. **Trinidad State Beach** (*off Trinity St, north of Main St; tel: (707) 677-3570*) is a good spot to watch a dramatic sunset behind jewel-sharp rocks rising from the sea, with diving and swooping black oystercatchers. Trinidad Scenic Drive (*south from Trinity St; parallel to Hwy 101*) provides access to **Luffenholtz Beach County Park**, with clamming and surf fishing, and **Houda Point**. The area is also known for great surfing.

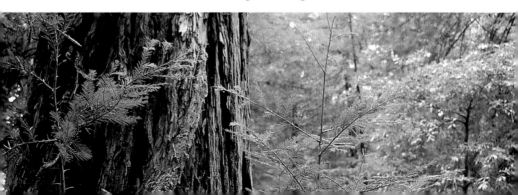

Suggested tour

Total distance: 221 miles.

Time: 6 hours' driving. Allow a day for the main route, two days with **Detour 2**. Add a minimum of three extra days to drive into and hike the Lost Coast (*see Also worth exploring*).

Links: From Fort Bragg, the beginning of this route, connect with the Mendocino Coast (*see page 184*). For direct access from San Francisco, take Hwy 101 180 miles north to Leggett and on to Crescent City.

Route: Take Hwy 1 north from **Fort Bragg ❶**, turning inland north of **Rockport ❷** for a 16-mile drive over the mountains to **Leggett ❸**. Continue north on Hwy 101 to **EUREKA ❹**, **ARCATA ❺** and **CRESCENT CITY ❻**.

Detour 1: Weaving in and out of the **AVENUE OF THE GIANTS ❼** for 31 miles between **Phillipsville ❽** and **Pepperwood ❾** will take 45 minutes longer than going straight through on Hwy 101.

Detour 2: Two miles north of **Weott ❿** at **Dyerville ⓫**, take the Rockefeller Forest exit west from Hwy 101. Follow the **Mattole Rd ⓬** from the redwood groves to **Honeydew ⓭**, a small apple-growing hamlet. Continue northwest on the same road to **Petrolia ⓮** and the coast south of **Cape Mendocino ⓯**. As Mattole Rd turns to rise steeply inland, the road narrows further, with 10mph speed limits to **FERNDALE ⓰**. Add half a day to the driving time for this scenic route.

Also worth exploring

The **Lost Coast ⓱** is little known because of its remoteness from roads and settlements. North of Rockport ❷ off Hwy 1 on Usal Rd, south from Honeydew ⓭ from Wilder Ridge/Kings Peak Rd, or west 24 miles from **Redway ⓲** to **Shelter Cove ⓳**, is a barely touched section of coast, with sheer mountain peaks and slate black sand.

The coast, park and conservation areas are not signposted from any highway. Ask rangers or locally for directions, as some north and south roads are unpaved, and can be treacherous from October to March from heavy rainfall when even 4WD vehicles can get stuck. RVs can't manoeuvre the steep, narrow, rugged roads.

Shelter Cove ⓳, with its working fishing fleet, has recently seen an influx of the rich and celebrated who are building homes on the hills.

South of Shelter Cove, the 7,367-acre **Sinkyone Wilderness State Park ⓴** (*PO Box 245, Whitethorn; tel: (707) 986-7711; www.parks.ca.gov*) has a 17-mile trail through the wilderness.

King Range National Conservation Area ㉑ (*Arcata Field Office, US Bureau of Land Management, 1695 Heindon Rd; Arcata; tel: (707) 825-2300 or (707) 986-5400; www.blm.gov/ca/arcata/kingrange*) has 64,000 acres of rugged hiking and camping.

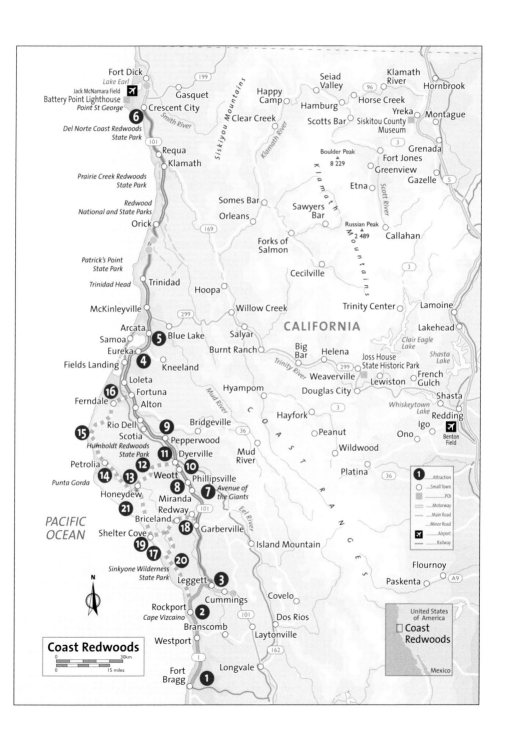

Fort Dick
Lake Earl
Jack McNamara Field
Battery Point Lighthouse
Point St George
Crescent City
Gasquet
199
Siskiyou Mountains
Happy Camp
Seiad Valley
Klamath River
96
Hornbrook
Hamburg
Horse Creek
Clear Creek
Scotts Bar
Yreka
Siskitou County Museum
Montague

Del Norte Coast Redwoods State Park
6
Smith River
101

Requa
Klamath

Boulder Peak
8 229
3
Grenada
Fort Jones
Greenview
Gazelle
5

Prairie Creek Redwoods State Park

Klamath River
Klamath
Siskiyou
Scott River

Etna

Redwood National and State Parks
Orick

Somes Bar
Orleans
169

Sawyers Bar

Russian Peak
2 489
Callahan

Forks of Salmon

Klamath Mountains

Patrick's Point State Park
Trinidad Head
Trinidad
Hoopa

Cecilville

McKinleyville
299
Willow Creek
Trinity Center
Lamoine

Arcata
Samoa
Eureka
Fields Landing
5 Blue Lake
4 Kneeland
Salyar
Burnt Ranch
CALIFORNIA
Big Bar
Helena
Trinity River
Joss House State Historic Park
Lakehead
Clair Eagle Lake
Shasta Lake
French Gulch
Weaverville
Lewiston
299

Loleta
16 Fortuna
Ferndale
Alton
Hyampom
Douglas City
Shasta
Whiskeytown Lake
Redding
Igo
Benton Field

Rio Dell
15
Scotia
Humboldt Redwoods State Park
9
Pepperwood
11 Dyerville
Bridgeville
36
Mud River
Hayfork
3
Peanut
Wildwood
Ono

Petrolia
Punta Gorda
14 13 Weott
12
10
8
Phillipsville
7 Avenue of the Giants
Honeydew
21 Miranda
Redway
101
Briceland
18 Garberville
Platina
36

C
O
A
S
T

R
A
N
G
E
S

Eel River

PACIFIC OCEAN
Shelter Cove
19
17
20
Island Mountain

Sinkyone Wilderness State Park
Leggett
3
Cummings
Covelo
Flournoy
Paskenta
A9

Rockport
Cape Vizcaino
2
Branscomb
Westport
Dos Rios
Laytonville
101
162

N

Coast Redwoods
0   30km
0   15 miles

Fort Bragg
1
Longvale

1 ── Attraction
○ ── Small Town
■ ── POI
── Motorway
── Main Road
── Minor Road
✈ ── Airport
── Railway

United States of America
☐ Coast Redwoods
Mexico

Monterey Peninsula

Ratings

History	●●●●●
Scenery	●●●●●
Food and wine	●●●●○
Children	●●●○○
Coastal villages	●●●○○
Wildlife	●●●○○
Art and craft	●●○○○
Beaches	●●○○○

Hwy 1 from San Francisco to the Monterey Peninsula is surrounded by flower fields and vast vegetable farms, fringed by an ever-changing panorama of lighthouses, beaches and crumbling cliffs. Coastal attractions run the gamut from the ponderous mating of elephant seals on the sands of Año Nuevo to the theme-park atmosphere of the Santa Cruz Beach Boardwalk, historical buildings in Monterey and the contrived artistic atmosphere of Carmel.

The whale-watching season runs from November to April, depending on location. Some areas, notably Point Reyes, Gualala and the north Mendocino Coast, offer good views of whales passing just offshore. Ports from San Diego to Crescent City offer closer views from whale-watching cruises. Whale-watching boats like those from Monterey aren't allowed to pursue whales, but if a canny captain manages to place his vessel ahead of the pod and a curious whale just happens to surface a few yards away, expect the view of a lifetime.

AÑO NUEVO STATE PARK

Año Nuevo State Park $ *Hwy 1, 22 miles north of Santa Cruz; tel: (650) 879-0227; www.parks.ca.gov. Open daily. Advance reservations required for mid-Dec–Mar, tel: (800) 444-4445 or (916) 638-5883 (international reservations). Guided walks.*

This state park is a 4,000-acre promontory of bluffs and beaches with the largest northern elephant seal rookery on the California mainland. There are always a few of these huge aquatic mammals in residence, but the main show is between winter and spring, when immense bulls (up to 2.5 tons) battle for harems, and females give birth. Access is by guided tour only, mid-December–March, self-guided April–November. Get a sneaky peek at the elephant seals en masse and the coastline in real time on the California State Park website's Elephant Seal live webcam (*www.parks.ca.gov/default.asp?page_id=25732*).

CARMEL-BY-THE-SEA

This one-time artists' colony has tried to legislate its rustic past. Local ordinances prohibit parking meters, street addresses, postal delivery, high-heeled shoes and digging on the beach unless building a sand castle. Instead of the usual franchise stores and T-shirt shops, the town

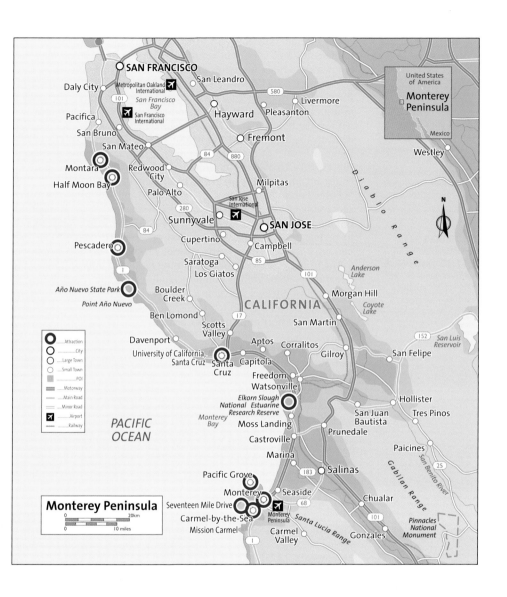

ⓘ Carmel Chamber of Commerce Visitor Center *Above Hog's Breath Inn, San Carlos, between 5th and 6th Sts; tel: (831) 624-2522; www.carmelcalifornia.org. Open Mon–Sat 1000–1700.*

centre, **Ocean Ave**, has mock Tudor art galleries, overpriced antique shoppes, traffic congestion and an unending stream of weekend events to keep the tourists coming. Parking is scarce, pavements uneven and prices high. The area from Junipero to the beach, between 5th and 8th Sts, is filled with unique homes, from ersatz adobe to shingled cottages and 'dolls houses' trimmed with Victorian finery.

Mission Carmel $
2080 Rio Rd; tel: (831)
624-1271; www.
carmelmission.org. Open
Mon–Sat 0930–1700, Sun
1030–1700.

**Point Lobos State
Natural Reserve $** Hwy
1, 3 miles south of Carmel;
tel: (831) 624-4909;
www.parks.ca.gov. Open daily.
Sea Lion Point Information
Station 0900–1700. Diving
information, tel: (831) 624-
8413.

Tor House $ 26304
Ocean View Ave; tel: (831)
624-1813; www.torhouse.
org. Tours hourly Fri–Sat
1000–1500, advance
reservation required.

The emerald-blue cove of **Carmel City Beach** (*foot of Ocean Ave*) is bordered by soft white sand and green cypress trees. Enjoy the sand, but beware, a fierce undertow makes swimming dangerous.

Mission Carmel (Mission San Carlos Borromeo del Rio Carmelo) is the very stereotype of a California mission (*see page 256*), with golden sandstone walls, Moorish towers and contemplative gardens splashed with scarlet bougainvillea. Mission founder Fra Junípero Serra is buried beneath the sanctuary of the rebuilt complex. Carmel is also one of the most-visited of the California missions; go early in the day before the crowds arrive. The church is closed during services, but the courtyard and grounds, including a museum, remain open.

Point Lobos State Natural Reserve has 6 miles of jagged shoreline above aquamarine coves favoured by scuba divers, known as much for rolling meadows as the sea lions, whales, sea otters, seals and seabirds in permanent residence. Rangers lead pre-arranged nature walks, but parking is limited. Arrive early, especially between May and October.

Tor House is Carmel's most imposing residence, a medieval-looking structure built of golden boulders hauled from the beach below by poet Robinson Jeffers. The family still lives in the house.

Accommodation and food in Carmel

Nothing in Carmel is inexpensive. **Hog's Breath Inn $$** (*San Carlos and 5th Sts; tel: (831) 625-1044; www.hogsbreathinn.net. Open daily 1130–2200*) was once owned by film star Clint Eastwood, and serves lunch and dinner with local specialities like Castroville artichoke soup. The **Tuck Box English Tea Room $$** (*Dolores St and Ocean Aves; tel: (831) 624-6365; www.tuckbox.com. Open daily 0730–1430*) is kitschy, entertaining and anything but English, tiny and known for scones. **Carmel Valley Ranch $$$** (*One Old Ranch Rd; tel: (877) 583-0052; www.carmelvalleyranch.com*), renovated in 2010, escapes the crowds (and coastal fog) in Carmel Valley, a few miles inland. The **Highlands Inn, A Hyatt Hotel $$$** (*120 Highlands Dr; tel: (831) 620-1234; www.highlandsinn.hyatt.com/hyatt/hotels*) sits above the coast just south of Point Lobos. Golfers gravitate to **Pebble Beach** and **The Inn at Spanish Bay $$$** or **The Lodge at Pebble Beach $$$** (*PO Box 567, Pebble Beach; tel: (800) 654-9300; www.pebble-beach.com*) on the famed Seventeen Mile Drive.

ELKHORN SLOUGH NATIONAL ESTUARINE RESEARCH RESERVE

**Elkhorn Slough
National Estuarine
Research Reserve $**
3 miles north of Castroville;
tel: (831) 728-2822;
www.elkhornslough.org. Open
Wed–Sun 0900–1700.

This is California's largest-surviving coastal wetland, teeming with birds, seals, sea otters and fish. Trails ($) provide shoreline access. **Elkhorn Slough Safari Nature Tours $$** (*tel: (831) 633-5555; www.elkhornslough.com*) offers boat tours; **Monterey Bay Kayaks $$$** (*tel: (800) 649-5357; www.montereybaykayaks.com*) offers guided or self-guided kayak tours. Advance bookings required for tours.

HALF MOON BAY

ⓘ Half Moon Bay Coastside Chamber of Commerce and Visitors Bureau *235 Main St; tel: (650) 726-8380; www.halfmoonbaychamber.org and tel: (866) 558-6823; www.visithalfmoonbay.org. Open Mon–Fri 0900–1700.*

Half Moon Bay is part old-fashioned farming town, part artistic community and part surfing destination. Bay and town are named after the half-moon-shaped beach stretching south from **Pillar Point Harbor** (staging point for late December–April whale-watching tours) and **Princeton-by-the-Sea**. **St Francis Beach** may be the most beautiful local beach; surfers head for **Surfer's Beach** (*El Granada*) and **Mavericks** (*off Pillar Point*), renowned for enormous and occasionally lethal waves. **Venice Beach** and **Dune Beach** are the least crowded. **San Mateo County Farm Bureau** (*765 Main St; tel: (650) 726-4485; http://sanmateo.cfbf.com*) publishes a free map to vegetable, fruit and flower farms in the area, many of which invite visitors to pick for themselves. October brings the world-renowned **Half Moon Bay Art & Pumpkin Festival** (*tel: (650) 726-9652*).

Accommodation and food in Half Moon Bay

Barbara's Fishtrap $$ *281 Capistrano Rd and Hwy 1, Princeton-by-the-Sea; tel: (650) 728-7049. Call for hours.* This rustic bayside cash-only diner is a long-time favourite with San Franciscans.

Cetrella $$$ *845 Main St; tel: (650) 726-4090; www.cetrella.com. Call for hours.* Serves award-winning Mediterranean cuisine, and has weekend jazz in the bar.

Oceano Hotel & Spa $$$ *280 Capistrano Rd, Princeton-by-the-Sea; tel: (650) 726-5400 or (888) 623-2661; http://oceanohalfmoonbay.com.* Has rooms with harbour or Montara Mountain views.

Old Thyme Inn $$$ *779 Main St; tel: (650) 726-1616 or (800) 720-4277; www.oldthymeinn.com.* This 1898 Victorian has an English herb and flower garden.

Pillar Point Inn $$$ *380 Capistrano Rd, Princeton-by-the-Sea; tel: (650) 728-7377 or (800) 400-8281; www.pillarpointinn.com.* More Bed & Breakfast than motel.

Ritz-Carlton Hotel Half Moon Bay $$$ *1 Miramontes Point Rd; tel: (650) 712-7000; www.ritzcarlton.com/resorts/half_moon_bay.* A sprawling resort with two golf courses.

MONTARA

ⓕ Fitzgerald Marine Reserve *Off Hwy 1, just north of Pillar Point, California and N. Lake Sts, Moss Beach; tel: (650) 728-3584; www.fitzgeraldreserve.org. Free.*

The coastal hamlet of **Montara** is known primarily for the **Point Montara Lighthouse Hostel** (*16th St and Hwy 1; tel: (650) 728-7177 or (888) 464-4872; www.norcalhostels.org/montara*), a former lighthouse converted to a youth hostel, and **Fitzgerald Marine Reserve**. At high tide, the reserve could be any stretch of rocky coastline, but low tide uncovers broad rocky terraces and innumerable tide pools.

Food in Montara

Moss Beach Distillery $$ *140 Beach Way and Ocean Blvd, Moss Beach; tel: (650) 728-5595; www.mossbeachdistillery.com. Open daily.* The 'distillery' was an illicit spirits storehouse and bar/restaurant/brothel during Prohibition and boasts its own Blue Lady ghost. The bar and restaurant remain, one of the better eating spots along the coast and a popular protected vantage point for sunsets.

MONTEREY

ℹ Monterey County Convention & Visitors Bureau PO Box 1770; tel: (877) 666-8379; www.seemonterey.com

Lake El Estero Visitor Center Franklin and Camino El Estero. Open daily. A 'Monterey County Film & Literary Map', keyed to locations, is available online: www. seemonterey.com/monterey-county-literary-and-film-map

🏛 Monterey Bay Aquarium $$$ 886 Cannery Row; tel: (831) 648-4800 or (800) 756-3737; www. montereybayaquarium.org. Open daily summer 0930–1800, rest of year 1000–1800.

Monterey Bay National Marine Sanctuary 299 Foam St; tel: (831) 647-4201; http://montereybay.noaa.gov. Open Mon–Fri. Free.

Monterey State Historic Park $ 20 Custom House Plaza; tel: (831) 649-7118 for current tour information; www.park.ca.gov

Monterey History & Maritime Museum 5 Custom House Plaza; www.montereyhistory.org. Will reopen after renovation in 2011.

Monterey was the capital of California under Spanish, Mexican and American flags. Overfishing in the 1940s killed the gritty sardine canneries immortalised in John Steinbeck's *Cannery Row*, but the town has been successfully trolling for tourists ever since.

Cannery Row (*west of Fisherman's Wharf; www.canneryrow.com*) lost its last cannery decades ago, but the area has been resurrected as Monterey's main tourist district. The mile-long bay-front street is lined with restaurants, art galleries, shops and similar attractions.

Fisherman's Wharf has a bevy of restaurants, galleries, handicraft shops, sport fishing boats and whale-watching operations.

Built around Monterey's last cannery at the edge of the tide pools, the **Monterey Bay Aquarium** explores the rich and varied sea life of the **Monterey Bay National Marine Sanctuary**. Time your visit to begin with watching divers clean the three-storey-tall glass of the **Kelp Forest** with interactive diver narration. Check out the cavorting sea otters, African penguins and the Splash Zone. There are sharks and rays from around the world. The aquarium has had jellyfish and sea horses moving in tanks. A giant Pacific octopus and wolf eels are in the Deep Reefs Gallery Stroll, a walk-through tunnel beneath tidal action coastal wetlands, and shorebird aviary.

The best way to see the real Bay is by kayak; **Monterey Bay Kayaks** (*see page 206*) is the biggest operator. **Monterey Bay National Marine Sanctuary** stretches 276 miles south along the California Coast from Marin to Cambria, the largest marine sanctuary in the country. Within its 5,322sq miles is a variety of marine habitats, including wetlands, beaches, kelp forests, sunken canyons and open ocean.

Monterey State Historic Park operates 37 historical buildings, sites and museums detailing Monterey from the 17th to 20th centuries. When offered, guided tours begin from the visitor centre at **Pacific House** on **Custom House Plaza**, next to Fisherman's Wharf. A 1½-mile **Path of History** walk connects the sites, most of the interiors of which are closed except to guided tours. **Monterey History & Maritime Museum**, covering seafaring in Monterey Bay, is closed for renovation until 2011.

Accommodation and food in Monterey

Quock Mui Tea Room $ *774 Wave St; tel: (831) 655-2033*. Has a warmed stone seating area by a cascading waterfall.

Rappa's Seafood Restaurant $$ *End of Fisherman's Wharf; tel: (831) 372-7562; www.rappas.com*. Combines good seafood with great views.

Casa Munras Hotel & Spa $$$ *700 Munras Ave; tel: (831) 375-2411; http://larkspurhotels.com/collection/casa-munras*. Incorporates one of the first homes built outside the walls of the original Presidio in 1824. If you absolutely *must* have a harbour view, try the **Monterey Bay Inn** $$$ *242 Cannery Row; tel: (800) 424-6242; http://montereybayinn.com*

PACIFIC GROVE

ⓘ Pacific Grove Chamber of Commerce *584 Central Ave; tel: (831) 373-3304 or (800) 656-6650; www.pacificgrove.org. Information Center, Central and Forest Aves. Open Mon–Fri 0930–1700, Sat 1000–1500.*

The most scenic way out of Monterey is Pacific Grove, via the **Seventeen Mile Drive** (*see page 210*), but the town has its own attractions. **Monarch Grove Sanctuary** (*Ridge Rd, between Lighthouse Ave and Short St; tel: (831) 648-5716; www.pgmuseum.org*) is winter home to millions of monarch butterflies, which congregate before migrating north. **Point Piños Lighthouse** $, in operation since 1855, shows how lighthouse keepers lived and worked in the 19th and early 20th centuries (*Asilomar and Lighthouse Aves; tel: (831) 648-5716; www.ci.pg.ca.us/lighthouse/default.htm. Open Thur–Mon 1300–1600*). **Asilomar Conference Grounds** $$ (*800 Asilomar Ave; tel: (888) 635-5310; www.visitasilomar.com*) is on the dunes, with historical buildings designed in Arts and Crafts style.

PESCADERO

ⓘ Duarte's $–$$ *202 Stage Rd; tel: (650) 879-0464; www.duartestavern.com. Open daily 0700–2100. This is one of the most talked-about fish restaurants, with famed home-made pies.*

This former Portuguese fishing and farming town presents a tidy face, but is best known for the 115ft-high **Pigeon Point Lighthouse** (*Pigeon Point Rd in Pigeon Point Light Station State Historic Park; tel: (650) 879-2120. Closed, awaiting repair*). A **Pigeon Point Lighthouse Hostel** $ (*210 Pigeon Point Rd; tel: (650) 879-0633; www.norcalhostels.org/pigeon*) stay includes a cliff-top hot tub. **Año Nuevo State Park** (*see page 204*) is nearby.

SANTA CRUZ

ⓘ Santa Cruz County Conference and Visitors Council *303 Water St, Ste 101; tel: (831) 425-1234 or (800) 833-3494; www.santacruz.org. Open daily.*

Perched on the north end of Monterey Bay, Santa Cruz began as a mission town in 1791 and boomed as a beach resort with the coming of the railway. A University of California campus adds one more layer to this blue-collar, intellectual and artistic surfer city. The city **beach** is one of the widest and busiest north of Santa Barbara. **Art galleries** and **studios** are concentrated along **Pacific Ave** (*between Water and Cathcart Sts*), rebuilt following the 1989 earthquake.

Seymour Marine Discovery Center $ 100 Shaffer Rd; tel: (831) 459-3800; www2.ucsc.edu/ seymourcenter. Open Jul–Aug daily; Sept–Jun Tue–Sat 1000–1700, Sun 1200–1700.

Roaring Camp Railroads PO Box G-1, Felton; tel: (831) 335-4484; www.roaringcamp.com

Santa Cruz Beach Boardwalk 400 Beach St; tel: (831) 423-5590; http://beachboardwalk.com. Open daily. Check website for details. Boardwalk free, rides $.

Santa Cruz Surfing Museum Ground floor of the lighthouse, 701 West Cliff Dr; tel: (831) 420-6289; www.santacruzsurfingmuseum. org. Open 4 Jul–mid-Sept Wed–Mon 1000–1700; mid-Sept–3 Jul Thur–Mon 1200–1600. Free.

Wilder Ranch State Park $ Hwy 1, 2 miles north of Santa Cruz; tel: (831) 423-9703 or (831) 426-0505; www.santacruzstateparks.org or www.parks.ca.gov. Open daily 0800–dusk.

Seymour Marine Discovery Center is part of the University of California's Joseph M Long Marine Laboratory. The museum and guided tours explain current research projects and provide ample time to explore aquaria, touch-tank creatures and marine mammal pools. The lab overlooks **Natural Bridges State Beach** (tel: (831) 423-4609) – also the location of the **Monarch Butterfly Natural Preserve**.

Roaring Camp Railroads is America's last steam-powered railway. Two lines take passengers through the redwood forests near Roaring Camp or between Roaring Camp and the Santa Cruz Beach Boardwalk (3 hours return). Rail buffs will opt for the narrow-gauge steam train to the summit of Bear Mountain (1 hour return).

Santa Cruz Beach Boardwalk was California's first beach boardwalk amusement park (1904) and the only one to survive. Top rides are the **Hurricane** roller coaster and the 1924 **Giant Dipper** wooden roller coaster, one of America's Top Ten Coasters. The 1911 Charles Looff **merry-go-round** has its original organ and ring toss. There are also free beach rock 'n' roll concerts on Friday nights in summer.

Exhibits hearkening back to 100lb redwood surfboards of the 1930s are on display at the **Santa Cruz Surfing Museum**.

Wilder Ranch State Park has 34 miles of coastal hiking, cycling and equestrian trails as well as preserved ranch buildings. Guides in period costume explain the life of early Central Coast ranchers.

Accommodation and food in Santa Cruz

Gabriella Café $$ (910 Cedar St; tel: (831) 457-1667; www.gabriellacafe. com. Open daily) is one of the area's best Northern Italian restaurants. **Casablanca Inn & Motel** $$$ (101 Main St; tel: (831) 423-1570; www.casablanca-santacruz.com) is a converted mansion across from the Beach Boardwalk. **The Dream Inn** $$$ (175 W. Cliff Dr; tel: (831) 426-4330; www.jdvhotels.com/hotels/centralcoast/dream) with balconies or patios is Santa Cruz's beachfront hotel.

SEVENTEEN MILE DRIVE

Seventeen Mile Drive $$ www. pebblebeach.com/page.asp? pageName=_17_Mile_Home

This is the scenic coastal route from Monterey (Pacific Grove) to Carmel by way of the coast, Pebble Beach and 21 marked points of interest. Don't miss **The Lone Cypress**, one of California's most-photographed trees clinging to a bare rock (with help from guy wires).

Suggested tour

Total distance: 90 miles.

Time: 2½ hours' driving. Allow a full day or overnight in Santa Cruz, plus a day exploring the Monterey Peninsula.

Santa Cruz Mountains
For information on wine
tours and tastings, contact
**Santa Cruz Mountains
Winegrowers Assn**
7605-A Old Dominion Court,
Aptos; tel: (831) 685-8463;
www.scmwa.com

Links: San Francisco and the Marin Coast to the north, Big Sur and Southern California to the south.

Route: From **San Francisco ❶**, follow Hwy 1 south over the spine of the San Mateo Peninsula to **Pacifica ❷**, the self-proclaimed Fog Capital of California. The road south follows cliffs and beaches fronted by rocky reefs and lighthouses at **MONTARA ❸** and **Pigeon Point**. Beach parks at Pomponio and **PESCADERO ❹** are local favourites. Continue past **AÑO NUEVO STATE PARK ❺** to **SANTA CRUZ ❻**.

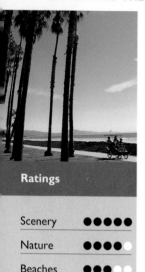

Big Sur and the Central Coast

Ratings

Scenery	●●●●●
Nature	●●●●○
Beaches	●●●○○
Children	●●●○○
Sport	●●●○○
Food	●●○○○
History	●●○○○
Architecture	●○○○○

Big Sur is elemental California, undeveloped and seemingly untouched. Hwy 1 is the sole access, a route frequently blocked by winter rains and mudslides and clogged with summer weekend traffic. South of Big Sur, the road becomes wider, straighter and less crowded, but no less scenic for the easier access. The Central Coast, Hearst Castle® to Santa Barbara, offers an alluring combination of good weather, easy driving and rolling countryside that invites leisurely exploration.

Big Sur and its series of state parks is one of the most visited parts of California, yet manages to retain an air of isolation, mystery and mysticism. The 90 rugged, craggy miles of Hwy 1 were carved into trackless cliffs by convict labour in the 1930s. Enjoy the ethereal magic of the cobalt and turquoise Pacific Ocean battering soaring mountains cloaked in swirling mists and dense forests.

BIG SUR

 Big Sur Chamber of Commerce
PO Box 87; tel: (831) 667-2100;
www.bigsurcalifornia.org

Big Sur Ranger Station
½ mile south of Pfeiffer Big Sur State Park; tel: (831) 667-2315. Open spring–autumn daily 0800–1630; winter Wed–Sun.

All **state parks** found on www.parks.ca.gov

For **Hwy 1 traffic and road information** from Carmel to Cambria, including Big Sur, call CalTrans: tel: (888) 836-0866.

The best views are southbound, driving on the ocean side of Hwy 1. The scenery is unendingly stunning, but the winding road demands full driving attention – drivers should wait for the frequent lay-bys before taking in the views. The most complete local guide is the *Big Sur Guide*, free from the **Chamber of Commerce** online or at ranger stations and shops. The best information stop is the **Big Sur Ranger Station** (*just south of Pfeiffer-Big Sur State Park*). Big Sur ends at **Piedras Blancas Lighthouse**, just north of **Hearst Castle®** (*see page 216*).

Andrew Molera State Park (*south of Point Sur Lighthouse; tel: (831) 667-2315*) is the largest and least developed of the Big Sur parks. Miles of trails wander its open beaches, meadows and hilltops.

Big Sur Valley (*25 miles south of Carmel*), the centre for tourist services, stretches for 6 miles along Hwy 1.

Bixby Creek Bridge (*3½ miles south of Garrapata State Park*), a solitary and much-photographed arch, soars high above Bixby Creek. Best **views** are from a viewpoint at the north end. **Esalen Institute** (*8 miles south of Julia Pfeiffer Burns State Park; tel: (831) 667-3000; www.esalen.org*) is

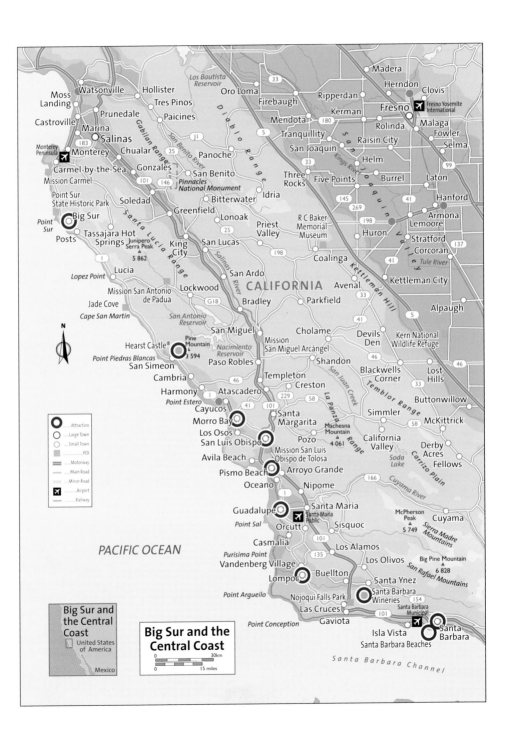

Big Sur and the Central Coast

PACIFIC OCEAN

N

Attraction
Large Town
Small Town
POI
Motorway
Main Road
Minor Road
Airport
Railway

Big Sur and
the Central
Coast

United States
of America

Mexico

Big Sur and the
Central Coast

0   30km
0   15 miles

CALIFORNIA

Madera
Herndon   Clovis
Ripperdan   Fresno   Fresno Yosemite
Kerman   International
Rolinda   Malaga
Mendota   180   Fowler
Tranquillity   Raisin City   Selma
San Joaquin   99
Helm
Three   Five Points   Burrel   Laton
Rocks
Idria   Hanford
Bitterwater   145
269   41
Armona
R C Baker   198   Lemoore
Lonoak   Priest   Memorial   Huron   Stratford
Valley   Museum   Corcoran   137
25   41   Tule River
Coalinga
Avenal   Kettleman City
Parkfield   33
Alpaugh
41
Cholame   Devils   Kern National
Mission   Den   Wildlife Refuge
San Miguel Arcángel   46
Shandon   Blackwells   Lost   46
Corner   Hills
Creston   33
Buttonwillow
Santa   Simmler   McKittrick
Margarita   Machesna   58
Mountain
Pozo   4 061   California
Mission San Luis   Valley   Derby
Obispo de Tolosa   Soda   Acres
Arroyo Grande   Lake   Fellows
Nipome   166
Cuyama River
Santa Maria   McPherson
Santa Maria   Peak   Cuyama
Sisquoc   5 749
Los Alamos
135   Los Olivos   Big Pine Mountain
6 828
Buellton   Santa Ynez   San Rafael Mountains
Lompoc   Santa Barbara   154
Nojoqui Falls Park   Wineries
Santa Barbara
Las Cruces   101   Municipal
Gaviota   Santa
Isla Vista   Barbara
Santa Barbara Beaches
Santa Barbara Channel

Los Bautista
Reservoir   33
Oro Loma
Firebaugh
180

5
San Joaquin
Panoche   33
San Benito
146   Pinnacles
National Monument

Watsonville   Hollister
Tres Pinos
Prunedale   Paicines
Moss
Landing
Castroville
Marina   183
Salinas
Monterey
Peninsula
Monterey   Chualar
Carmel-by-the-Sea   Gonzales
Mission Carmel   101
Point Sur   Soledad
State Historic Park
Big Sur   Greenfield
Point
Sur   Posts   Tassajara Hot
Springs   Junipero
Serra Peak   King
5 862   City
San Lucas   198
Lopez Point   Lucia
Mission San Antonio   Lockwood
de Padua   G18   Bradley
Jade Cove
Cape San Martin   San Antonio
Reservoir
Hearst Castle   Pine
Mountain   Nacimiento
3 594   Reservoir
Point Piedras Blancas
San Simeon   Paso Robles
Cambria   46   Templeton
Harmony   Atascadero
Point Estero   41   101   229   58
Cayucos
Morro Bay
Los Osos
San Luis Obispo
Avila Beach
Pismo Beach
Oceano   1
Guadalupe
Point Sal   Orcutt
Casmalia
Purisima Point
Vandenberg Village
Point Arguello
Point Conception

25
11
Gabilan Range
San Benito River
Diablo Range
Santa Lucia Range
Salinas River
Kettleman Hills
La Panza Range
Temblor Range
Carrizo Plain
Sierra Madre Mountains

San Joaquin Valley
Kings River

Chualar
Panoche
San Benito
Idria

25
1

La Panza Range
San Juan Creek

Henry Miller Memorial Library
35 miles south of Carmel; tel/fax: (831) 667-2574; www.henrymiller.org. Open Wed–Mon 1100–1800. Free.

Julia Pfeiffer Burns State Park *12 miles south of Pfeiffer Big Sur State Park; tel: (831) 667-2315. Open daily ½ hour before dawn to ½ hour after dusk.*

Point Sur State Historic Park *19 miles south of Carmel; tel: (831) 625-4419; www.pointsur.org. Guided tours on a first come, first served basis; call or check the website for tour information.*

Nepenthe $$ *South of Big Sur Valley; tel: (831) 667-2345; www.nepenthebigsur.com. Open daily for lunch and dinner.*

Below
Big Sur's scenic coastline

America's original New Age retreat. The public are allowed as far as the famed hot springs $$ *(tel: (831) 667-3047; www.esalen.org/place/hot_springs.shtml. Open daily 0100–0300).*

Garrapata State Park *(10 miles south of Carmel; tel: (831) 624-4909)* contains 4 miles of undeveloped coast, but has no car parks or other facilities. Park paths from lay-bys around **Soberanes Point** headlands run to beaches, through stands of cacti and into dense redwood groves. **Henry Miller Memorial Library** is a shrine to the infamous writer who lived in Big Sur for 18 years. The library is filled with Miller memorabilia, much of it for sale. The toilet has erotic tiles by local artist Ephraim Doner, and oversized sculptures grace the lawn.

Julia Pfeiffer Burns State Park includes some of Big Sur's best coastline. Don't miss the easy ½-mile return trail to **McWay Waterfall**, if accessible, which drops from a bluff into the ocean. Follow the Waterfall Overlook Trail for whale-watching in December and January. Another easy ½-mile return trail leads from Hwy 1 to **Partington Point**, overlooking the surging, kelp-filled waters of Partington Cove. **Nepenthe** is a restaurant best known for its **views**. The multi-storey structure, 800ft above the crashing surf, was built by Hollywood director Orson Welles for his bride, Rita Hayworth, in the 1940s. **Café Kevah** has the best views.

Pfeiffer Beach *(no sign; off Sycamore Canyon Rd, the only paved road west off Hwy 1 between the Big Sur Post Office and Pfeiffer Big Sur State Park)* is Big Sur's best and hardest-to-find beach. The white strand is dominated by a rock hump that changes from brown to fiery orange as the sun sets. Richard Burton and Elizabeth Taylor produced some of their steamier cinematic love scenes here for *The Sandpiper* in 1965. Their beach scenes notwithstanding, a fierce undertow makes swimming extremely hazardous.

Pfeiffer Big Sur State Park *(tel: (831) 667-2315)* sits in the midst of the Big Sur Valley, groves of redwoods, conifers and oaks interspersed with open meadows along the Big Sur River. There are miles of hiking trails and deep, clear river swimming-holes among the boulders in summer. Pfeiffer Big Sur is headquarters for all of the Big Sur state parks, with the best visitor and information centre.

Point Sur State Historic Park contains the **Point Sur Lightstation**, in operation since 1889. The light is automated, but the building's interiors are being restored to their turn-of-the-20th-century appearance. The station is open only for guided tours (*www.pointsur.org*) as part of a 3-mile return hike, with moonlight tours in summer.

Accommodation and food in Big Sur

High demand and low supply tends to keep prices high. Advance bookings are essential. **Deetjen's Big Sur Inn $$** (*48865 Hwy 1, tel: (831) 667-2377; www.deetjens.com*) is a rambling, old-fashioned inn popular with long-time visitors. **Deetjen's Big Sur Inn Restaurant $$** serves good Euro-Californian cuisine with larger-than-average portions. **Big Sur Lodge $$–$$$** (*Pfeiffer Big Sur State Park; tel: (831) 667-3100 or (800) 424-4787; www.bigsurlodge.com*) is the only non-camping accommodation in the Big Sur state parks, with modern cottages around a swimming pool. **The Restaurant at Ventana $$$** (*Ventana Inn – see below*) on a sunny day has 50-mile views. **Post Ranch Inn $$$** (*tel: (831) 667-2200 or (888) 524-4787; www.postranchinn.com*), a postmodernist retreat below Hwy 1, has stunning views, rooms and restaurant. **Sierra Mar $$$** (*tel: (831) 667-2800 (Post Ranch Inn – see above)* keeps to cutting-edge California dishes. **Treebones Resort $$$** (*71895 Hwy 1; tel: (877) 424-4787; http://treebonesresort.com*) has luxury Mongolian-style yurts. **Ventana Inn & Spa $$$** (*tel: (831) 667-2331 or (800) 628-6500; www.ventanainn.com*) is another posh equivalent above Hwy 1.

GUADALUPE

Rancho Guadalupe Dunes County Park *Hwy 166 west of Guadalupe; tel: (805) 343-2354; www.countyofsb.org/parks/parks02.aspx?id=13422*

Guadalupe-Nipomo Dunes National Wildlife Refuge *1045 Guadalupe St; tel: (805) 343-9151; www.fws.gov/hoppermountain/GuadalupeNDNWR/GuadalupeNipomoDunesNWR.html. North entrance from Oso Flaco Rd, 3 miles north of Guadalupe; south entrance west on Hwy 166 (Main St).*

Guadalupe-Nipomo Dunes Center *1055 Guadalupe St; tel: (805) 343-0442; www.dunescenter.org. Open Wed–Sun 1000–1600.*

Guadalupe is a California time capsule, a town that never lost its past. The traditional **Italian Cemetery** at the intersection of Hwys 1 and 166 is filled with ornate funerary monuments; the brick shopfronts lining Main St still display the names of the Italian, Mexican, Chinese and Basque merchants who erected them. **Rancho Guadalupe Dunes County Park** has biking, hiking, fishing and an uncrowded beach. **Guadalupe-Nipomo Dunes National Wildlife Refuge** has the West Coast's tallest dunes (550ft), birdwatching, Oso Flaco (freshwater) Lake and a dunes vehicular area.

Food in Guadalupe

Santa Maria Barbecue, a hangover from *Californio* days, is the best reason to stop here. The **Far Western Tavern $–$$** (*899 Guadalupe St; tel: (805) 343-2211; www.farwesterntavern.com. Open Tue–Sun, call for hours*) specialises in thick steaks, grilled with salt, pepper, garlic and olive oil.

HEARST CASTLE®

Hearst San Simeon State Historical Monument
$$ *750 Hearst Castle Rd, San Simeon; tel: (805) 927-2020 or (800) 444-4445; international reservations: tel: (916) 414-8400, ext. 4100; www.hearstcastle.org. Advance bookings essential in summer and recommended all year. Walk-in space may be available mid-Nov–mid-May midweek. A self-guided Gardens and Vistas Tour, with no visits to interiors, is offered Mar–Labor Day weekend.*

The rolling hills of the Central Coast have long been a magnet for dreamers with money to bring their fantasies to life – none with more extravagance than William Randolph Hearst. Hearst called his 165-room Renaissance-Moorish-medieval holiday house 'The Ranch'. The official name was *La Cuesta Encantada*, The Enchanted Hill, but the world knew it as Hearst Castle®.

More estate than castle, *Casa Grande*, the Big House, is surrounded by guesthouses and an outdoor swimming-pool complex, the whole set within lush gardens and a private zoo with free-roaming zebras and other exotic creatures.

Hearst, an only child, inherited a failing *San Francisco Examiner* and turned it into a hugely profitable chain of papers. In the euphoria following World War I, America's most famous media personality decided to build America's most famous house. With the help of architect Julia Morgan, Hearst got an eclectic pastiche of European treasures. The grand façade to *Casa Grande* once graced a Spanish cathedral; the ceilings were pulled from European monasteries. No museum of the day could outbid Hearst's buyers, who filled the castle with priceless treasures.

Never one to underplay his own success, Hearst invited the social and political elite of the world to visit The Ranch for as long as they wished. Charlie Chaplin, Winston Churchill, Greta Garbo, Clark Gable, Charles Lindbergh, George Bernard Shaw and hundreds more accepted. Hearst's 'home movies', seen as part of the tour, show just how carefree life could be at The Ranch; Orson Welles's 1941 film *Citizen Kane* gives an equally accurate – if fictionalised – rendition of Hearst, castle and company.

The property eventually passed to the State of California and became **Hearst San Simeon State Historical Monument** (*tel: (805) 927-2020*), open by guided tour. **Tour One** is an overview of the property. **Tour Two** concentrates on the upper floors of *Casa Grande*, including the art collection and Hearst's library and bedroom suite. **Tour Three** looks at one of the guesthouses in detail. **Tour Four** (*Apr–Oct*) inspects the grounds and gardens. It's possible – but ill-advised – to cram all four tours into a single day. After the first few hours, one Baroque tapestry starts looking much like any other. A **Gardens and Vistas Tour**, offered from March to Labor Day weekend after the other tours, allows for self-guided garden wandering. The **Visitor Center** is worth a visit even if tours are fully booked. The free museum provides a good overview of the castle and architect Julia Morgan's other and far more original work.

The **Coastal Discovery Centre** (*tel: (805) 927-6577; www.coastaldiscoverycenter.org*) at San Simeon Bay across Hwy 1 from Hearst Castle® has information, live rainbow trout, and a talking tide-pool sculpture. Four miles north at **Piedras Blancas** (*www. elephantseal.org*) is a vista point for northern elephant seal-watching.

Below
Sybaritic luxury – the Neptune Pool at Hearst Castle

LOMPOC

ⓘ Lompoc Valley Chamber of Commerce and Visitors Bureau *111 S. 1 St; tel: (805) 736-4567 or (800) 240-0999; www.lompoc.com. Open Mon–Fri 0900–1700.*

ⓗ La Purisima Mission State Historic Park *$ 2295 Purisima Rd; tel: (805) 733-3713; www.parks.ca.gov or www.lapurisimamission.org. Open daily 0900–1700.*

Lompoc Museum *$ 200 S. H St; tel: (805) 736-3888; www.lompochistory.org/ lompocmuseum.html. Open Tue–Fri 1300–1700, Sat–Sun 1300–1600. Tour daily 1300.*

Many of the flower seeds sold in America are grown on acres of fields in Lompoc, which blaze with colour between June and August. The town also boasts more than 70 wall murals (*www.lompocmurals.com*), inspired by Chemainus in British Columbia, Canada.

La Purisima Mission State Historic Park (*see page 257*) is the most authentically restored of the 21 California missions. The park includes ten buildings restored to their 1820s glory, the historical water system, replanted gardens and period barnyard animals. **Lompoc Museum** has a large collection of artefacts from local Native American bands, including the Chumash. **Santa Rita Hills** is a new wine region with open tasting rooms between Lompoc and Buellton (*www.staritahills.com*).

Right
Commercial flower farms blaze with colour in the Californian summer

MORRO BAY

ⓘ Morro Bay Chamber of Commerce and Visitor Center *845 Embarcadero Rd, Ste D; tel: (805) 772-4467 or (800) 231-0592; www.morrobay.org. Open Mon–Fri 0900–1700, Sat 1000–1600.*

Once a lively port for the area's ranchers, Morro Bay has become a busy fishing port and holiday destination. The town and Bay are named after **Morro Rock**, first in a line of volcanic cores stretching south to San Luis Obispo. The sand spit which protects the harbour is accessible only by boat. Kayaking around the protected estuary at the south end of the Bay is popular in all seasons.

The Embarcadero is the town's main tourist and commercial fishing area. Many fishing boats unload directly into restaurant kitchens or sell straight to consumers. **Chablis Cruises's** riverboat *Chablis* passes Morro Rock, the Embarcadero and Morro Back Bay. **Sub Sea Tours $$** (*tel: (805) 772-9463; www.subseatours.com*) offers 45-minute Bay tours on a semi-submerged vessel with view windows beneath the waves.

Montaña de Oro State Park, 'Mountain of Gold' in Spanish, was named after the mounds of golden California poppies, wild mustard

Chablis Cruises $$ *Embarcadero; tel: (805) 772-2128; www.chabliscruises.com. One-hour trips – call for cruise times.*

Montaña de Oro State Park $ *End of Los Osos Valley Rd, south of Morro Bay; tel: (805) 528-0513 or (805) 772-7434.*

Morro Bay State Park and Museum of Natural History $ *South end of Morro Bay; tel: (805) 772-2560. Museum, tel: (805) 772-2694. Open daily 1000–1700.*

and other wild flowers that bloom each spring. There are more than 50 miles of walking paths in the park; among the most popular is **Hazard Canyon**, ½ mile from gum forests to tide pools.

Morro Bay State Park takes in most of the south end of Morro Bay, including a public golf course. The **Museum of Natural History** covers the Bay's complex ecosystem, including a network of walking paths.

Morro Rock (578ft) has been mined for building materials for nearly four centuries, but still dominates the Bay and town. The Rock itself is closed to protect peregrine falcons nesting on the upper slopes. Morro Bay's estuary is a major stopover point for birds on the Pacific flyway, especially in winter. The **Morro Bay Harbor Walk** extends from the Embarcadero to Morro Rock.

Food in Morro Bay

Fish is the obvious best choice in town. **Windows on the Water $$$** *(699 Embarcadero; tel: (805) 772-0677; www.windowsonthewater.net. Open daily from 1700)* has a wide variety of excellent seafood, an extensive wine list and Bay views.

PISMO BEACH

Pismo Beach Visitors Information Center *581 Doliver St; tel: (805) 773-4382 or (800) 443-7778; www.pismochamber.com or www.classiccalifornia.com. Open Mon–Fri 0900–1700, Sat 1100–1600.*

Pismo State Beach $ *2 miles south; tel: (805) 489-1869.*

The town took its name from the Pismo clam, a local mollusc once so plentiful that newspapers talked of 45,000 clams being dug in a single day. Few legal-sized clams survived decades of depredation, though hardware stores hire digging gear and sell the requisite fishing licences. The fishing pier offers excellent views of surfers riding the waves towards shore.

At the **Monarch Butterfly Grove** *(www.monarchbutterfly.org)*, in the **Pismo State Beach North Beach Campground** between Pismo Beach and Grover City, the orange and black butterflies hang in great clusters from the gum trees and Monterey pines from late October to February.

Pismo Beach, Grover City and Oceano are often lumped together as the **Beach Cities**. The **Nipomo Dunes** begin south of the Beach Cities, a sand sea stretching 18 miles to **Point Sal**. Cecil B DeMille filmed the original *Ten Commandments* in the dunes beyond West Main St (Hwy 166) in Guadalupe *(see page 215)*. Bits of his faux-Egypt set occasionally reappear as the dunes shift.

Food in Pismo Beach

Splash Café $ *197 Pomeroy Ave; tel: (805) 773-4653; www.splashcafe. com. Open daily 0800–2000 or 2100.* Famous for clam chowder, its surfing murals inside and out and a surfboard above the entrance.

Below
San Luis Obispo County
coastline

Cracked Crab $$–$$$ *751 Price St; tel: (805) 773-2722; www.crackedcrab.com.* Dumps the bucket of shellfish – among many other fish specialities – on the table with mallet and crab cracker for ultimate dining.

SAN LUIS OBISPO

ℹ San Luis Obispo Chamber of Commerce Visitor Center *1039 Chorro St, San Luis Obispo, CA 93401; tel: (805) 781-2777; www.VisitSLO.com. Open Sun–Wed 1000–1700, Thur–Sat 1000–1900.*

San Luis Obispo County Visitors and Conference Bureau *811 El Capitan Way, Ste 200; tel: (800) 634-1414 or (805) 541-8000; www. sanluisobispocounty.com. Open Mon–Fri 0900–1700, for area information.*

ⓒ California Polytechnic University *Tel: (805) 756-5734; www. ess.calpoly.edu/_admiss/visit/ guided.html. GPS or device-download tours, or guided tour, Mon–Fri 1110. Free.*

Mission San Luis Obispo de Tolosa *Chorro at 782 Monterey St; tel: (805) 781-8220; www. missionsanluisobispo.org. Open daily 0900–1700. Free.*

ⓒ San Luis Obispo County Historical Museum $ *696 Monterey St; tel: (805) 543-0638; www.slochs.org. Open Wed–Sun 1000–1600.*

San Luis grew up as a mission farming community that blossomed when the railway arrived in 1894. The mission heritage remains, both in the pronunciation ('Lou-iss', Spanish-style) and in the town's common appellation, SLO, as in 'slow', the relaxed pace of life.

The town centre, **Higuera and Monterey Sts**, contains some of the finest small-town commercial architecture in the state, from adobes to Art Deco and Frank Lloyd Wright. The **Chamber of Commerce** has free self-guided walking, hiking, biking and driving maps, or ride the inexpensive **SLO Trolley** around a circular route covering the main tourist sites, Thursday–Sunday.

California Polytechnic University, usually called Cal Poly, offers free 80-minute campus tours. Don't miss the **Leaning Pine Arboretum** (*www.leaningpinearboretum.calpoly.edu*) or **Poly Canyon**, an outdoor laboratory for experimental architecture and construction.

Generations of teenagers have festooned **Bubblegum Alley** (*between Chorro and Broad Sts*) with graffiti, names and free-form designs, all carefully executed in well-used chewing gum. The oral appliqué changes slightly almost every night. Every Thursday night, Higuera St becomes a pedestrians-only **Farmers' Market** with food and produce stalls, pavement restaurants and free entertainment.

Mission San Luis Obispo de Tolosa pioneered the red-tile roof that became the Mission hallmark – the 1772 mission needed something more substantial than thatching to withstand fiery attacks by local Native American tribes (*see page 259*). **Mission Plaza**, fronting the mission, is a shady park sloping down to **San Luis Creek** and the business district. Music wafts through the trees from several restaurant patios that open on to the plaza. **San Luis Obispo County Historical Museum** has a collection of local artefacts in the historic Carnegie Library building.

Accommodation and food in San Luis Obispo

Big Sky Café $$ *1121 Broad St; tel: (805) 545-5401; www.bigskycafe. com.* Has fresh seasonal ingredients with cuisine spanning Europe to Morocco.

Madonna Inn $$–$$$ *100 Madonna Rd; tel: (805) 543-3000 or (800) 543-9666; www.madonnainn.com.* A shocking pink temple of kitsch, from the 200-ton boulders in the Jungle Rock Room to the crimson silk Love Nest and equally whimsical décor in the Fabulous 50s, Caveman and other theme rooms.

Koberl at Blue $$$ *998 Monterey St; tel: (805) 783-1135; www. epkoberl.com.* Has fine dining with Wine Country cuisine and finely crafted Martinis.

Santa Barbara

**ⓘ Santa Barbara
Conference and
Visitors Bureau** *1601
Anacapa St; tel: (800) 676-
1266 or (805) 966-9222;
www.santabarbaraca.com*

**Santa Barbara
Chamber of
Commerce Visitor
Center** *1 Garden St; tel:
(805) 965-3021. Open
Mon–Fri 0900–1700, Sat
1000–1700.*

**ⓗ El Presidio de
Santa Barbara
State Historic Park $**
*100–200 E. Canon Perdido
St; tel: (805) 965-0093.
Call for hours.*

**Mission Santa Barbara
$** *E. Los Olivos at 2201
Laguna St; tel: (805) 682-
4713; www.sbmission.org.
Open daily 0900–1700.*

Santa Barbara began as a mission town, but the mission-look of downtown, red-tile roofs, whitewashed plaster walls and colourful wall tiles, dates from a 1925 earthquake. Faced with rebuilding nearly the entire city centre, authorities opted to create their own historical look with a strict architectural code. The result is one of the most gracious, visually pleasing cities in Southern California. Built on a series of rolling hills between broad beaches and the rugged Santa Ynez Mountains, Santa Barbara happily lives up to the name 'Lotusland' bestowed by an early opera diva who retired here.

El Paseo and State St are centrepieces of the 1920s reconstruction. **El Paseo** is an early shopping arcade, filled with delightfully sunny niches and fountains. **El Paseo Nuevo** is an updated version with the same mission motif, while **State St** is Santa Barbara's high street.

El Presidio de Santa Barbara State Historic Park is the site of the 1782 Spanish fort that first lured settlers to Santa Barbara. The restored **El Cuartel** is among the oldest structures in California. The padres' quarters, chapel, commandant's office and other buildings are reconstructions.

Mission Santa Barbara (*see page 261*), the 'Queen of the Missions', starred in numerous early cinematic epics. Buildings, gardens and the church interior are beautifully preserved.

Santa Barbara Botanic Garden is devoted to native trees, cacti, shrubs and flowers.

Santa Barbara County Courthouse, in an extravagant take on the mission style, has tiled corridors, heroic furnishings and a red-tiled roof. The courthouse has a Moorish tower with fine views of city and sea.

Santa Barbara Historical Museum offers local historical exhibits, while the **Santa Barbara Museum of Natural History** specialises in Native American tribal artefacts, as well as local flora and fauna.

Stearns Wharf (*foot of State St; www.stearnswharf.org*), originally built in 1872, now houses small speciality shops, restaurants and the

Santa Barbara Botanic Garden $ *1212 Mission Canyon Rd; tel: (805) 682-4726; www.sbbg.org. Open daily Mar–Oct 0900–1800; Nov–Feb 0900–1700.*

Santa Barbara County Courthouse *1100 Anacapa St; tel: (805) 962-6464. Open Mon–Fri 0800–1700, Sat 1000–1700. Free tours Mon–Sat 1400 & Mon, Tue & Fri 1030.*

Santa Barbara Historical Museum $ *136 E. De La Guerra St; tel: (805) 966-1601; www.santabarbaramuseum.com. Open Tue–Sat 1000–1700, Sun 1200–1700.*

Santa Barbara Museum of Natural History $ *2559 Puesta del Sol Rd; tel: (805) 682-4711; www.sbnature.org. Open Daily 1000–1700.*

Ty Warner Sea Center $ *(tel: (805) 962-2526. Open daily 1000–1700)*, a small museum devoted to marine life and birdlife of the Channel Islands National Marine Sanctuary.

Accommodation and food in Santa Barbara

Santa Barbara's popularity as a quick getaway for Los Angelenos keeps accommodation demand and prices high.

Wine Cask $$ *813 Anacapa St (El Paseo); tel: (805) 966-9463; www.winecask.com. Open daily from 1730.* Has one of Santa Barbara's best wine lists from the Central Coast and elsewhere. Don't miss the tasting menu on request.

Bouchon $$$ *9 W. Victoria St; tel: (805) 730-1160; www.bouchon.net. Open daily.* Combines local farm-to-table ingredients with many Santa Barbara County wines by the glass.

Hotel Santa Barbara $$$ *533 State St; tel: (805) 957-9300 or (800) 549-9869; www.hotelsantabarbara.com.* A posh stop in the city centre.

The Hungry Cat $$$ *1134 Chapala St; tel: (805) 884-4701; www.thehungrycat.com. Open Tue–Sun.* Has intricate fish dishes, and in-the-shell, on-the-half-shell and create-your-own seafood platter appetisers.

The Upham Hotel $$$ *1404 De la Vina St; tel: (805) 962-0058 or (800) 727-0876; www.uphamhotel.com.* Santa Barbara's oldest operating hotel, in the midst of gardens, with breakfast and an afternoon wine and cheese service.

SANTA BARBARA BEACHES

El Capitan, **Gaviota** and **Refugio State Beaches** (*Hwy 101, north of Santa Barbara; tel: (805) 968-1033*) are three of Santa Barbara's most popular beach parks. **El Capitan** has rocky tide pools, a sandy beach and stands of sycamore and oak trees. **Gaviota** boasts a wooden fishing pier. **Refugio** offers palm trees along a small creek. Two luxury resorts have appeared in recent years: **El Capitan Canyon $$$** *11560 Calle Real, Gaviota; tel: (866) 352-2729; www.elcapitancanyon.com*, with cedar cabins, safari tents and spa treatments; and one of California's largest spa resorts, **Bacara Resort & Spa $$$** *8301 Hollister Ave; tel: (877) 422-4245; www.bacararesort.com*

SANTA BARBARA WINERIES

Santa Barbara County has more than 100 wineries, many of them in the Santa Ynez Valley, off Hwys 154 and 246 near Solvang, or near Foxen Canyon Rd in the **Santa Maria Valley** (*tel: (800) 331-3779;*

www.santamariawines.com). For information on visits and tasting facilities, contact the **Santa Barbara County Vintners' Association**, *PO Box 1558, Santa Ynez; tel: (805) 688-0881; www.sbcountywines.com*. The **San Luis Obispo Vintners Association** (*tel: (805) 541-5868; www.slowine.com*) represents San Luis Obispo, Edna Valley and Arroyo Grande wineries. **Paso Robles Wine Country Alliance** (*tel: (805) 239-8463; www.pasowine.com*) covers Paso Robles wineries.

Suggested tour

Total distance: 245 miles.

Time: 6 hours' driving. Big Sur deserves at least a day to itself. Allow half a day to tour Hearst Castle®, with an overnight stop in Morro Bay or San Luis Obispo.

Links: Monterey Peninsula (north), Southern California (south).

Route: Follow Hwy 1 south from **Monterey ❶**/Carmel ❷ past **Point Lobos ❸** into **BIG SUR ❹**. **HEARST CASTLE® ❺** marks the start of the San Luis Obispo coast. From **MORRO BAY ❻**, Hwy 1 runs inland to join Hwy 101 at **SAN LUIS OBISPO ❼**. Hwy 1 returns to the coast at **PISMO BEACH ❽** and runs south towards **GUADALUPE ❾** and **LOMPOC ❿** before rejoining Hwy 101 28 miles north of **SANTA BARBARA ⓫**.

Also worth exploring

San Luis Obispo to Port San Luis

Take San Luis Bay Rd west from Hwy 101 just south of San Luis Obispo to Avila Beach Dr. **Avila Hot Springs Resort $$** (*250 Avila Beach Dr; tel: (805) 595-2359; www.avilahotsprings.com*) was a favourite party stop for Hollywood stars on their way to Hearst Castle® (*see page 216*). Today the resort is a family stop.

Sycamore Mineral Springs Resort $$$ (*1215 Avila Beach Dr; tel: (805) 595-7302* or *(800) 234-5831; www.sycamoresprings.com*) offers a full-service spa, in-room hot tubs, a labyrinth and an excellent restaurant, **The Gardens of Avila $$**.

The fishing village of **Avila Beach** has been dug up and largely rebuilt to remove decades of petroleum pollution and is one of the few beaches on this section of coast known for soft sand and no undertow. **Point San Luis Lighthouse $** (*tel: (805) 546-4904; www.sanluislighthouse.org*) has 3½-mile docent-led hikes on the Pecho Coast Trail to the lighthouse on Saturdays and Sunday van tours.

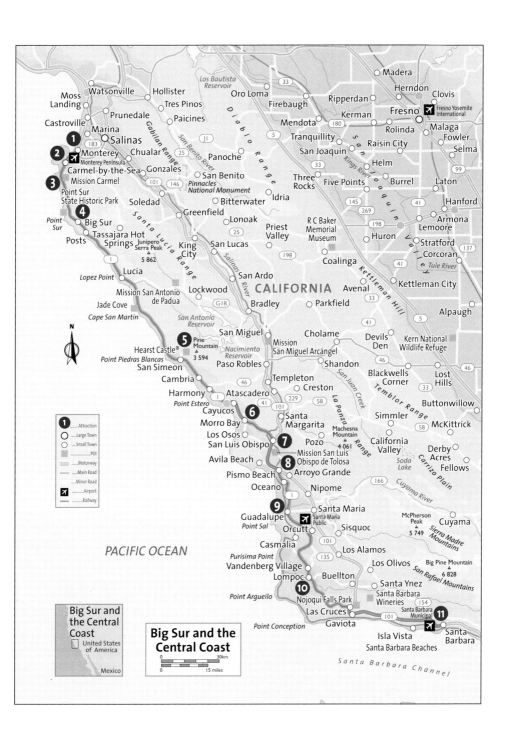

Big Sur and the Central Coast

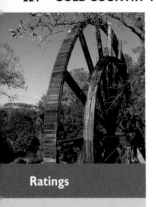

Gold Country to Yosemite

Ratings

Scenery	●●●●●
History	●●●●○
Mountains	●●●●○
Children	●●●○○
Food	●●●○○
Museums	●●●○○
Wine	●●○○○
Architecture	●○○○○

The discovery of gold in 1848 catapulted California from backwater to powerhouse and created Sacramento as its capital. Gold Country, the Sierra Nevada foothills from Sierra City south to Mariposa, shaped the California psyche far more dramatically than today's placid landscape would suggest. The rough-and-tumble promise of riches just over the next hill was fulfilled often enough that Californians still embrace calculated risks that many Americans might consider foolhardy. Try to visit in spring or early autumn; winding roads are congested in summer and most attractions are closed Monday to Wednesday in winter. Yosemite Valley is a summertime city, complete with crowds, traffic, noise and pollution, but the rest of the park is delightfully calm.

ANGELS CAMP

ⓘ Calaveras Visitors Bureau *1192 S. Main St, Angels Camp; tel: (209) 736-0049; www.gocalaveras.com. Open Mon–Fri 0900–1700, Sat 1000–1700, Sun 1100–1600.*

◎ Calaveras County Fair $ *Calaveras County Fairgrounds, 2 miles south; tel: (209) 736-2561; www.frogtown.org*

 Angels Camp Museum & Carriage House $ *753 Main St; tel: (209) 736-2963; www.angelscamp.gov. Open Mar–Dec Thur–Mon; Jan–Feb Sat–Sun.*

A young prospector with literary ambitions heard the story of a jumping frog contest here, and *The Celebrated Jumping Frog of Calaveras County* brought fame and the beginnings of fortune to Mark Twain. Twain may have written the short story in a rebuilt cabin just outside of town. Fans flock to the **Jumping Frog Jubilee** on the third weekend in May at the **Calaveras County Fair** *(tel: (209) 736-2561)*. Bring your own frog or hire a jumper on the spot.

Angels Camp Museum & Carriage House has photographs, carriages and relics of gold-mining equipment from the old days, a taste of the romance – and the back-breaking labour – of panning gold by swirling gravel, sand, mud and water in an oversized pie tin to wash away the dross and recover a few flecks of precious metal.

OARS *(tel: (209) 736-4677 or (800) 346-6277; www.oars.com)* offers river trips from local half-day floats to white-water expeditions. In-shape adventurers hike, climb, crawl and raft through **Gold Cliff Mine** tours $$$ *(tel: (866) 762-2837 or (209) 736-2708; http://caverntours.com/Gold_Cliff.html)*. Calaveras winery tours make pleasant terrestrial expeditions *(Calaveras Winegrape Alliance; tel: (866) 806-9463; www.calaveraswines.org)*.

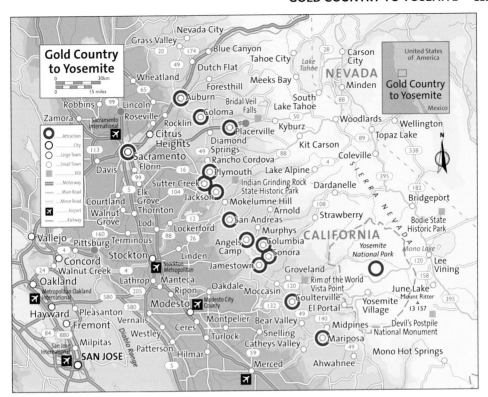

Accommodation and food in Angels Camp

Angels Inn Motel $$ (*600 N. Main St; tel (888) 753-0226, (209) 736-4242 or (888) 753-0226; www.angelsinnmotel.com, on Hwy 49*) has modern facilities. Crusco's $$$ (*1240 S. Main St; tel: (209) 736-1440; www.cruscos.com. Open Thur–Mon*) in a 150-year-old building has freshly made Italian-influenced fare.

AUBURN

ⓘ Placer County Information Center and **California Welcome Center Auburn** *13411 Lincoln Way; tel: (530) 887-2111; www.visitplacer.com. Open Mon–Sat 0930–1630, Sun 1100–1630.*

ⓑ Placer County Museum *101 Maple St; tel: (530) 889-6500; www.placer.ca.gov. Open daily 1000–1600. Free.*

Like most Gold Country towns, Auburn was an accident. Prospectors headed somewhere else hit pay dirt here first, but unlike hundreds of ragtag tent camps that disappeared as quickly as they sprouted, Auburn endured. Placer gold, panned from stream beds, gave way to hard rock gold, mined underground, which in turn gave way to more enduring riches from the Transcontinental Railroad in the 1860s.

Placer County Museum has excellent regional gold displays and Native American baskets. The real Gold Rush was in **Old Town** (*Lincoln Way*), a warren of narrow streets and 19th-century buildings surrounding the red-and-white-striped **Old Town Firehouse** (*Lincoln Way; tel: (530) 505-7725*) and an 1849 **Post Office** (*1583 Lincoln Way; tel: (530) 889-2120*), California's oldest. The **Gold Country Museum** has a demonstration mine shaft as well as period equipment.

Gold Country Museum *Gold Country Fairgrounds, 1273 High St; tel: (530) 889-6500; www.oldtownauburnca.com/list.php?cat=5&sub=5. Open Tue–Sun 1100–1600. Free.*

Accommodation and food in Auburn

Ikeda's $ *13500 Lincoln Way; tel: (530) 885-4243; www.ikedas.com. Open daily 0800–1900, 2000 or 2100, depending on season.* The best stop for burgers and milkshakes, especially fresh peach milkshakes.

Bootlegger's Old Town Tavern & Grill $$ *210 Washington St; tel: (530) 889-2229; www.bootleggersauburn.com. Open Tue–Sun.* Serves an eclectic mix including steaks in Auburn's 1870 City Hall building.

Power's Mansion Inn $$$ *195 Harrison Ave; tel: (530) 217-6031; www.powersmansioninn.com.* A bright pink mansion built in 1898, with 16 rooms and Bed & Breakfast service.

COLOMA

Marshall Gold Discovery State Historic Park $ *310 Back St; tel: (530) 622-3470; www.parks.ca.gov. Call or check online for current seasonal hours and opening dates for the park and museum. In summer or on warm weather weekends Coloma is awash with school groups, family picnickers and river rafters.*

The California Dream started in Coloma, when a sawmill contractor named James Marshall spotted a few shiny flecks in January 1848. **Marshall Gold Discovery State Historic Park** *(surrounding Hwy 49)* contains about 70 per cent of the once-booming town. Historical buildings are concentrated along Main, Back and Brewery Sts; Marshall's restored cabin is below his hilltop grave and monument.

Start with the visitor centre and an excellent video about the geology of California gold, Gold Rush history and the often-ruinous impact of miners digging, blasting and washing everything in sight – 150 years have barely begun to heal the environmental havoc that set California on the path to riches. A working replica of Marshall's sawmill sits on the banks of the American River, which has changed course since 1848. Trails lead to the site of the original mill. Visitors still find traces of gold by panning the riverbank using pans from the visitor centre.

COLUMBIA

Columbia California Chamber of Commerce *Tel: (209) 536-1672; www.columbiacalifornia.com*

Columbia State Historic Park *Tel: (209) 588-9128; www.parks.ca.gov*

Museum and Visitor Center *Main and Spring Sts; tel: (209) 588-9128. Open daily 1000–1600. Free.*

California's most appealing Gold Rush relic is an almost-ghost town, complete with brick shopfronts, iron shutters, wooden pavements, spreading trees, stagecoaches and men (plus a few women) in real frontier garb. The park museum and ranger office have free self-guiding tours to the dozens of restored Gold Rush structures and businesses in a real town that never closes.

Accommodation and food in Columbia

Two restored historical hotels were closed in 2009 because of cuts in the California State Parks budget. Check online (*www.parks.ca.gov*, **Columbia State Historic Park**) for the possible reopening of the City Hotel and Fallon Hotel.

Fitting for the 'Gem of the Southern Mines' location, **Columbia Kate's** **$$** (*22727 Columbia St; tel: (209) 532-1885; www.columbiakates.com. Open Wed–Sun 1100–1600*) is a full tearoom with lace curtains, cabinets of small treasures for sale and a variety of teas served with small sandwiches. You can also indulge in scones from a home-made menu.

COULTERVILLE

Northern Mariposa County History Center *10301 Hwys 49 and 132; tel: (209) 878-3015; http://home.inreach.com/nmchc/ or www.coultervillemuseum.org. Open Wed–Sun 1000–1600. Free.*

Coulterville remains a very small mining, ranching and tourist supply town. The **Northern Mariposa County History Center** is a pair of 1865 brick and stone buildings with period guns, Paris gowns, local Chinese furnishings and a John Muir exhibit. The 1851 **Sun Sun Wo Company Store** (*Main and Kew Sts*) is the sole survivor of a once-thriving Chinatown. The 1920s goods on the shelves here disguise an opium den behind. The **Whistling Billy** locomotive engine, under the **Hanging Tree** in front of the History Center, once hauled ore from a nearby mine. Gold is still found in town along Maxwell Creek.

Accommodation and food in Coulterville

The **Hotel Jeffery $$** (*1 Main St; tel: (209) 878-3471; www. hoteljefferygold.com*) began as a Yosemite stage stop. Walls are still covered in the original stamped tin.

Right
Brewing up around the campfire, Columbia State Historic Park

JACKSON

ⓘ Amador County Chamber of Commerce and Visitors Bureau 571 S. Hwy 49; tel: (209) 223-0350 or (800) 649-4988; www. amadorcountychamber.com. Open Tue–Fri 0900–1630.

ⓗ Kennedy Mine Tailing Wheels N. Main St, in Jackson Kennedy Wheels City Park. 1 mile north of downtown. Open daily dawn–dusk. Free.

Kennedy Mine Tours $ Tel: (209) 223-9542; www. kennedygoldmine.com. Self-guided or guided tours mid-Mar–Oct Sat, Sun & holidays, bookings required.

Jackson grew and prospered with the Kennedy and Argonaut Mines, which survived until World War II. The most striking remnant of the past is the **Kennedy Mine Tailing Wheels**, ruins of wooden wheels used to move mine debris (tailings) over several ridges to a holding pond. A well-marked **viewpoint** 1½ miles north of town overlooks what remains of the mine headframe at the top of an abandoned 6,000ft shaft, once the deepest in North America. **Kennedy Mine Tours** explores the surface structures. White **St Sava Serbian Orthodox Church** (724 N. Main St; tel: (209) 223-2700) is the oldest Serbian Orthodox church in America.

Accommodation and food in Jackson

Linda Vista Motel $$ (10708 N. Hwy 49, Martell, 1 mile north of Jackson; tel: (209) 223-1096) is outstanding value accommodation. **Gate House Inn $$–$$$** (1330 Jackson Gate Rd; tel: (209) 223-3500 or (800) 841-1072; www.gatehouseinn.com) is a Queen Anne Victorian Bed & Breakfast with a pool and bocce ball court. The **Jackson Rancheria Casino & Hotel $$–$$$** (12222 New York Ranch Rd, Jackson; tel: (800) 822-9466; www.jacksoncasino.com), Amador County's largest employer, offers (Native American-operated) gaming, lodging and dining.

JAMESTOWN

ⓗ Gold Prospecting Adventures $$ 18170 Main St; tel: (209) 984-4653 or (800) 596-0009; www.goldprospecting.com. Advance booking required.

Railtown 1897 State Historic Park $ Two blocks east of Historic Downtown Jamestown on 5th Ave; tel: (209) 984-3953; www.railtown1897.com. Grounds open daily Apr–Oct 0930–1630; Nov–Mar 1000–1500 for self-guided tours. Call in advance to book weekend steam-train excursions Apr–Oct.

'Jimtown' still uses original false-front buildings and wooden pavements, many of which have featured prominently in films such as Butch Cassidy and the Sundance Kid. Jamestown's working gold mine, an open-pit operation outside town, is off-limits, but **Gold Prospecting Adventures** sells prospecting and panning trips for individuals and families. These can be great fun, but expect to get dirty and wet, and dress accordingly.

Locomotive engines and carriages from **Railtown 1897 State Historic Park** have appeared in more than 200 films. The museum contains the original roundhouse and workshops of the Sierra Railroad, organised in 1897 to serve the Mother Lode.

Accommodation in Jamestown

The **National Hotel $$** (18183 Main St; tel: (209) 984-3446 or (800) 894-3446; www.national-hotel.com) is an 1859 antique; many of the furnishings are original to the building. The **Jamestown Hotel $$** (18153 Main St; tel: (209) 984-3902 or (800) 205-4901; www.jamestownhotel.com) is an 11-room Bed & Breakfast of similar vintage.

MARIPOSA

ℹ️ **Mariposa County Visitors Center** *5158 Hwy 140; tel: (209) 966-7081 or (866) 425-3366; www. homeofyosemite.com. Open daily.*

This southern gateway to Gold Country is the home of the **California State Mining and Mineral Museum $** (*Fairgrounds Rd; tel: (209) 742-7625; www.parks.ca.gov. Open May–Sept daily 1000–1700; Oct–Apr Wed–Mon 1000–1600, call to check opening dates*), one of the world's finest mineral and gem museums. Government has been holding court in the white **Mariposa County Courthouse** (*Bullion St between 9th and 10th Sts*), the state's oldest official building still in use, since 1854. Most courtroom furnishings are original, including the potbellied stove. **St Joseph's Catholic Church** (*top of Bullion St*) is a striking example of traditional Gold Country church architecture. The **Mariposa County Museum and History Center $** (*5119 Jesse St, tel: (209) 966-2924; www.mariposamuseum.com. Call for hours*) has an exhaustive collection, from a working stamp mill to ancient bottles of Guinness®.

PLACERVILLE

ℹ️ **El Dorado County Visitors Authority Chamber of Commerce** *542 Main St; tel: (530) 621-5885 or (800) 457-6279; www.visit-eldorado.com. Open Mon–Fri 0900–1700, Sat 1100–1500.*

🏛️ **El Dorado County Historical Museum $** *Next to the Fairgrounds, 104 Placerville Dr; tel: (530) 621-5865; www.co.el-dorado.ca.us/ museum. Open Wed–Sat 1000–1600, Sun 1200–1600.*

Once known as 'Hangtown' for its favoured method of law enforcement, Placerville was more supply centre than mining town, a breeding ground for early entrepreneurs. The town's most famous product is the 'Hangtown Fry', eggs scrambled with bacon and oysters. Look for the historical saloon on Main St with a 'hangman' suspended outside, visible across the street from the balcony of the beautifully restored 1857 **Cary House Hotel $$** (*300 Main St; tel: (530) 622-4271; www.caryhouse.com*). The **El Dorado County Historical Museum** focuses on local manufacturing and other mining support services. **Hangtown's Gold Bug Park & Mine** (*1 mile north via Bedford Ave and Hwy 50; tel: (530) 642 5207; www.goldbugpark.org. Open Apr–Oct daily 1000–1600; Nov–Mar Sat–Sun 1200–1600*) has 352ft of lighted tunnel with wooden floors for self-guided tours, a stamp mill, museum and hiking trails. Nearby **El Dorado wine** valleys are best known for Zinfandel, Syrah and Merlot. The **El Dorado Winery Association** (*tel: (800) 306-3956; www.eldoradowines.org*) has free winery maps and touring suggestions.

PLYMOUTH

Plymouth is a convenient starting point for tours of the **Amador wine country**. **Amador Vintners' Association** (*Box 667; tel: (209) 245-6992 or (888) 655-8614; www.amadorwine.com*) has free tasting and touring information in a region renowned for Zinfandel.

SACRAMENTO

Sacramento Convention and Visitors Bureau 1608 I St; tel: (916) 808-7777; www.discovergold.org. Open Mon–Fri 0800–1700.

Old Sacramento Visitors Center 1002 2nd St; tel: (916) 442-7644; . www.oldsacramento.com. Open daily 1000–1700.

Sutter's Fort State Historic Park $ 27th and L Sts; tel: (916) 445-4422; www.parks.ca.gov. Open Tue–Sun 1000–1700.

California State Indian Museum $ 2618 K St at Sutter's Fort; tel: (916) 324-0971; www.parks.ca.gov. Open Tue–Sun 1000–1700.

California Museum $$ 1020 O St; tel: (916) 653-7524; www.californiamuseum.org. Open Mon–Sat 1000–1700, Sun 1200–1700.

California State Capitol 10th St between L and N Sts; tel: (916) 324-0333; www.parks.ca.gov or www.capitolmuseum.ca.gov. Open daily 0900–1700, free guided tours hourly.

Old Sacramento 28 acres west of 3rd St to the Sacramento River.

California State Railroad Museum $$ 2nd and I Sts in Old Sac; tel: (916) 445-6645; www.csrmf.org. Open daily 1000–1700. Train excursions $, Apr–Sept Sat–Sun.

California's capital city began as **Sutter's Fort**, built by Swiss immigrant John Sutter, whose Coloma sawmill sparked the Gold Rush. Sutter's adobe administration building is largely original, but the rest of the fort is reconstructed. The self-guided audio tour is a lively introduction to daily life of the era, aided by interpreters in period dress during summer and holiday periods. The adjoining **California State Indian Museum** has a rich collection of photographs and artefacts. The **California Museum** draws upon the 120 million items in state archives.

The domed **California State Capitol** is one of the West's most elegant public buildings. It is also an outstanding museum, thanks to extensive 1980s renovations that returned gubernatorial and admin offices to turn-of-the-20th-century splendour. Visitors can watch Senate and Assembly sessions, but the magnificent **Capitol Park** around the building can be more revealing than legislative debates.

Old Sacramento, or 'Old Sac', is Sacramento's original city centre, now almost all a state historic park and national historic landmark. Brick buildings date to the 1850s, skilfully mixed with modern construction, wooden pavements and shade trees. The **California State Railroad Museum** is America's largest railway museum, filled with splendidly restored locomotive engines, luxurious private carriages, sleepers and extensive displays on America's first transcontinental railway. A **Waterfront Promenade** links Old Sacramento and the **Crocker Art Museum**, the oldest art gallery west of the Mississippi. Guided tours of the **Governor's Mansion**, built during the Victorian era and used until Ronald Reagan refused to live in it, show the daily life of state executives and their families. The **Aerospace Museum of California**, north of downtown, displays 30 military and civilian aircraft with a flight ride simulator.

Accommodation and food in Sacramento

The **Delta King Hotel** $$ (1000 Front St; tel: (916) 444-5464 or (800) 825-5464; www.deltaking.com) is an original paddle-wheel steamboat with hotel, restaurant overlooking the river, and a saloon,

Early Tourism

California has been a popular tourist destination since the 1870s. Thomas Cook included California in its first round-the-world tour in 1872–3, and in 1876 the company ran the first tour of California in its own right. Early tourists visited the Yosemite Valley by stagecoach, before continuing on to San Francisco by train – in fact, only Los Angeles (which began to grow as late as the 1880s) and Disneyland® Resort would have been missing from the list of sights that remain popular to this day.

Crocker Art Museum $ 216 O St; tel: (916) 808-7000; www.crockerartmuseum.org. Open Tue–Sun 1000–1700, first and third Thur 1000–2100. Free Sun 1000–1300.

Governor's Mansion State Historic Park $ 1526 H St; tel: (916) 323-3047; www.parks.ca.gov/?page_id=498. Open Tue–Sun, tours hourly 1000–1600.

Aerospace Museum of California $ 3200 Freedom Park Dr; tel: (916) 643-3192; www.aerospacemuseumofcalifornia.org. Open Tue–Sat 0900–1700, Sun 1000–1700.

permanently moored at Old Sacramento. **Lucca $$** (1615 J St; tel: (916) 669-5300; www.luccarestaurant.com. Open daily) is a Californian-Italian favourite of recent governor Arnold Schwarzenegger. **Amber House Bed & Breakfast $$–$$$** (1315 22nd St; tel: (916) 444-8085; www.amberhouse.com), comprising two historical homes, has the latest hotel amenities. **Biba $$$** (2801 Capitol Ave; tel: (916) 455-2422; www.biba-restaurant.com. Open Mon–Sat) is one of Northern California's better Italian restaurants; its owner writes cookbooks and has hosted a television cooking programme. **Il Fornaio $$$** (400 Capitol Mall; tel: (916) 446-4100; www.ilfornaio.com. Call for hours) serves traditional Italian in a white froth of a dining room, next to the Wells Fargo Museum. **Le Rivage Hotel $$$** (4800 Riverside Blvd; tel: (916) 433-8400; www.lerivagehotel.com) is luxury with a marina and bocce ball court along the Sacramento River. The sleek **Sterling Hotel $$$** (1300 H St; tel: (916) 448-1300; www.sterlinghotel.com) is even better known for its stunning **Chanterelle** restaurant $$$ (tel: (916) 442-0451).

SAN ANDREAS

This tiny mining camp was known largely for the capture, trial and conviction of notorious highwayman Black Bart, famous for his courtesy and poetry. The courthouse where the trial was held is now the **Calaveras County Historical Museum $** (30 N. Main St; tel: (209) 754-1058; www.calaverascohistorical.com/museum.html. Open daily 1000–1600).

SONORA

Tuolumne County Visitors Bureau 542 W. Stockton Rd; tel: (209) 533-4420 or (800) 446-1333; www.tcvb.com. Open daily.

Tuolumne County Museum & History Center $ 158 W. Bradford Ave; tel: (209) 532-1317; www.tchistory.org. Open Mon–Fri 1000–1600, Sat 1000–1530.

Once the wildest town on the Southern Mother Lode, Sonora has remained a busy crossroads with skiers, snowboarders, hikers and loggers mixing with Gold Country tourists.

The **Tuolumne County Museum & History Center**, in the 1857 county jail, has an interesting mix of old photos and curios. **Old Sonora** stretches along **Washington St** from the dark red **St James Episcopal Church** into the town centre. The County Museum has self-guiding walking maps.

Accommodation and food in Sonora

The Gunn House $$ (286 S. Washington St; tel: (209) 532-3421; www.gunnhousehotel.com), built in 1850, is within walking distance of restaurants and two live theatres. **Diamondback Grill $** (93 S. Washington St; tel: (209) 532-6661; www.thediamondbackgrill.com) serves burgers and is renowned for its sweet potato fries.

SUTTER CREEK

ℹ **Sutter Creek Visitors Center** *71 Main St; tel: (800) 400-0305 or (209) 267-1344; www.suttercreek.org. Open daily, call for hours.*

Sutter Creek does not have a very Gold Rush-like appearance. Main St is filled with galleries and antique shops in 19th-century storefronts; side streets are lined with still more original buildings. **Knight Foundry** (*81 Eureka St*) was the last water-powered foundry in America.

Accommodation and food in Sutter Creek

Grey Gables Inn $$ *161 Hanford St; tel: (209) 267-1039 or (800) 473-9422; www.greygables.com.* Victorian-style accommodation run by a pair of British expatriates.

The Foxes Inn $$–$$$ *77 Main St; tel: (209) 267-5882 or (800) 987-3344; www.foxesinn.com.* One of Gold Country's most popular Bed & Breakfasts.

J&D's Steakhouse $$–$$$ *1860 Main St; tel: (209) 267-0535; www.janddsteakhouse.com.* Has traditional Western fare, from burgers to prime rib.

Sutter Creek Palace $$$ *76 Main St; tel: (209) 267-1300; www.thesuttercreekpalace.com. Open Fri–Tue.* Known for steaks and the appearance of occasional ghosts in the Victorian dining room.

YOSEMITE NATIONAL PARK

ℹ **Yosemite Valley Visitor Center** *Yosemite Village; tel: (209) 372-0200. Open summer daily 0900–1900.*

Tuolumne Meadows Visitor Center *Tuolumne Meadows; tel: (209) 372-0263. Open early summer–Sept.*

🏛 **Yosemite National Park $$** *PO Box 577; tel: 209-372-0200; www.nps.gov/yose*

◑ **Accommodation** *Delaware North Companies Parks & Resorts at Yosemite; tel: (801) 559-4884; www. yosemitepark.com*

Yosemite has been the target of adoring adjectives since the 1850s – all of them pertaining to waterfalls cascading down sheer, ½-mile-high granite walls, meadows laced with oak, cedar and maple trees, stupendous stands of sequoia redwoods and mountain vistas punctuated by rocky domes and spires.

The only problem is that the most famous sights, **Half Dome, El Capitan, Yosemite Falls, Bridalveil Fall** and more, are in Yosemite Valley. Nearly all of the 3.7 million-plus people who come to Yosemite each year come to Yosemite Valley. The rest of the park is practically deserted, including hiking trails barely beyond shouting distance of the gridlocked valley floor.

If possible, *don't* visit the valley in summer, but if you absolutely must come during high season, park your car, hire a bicycle (about $20 per day) and bypass the traffic jams. Free shuttles make non-stop loops around the valley from 0700 to 2200 in summer, an even easier alternative to driving. The main visitor centre, as well as most accommodation, restaurants and services, are in **Yosemite Village**.

Instead of crawling through the valley, visit **Glacier Point**. The view is better than anything in the valley, spanning **Vernal Fall, Nevada**

Fall, **Little Yosemite Valley**, **Yosemite Falls** and more. The vista is even better in winter, when the only access is by ski or snowshoe. The 60 miles across Yosemite National Park from **Crane Flat** over **Tioga Pass** and down to **Lee Vining** is one of California's best short drives, threading through lush alpine meadows along the spine of the Sierra Nevada. The road is usually closed by snow in October or November and seldom reopens before the end of May.

Accommodation and food in Yosemite National Park

All accommodation in Yosemite National Park is run by DNC Parks & Resorts at Yosemite. Advance bookings are essential April–September and at weekends and during holidays all year *(tel: (801) 559-4884; www.yosemitepark.com)*. Valley choices include **The Ahwahnee $$$**, motel-like **Yosemite Lodge at the Falls $$** and several clusters of tent-cabins, cabins and campsites. Choices at the south end of the park include the **Wawona Hotel $$$** and camping. Towns surrounding the park also offer accommodation.

Eating choices within Yosemite are limited to the same concessionaire-operated facilities, ranging from posh at **The Ahwahnee $$$** to fast food and supermarket fare.

Right
Yosemite National Park's
Bridalveil Fall

Suggested tour

1 **Grass Valley**
Nevada County
Chamber of
Commerce 248 Mill St;
tel: (530) 273-4667 or
(800) 655-4667; www.
grassvalleychamber.com.
Open Mon–Fri 0900–1700,
Sat 1000–1500.

2 **The Northstar**
Mine Powerhouse
& Pelton Wheel
Museum $ Across Hwy 49;
tel: (530) 273-4255;
www.nevadacountyhistory.org
/htmls/northstar.html. Open
May–Oct daily 1000–1700.

3 **Nevada City**
Chamber of
Commerce 132 Main St;
tel: (530) 265-2692 or
(800) 655-6569; www.
nevadacitychamber.com.
Open Mon–Fri 0900–1700,
Sat 1100–1600, Sun
1100–1500.

4 **Firehouse No 1**
Museum $ 215 Main
St; tel: (530) 265-5468;
www.nevadacountyhistory.
org/FirehouseMuseum.aspx.
Open May–Oct daily
1300–1600.

Miners Foundry
Cultural Center 325
Spring St; tel: (530) 265-
5040; www.minersfoundry.
org. Museum open Mon–Fri
0900–1600. Free.

Total distance: 175 miles.

Time: Two days, plus at least one night in Yosemite.

Links: Lake Tahoe to the north, Spine of the Sierra to the east.

Route: From **SACRAMENTO ①**, take I-80 east across the flat Sacramento Valley **②** to AUBURN **③** and the foothills of the **Sierra Nevada ④**. Follow Hwy 49 south through Gold Country to COLOMA **⑤**, where gold was discovered in 1848, PLACERVILLE **⑥**, PLYMOUTH **⑦**, JACKSON **⑧**, SAN ANDREAS **⑨**, ANGELS CAMP **⑩**, COLUMBIA **⑪**, SONORA **⑫**, JAMESTOWN **⑬** and MARIPOSA **⑭**. Turn east on Hwy 140 to the canyon of the Merced River and follow the river into YOSEMITE NATIONAL PARK **⑮**, or take Hwy 120 from south of Jamestown to **Groveland ⑯** and head for Yosemite **⑰**.

Detour 1: Grass Valley and Nevada City prospered on deep mines drilled by immigrants from Cornwall and other European mining centres; Cornish pasties remain a local speciality. Follow Hwy 49 north from Auburn to Nevada City; either return to Auburn on Hwy 49 or take scenic Hwy 20 to I-80 and loop back to Auburn.

Grass Valley grubbed more than $400 million in bullion from tunnels beneath the town. **Empire Mine State Historic Park** $ (*10791 E. Empire St; tel: (530) 273-8522; www.parks.ca.gov. Open Mar–Nov daily; Dec–Feb Thur–Mon*) has tours of the mine entrance, the 1850 owner's home, formal gardens and other buildings. The **Northstar Mine Powerhouse & Pelton Wheel Museum** is one of the most comprehensive mining museums in the Mother Lode.

Nevada City, 4 miles north, is quieter and more scenic. Don't miss admiring the filagree-balconied **National Hotel** (*211 Broad St; tel: (530) 265-4551*). The white wedding-cake **Firehouse No 1 Museum** has pioneer relics, including Donner Party artefacts (*see page 34*). The **Miners Foundry Cultural Center** is an arts centre. **Malakoff Diggins State Historic Park** $ (*54-mile return trip; Hwy 49 11 miles to Tyler Foot Crossing Rd, turn right for 17 miles and follow the signs; tel: (530) 265-2740; www.parks.ca.gov*) is a rust-red badlands created by mining that washed away entire mountains.

Detour 2: Follow Hwy 88 east from Jackson to **Indian Grinding Rock State Historic Park** $ (*14881 Pine Grove–Volcano Rd; tel: (209) 296-7488; www.parks.ca.gov. Call for hours*). The park protects an immense limestone slab with nearly 1,200 holes worn by generations of Miwok women grinding meal, a reconstructed Miwok village, the **Chaw'Se Regional Indian Museum** (*Open Thur–Mon*) and primitive camping in bark houses.

Less than 2 miles away, **Volcano's Daffodil Hill** turns golden with more than 300,000 daffodils in March and April.

Also worth exploring

This backroads route to Columbia passes two of California's finest public caves. **Mercer Caverns $$** (*tel: (209) 728-2101; www. mercercaverns.com. Open daily, call for hours; arrive early for tour time and be prepared for stair climbing*) is an intimate hole filled with dripping stalactites, towering stalagmites, congealed waterfalls and delicate strands of limestone pasta. **Moaning Cavern $$** (*5350 Moaning Cave Rd, Vallecito; tel: (866) 762-2837 or (209) 736-2708; www.caverntours.com. Call for hours*) has a free-standing 234-step spiral staircase; the more adventurous explorers can abseil 165ft to the bottom. The moaning emanates from bottle-shaped holes at the bottom of the cave. A zipline entertains above ground.

    Murphys is centred around the 1865 **Murphys Historic Hotel $$** (*457 Main St; tel: (800) 532-7684 or (209) 728-3444; www.murphyshotel.com*), temporary home to Mark Twain, Brett Harte, J P Morgan, Horatio Alger and other Gold Rush luminaries who left bullets in the woodwork. Galleries and wine-tasting rooms are legion.

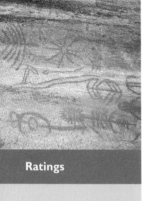

Sequoia and Kings Canyon National Parks

Ratings

Children	●●●●●
Outdoor activities	●●●●●
Scenery	●●●●●
Geology	●●●●○
History	●●●●○
Wildlife	●●●○○
Architecture	●○○○○
Food	●○○○○

These two contiguous parks contain some of California's most spectacular mountain scenery, from the biggest living things on earth to vast tracts of Sierra Nevada wilderness. The human-made attractions of Sequoia and Kings Canyon are warnings: valleys filled with rotting stumps larger than houses, fallen logs big enough to support a car, awe-inspiring views very nearly turned into theme-park ski-runs. Tortuous trails lead eastwards over the spine of the Sierra to Mount Whitney and the Owens Valley, but innumerable easier paths wandering a few miles into the wilderness are an indelible introduction to the glories of outdoor California.

BOYDEN CAVERN

Festooned with marble draperies, stalactites and stalagmites, the interior of Boyden Cavern $$ (*Hwy 180, 22 miles northeast of Grant Grove, Kings Canyon NP in Sequoia National Monument; tel: (866) 762-2837 or (559) 338-0959; www.caverntours.com/BoydenRt.htm. Open May–Oct; call for tour times*) is a constant 55°F (13°C), which sends birds, small animals and underdressed tourists into quick hibernation. Walking, rappelling and canyoneering tours are offered. Entrance through Sequoia National Park requires separate admission charges to the park and Boyden Cavern.

CRYSTAL CAVE

Crystal Cave $ is more difficult to reach. Vehicles over 22ft are prohibited on the access road and a steep ½-mile trail leads from the car park to the cave entrance. Marble stalactites, stalagmites and

Sequoia and Kings Canyon National Parks

flowstone adorn the chilly 48°F (9°C) caverns (*off General's Hwy, 8 miles south of Giant Forest (Sequoia National Park); tel: (559) 565-3759; www.sequoiahistory.org/cave/cave.htm. Open mid-May–Oct daily*). Day-of-tour advance tickets required from Foothills Visitor Center or Lodgepole Visitor Center (*see pages 241 and 242*).

FRESNO

ℹ Fresno Convention and Visitors Bureau, Water Tower Visitor Center
2444 Fresno St; tel: (559) 445-8300 or (800) 788-0836; http://playfresno.org. Open Mon–Fri 1100–1500, Sat 1100–1400.

The agricultural heart of California is blazing in summer and blanketed by thick fogs in winter. A third of all US-grown grapes and over half the figs, cotton, nectarines and turkeys come from local farms.

The **Fresno Art Museum $** (*2233 N. 1st St (Radio Park); tel: (559) 441-4221; www.fresnoartmuseum.org. Open Thur–Sun 1200–1600*) has collections of French Post-Impressionist prints as well as American, Asian and Mexican art and sculpture.

Forestiere Underground Gardens (*5021 W. Shaw Ave; tel: (559) 271-0734; www.undergroundgardens.com*) is an underground labyrinth of 50-odd rooms created between 1905 and 1946 to protect fruit orchards and other crops from the blistering summer sun. Descendants of builder Baldassare Forestiere conduct the tours.

The **Kearney Mansion Museum $** (*Fresno Historical Society; 7160 W. Kearney Blvd; tel: (559) 441-0862; www.valleyhistory.org. Open Fri–Sun for*

ⓕ Forestiere Underground Gardens $$ *5021 W. Shaw Ave; tel: (559) 271-0734; www. undergroundgardens.info. Open Apr–Nov, call for hours.*

Meux Home Museum $ *1007 R St; tel: (559) 233-8007; www.meux.mus.ca.us. Open Fri–Sun 1200–1530.*

tours 1300, 1400, 1500) began as an opulent French Renaissance-style mansion for turn-of-the-20th-century raisin mogul M Theo Kearney. Kearney's extensive canal system introduced industrial-scale vineyards and orchards to Fresno.

Meux Home Museum brought Fresno the latest in urban elegance, 1889-style. The town's first two-storey home and the first embellished with Victorian finery, it remains Fresno's most stylish building.

Ask for details of the **William Saroyan Walking Tour** *(from the William Saroyan Society; tel: (559) 221-1441; www.williamsaroyansociety. org)*, which explores many of the sites used by native son and novelist William Saroyan in his tales of Armenian immigrant life in America. Saroyan is best known for *The Human Comedy* and the stage play *The Time of Your Life*.

KINGS CANYON NATIONAL PARK

ⓘ Kings Canyon Park Visitor Center *Grant Grove Village; tel: (559) 565-4307. Open daily, call for hours.*

Cedar Grove Visitor Center *Next to Sentinel Campground; tel: (559) 565-3793. Open late May–early Sept daily.*

ⓕ Kings Canyon National Park $ *Sequoia and Kings Canyon National Parks, Three Rivers; tel: (559) 565-3341; www.nps/gov/seki*

The park is named after a gaping canyon ripped into the salt-and-pepper granite of the High Sierra by the raging torrent of the Kings River, then gouged into a broad valley by ponderous glaciers. Just downstream from the confluence of the middle and south forks of the Kings River, the canyon plunges 8,200ft from the peak of Spanish Mountain, the deepest gorge in North America.

Kings Canyon's most popular attractions are concentrated around Grant Grove. Just one road penetrates the park proper, the Kings Canyon

Right
Kings Canyon Highway

Highway (*Hwy 180*), open only in summer. From the flat river meadow at Roads End, canyon cliffs soar nearly another mile straight up.

Cedar Grove is as close as Kings Canyon comes to civilisation. The seasonal village and visitor centre are named after surrounding groves of incense cedars. The flat valley floor is ideal for leisurely cycling 5 miles to Roads End.

The 'U' shape of Kings Canyon, the unmistakable sign of past glacial activity, is most obvious from **Canyon Viewpoint** (*1 mile east of Cedar Grove*). The 'V' shape of the lower canyon, beyond the reach of glaciers, is typical of canyons carved by rivers.

Knapp's Cabin (*1 mile east of the viewpoint*) stored equipment for opulent fishing expeditions staged by Santa Barbara businessman George Knapp during the 1920s. One mile east of the cabin is the car park for **Roaring River Falls**. An easy 5-minute paved path leads to the Falls, roaring (and sometimes trickling) through a narrow granite chute.

The 1½-mile loop trail through **Zumwalt Meadow** is one of the most scenic walks in either park. The trail crosses a suspension bridge to a view over the grassy meadow and **North Dome** (8,717ft), then descends through the meadow. Expect to see a variety of birds, as well as a profusion of wild flowers – leopard lilies, shooting stars, violets, Indian paintbrush, lupins and others, depending on the season. Pick up a self-guiding map at the visitor centre.

Just beyond is **Grand Sentinel Viewpoint**, with clear views of one of the most striking rock formations in the area, the Grand Sentinel (8,504ft).

Roads End is the literal end of the road and the start of a vast network of trails. Gruelling tracks cross the Sierra over passes above 11,000ft and into the Owens Valley (*see page 114*). The 9-mile return hike to **Mist Falls** is an easier glimpse of the backcountry. The sandy trail is relatively flat, but gains 600ft in the final mile to the largest waterfall in the twin parks. Allow between 4 and 6 hours.

Return to Cedar Grove on the road, or, more interestingly, via the **Motor Nature Trail** on the north side of the river. The rough corrugated road is passable by passenger vehicles but is *not* recommended for RVs.

Grant Grove is administratively part of Kings Canyon National Park, but the dense stand of sequoia, sugar pine, incense cedar, black oak and mountain dogwood looks more like Sequoia National Park. The grove is named after the **General Grant Tree**, officially the world's third-largest giant sequoia and the nation's Christmas Tree at 267ft tall and 107ft in circumference. A ⅓-mile paved path wanders through the grove. Most of the major trees have been fenced off to protect their shallow root systems from trampling by enthusiastic crowds.

The trail also passes the **Fallen Monarch**, which has been a house and a stable, and the **Gamlin Cabin**, a rebuilt 1872 loggers' cabin. A quieter alternative is the seldom-visited **North Grove Loop**, a 1½-mile trail from the Grant Grove car park. The 1½-mile **Dead Giant Loop** (*lower end of Grant Grove car park*) passes a historical lumber mill pond on the way to a giant sequoia that was killed by girdling, or cutting through the living cambium layer (just beneath the bark), which cut the flow of nutrients to the tree. The walk offers an instructive comparison between the ways national park and national forest lands are managed.

Big Stump Basin (*Hwy 180, 2½ miles southwest of the visitor centre*) is just what the name suggests, a valley filled with gigantic stumps – how Grant Grove would appear today had early loggers been allowed to continue. A self-guiding 1-mile **loop trail** highlights regenerating sequoias and other natural features.

The **Mark Twain Stump** is what remains of a giant sequoia felled in 1891 so sections could be displayed in the American Museum of Natural History in New York and the British Museum in London. A similar tree-cutting exercise was conducted for the 1876 Centennial Exhibition in Philadelphia.

The **Kings Canyon Highway** runs from Grant Grove to Cedar Grove. Much of the road follows the canyon of the Kings River, here a sharp 'V' filled with the rushing boom of the river. The sheer granite walls are laced with blue marble, pocked with yellow yucca plants and splattered with green and orange lichen, more easily visible beyond **Junction View**. Numerous lay-bys offer excellent views of the canyon and high Sierra peaks rising in the distance.

Panoramic Point is one of the most accessible vistas across the spine of the high Sierra, with **Lake Hume** to the north below. The 5-mile return **Park Ridge Trail** offers views from the high peaks to the east down the descending western ranges into the Central Valley.

Accommodation and food in Kings Canyon National Park

All accommodation is booked through **Sequoia-Kings Canyon Park Services Company**, *PO Box 907, Kings Canyon National Park; tel: (559) 335-5500 or (866) 522-6966; www.sequoia-kingscanyon.com*

John Muir Lodge $$ is open all year; **Cedar Grove Lodge $$** is open May–October and **Grant Grove Cabins $$**, both rustic and tent, are open in summer. Accommodation is also available outside the park, including **Stony Creek Lodge $$$**. Advance booking is necessary all year.

In summer, picnic supplies and restaurant meals are available in **Cedar Grove Village $$** and **Grant Grove Village $$**. Grant Grove stays open in winter. There are no petrol stations in the park, but Stony Creek Village and Kings Canyon Lodge have a limited supply at premium prices.

SEQUOIA NATIONAL PARK

ⓘ Sequoia National Park $ *Sequoia and Kings Canyon National Parks, Three Rivers; tel: (559) 565-3341; www.nps/gov/seki*

ⓘ Foothills Visitor Center *Generals Highway and Hwy 198; tel: (559) 565-4212. Open summer daily.*

ⓠ Free summertime Sequoia National Park shuttles provide easy access to main areas: Green shuttle line: Giant Forest Museum–Wuksachi; Gray shuttle line: Giant Forest Museum–Crescent Meadow–Moro Rock. A 2-hour shuttle $ *(tel: (877) 287-4453; www.ci.visalia. ca.us/depts/transit/sequoia_ shuttle/general_info.asp)* from Visalia saves driving and fuel.

Sequoia has a variety of natural attractions, from caves and Mount Whitney to alpine meadows and crashing rivers – all of which pale next to the dense stands of giant sequoia redwood trees (*Sequoiadendron giganteum*), the largest living things on earth.

Sequoia was created in 1890 to protect these massive trees, then in danger of extinction by logging. **Big Stump Basin**, near the entrance to Kings Canyon National Park, and the **Generals Highway**, which leads to Sequoia National Park, is the result of still-current logging techniques.

Three-mile **Crescent Meadow Rd** leaves the main road from the former Giant Forest Village. The scenic detour passes several famous sites, but is not recommended for RVs. **Auto Log**, a sequoia felled and flattened for drive-on passenger cars, gives visitors a sense of just how huge sequoias can grow. A set of nearly 400 concrete steps leads 300ft up the side of **Moro Rock** (6,725ft) and to a splendid 360-degree view stretching 150 miles from the spine of the Sierra to the Central Valley – save the staircase climb for clear days when valley vistas are visible rather than swathed in haze.

Tunnel Log fell across the road in 1937; crews cut an 8ft-high tunnel through the log the next summer. A bypass accommodates taller vehicles. **Crescent Meadow**, like most naturally grassy areas in the park, is actually a marsh, too wet to support sequoias and other trees. A flat 1½-mile trail circles the meadow to **Tharp's Log**, a sequoia

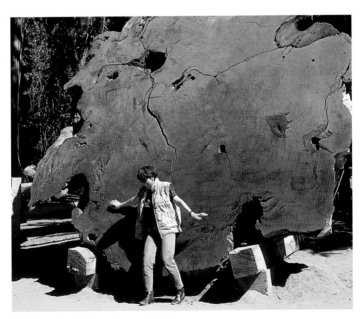

Right
A few centuries of growth – section through a giant sequoia tree

ℹ️ **Lodgepole Visitor Center** *2 miles north of General Sherman Tree;* tel: *(559) 565-4436. Open early spring–late autumn; winter Sat–Sun, call for hours.*

Mineral King Ranger Station *24 miles up Mineral King Rd. Open approximately May–Sept daily.*

Giant Forest Village

Giant Forest Village was Sequoia's original centre for visitor services. Recognising that the year-round pounding of traffic and visitors was harming Giant Forest trees, the US Park Services removed accommodation and other services to **Wuksachi**, near the **Lodgepole Visitor Center**, in 1998 and 1999. Car parks and **Giant Forest Museum** *(tel: (559) 565-4480)* remain, but most of the Village site is being re-seeded and returned to the Giant Forest.

hollowed into a cabin for Hale Tharp, who grazed sheep in the meadow in the 1850s. **Chimney Tree** is a still-living sequoia hollowed out by fire; look inside from the base to see blue sky through the crown. The **John Muir Trail**, which follows the crest of the Sierra Nevada, crosses 71 rugged miles to Mount Whitney.

Giant Forest (*30 miles from Big Stump Entrance, 16 miles from Ash Mountain Entrance*) was named by John Muir. Four of the largest known sequoias grow in this grove. Most visitors spend their time staring in awe at named trees and dodging other visitors. Fortunately, the many hiking trails through Giant Forest provide a serene, almost deserted introduction to the 8,000 or so mature sequoias in the area.

The biggest of them all is the **General Sherman Tree**, 275ft tall and 103ft in circumference. The trunk alone contains more than 52,000 cubic feet of wood, but with so many other slightly less monstrous trees nearby, it's hard to grasp General Sherman's extraordinary dimensions. One of the best easy walks is the 2-mile paved **Congress Trail** (*from the Sherman Tree*); pick up a self-guiding trail guide at the Sherman tree or the **Lodgepole Visitor Center**, just north.

Hospital Rock (*5 miles beyond Ash Grove Entrance towards Giant Forest*) marks an ancient Native American village site. Look for **pictographs** on surrounding boulders and 71 mortar holes once used to grind acorns and seeds into flour.

Mineral King (*turn off 5 miles north of Three Rivers; no RVs or trailers*) is a scalloped bowl at 7,800ft, the only bit of the park's Sierra high country accessible by vehicle. Walt Disney tried to turn the scenic bowl into a ski resort in 1965. Thirteen litigious years later, it was added to Sequoia National Park instead.

Seven hundred-odd twists and turns in 25 miles of part-paved, part-gravel road discourage most visitors, but the summer-only route along the East Fork of the Kaweah River is worth the time, the driving effort and the occasional terror of meeting another vehicle on a blind corner with neither verge nor guardrail.

Silver City has general supplies, petrol and food, but the only facilities in Mineral King itself are a seasonal ranger station and a basic campsite. Hiking into the golden **Sawtooth Mountains** to the east is superb. The ¼-mile **Cold Springs Nature Trail** is a less strenuous alternative.

Accommodation and food in Sequoia National Park

Sequoia National Park campgrounds
www.nps.gov/seki/ planyourvisit/campgrounds. htm. Gives details of the advance reservation procedure for the Lodgepole and Dorst Creek campgrounds.

The Sequoia High Sierra Camp $$$ *Giant Sequoia National Monument; tel: (866) 654-2877; www. sequoiahighsierracamp.com, operates mid-Jun–early Oct.* Rates include well-appointed canvas tent cabins and three daily meals

The park hotel, restaurants and other commercial services, including **Wuksachi Lodge $$$**, open all year, are operated by **Delaware North Companies Parks & Resorts at Sequoia, Inc.** (*PO Box 89; tel: (866) 807-3598; www.visitsequoia.com*). There are seven campsites in Sequoia National Park; three are open year-round. Only two campsites, Lodgepole and Dorst Creek, can be reserved in advance. Intrepid hikers go 11½ miles into the Sierra backcountry and stay at **Bear Paw High Sierra Camp $$$** (*www.visitsequoia.com/bearpaw.aspx*) tent cabins.

Montecito-Sequoia Lodge $$–$$$ (*63410 Hwy 180 (Generals Hwy) between Sequoia and Kings Canyon; reservations, tel: (800) 227-9900; www.mslodge.com*) is open all year, as are motels in the town of **Three Rivers** (*Hwy 180, south of Ash Mountain Entrance*).

Silver City Mountain Resort $$–$$$ (*tel: (559) 561-3223 (summer)* or *(559) 734-4109 (winter); www.silvercityresort.com*) has cabins and chalets on the road to Mineral King in summer.

Meals and picnic supplies are available in Wuksachi Village, Lodgepole and Montecito-Sequoia all year. **Silver City Bakery and Restaurant $$** near Mineral King and an adjoining general store are open in summer.

In 2000, US President Bill Clinton proclaimed a section of national forest south of Sequoia National Park's former Giant Forest Village as **Giant Sequoia National Monument**. The forest service, the timber industry and environmentalists have been at odds over logging in the monument. The monument is accessible from Kernville, near Lake Isabella east of Bakersfield. For information, contact the **Sequoia National Forest** office (*tel: (559) 784-1500; www.fs.fed.us/r5/sequoia/ gsnm.html*). A major draw is the **Trail of a Hundred Giants** within a 355-acre grove (*www.kernvalley.com/news/trail100.htm*). The **Sequoia High Sierra Camp** is open in mid-June–early October for hiking and fly fishing.

Giant Sequoias

Sequoiadendron gigantea aren't the tallest living things – coastal redwoods top them by 100ft – nor the largest around – a Montezuma cypress in Oaxaca, Mexico, has a larger girth. But in sheer volume, giant sequoia redwoods are the largest living things on earth, and Sequoia National Park has more of them than anywhere else.

Sequoias have high tannin levels that discourage insects and rot; bark nearly 3ft thick is impervious to fire. Even if the heartwood burns away, the tree can survive. The intense heat releases its tiny seeds and burns away brush that would compete with its seedlings.

The sequoia's weakness is its roots, which penetrate only 3–5ft into the soil. High winds or heavy snows can topple the top-heavy giants. Foot or vehicle traffic atop the fragile roots can further weaken the trees.

Cascade Volcanoes

Ratings

Geology	●●●●●
Scenery	●●●●●
Lakes	●●●●
Waterfalls	●●●●
Children	●●●
Steam trains	●●●
Walking	●●●
Wildlife	●●●

California's Cascade peaks, Lassen and Shasta, begin a string of active volcanoes stretching north into British Columbia. This jumble of volcanic peaks, razor-edged river valleys and deep forests is one of California's most alluring – and forbidding – natural areas. Don't be deceived by mild Sacramento Valley weather. A few miles east – and a few thousand feet up – temperatures can drop to freezing in any month. The highway through Lassen Volcanic National Park is closed in winter, though snowploughs keep most other paved roads open.

The Sierra Nevada volcanoes are largely dormant, but the Cascades are very much alive. Mount Shasta last erupted around 1786, but steam vents near the peak are still hot. Lassen Peak erupted between 1915 and 1917, the most recent eruption in the continental US until Mount St Helens (in southern Washington State) blew up in 1980. Bookmakers aren't fixing odds, but geologists are betting on another major California eruption in the next few centuries.

CASTLE CRAGS

Castle Crags State Park *Castella exit from I-5; tel: (530) 235-2684; www.parks.ca.gov. Ranger station usually open summer and weekends.*

The granite ramparts of Castle Crags rise dramatically from the west side of I-5, resembling the remnants of some enormous castle wall towering more than 4,000ft above. A narrow road twists 2 miles from the park entrance to a wooded **Vista Point** and a cluster of picnic tables with unobstructed views of the Crags and Mount Shasta. The best views are late in the day (Mount Shasta) and early morning (Castle Crags), when the setting sun casts a rich, smouldering glow.

DUNSMUIR

The railway made Dunsmuir a popular mountain resort between the 1920s and 1940s, known as much for its wonderful fly fishing and mineral water as the pristine mountain scenery and a cinema palace called the California Theater. Celebrities pulled into town by the carriage-load, from baseball home-run king Babe Ruth to Hollywood

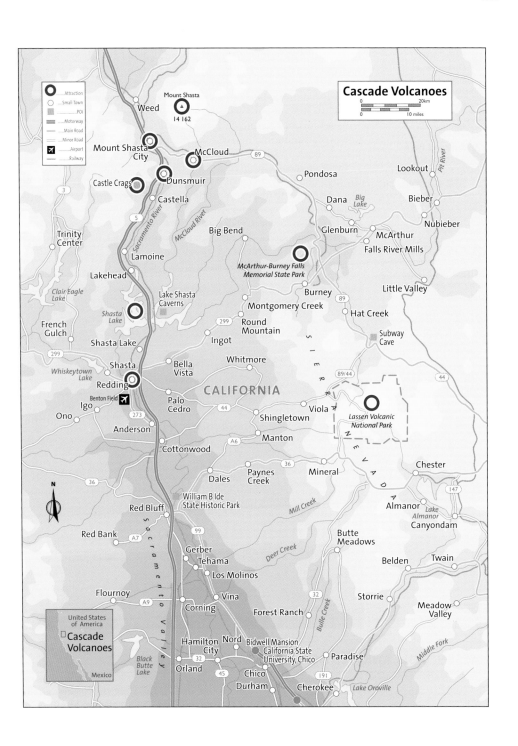

Cascade Volcanoes

Dunsmuir Chamber of Commerce and Visitors Center *5915 Dunsmuir Ave, Ste 100; tel: (530) 235-2177 or (800) 386-7684; www.dunsmuir.com*

Railroad Park Resort *$$ 100 Railroad Park Rd; tel: (530) 235-4440; www.rrpark.com.* Features accommodation in boxcars with bay windows or rooftop cupolas.

Café Maddalena *$$ 5801 Sacramento Ave; tel: (530) 235-2725; www.cafemaddalena.com. Open mid-Feb–Dec Thur–Sun for dinner.* Serves Mediterranean dishes to rival anything San Francisco can offer.

luminary Clark Gable. As more powerful diesel-electric locomotives replaced steam in the 1950s, Dunsmuir sank into obscurity.

Once I-5 bypassed the town in 1961, most of California forgot it ever existed, until 1991, when the railway put Dunsmuir back in the spotlight. A Southern Pacific train derailed, spilling tank cars loaded with a powerful herbicide into the Sacramento River. The poison killed everything in the river for 45 miles downstream into Shasta Lake, and nearly killed off the town.

The Sacramento River eventually recovered. So did Dunsmuir, with the help of a hefty financial settlement from the railway. Trophy-sized trout returned to the river while the town refurbished and rebuilt Dunsmuir and Sacramento Aves.

Don't miss **Hedge Creek Falls** (*north edge of town, Frontage Rd*), a 30ft waterfall cutting through basaltic lava that once flowed down the slopes of Mount Shasta. A gazebo next to the trailhead offers a pleasant view of the Sacramento River Canyon.

Right
Marsh and mountain in Lassen Volcanic National Park

LASSEN VOLCANIC NATIONAL PARK

Lassen Peak is the southernmost link in the Cascade volcano chain that runs through **Mount Shasta** and **Lava Beds National Monument** in California, north to British Columbia. It is also one of California's least-visited national parks, an eerie, volcanic landscape that is virtually devoid of people, even at the height of summer.

Lassen Peak, the mountain (10,457ft), is a fraction of **Lassen Volcanic National Park**, 100,000 jumbled acres where Cascade volcanoes meet the Sierra Nevada. Prominent features include Lassen Peak and smaller volcanoes, as well as mud pots, fumaroles, hot springs, boiling lakes, emerald-green meadows and stupendous wildflower displays – and that's just what's visible from the highway. Drive slowly (the speed limit is 35mph) and buy the *Road Guide to Lassen Volcanic National Park* ($) at park entrances.

Unfortunately, the road, Hwy 89, is covered by 50ft of snow in winter. From November to June, it's possible to explore both the north (from Redding) and south (from Red Bluff) edges of the park, but the only permitted forms of transport across this road in winter are snowshoes and cross-country skis.

From the north, the **Loomis Museum** covers regional geology and history. Lassen erupted around 1700, creating the **Chaos Crags**, which were still steaming in 1850, and a vast rockfield called the **Chaos Jumbles**. The mountain went into violent action in 1914, with an earth-shattering eruption in 1915 and small bursts that continued through 1921. The 1915 eruption blasted boulders to Reno, Nevada, shot a plume of dust 25,000ft into the air and cast a pall over Sacramento. Time and advancing vegetation have hidden most visible signs of that last eruption. The best views are from the ½-mile **Devastation Trail** (*Road Marker 44*).

Park rangers lead free naturalist June–August programmes (guided walks and hikes), and January–April snowshoe programmes. There are also many self-guiding walks. Remember, though, that nature has a thin skin in Lassen – literally. Most areas of visible thermal activity are vast pools of boiling mud covered by a solid-seeming, but fragile, crust.

One of Lassen's otherworldly sights, **Bumpass Hell** (*3 miles return from Marker 17*), is named after an early Danish explorer who put a foot through the crust and saw his leg cook before he could pull away. *Stay on marked trails and boardwalks!*

One of the best high hikes is the 5-mile return **Lassen Peak Trail** (*5 hours from Marker 22*), a windy, sun-blasted trail that gains 2,000ft. Bring sunblock, a hat and plenty of water. An easier 7½-mile return trail climbs **Brokeoff Mountain** near the south entrance. The peak is 1,200ft lower than Lassen, but the trail is shaded until the summit.

Best stops for non-hikers are **Manzanita Lake** and **Reflection Lake** (*near the north entrance*), which provide serene reflections of Lassen Peak in late afternoon. Thousands of 19th-century migrants walked **Nobles Emigrant Trail** (*Marker 60*) through the park. The trail can be seen through the chaparral to the northeast. Beyond the **Devastation Area**, look for trees with a curve at their base, the 'snow bend', caused by winter snows bending the trees as saplings.

Deep blue **Lake Helen**, between the Lassen Peak and Bumpass Hell car parks, is frozen white at least eight months of the year. The lake was named after Helen Brodt, the first woman known to have climbed Lassen Peak. Lassen's most accessible thermal field is **The Sulphur Works**, a miniature Bumpass Hell near the south entrance. An easy boardwalk winds past small mud pots and fumaroles.

Accommodation and food near Mount Lassen

☽ Drakesbad Guest Ranch *California Guest Services; tel: (530) 529-1512 or (866) 999-0914; www.drakesbad.com.* A national historic landmark.

Sleeping in the park means camping. For a real roof (all must be booked well in advance), try **Hat Creek Resort $$** (*Hwys 44 and 89, Old Station; tel: (530) 335-7121; www.hatcreekresortrv.com; year-round*); **Lassen Mineral Lodge $$** (*Hwy 36 E., Mineral; tel: (530) 595-4422; www.minerallodge.com*); cabins at **Rim Rock Ranch $$** (*13275 Hwy 89, Old Station; tel: (530) 335-7114; www.rimrockcabins.com*); or secluded **Drakesbad Guest Ranch $$$** (*Warner Valley Rd, Chester*). Most visitors drive up from Redding or Red Bluff. The only food in the park is at **Manzanita Lake $$** (*north entrance*) and at the **Kohm Yah-mah-nee Visitor Center** restaurant.

Right
Burney Falls

McArthur-Burney Falls Memorial State Park

McArthur-Burney Falls Memorial State Park $ 24898 Hwy 89, Burney; tel: (530) 335-2777; www.parks.ca.gov. Open year-round for camping and day use.

The 129ft double cataract of **Burney Falls** cuts through millions of years of moss-covered lava flows in a lush conifer forest. Halfway between Shasta and Lassen, the Falls, like the rest of the region, owe their existence to volcanoes. Shasta, Lassen and other Cascade peaks are noted for their explosive power, generated when thick, sticky lava builds up pressure in underground chambers until it blasts through to the surface.

Shield volcanoes such as these begin life belching a mixture of magma, superheated steam and other gases. Magma shoots into the air, cools quickly and falls back to earth to form steep-sided hills called cinder cones. In later stages, lava floods from vents in vast sheets, building up successive layers called shields. Hwy 89 between Lake Britton and the park entrance cuts through a shield, as do the Falls.

An easy 1-mile **Falls Trail Loop** winds to the bottom of the Falls and back up. The slightly more difficult 1½-mile **Headwaters Loop** passes the point where underground rivers emerge to feed the Falls. **Lake Britton**, a reservoir popular for fishing, swimming and boating, is a 1-mile walk or 1½ miles by road (Hwy 89) from the park entrance.

McCloud

McCloud Chamber of Commerce 205 Quincy St; tel: (530) 964-3113; www.mccloudchamber.com

McCloud Ranger District 2019 Forest Rd, Hwy 89 east of McCloud; tel: (530) 964-2184. Open summer Mon–Sat 0800–1630; rest of the year Mon–Fri 0800–1630.

McCloud Railway and Shasta Sunset Dinner Train $$–$$$ Across from the McCloud post office; tel: (530) 964-2142; www.shastasunset.com. Offers Jun–Dec excursions.

McCloud looks much as it did in 1965, when the McCloud River Lumber Company abandoned the town it had built. Heavy winter snows can cut power and phone lines for days, but urban refugees have revitalised a town that most expected to die.

Among McCloud's most popular attractions are the Upper, Middle and Lower **Falls of the McCloud River** (*near River Loop Rd and Fowlers Campground off Hwy 89, 5 miles east of McCloud*), torrents shooting from crevices in the rock. Lower Falls has carved a deep swimming hole. **Jot Dean Cave** (*9 miles south of Medicine Lake on County Rd 49*), a shallow, collapsed lava tube, is usually cool enough to hold ice in summer but shallow enough to explore without a torch.

The easiest way to enjoy off-road sights is aboard open-air carriages on the **McCloud Railway** Excursion Train, sightseeing trips, or its 3-hour Friday- and Saturday-night **Shasta Sunset Dinner Train**.

Accommodation and food in McCloud

The carefully restored 1916 **McCloud Hotel $$** (*408 Main St; tel: (530) 964-2822 or (800) 964-2823; www.mccloudhotel.com*), a national historic landmark building, was originally company-owned housing for mill workers and town teachers. The hotel now offers bed with breakfast in the garden as an option. The **McCloud River Inn Bed and Breakfast $$–$$$** (*325 Lawndale Ct; tel: (800) 261-7831 or (530) 964-2130; www.riverinn.com*) is a historical five-room Victorian inn.

MOUNT SHASTA AND MOUNT SHASTA CITY

ℹ Mount Shasta Chamber of Commerce and Visitors Bureau *300 Pine St, Mount Shasta; tel: (530) 926-4865 or (800) 926-4865; http://mtshastachamber.com/index.php*

◉ Mount Shasta Ranger Station *204 W. Alma St; tel: (530) 926-4511.*

Below
Serene Mount Shasta

Mount Shasta City is a former railway and lumber centre that has turned its attention to tourists and New Age believers. The latter revere 14,162ft **Mount Shasta** as an energy and spiritual centre inhabited by Limurians, ancient escapees from the lost continent of Mu. The rest of us see the tallest and most spectacular peak in Northern California, the source of the Sacramento River and a climbing challenge.

Mt. Shasta Ski Park (*off Hwy 89; tel: (530) 926-8610 or (800) 754-7427; www.skipark.com*) is a pleasant local ski area in winter, popular with mountain bikers in summer and a lift up the mountain in any season. It's also possible to climb the peak in summer, a strenuous, occasionally fatal, trek. Stop at the **Ranger Station** for advice on climbing, equipment hire or lessons. **Bunny Flat Scenic Trail** (*from Bunny Flat car park*) is a gentle alternative that climbs to Horse Camp, the usual base for peak climbs. A still less strenuous outing is **Mount Shasta City Park** (*north end of town*), where Sacramento River headwaters gush from a lava tube.

Accommodation and food in Mount Shasta

Lily's $$ (*1013 S. Mt Shasta Blvd; tel: (530) 926-3372; www.lilysrestaurant.com. Open daily*) serves Californian food with Asian touches. Best bets for accommodation are the **Mount Shasta Ranch Bed and Breakfast $$** (*1008 W.A. Barr Rd; tel: (530) 926-3870; www.stayinshasta.com*), a 70-year-old ranch, and **Mount Shasta Resort $$** (*1000 Siskiyou Lake Blvd; tel: (800) 958-3363; www.mountshastaresort.com*), a golf resort near Lake Siskiyou.

REDDING

ℹ Redding Convention and Visitors Bureau *777 Auditorium Dr; tel: (800) 874-7562 or (530) 225-4100; www.visitredding.com. Open summer Mon–Fri 0900–1700, Sat 1000–1700; winter Mon–Fri 0900–1700.*

A railway town that never stopped growing, Redding is the primary gateway to mountain escapes in three directions. The top historic sight is **Shasta State Historic Park** (*Hwy 299, 6 miles west; tel: (530) 243-8194; www.parks.ca.gov. Open Thur–Sun 1000–1700*). Originally Shaster, the area's Gold Rush settlement, was the richest, busiest town in the region until the railway route was built in Redding in 1872. The 1861 **County Courthouse** has been restored as an excellent museum.

Turtle Bay Exploration Park
$$ 840 Auditorium Dr; tel: (800) 887-8532; www.turtlebay.org. Call for hours.

The best stop in Redding itself is **Turtle Bay Exploration Park**. The civic complex includes the well-designed **McConnell Arboretum & Botanical Gardens**, 200 acres of oak savanna and wetlands laced with walking paths, **Paul Bunyan's Forest Camp**, which celebrates the logging industry, and the **Turtle Bay Museum** with a river aquarium with trout, native perch and sturgeon, and combined collections from the Redding Museum of Art and History and the Carter House Natural Science Museum. Spanish architect Santiago Calatrava designed the **Sundial Bridge**, a translucent glass and tile-covered concrete pedestrian bridge with a sundial-like support pylon, to connect Turtle Bay Exploration Park to the Sacramento River Trail and with the Mediterranean-climate botanic gardens addition to McConnell Arboretum.

Accommodation and food in Redding

Redding used to be a stop for petrol between the San Francisco Bay Area and Oregon. With the Turtle Bay complex, it has come into its own, but still boasts many moderately priced motels, mostly clustered around I-5 freeway services at Hilltop Dr. **Jack's Grill $$** (*1743 California St; tel: (530) 241-9705; www.jacksgrillredding.com. Open Mon–Sat 1700–2300*) is a Redding institution for 16oz steaks.

SHASTA LAKE

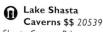

Shasta Lake Visitor Information Center
14250 Holiday Rd, Redding; tel: (530) 275-1589; www.fs.fed.us/r5/shastatrinity/recreation/nra/index.shtml. Open summer.

Shasta Dam Visitor Center Tel: (530) 275-4463; www.shastalake.com/visitorcenters. Open for tours, call for location and hours. Free.

Lake Shasta Caverns $$ 20539 Shasta Caverns Rd, Shasta Dam Blvd exit from I-5; tel: (530) 238-2341 or (800) 795-2283; http://lakeshastacaverns.com. Advance booking required for daily tours.

When full, Shasta Lake has more shoreline than San Francisco Bay. Shasta Lake is used by more than 2 million people every year, many of whom stay in a houseboat, among the world's largest fleet of flat-bottom homes on water. Activities include trout and salmon fishing, jet-skiing, waterskiing, wakeboarding, and hiking around the shore, resulting in a surfeit of whining jet-skis and roaring motorboats near the lake's dozen or so marinas.

Shasta Dam, 3,460ft long at its crest, 602ft high and 883ft thick at the base, contains enough concrete to build a 3ft path around the equator. Behind the dam are five watery arms, stumps of the Sacramento, Pit and McCloud Rivers, dammed for power and irrigation in 1945. The **Visitor Information Center** tells the story of this engineering feat.

It's possible to plumb nature's bowels at **Lake Shasta Caverns**, one of the state's more spectacular caves, complete with 'waterfalls' of solid calcium carbonate, masses of mineral straws that seem to defy gravity and delicate fluted columns. The 2-hour tour begins with a 15-minute catamaran ride across the lake and an 800ft climb by bus before descending into the chilly cave on foot.

Suggested tour

Vulcanism in California

California was born of a 200-million-year collision between North America and the floor of the Pacific Ocean. As the Pacific Plate, one of the great tectonic plates that make up the earth's crust, was forced beneath the North American Plate, islands and mountains scraped off against the edge of the continent. At the same time, a fraction of the titanic forces driving the Pacific Plate downwards escaped to the surface as volcanic activity. The Sierra Nevada mountain range emerged about 170 million years ago, while the Cascade peaks are still emerging.

In Southern California, vulcanism is most obvious around Mammoth Lakes. Devil's Postpile National Monument is an ancient basalt flow that cooled into striking vertical columns. The hot springs dotting the Sierra are fuelled by geothermal activity, including mineral springs that created the striking tufa towers of Mono Lake. Mountains of black volcanic obsidian, once the source of arrowheads, are now used for fine surgical scalpels.

Total distance: 225 miles.

Time: One day with no stops, but three days recommended.

Links: The Gold Country (*see page 224*) and Lake Tahoe (*see page 120*); both lie to the south (follow I-5 to Sacramento, or Hwy 89 to Truckee). The Coast Redwoods (*see page 194*) are to be found by driving due west from Redding.

Route: Take I-5 north from **REDDING**, climbing from soporific Sacramento Valley scenery towards **SHASTA LAKE** ❶, **CASTLE CRAGS** ❷ and the riverside town of **DUNSMUIR** ❸ to **MOUNT SHASTA CITY** ❹, at the base of **MOUNT SHASTA** ❺. Follow scenic Hwy 89 east into the Cascades to the former logging town of **McCLOUD** ❻, then gradually turn south along the federally designated Volcanic Legacy Scenic Byway through lava flows and pine forests to **McARTHUR-BURNEY FALLS MEMORIAL STATE PARK** ❼, **Hat Creek** ❽ and **Old Station** ❾ to **LASSEN VOLCANIC NATIONAL PARK** ❿. In winter, take Hwy 44 west to Redding. In summer, continue south through the park to Hwy 36, then turn west to **Red Bluff** ⓫.

Also worth exploring

Mount Shasta Loop
A network of gravel roads loops around the north and east sides of Mount Shasta, making it possible to circumnavigate the mountain in a single day – but only in good summer weather and never in an RV. Check road conditions and maps before setting out. Local vehicles travel the back roads regularly, but most have high clearance and 4WD. If rangers or the Visitors Bureau advise against the drive, heed their caution – blizzards can occur in summer.

Fortunately, paved roads offer a taste of Mount Shasta's more spectacular north face. Take I-5 north from Mount Shasta City past **Black Butte** ⓬ (6,325ft), a volcanic plug cloaked with broken rock called talus. A 2½-mile trail leads to the peak, with sweeping views of Mount Shasta just east, the Sacramento Valley south, the Klamath Mountains west and **Weed** ⓭ just north. Continue 5½ miles north to the Central Weed exit, Hwy 97.

A lumber baron named Weed picked the windiest spot in the upper Sacramento Valley for a mill so the newly sawn lumber would dry quickly. Hwy 97 bypasses the late 19th-century town centre, which remains largely intact. The best Shasta views lie along the first 15 miles of Hwy 97 between I-5 and Military Pass Rd, just beyond the Hwy 99–Hwy 97 cut-off.

Cascade Volcanoes

- ●..........Attraction
- ○..........Small Town
- ■..........POI
- ━━━..........Motorway
- ━━━..........Main Road
- ━━━..........Minor Road
- ✈..........Airport
- ━━━..........Railway

0 ————— 20km
0 ————— 10 miles

13 Weed
5 Mount Shasta ▲ 14 162
12
4 Mount Shasta
3 McCloud
Castle Crags ■
2 Castella
6 Dunsmuir
Pondosa
Lookout
Pit River
Trinity Center
Lamoine
Dana   Big Lake
Bieber
Nubieber
Castella
Big Bend
Glenburn
McArthur Falls River Mills
Lakehead
7 McArthur - Burney Falls Memorial State Park
Clair Eagle Lake
Shasta Lake
Lake Shasta Caverns
1
Montgomery Creek
Burney
Little Valley
French Gulch
Shasta Lake
Round Mountain
8 Hat Creek
Whiskeytown Lake
Shasta
Ingot
Whitmore
Subway Cave ■
Old Station
Redding
Benton Field ✈
Bella Vista
CALIFORNIA
9
Igo
Palo Cedro
Viola
10 Lassen Volcanic National Park
Ono
Anderson
Shingletown
Manton
Cottonwood
Dales
Paynes Creek
Mineral
Chester
William B Ide State Historic Park
Mill Creek
Almanor   Lake Almanor
Canyondam
Red Bluff
11
Red Bank
Butte Meadows
Belden   Twain
Gerber
Tehama
Deer Creek
Los Molinos
Storrie
Meadow Valley
Flournoy
Vina
Corning
Forest Ranch
Bulle Creek
United States of America
□ Cascade Volcanoes
Hamilton City   Nord
Bidwell Mansion California State University, Chico
Paradise
Middle Fork
Black Butte Lake
Orland
Chico
Durham
Cherokee   Lake Oroville
Mexico

Sacramento River
McCloud River
Shasta Lake
Sacramento Valley
SIERRA NEVADA

N

California Missions

'Always go forward and never look back' was the personal credo espoused by Fra Junípero Serra, the 18th-century Franciscan priest, university professor and missionary who created California.

Serra's missions are California's most visible link to the past, a chain of 21 whitewashed churches that define the state's most important highway as well as its very existence. For despite its secular excesses, modern California was born as a religious enterprise whose branches still flower in popular mythology and architecture.

In 1769, the Spanish crown sent Serra and military commander Gaspar de Portolá to head Spain's first attempt to settle Alta, or upper, California. It was called The Sacred Expedition, a gruelling desert march from Baja (lower) California to San Diego in midsummer.

Serra's mission was simple and direct: Christianise the local tribes, teach them the Spanish language and European mores, put them to work and then start over again until California had been civilised under Spanish rule.

Visiting California's Missions All the missions described here lie off Hwy 101. If time is short, Carmel, La Purísima, San Juan Capistrano, San Luis Rey and Santa Barbara are easily accessible.

User-friendly websites provide historical and cultural information – some even have samples of Native Americans' purported plainsong! Here are some sites to enhance the mission experience: *missions.bgmm.com, www.californiamissions.com, www.ca-missions.org, www.parks.ca.gov/ ?page_id=22722*

History

Serra founded a chain of 21 missions, stretching 600 miles north to Sonoma, just below Russia's southernmost settlement of Fort Ross (*see page 187*). Each outpost was a day's travel from the next, linked by **El Camino Real**, The King's Highway, a rough trail that became Hwy 101. Individual missions flourished and grew wealthy, but the system failed.

Supplies and equipment from Mexico often arrived late or disappeared. Earthquakes levelled adobe buildings. Imported diseases killed Native American converts, called 'neophytes', by the thousands.

The final blow came in 1834, when a then-independent Mexico secularised Church property. Mission holdings were sold or given as land grants. Most of the mission buildings dissolved back into the adobe mud from which they had sprung, surviving only as the names of the towns which had grown up around the long-vanished churches.

Nostalgic 19th-century artists pushed for the missions' restoration, aided by commercial interests, recognising profit in 'Old California'.

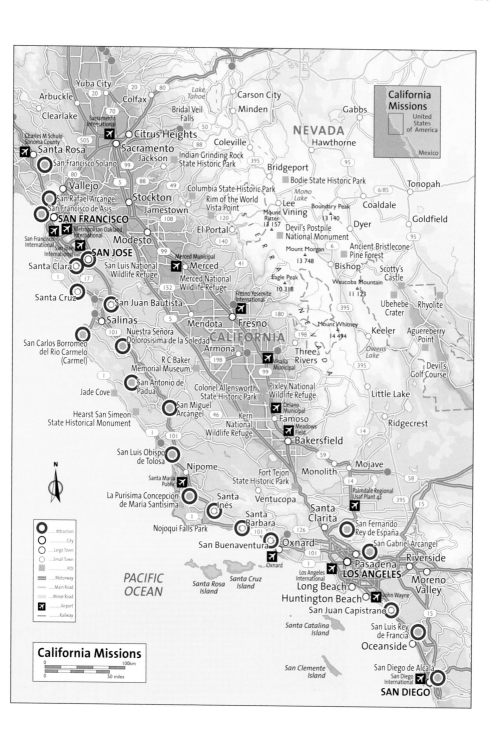

Yuba City
Arbuckle   20   Colfax   80   Lake Tahoe   Carson City   California Missions
Clearlake   70   Bridal Veil Falls   Minden   Gabbs   United States of America
Charles M Schulz Sonoma County Sacramento International   505   Citrus Heights   50   Coleville   NEVADA   Mexico
Santa Rosa   Sacramento   88   Hawthorne
San Francisco Solano   Jackson   Indian Grinding Rock State Historic Park   395   Bridgeport   95
80   99
Vallejo   5   88   49   Columbia State Historic Park   Bodie State Historic Park   Tonopah
San Rafael Arcangel   Stockton   Rim of the World   Mono Lake   6/85
San Francisco de Asis   Jamestown   Vista Point   Lee   Boundary Peak   Coaldale
SAN FRANCISCO   108   120   Mount Ritter   Vining   13 140   Goldfield
San Francisco International   Metropolitan Oakland International   El Portal   13 157   Devil's Postpile National Monument   Dyer
Modesto   140
San Jose International   SAN JOSE   99   Mount Morgan   6   Ancient Bristlecone
Santa Clara   San Luis National Wildlife Refuge   Merced Municipal   Merced   41   13 748   Pine Forest
1   17   152   Merced National Wildlife Refuge   Eagle Peak   Bishop   Scotty's Castle
Santa Cruz   10 318   Waucoba Mountain
San Juan Bautista   Fresno Yosemite International   11 123
Salinas   5   Mendota   Fresno   180   Ubehebe Crater   Rhyolite
Nuestra Señora Dolorosisima de la Soledad   101   CALIFORNIA   198   Mount Whitney   14 494   Keeler   Aguereberry Point
San Carlos Borromeo del Rio Carmelo (Carmel)   Armona   Three Rivers   Owens Lake   395   Devil's Golf Course
R C Baker Memorial Museum   198   Visalia Municipal   99
Jade Cove   San Antonio de Padua   Colonel Allensworth State Historic Park   Pixley National Wildlife Refuge   Little Lake
San Miguel Arcangel   46   Delano Municipal
Hearst San Simeon State Historical Monument   Kern National Wildlife Refuge   Famoso   Meadows Field   Ridgecrest
1   101   Bakersfield   14
San Luis Obispo de Tolosa   59
Nipome   Fort Tejon State Historic Park   Monolith   Mojave   58
Santa Maria Public   Palmdale Regional USAF Plant 42   395   15
La Purisima Concepción de María Santisima   Santa Inés   Ventucopa   Santa Clarita   San Fernando Rey de España
1   Santa Barbara   126   San Gabriel Arcangel
Nojoqui Falls Park   101   Pasadena   Riverside
San Buenaventura   Oxnard   Los Angeles International   LOS ANGELES   Moreno Valley
Oxnard   101   Long Beach   John Wayne
PACIFIC   Santa Rosa Island   Santa Cruz Island   Huntington Beach
OCEAN   San Juan Capistrano   15
Santa Catalina Island   San Luis Rey de Francia
Oceanside
California Missions
0   100km   San Clemente Island   San Diego de Alcalá
0   50 miles   San Diego International   SAN DIEGO

N

O ... Attraction
O ... City
O ... Large Town
O ... Small Town
■ ... POI
— ... Motorway
— ... Main Road
— ... Minor Road
✈ ... Airport
— ... Railway

San Juan Capistrano was converted back from a hay barn, San Luis Obispo from a jail, while Carmel was rebuilt from a rubble heap.

The mission style, whitewashed walls, red-tile roofs, rounded arches and massive sprays of bougainvillea, became the architectural rage from California to Florida. Generations of cinema-goers grew up with the imposing façade of Mission Santa Barbara as their image of Early California – modern pink paint apparently photographed better than the original whitewash.

Many missions have common names, shown below in parenthesis.

Missions

Mission Carmel (San Carlos Borromeo del Rio Carmelo) $ 3080 Rio Rd, Carmel; tel: (831) 624-1271; www.carmelmission.org. Open Mon–Sat 0930–1700, Sun 1030–1700.

Nuestra Señora Dolorosísima de la Soledad 36641 Ft Romie Rd, Soledad; tel: (831) 678-2586. Call for hours. Admission by donation.

San Carlos Borromeo del Rio Carmelo (Mission Carmel)

Carmel (1770) is a nearly perfect image of what a mission ought to be – golden sandstone, Moorish towers and contemplative gardens, all set off by splashes of brilliant bougainvillea. Fra Serra is buried beneath the floor in front of the main altar; the rebuilt padre's quarters include Serra's spartan cell and a library with volumes dating to 1534. Carmel is also one of the most visited of the missions. Try to go early in the day before the crowds arrive. The church is closed during services, though the large courtyard remains open and popular.

Nuestra Señora Dolorosísima de la Soledad (Mission Soledad)

Soledad (1791) is better known for its state prison than its mission, which is little more than a restored chapel, museum and adobe ruins in a pleasant, pastoral setting.

Right
Father Serra's parlour in the Mission San Carlos Borromeo del Rio Carmelo

Why Missions?

Spain had little interest in California when Serra and Portolá were sent north to establish a chain of missions. Generations of Spanish monarchs had happily ignored Alta California since Sebastián Vizcaíno visited Monterey in 1602. But in the 1760s, Spain saw a new threat in the Pacific: Russia.

Russian fur-seal hunters were slowly making their way south from Alaska, posing a potential threat to undefended Alta California. A chain of missions and presidios, military forts, could block Russian advances.

The Russians got as far south as Fort Ross (see page 187) in 1812. What impact the missions had is unclear. After Mission Solano (Sonoma) was established a decade later, Fort Ross became a major buyer of California flour, beef and wine to provision Alaskan fur bases.

When the fur trade declined from overhunting along the entire Pacific Coast, the Russians unloaded Fort Ross on John Sutter, best known as the owner of Sutter's Fort where the Gold Rush began in 1848. Sutter returned the favour by neglecting to pay most of the agreed selling price. The missions themselves went out of business in 1834, when Mexico secularised Church property.

La Purísima Concepción de María Santísima $
La Purisima Mission State Historic Park, 2295 Purisima Rd, 4 miles north of Lompoc; tel: (805) 733-3713; www.lapurisimamission.org. Open daily 0900–1700.

San Antonio de Padua
$ 23 miles southwest of King City, Mission Rd, Jolon; tel: (831) 385-4478; www.missionsanantonio.net. Call for hours.

San Buenaventura $
211 E. Main St, Ventura; tel: (805) 643-4318; www. sanbuenaventuramission.org. Open Mon–Fri 1000–1700, Sat 0900–1700, Sun 1000–1600. Admission by donation.

La Purísima Concepción de María Santísima (La Purísima)
La Purísima (1787) was rebuilt as a public works project in the 1930s, but it is the most authentic restoration among the missions. Workers used period tools and methods to bring an archaeological site back to life. The darkly ornate (but unconsecrated) church is furnished and painted as it would have been at its height in the 1820s. The kitchen garden is planted with typical food and medicinal plants, from garlic and chillies to elderberries and myrtle. Even the farm animals are period, down to the four-horned churro sheep that have come closer to extinction than the missions themselves.

San Antonio de Padua
Sitting in a small valley surrounded by Fort Hunter Liggett, a quiet military reservation, San Antonio (1771) is more serene now than when it was a famed horse-breeding centre. The founding Franciscans are long gone, though the rough, rebuilt adobe arches and promenades match 19th-century photographs of the original building. Modern renovators have removed the candles, flowers and other devotional objects that once crowded the simple chapel, and stencilled designs along the walls and altar are based on original colours.

San Buenaventura
The stone church and surrounding gardens have been restored to a good approximation of their original appearance (1782). The tiered bell tower, topped by a striped dome, echoes Moorish motifs that distinguish California mission styles from similar Mexican buildings. The museum has many of the mission's original furnishings, including the only wooden bells used in any of the 21 missions.

🔘 San Diego de Alcalá $ *10818 San Diego Mission Rd, San Diego; tel: (619) 281-8449; www.missionsandiego.com. Open daily 0900–1645.*

San Fernando Rey de España *15151 San Fernando Mission Blvd, Mission Hills; tel: (818) 361-0186. Open daily 0900–1700.*

San Francisco de Asís $ *3321 16th St, San Francisco; tel: (415) 621-8203; www.missiondolores. org. Open daily 0900–1600, or to 1430.*

San Francisco Solano $ *114 E. Spain St, Sonoma State Historic Park, Sonoma; tel: (707) 938-9560; www.parks.sonoma.net/ sonoma.html. Open daily 1000–1700.*

San Gabriel Arcángel $ *428 S. Mission Dr, San Gabriel; tel: (626) 457-3035; www.sangabrielmission.org. Open daily 0900–1630.*

San Jose de Guadalupe $ *43300 Mission Blvd, Fremont; tel: (510) 657-1797; www.missionsanjose. org. Open daily 1000–1700.*

San Diego de Alcalá (Mission San Diego)

This was California's first mission (1769), and the first to be moved out of the reach of presidio soldiers. Not a wise move in San Diego's case, for the mission was sacked by neophytes (see page 254) and unconverted tribes in 1775. Rebuilt with high adobe walls, the mission prospered until secularised in 1834, when it fell into ruin. The blindingly white walls were raised again in the early 20th century. San Diego buildings were particularly narrow because of the acute shortage of tall timber needed to span wider structures.

San Fernando Rey de España (San Fernando Rey)

The graceful buildings and lush gardens of San Fernando (1797) seem to have survived the test of time, but the church is actually the youngest in the mission system. It is a copy of an 1806 church demolished by an earthquake in 1971. The mission once grazed more than 21,000 head of cattle in the San Fernando Valley, supplying candles, soap and leather goods to other missions. San Fernando's *convento*, or guest and missionary quarters, is the largest-surviving mission building in the state. Bob Hope is buried at the San Fernando Mission Cemetery.

San Francisco de Asís (Mission Dolores)

Usually called 'Mission Dolores' after a nearby lake that disappeared decades ago, the mission (1776) is San Francisco's oldest building. It is also among the most ornate, with a chapel restored to the 1791 period. The small mission museum holds artefacts from the colonial period, as does the cemetery, including California's first native-born Mexican governor (Luís Antonio Arguello), the city's first Mexican mayor (Francisco de Haro) and last Mexican mayor (José Noé).

San Francisco Solano (often called Sonoma Mission)

This last of the missions to be established (1823) was also destroyed by a Native American uprising and rebuilt in more durable adobe. All that remains of the rebuilt complex are the chapel and part of the priests' quarters, restored about 1913.

San Gabriel Arcángel (Mission San Gabriel)

San Gabriel (1771) has the oldest cemetery in Los Angeles County (1778) and has survived more earthquake damage than any major structure still in use locally. The original vaulted roof was damaged by a quake in 1804, as were the replacement in 1812 and its replacement in 1987. The choir loft, baptistery, sanctuary, sacristy and pulpit are all original. Landscaped grounds contain numerous ruins, including the original bell tower, which collapsed in an early earthquake.

San Jose de Guadalupe (Mission San Jose)

This copy was built on the site of the original mission church (1797). The interior shows the 1830s–1840s period, complete with ornate sculptures and gold-leaf replica furnishings.

San Juan Bautista $
406 2nd St, San Juan Bautista Historic Park, centre of town; tel: (831) 623-4528; www.oldmissionsjb.org. Open daily 0930–1630.

San Juan Capistrano $$
26801 Ortega Hwy, San Juan Capistrano; tel: (949) 234-1300; www.missionsjc.com. Open daily 0830–1700.

San Luis Obispo de Tolosa Chorroat 782 Monterey St, San Luis Obispo; tel: (805) 781-8220; www.missionsanluisobispo.org. Open daily 0900–1700. Free.

San Juan Bautista

If this largest of the California missions looks familiar, with its ponderous bells in the tower and an extended arcade fronting the monastery wing, it probably is. San Juan Bautista (1797) was used for the climactic stairway chase in Alfred Hitchcock's classic *Vertigo*. The bear and coyote tracks in the tiles along the church's central aisle were made while the tiles were drying in the sun nearly three centuries ago. The mission and surrounding square are one of the best-surviving examples of an early 19th-century California town.

San Juan Capistrano

Forget the syrupy song and made-up legend about the swallows returning to Capistrano on 19 March. The mission (1775) is better remembered for its fountains, lush gardens, peaceful courtyards, the 1777 Serra Chapel, the oldest building still in regular use in California, and the ruins of the Great Stone Church, which collapsed during morning Mass in an 1812 earthquake. San Juan Capistrano is also one of the most popular missions. Get there at opening and flee when the tour buses start arriving.

San Luis Obispo de Tolosa (Mission San Luis Obispo)

You'd never know by looking that Mission San Luis Obispo (1772) served time as the town jail. Once among the richest of the missions (renowned for its wines), an 1830 earthquake sent San Luis's fortunes tumbling. It was eventually returned to the Roman Catholic Church, renovated into a vaguely New England-ish chapel, and finally returned to its adobe form from the 1930s. The imitation marble reredos, the decorated area behind the altar, is especially dramatic. So are the outstanding Chumash Native American exhibits that are displayed in the mission museum.

Mission Organisation

Spain had more than a century of mission experience in New Mexico, Texas, Baja California and elsewhere before moving into California. The basic scheme combined religious, military and civilian authority.

Missionaries were to Christianise and Hispanicise the natives and turn them into a docile workforce. Civilian settlers were responsible for creating a pueblo, or town, to instil civil authority, while soldiers built a presidio, or fort, to protect mission and town.

The scheme fared poorly in California. Early settlers and soldiers were largely conscripts who deserted at the earliest possible moment. The padres soon learnt to establish missions as far from pueblo and presidio as possible to avoid abuse of their converts. Civilian and military authorities were just as distrustful of the missions, which seemed to concentrate on amassing wealth rather than building a new order.

None seemed to give more than a passing thought to the Native Americans they subdued, converted and unknowingly killed by way of imported diseases, poor sanitation and worse diet. Whether by design or by accident, the missions effectively destroyed every Native American group they encountered.

Right
Mission Santa Barbara

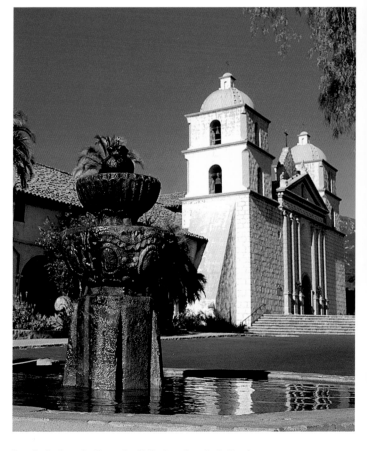

San Luis Rey de Francia (Mission San Luis Rey)
The King of the Missions (1798) was the largest building in all of California for more than half of the 19th century. It is still the largest mission, its scalloped white façade almost a glaring mirage beneath the Southern California sun. The quadrangle once sprawled across 6 acres and mission fields stretched 15 miles. A unique wooden dome sits atop the cruciform church, an eight-sided lantern with 12 dozen panes of glass. The mission museum claims America's largest collection of old Spanish vestments and the sole-surviving mission-era walking staff and padre's hat.

San Miguel Arcángel
San Miguel (1797) is a beloved mission, but was a structurally poor church building with the 21 missions' best-preserved original interior artwork – murals with mineral pigment bound with cactus juice – before it took a heavy hit in a 6.5 Richter-scale earthquake on

San Rafael Arcángel *1104 5th Ave, San Rafael; tel: (415) 454-8141; www.saintraphael. com. Open daily 0630–1830. Free.*

Santa Barbara $ *E. Los Olivos at 2201 Laguna St, Santa Barbara; tel: (805) 682-4713; www.sbmission.org. Open daily 0900–1700.*

Santa Clara de Asís *Santa Clara University, 500 El Camino Real, Santa Clara; tel: (408) 554-4023; www.scu.edu/mission. Open daily.*

Santa Cruz Mission State Historic Park *Santa Cruz; tel: (831) 425-5849; www.santacruzstateparks.org/ parks/mission. Open Thur–Sat 1000–1600.*

Santa Inés $ *1760 Mission Dr, Solvang; tel: (805) 688-4815; www.missionsantaines.org. Open daily 0900–1700.*

22 December 2003. The church still stands. Moisture swelled the cracked adobe and damaged the murals. Restoration was finished in 2009.

San Rafael Arcángel (Mission San Rafael)

Built as an *asistencia*, or branch, to Mission Dolores, San Rafael (1817) was primarily a sanatorium for its San Francisco parent house. The original mission was razed in 1870; the replica – on approximately the same site – was built in 1949.

Santa Barbara

Unique among the missions, Santa Barbara (1786) has remained a parish church from the day it was consecrated. Called 'Queen of the Missions' for its classic Roman façade (borrowed from a 27 BC architectural encyclopedia), the mission starred in dozens of early films – it was convenient to Hollywood's favourite holiday destination, Montecito. The pink-hued, sandstone church is complemented by the lush courtyard gardens within and a spectacular city rose garden in front.

Santa Clara de Asís (Mission Santa Clara)

The current church, built after fire destroyed the earlier building (1777) in 1926, mirrors an impressive mission building. The roof is covered in red tiles salvaged from the ruins of earlier mission structures. The wooden cross (inside a redwood frame) standing in front of the church dates to the founding of the original mission. Olive trees, roses and wisteria around the quadrangle beside the church have been growing since the mission days.

Santa Cruz

Santa Cruz (1791) was the smallest of the missions, but not this small – what you now see is a half-size replica built in 1931 to house a mission museum. The mission itself collapsed in 1857 from earthquake damage. The best reason to visit is **Santa Cruz Mission State Historic Park** (*144 School St; tel: (831) 429-5849*). A seven-room barracks is California's only remaining housing for mission neophytes (*see page 254*). The building was later used by *Californio* and Irish residents.

Santa Inés

Santa Inés (1804) was admired for its cattle herds, fine leatherwork and delicate jewellery until 1824, when a guard chastised a convert with too much obvious enthusiasm. The neophyte (*see page 254*) community set fire to the church and mission affairs never recovered. Restoration began around the turn of the 20th century, including a *trompe l'œil* painting behind the sanctuary. The marble panels separated by Ionic columns are actually flat plaster.

Greater Las Vegas

The ads claim that Las Vegas never sleeps. It's true. The lure of 'easy' money, clattering slot machines and flashing neon may slow in the hours just before dawn, but 'Vegas' has barely paused for breath since Nevada legalised gambling in the early 1930s.

'Show the suckers a good time and send 'em home broke' is how an early casino-owner might have put it. The public responded by turning what was once a dusty, sun-blasted oasis in the middle of nowhere into one of the most visited, most talked-about cities on earth.

Vegas mirrors America's changing visions of itself, especially the 3-mile stretch of Las Vegas Blvd South lined with 40-plus casinos known simply as The Strip.

In the 1990s, circus acts and fairy-tale castles pushed half-naked showgirls and other more traditional attractions into the background. The social pendulum is swinging back with shows and nightclubs that expand the limits of public sensuality. Extravagance, opulence and entertainment are today's watchwords, concepts that Las Vegas is more than happy to indulge with yet another round of bigger, grander and glitzier hotel-casinos.

Ratings

Gambling	●●●●●
Nightlife	●●●●●
Scenery	●●●●●
Architecture	●●●●○
Children	●●●●○
Shopping	●●●○○
Food and drink	●●○○○
History	●○○○○

Getting there and getting around

McCarran International Airport (LAS) (*tel: (702) 261-5211; www.mccarran.com*) is south of The Strip, 5 miles from the city centre. Taxi to Strip hotels averages $13–$25. **Gray Line** (*tel: (800) 634-6579 or (702) 384-1234; http://graylinelasvegas.com/airportshuttles.shtml*) airport bus is slightly less for a return journey. **I-15** is the main access highway from California and the Grand Canyon.

Public transport

The Regional Transportation Commission of Southern Nevada (*tel: (800) 228-3911 or (702) 228-7433; www.rtcsnv.com/transit*) offers **RTC** bus service to most of Las Vegas; a **Deuce** double-decker bus down the Las Vegas Strip; and **ACE** rapid transit bullet-shaped buses with dedicated lanes and stops adjusted for passenger flow between downtown, the convention centre, and The Strip. The **Las Vegas Monorail** (*$5 per ride*) connects seven hotel-casinos along the east side of Las Vegas Blvd South. The elevated line runs *behind* resorts from the MGM Grand (*at*

ℹ **Las Vegas Convention and Visitors Authority (LVCVA) Visitor Information Center** *3150 Paradise Rd; tel: (702) 892-7575 or (877) 847-4858; www. visitlasvegas.com. Open daily 0800–1700.*

🚊 **Las Vegas Monorail** *$ East of The Strip from MGM Grand to the Sahara; tel: (702) 699-8200; www.lvmonorail.com. Trains run daily Mon–Thur 0700–0200, Fri–Sun 0700–0300.*

Tropicana Ave) to the Sahara (*at Sahara Ave*), with stops for Bally's and Paris; Flamingo and Caesars Palace; Imperial Palace and Harrahs; the Las Vegas Convention Center, Hilton and the Sahara. Riding the air-conditioned carriages beats inching through Strip traffic, especially in summer, but stations are at the rear of each hotel stop. Allow for a 15–20-minute hike to get from the monorail to The Strip. Traffic along The Strip grinds to a crawl mid-afternoon to late evening.

Parking
Parking is plentiful, convenient and cheap. Casino car parks are well lit, patrolled 24 hours daily and almost always free. Free valet parking is available at the main entrance to all casinos; tip the attendant $2–$5 when the vehicle is returned. Car parks which do charge, such as the **Fremont Street Experience** (*see page 264*) lot, normally waive the fee with validation (a stamp or paste-on sticker) from a nearby casino or merchant.

⬛ **Fremont Street Experience**
Downtown, 425 Fremont St; tel: (702) 678-5777; www. vegasexperience.com. Light and sound shows nightly.

⬛ **Hoover Dam and Lake Mead** *30 miles southeast of Las Vegas on Hwy 93; tel: (702) 494-2517 or (866) 730-9097; www.usbr.gov/lc/hooverdam. Dam visitor centre open daily 0900–1800. Tours $$. Lake Mead National Recreation Area is open 24 hours.*

Imperial Palace Auto Collection $$ *Imperial Palace, 3535 Las Vegas Blvd S.; tel: (702) 794-3174; www.autocollections.com. Open daily 1000–1800.*

Sights

Fremont Street Experience
Four blocks of Fremont St have been transformed into the Fremont Street Experience, a walking street topped by a 90ft canopy set with 12.5 million synchronised LED modules that explode into light and sound shows after dark. Downtown casinos are generally less flashy than their Strip counterparts, less expensive and less noisy.

Hoover Dam
About 726ft from base to dam-top highway, Hoover Dam is one of the highest concrete dams ever built. Finished in 1936, it backs the Colorado River into **Lake Mead**, a 140-mile strip of blue in the beige, grey and red landscape of the Mojave, Great Basin and Sonoran Deserts that meet along its shores. The lake is a popular boating and outdoor recreation area from spring to autumn.

The **Dam Visitor Center** offers a Dam Tour and a Powerplant Tour. Several river-rafting companies in Las Vegas offer easy whole- or half-day raft and canoe trips down the Colorado River from just below the dam *(tel: (702) 294-1414).*

Imperial Palace Collection
One of the West's finer car collections (many vehicles are for sale!) includes an 1897 Haynes-Apperson. Rotating exhibits have featured a 1928 Delage limousine owned by the late King of Siam, US President Dwight Eisenhower's parade limo and one of the world's largest collections of Model J Duesenbergs.

Above
Las Vegas pastiche – the skyline of the New York New York Hotel

⓪ Las Vegas Natural History Museum $
900 N. Las Vegas Blvd; tel: (702) 384-3466; www.lvnhm.org. Open daily 0900–1600.

Liberace Museum $$
1775 E. Tropicana Ave; tel: (702) 798-5595; www.liberace.org. Open Mon–Sat 1000–1700, Sun 1200–1600.

Old Las Vegas Mormon State Historic Park $
Washington Ave and Las Vegas Blvd; tel: (702) 486-3511; http://parks.nv.gov/olvmf.htm. Open Tue–Sat 0800–1630.

Red Rock Canyon National Conservation Area $ *20 miles west, off Charleston Blvd; tel: (702) 515-5350; www.nv.blm.gov/redrock canyon. Scenic Drive loop open 0600–2000. Visitor Center open daily 0800–1630.*

Springs Preserve $$
333 S. Valley View Blvd at Alta Dr; tel: (702) 822-7700; www.springspreserve. org. Gardens 3701 W. Alta Dr. Both open daily 0800–1800.

⬣ The Strip *Las Vegas Blvd S., Stratosphere to Mandalay Bay. Never closed.*

Above
Man versus mountain in Red Rock Canyon

Las Vegas Natural History Museum
The museum is a good introduction to the plants and animals indigenous to Nevada as well as marine life from around the world.

Liberace Museum
Liberace was a classically trained pianist, technically astute and addicted to grand gestures of dazzling spectacle – audiences loved him. The museum displays many of his flashiest costumes, jewelled accessories, cars, pianos and other accoutrements.

Old Las Vegas Mormon State Historic Park
This is where the entertainment began. In 1855, Mormon traders opened a fort in an isolated desert meadow ('Las Vegas' is 'Meadows' in Spanish) to cater to pioneer wagon trains headed for California. The fort was eventually selected as a railway stop (steam locomotive engines needed regular infusions of water), which prompted an initial round of land speculation that resulted in today's Las Vegas. The museum includes a late-19th-century Mormon living room.

Red Rock Canyon National Conservation Area
Best known for a 13-mile driving loop that winds through some of the most spectacular desert scenery within easy reach of Las Vegas, the conservation area is named after the 3,000ft-high Red Rock Escarpment, as popular with rock climbers as with sightseers. Self-guided hiking trails lead to a spring, a waterfall, several small canyons and what remains of an old homestead. Wild burros frequent the loop road in search of handouts.

Springs Preserve
The Strip has an antidote: a 180-acre stop west of downtown with botanic gardens; trails; a desert living centre; Mojave Desert ecology; Native American history; and water use in an ORIGEN centre, and concert space constructed on a historic water-source landmark area that still provides most of Downtown Las Vegas's water supply.

The Strip
The Strip *is* Las Vegas for most visitors, 3 miles of boulevard glitz lined with more than 40 hotel-casinos and acres of neon. Traffic tends to move slowly, but the only way to see the full scope of creative casino architecture is to park and walk, or take the monorail.

Valley of Fire State Park
This rugged valley is filled with eroded red sandstone formations that
seem to catch fire in the sunlight – the effect is most spectacular at
dawn and sunset. Some rocks and cliffs are covered with prehistoric
petroglyphs. The most easily accessible set of petroglyphs lies along
the ¼-mile trail to **Mouse's Tank**, a natural basin named for a Paiute
Indian who successfully eluded capture in the natural maze.

Shopping in Las Vegas

Most stores and shops in Las Vegas open at 1000; along The Strip,
most remain open to 2300 or 2400. As shopping evolved to become
one of America's favourite forms of entertainment, casinos began to
create their own themed shopping opportunities. Among the glitziest
of the shoppertainment palaces are **The Grand Canal Shoppes** (*The
Venetian, 3377 Las Vegas Blvd S.; tel: (702) 414-4500; www.
thegrandcanalshoppes.com*) and **The Forum Shops at Caesars** (*Caesars
Palace, 3500 Las Vegas Blvd S.; tel: (702) 893-4800; www.
simon.com/mall/?id=224*). The Grand Canal is modelled on Venice,
complete with gondoliers in red-and-white striped shirts poling
gondolas along meandering canals, St Mark's Square, living statues,
and Renaissance-inspired singers and actors. The Forum Shops offers
Italianate streetscapes beneath hand-painted barrel vaulting that
cycles through the day from sunrise to sunset. Faux-marble statues
come to life on the hour with Vegas's own twist on Roman
mythology. **The Shoppes at the Palazzo** (*The Palazzo, 3327 Las Vegas
Blvd S.; tel: (702) 414-4525; www.palazzolasvegas.com/the_shoppes.html*)
touts 60 upmarket shops including Barneys New York. **Miracle Mile
Shops** (*Planet Hollywood, 3667 Las Vegas Blvd S.; tel: (888) 800-8284;
www.miraclemileshopslv.com*) boasts a regularly scheduled rainstorm at
Merchant's Harbor.
  Fashion Show Las Vegas (*3200 Las Vegas Blvd S.; tel: (702) 784-7000;
www.thefashionshow.com*) is the largest mall on The Strip, with more
than 250 speciality and department stores. A few blocks west of
Downtown Las Vegas, the **Las Vegas Premium Outlets** (*875 S. Grand
Central Parkway; tel: (702) 474-7500; www.premiumoutlets.com*) provides
a chance to 'collect' from more than 150 designer stores.

Accommodation and food
in Las Vegas

Las Vegas is the hotel capital of the planet, with 149,000 rooms and
still counting. Accommodation is concentrated along **The Strip** (*Las
Vegas Blvd S.*) and **downtown** (*Fremont St and nearby*). New Strip hotels
are the most luxurious, the most touted and the most expensive;

ℹ **The Word**
    The best single source of practical and up-to-the-minute Vegas information is **Anthony Curtis' Las Vegas Advisor**
3665 S. Procoyon Ave;
tel: (702) 252-0655 or (800) 244-2224;
www.lasvegasadvisor.com.
The monthly newsletter is filled with accommodation and show deals, gambling strategies, non-gaming activities and tips on local bargains – no adverts allowed.

downtown hotels are less expensive. Prices drop even further at motels west of I-15.

Visit midweek for the best value, but always book ahead to avoid major conventions or sporting events, which drive accommodation prices sky-high. The Sunday *Los Angeles Times* travel section is the single best source of current accommodation deals.

Casino food and drink prices have crept upwards in recent years, but casino buffets are still good value for any meal. The **Fiesta**, **Rio** and **Station** (**Boulder**, **Palace**, **Sunset**, **Texas** and **Santa Fe**, plus the **Green Valley Ranch**) casinos get high marks for good food as well as good buffet prices.

Drinks are free to gamblers, though service is generally slow. Expect to pay standard prices at casino bars, where service is generally very good. The drinking and gambling age is 21 and alcohol may be served 24 hours a day.

Gambling

Gambling, or 'gaming' as the politically correct prefer, fuels the flash, the glitter and the hype that keeps Las Vegas moving. Take the rows of slot machines standing like sentries at the airport (locals warn the odds are terrible), petrol stations, supermarkets and wedding chapels as a hint: Vegas is a money machine oiled by the mathematical certainty that, in the long run, the player *always* loses. The only question is how long it takes.

Below
Antique slot machine in Las Vegas

In general, the easier the game, the higher the house edge, or advantage. The house keeps around 45 per cent of the money bet on keno, less than 0.5 per cent of the cash bet on blackjack, Vegas's most popular card game. Most casinos offer free lessons for **blackjack** (also called '21' for the perfect hand) and **craps** (a high-speed dice game). Try to graduate to low-stakes tables at slack periods, breakfast to mid-afternoon, before jumping into the heady night-time whirl.

Most gamblers opt for the ubiquitous **slot machines**, which require neither skill nor a rulebook. Pump in quarters, dollars or banknotes (occasional nickel slots are around) and pull the handle or push a button to set the reels spinning. If a winning combination appears, bells ring, lights flash and coins clatter reassuringly into a metal hopper. **Video poker** machines operate similarly, but require some knowledge of the rules of poker.

Other popular games include **baccarat**, a European card game similar to blackjack where the goal is nine rather than twenty-one; **keno**, a lotto-like game; **roulette** and a number of different **poker** games. It is also possible to bet on sporting events at any casino sport book.

Casino themes

Most Vegas casinos have become gigantic theme parks in order to set themselves apart in a highly competitive market. The basic amenities are the same – accommodation, casino, restaurants, bars, cabarets and shows – but the packaging varies dramatically to lure different kinds of punters. And there are always new hotel-casinos opening or changing themes.

Aria *3730 Las Vegas Blvd S.; tel: (866) 359-7757; www.arialasvegas.com.* Modern, spare and spacious in The Strip's CityCenter complex.

Bellagio *3600 Las Vegas Blvd S.; tel: (702) 693-7111 or (888) 987-6667; www.bellagio.com.* An opulent village transplanted from Italy's Lake Como to Nevada. No one under 18 is admitted except registered guests, unless eating at a resort restaurant or attending a show or event.

Caesars Palace *3570 Las Vegas Blvd S.; tel: (800) 634-6001; www.caesarspalace.com.* Togas and other glories of Imperial Rome plus fabulous shopping.

Circus Circus *2880 Las Vegas Blvd S.; tel: (702) 734-0410; www.circuscircus.com.* Vegas's original family casino with circus acts, games and the **Adventuredome $$** (*www.adventuredome.com*) theme park to keep the kids occupied.

Encore *3121 Las Vegas Blvd S.; tel: (888) 320-7125; www.encorelasvegas.com.* Capitalising on the success of Wynn, a posh mirror-image high-rise that sits adjacent.

Excalibur *3850 Las Vegas Blvd S.; tel: (877) 750-5464; www. excalibur.com.* Camelot on The Strip, complete with strolling dragons.

Luxor *3900 Las Vegas Blvd S.; tel: (877) 386-4658; www.luxor.com.* Ancient Egypt within a black glass pyramid, complete with a Sphinx crouching over the entrance.

Mandalay Bay *3950 Las Vegas Blvd S.; tel: (877) 632-7800; www. mandalaybay.com.* The world's top tropical resorts distilled in the desert, with a separate no-gaming **Four Seasons Hotel $$$** (*3960 Las Vegas Blvds; tel: (702) 632-5000 or (877) 632-5000; www.fourseasons.com/ lasvegas*) to raise the tone.

MGM Grand *3799 Las Vegas Blvd S.; tel: (702) 891-7777 or (877) 880-0880; www.mgmgrand.com.* Cinema magic made real inside.

The Mirage *3400 Las Vegas Blvd S.; tel: (702) 791-7111 or (800) 374-9000; www.mirage.com.* Look for the erupting volcano outside at night, the tropical rainforest inside and white tigers in the Secret Garden.

New York New York *3790 Las Vegas Blvd S.; tel: (702) 740-6969 or (866) 815-4365; www.nynyhotelcasino.com.* The New York City skyline compressed around a casino. The roller coaster looping round the Statue of Liberty is real.

Palms Casino Resort *4321 W. Flamingo Rd; tel: (702) 942-7777 or (866) 725-6773; www.palms.com.* A season starring in MTV's *Real World* put The Palms on the map as Las Vegas's hippest, sexiest, must-be-seen party hotel, complete with a bookable recording studio.

Paris *3655 Las Vegas Blvd S.; tel: (877) 796-2096; www.parislasvegas.com.* All the romance of early-20th-century Paris, from steak frites to cobblestone streets, plus every mod con a casino can dream up. The **Eiffel Tower $$$** (*tel: (702) 948-6937*) is one of the hottest restaurants in town.

Rio All-Suite Hotel & Casino *3700 W. Flamingo Rd; tel: (866) 746-7671; www.riolasvegas.com.* Mardi Gras takes off seven days a week just west of The Strip.

Treasure Island *3300 Las Vegas Blvd S.; tel: (702) 894-7111 or (800) 288-7206; www.treasureisland.com.* Caribbean fantasies for adults, including an epic sea battle in front. In *Sirens of TI®*, sexy shipboard sirens vanquish renegade pirates four times nightly.

Vdara Hotel & Spa *2600 W. Harmon Ave; tel: (866) 745-7111; www. vdara.com.* The CityCenter complex's non-gaming, non-smoking hotel.

The Venetian *3355 Las Vegas Blvd S.; tel: (702) 414-1000; www. venetian.com.* Renaissance Venice, complete with St Mark's Square, gondolas, the Doge's Palace and the Grand Canal.

Wynn *3131 Las Vegas Blvd S.; tel: (877) 321-9966; www.wynnlasvegas.com.* Awards abound for this top-of-the-line high-rise casino resort.

That's entertainment!

Entertainment is the name of Las Vegas's game. The idea began with mobster Bugsy Segal, who imported musicians and comedians to give customers another reason to gamble in *his* casino. The ploy worked, then started feeding on itself. Casinos competed to create the flashiest shows and the most outlandish décor. Elegant drives were eclipsed by acres of neon, which gave way to erupting volcanoes, battling frigates and crooning gondoliers. Fantasy became a prelude to reality.

Big-name stars, 'headliners' in Vegas-speak, come and go regularly. Traditional shows such as **Jubilee $$** (*Bally's; tel: (800) 237-7469; www.ballyslasvegas.com*) and **Crazy Horse Paris $$** (*MGM Grand; tel: (866) 740-7711; www.mgmgrand.com*) rely on lavish sets, singing, dancing and bare breasts. Most offer early-evening covered versions with topless shows later. Sextravaganzas such as **Zumanity $$$** (*New York New York; tel: (866) 606-7111; www.nynyhotelcasino.com*) or **Fantasy $$** (*Luxor; tel: (800) 557-7428 or (702) 262-4400; www.luxor.com*) are adult-only and uncovered.

There are magicians, comedians and music acts, rendered with flash and pyrotechnics. A few casinos have held on to child-orientated spectacles. The most lavish is the **Tournament of Kings $$** (*Excalibur; tel: (702) 597-7600; www.excalibur.com*), a dinner show with jousting.

Lavish productions, like those by the **Cirque du Soleil** (*www.cirquedusoleil.com*), are expensive supershows with elaborate technical effects and superb athletic performances. Cirque's Las Vegas productions, all $$$ and among the most popular entertainment in town, include: **The Beatles LOVE** (*The Mirage; tel: (800) 963-9634 or (702) 792-7777; www.mirage.com*), **Kà** (*MGM Grand; tel: (866) 740-7711 or (702) 531-3826; www.mgmgrand.com*), **Mystère** (*Treasure Island; tel: (800) 392-1999 or (702) 894-7722; www.treasureisland.com*), **O** (*Bellagio; tel: (888) 488-7111 or (702) 693-7722; www.bellagio.com*), **CRISS ANGEL Believe** (*Luxor (see above)*), **Viva ELVIS** (*Aria; tel: (877) 253-5847 or (702) 590-7760; www.arialasvegas.com*), and **Zumanity** (*New York New York (see above)*).

The glitz capital also has high culture: **Bellagio Gallery of Fine Art $$** (*Bellagio; tel: (877) 957-9777 or (702) 693-7871; www.bellagio.com/amenities/gallery-of-fine-art.aspx*) has several exhibitions each year.

Vegas for kids

Vegas is the archetypal playground for adults, but children don't get left out entirely. Easy hikes at **Springs Preserve, Red Rock Canyon $, Valley of Fire $** and **Lake Mead/Hoover Dam** are a good way to run off excess energy. Nearby Henderson (on the way to Hoover Dam) has a free attraction for kids of all ages; **Ethel M® Chocolate Factory & Botanical Cactus Garden** (*2 Cactus Garden Dr, Henderson; tel: (702)*

435-2655; www.ethelschocolate.com. Factory tours Mon–Thur 0830–1630) has free tours and samples of fine chocolate production, with a well-labelled cactus garden outside.

Thrill rides are Vegas's latest attraction for grown-up kids. **Adventuredome $$** (*Circus Circus; tel: (702) 794-3939; www.adventuredome.com*) has its share of screamers, but the top ride is the **Stratosphere Tower $$** (*Stratosphere; tel: (702) 380-7777; www.stratospherehotel.com*), with a roller coaster, two free-fall rides and a jump-off atop the 1,149ft tower. Best indoor-outdoor roller coaster is **New York New York $** (*www.nynyhotelcasino.com/entertainment/ entertainment_therollercoaster.aspx*), which runs through the lobby and around the New York skyline.

For artificial reality, kid-style, **Excalibur $** (*www.excalibur.com/ attractions/spongebob4d.aspx*) has the SpongeBob Squarepants 4D™ ride. **Popovich's Comedy Pet Theater $$** (*Planet Hollywood; tel: (866) 932-1818* or *(702) 260-7200; www.varietytheater.com/comedypet.htm*) combines a human juggler and trained rescue shelter dogs and cats in a Vegas showroom experience.

For free attractions, check out the dancing **Fountains of Bellagio** (*Bellagio*) that perform afternoon and night, and the **Volcano** (*The Mirage*) that erupts every 15–30 minutes after dark. **St Mark's Square** (*The Venetian*) offers a variety of strolling minstrels to keep the crowds amused; or look for buskers in quiet corners throughout the Grand Canal Shoppes. Downtown, the **Fremont Street Experience** (*425 Fremont St; tel: (702) 678-5777; www.vegasexperience.com*) explodes into an overhead parade of moving images at dusk.

The Mirage offers animal attractions from Siegfried & Roy: the **Secret Garden $** is a small zoo with white tigers and other endangered large cat species, and **Dolphin Habitat $** is a large pool with trained bottlenose dolphins. **Shark Reef Aquarium $** (*Mandalay Bay; www.sharkreef.com*) has two walk-through tunnels for viewing of 30 sharks and several thousand other inhabitants, and exhibits of rare golden crocodiles and piranhas.

Below
Excalibur Hotel, Las Vegas

Showcase Mall (*3785 Las Vegas Blvd S.*) has three child-friendly attractions. **GameWorks $–$$** (*tel: (702) 432-4263*) is Vegas's largest video arcade, designed primarily for teenagers and young adults. **Everything Coca-Cola $** (*tel: (702) 270-5952*) is everything you ever wanted to buy (or to know) about Coca-Cola. **M&M's World** (*tel: (702) 736-7611*) is the ultimate M&M's sweet shop, with colours available nowhere else.

Grand Canyon, Bryce and Zion

The Painted Desert vision of the American Southwest springs to life in these three national parks. All were regarded as aberrations of nature and roadblocks to orderly development until recent decades. Today's visitors are more likely to stare with awe and vertigo into the mile-deep Grand Canyon, wonder at the fairy-like hoodoos of Bryce Canyon and gaze in silence at the mountain patriarchs of Zion – at least until the next tour bus or RV caravan pulls into the car park.

'The region ... is altogether valueless. It can be approached only from the south, and after entering it, there is nothing to do but leave. Ours has been the first, and will doubtless be the last, party ... to visit this profitless locality.'

Thus wrote a member of the 1858 US government survey team, summing up the perceived economic value of the Grand Canyon. Today the canyon receives more than four million visitors annually, all come to wonder at the red, white, buff, grey, yellow, orange, brown, pink and black rock.

BRYCE CANYON NATIONAL PARK

ⓘ Visitor Center
1½ miles south of Park Entrance. Open Nov–Mar 0800–1630; Apr & Oct 0800–1800; May–Sept 0800–2000; verify hours in the Hoodoo park newspaper, also normally online at the park website.

ⓝ Bryce Canyon National Park $$
PO Box 640201; tel: (435) 834-5322; www.nps.gov/brca

Bryce is an 18-mile canyon lined with hoodoos – ancient cliffs that have been eroded into parallel rows of sharp-edged pinnacles tinged with red, gold and chalk. Endless ranks of hoodoos form fanciful forests of stone that seem at times to resemble natural amphitheatres rimmed by fairy-tale cities of sheer-sided minarets, turrets, steeples and towers.

The drive south from the Park Entrance rises 1,100ft to **Rainbow Point**. The road (Hwy 63) offers numerous lay-bys where you can pull in and enjoy the view, but longer-term parking is extremely limited. Arrive before 1000 if you are planning to park and explore from **Sunrise, Sunset, Inspiration, Bryce** or **Paria viewpoints** during the spring to autumn. Trailers are not permitted beyond Sunset Campground, midway along the canyon drive. RVs longer than 25ft are prohibited from Paria View, at the end of the road, because of lack of turning space.

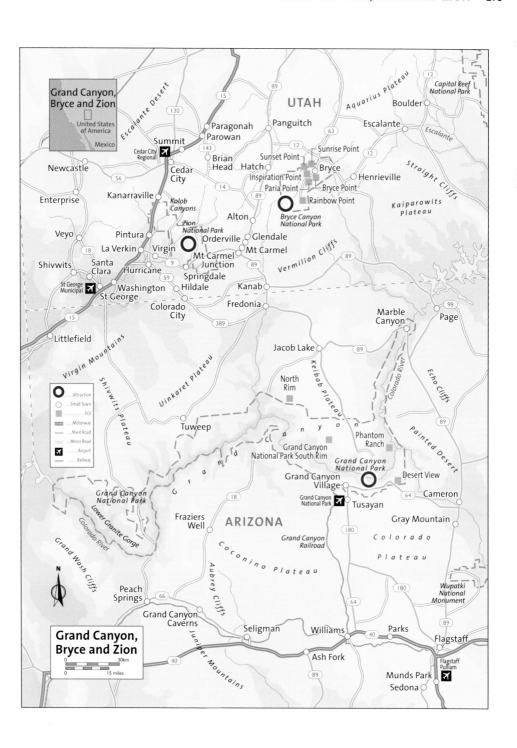

Grand Canyon, Bryce and Zion

United States of America

Mexico

Grand Canyon, Bryce and Zion

0   30km
0   15 miles

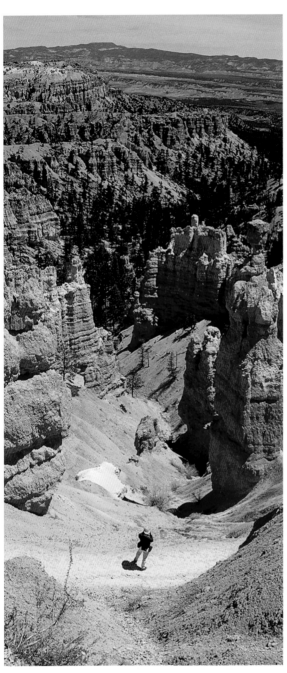

Arriving at dawn

Sunrise is one of the most striking times of day to see the hoodoos and the easiest time of day to park. Park at **Sunrise Point** (*less than a mile beyond the Visitor Center*) to watch the low rays of light begin to pick out the spires, then follow the **Rim Trail** down between the hoodoos to **Sunset Point, Inspiration Point** or **Bryce Point**. Return via the main road.

During the day

Drive directly to **Rainbow Point**, where visibility can exceed 100 miles and early visitors occasionally spot mountain lions. The 1-mile **Bristlecone Loop Trail** threads through stands of rare bristlecone pines.

The return drive offers many lay-bys, most with hiking trails. **Agua Canyon** has several named hoodoos, including **Hunter** and **Rabbit**. One of the park's biggest draws is **Natural Bridge**, an 85ft arch 6 miles north of Rainbow Point.

Bryce Point was named for Mormon settler Ebenezer Bryce, who farmed the Paria Valley for a short time in the 1870s and told the world of the mystical wonders that lay just to the south. **Inspiration Point** is best known for **Silent City**, a formation of 200ft hoodoos packed in dense rows like some high-rise city emptied of people.

Arriving at sunset

Sunset Point is the obvious point from which to enjoy the sunset, though parking is a problem in summer. Vistas curve east towards **Queen's Garden, Wall Street** and an illusory balanced rock called **Thor's Hammer**. Allow 2 hours to

Bryce Canyon Shuttle provides free transport *early May–mid-Oct daily 0800–2000* between the Ruby's Inn business area (*Hwy 63*), the park Visitor Center and the most famous viewpoints and trailheads in the Main Amphitheater. Park roads remain open to private vehicles, but summer traffic moves slowly.

ⓘ Garfield County Tourism Office
55 S. Main St, Panguitch; tel: (435) 676-1102 or (800) 444-6689; www. brycecanyoncountry.com

Opposite
Walking the Navajo Trail in Bryce Canyon National Park

walk the 1¼-mile **Navajo Loop Trail**, which wanders past Thor's Hammer, through the narrow clefts separating the hoodoos and through forests of pygmy Douglas fir trees. The easiest canyon trail is a 1¾-mile stroll through Queen's Garden from Sunset Point.

If schedules are tight, the best 1-hour park visit is **Fairyland Point**, just beyond the Visitor Center (also good for Nordic skiers). The stunning view is a preview of the magical scenery that lies beyond. Astronomy programmes and full-moon walks are popular, and Bryce Canyon horse riding (*www.canyonrides.com/bryce_canyon_rides.html*) is a unique way to see the hoodoos.

Accommodation and food in Bryce

The only non-camping accommodation in the park is **Bryce Canyon Lodge $$** (*Forever Resorts, PO Box 640041, Bryce; tel: (877) 386-4383 or (435) 834-8700; www.brycecanyonforever.com. Open Apr–Oct*). Nearby choices include **Best Western Ruby's Inn $$** (*1 mile north of the Park Entrance on Hwy 63, Bryce Canyon City; tel: (435) 834-5341 or (866) 866-6616; www.rubysinn.com*) and **Bryce Canyon Pines $–$$$** (*12 miles west on Hwy 12; tel: (800) 892-7923; www.brycecanyonmotel.com*). Other accommodation is available in **Tropic** (*east of the park on Hwy 12*).

Best local restaurant, and well worth the 6-mile drive, is **Cowboy's Smokehouse Bar-B-Q $$** (*95 N. Main St, Panguitch; tel: (435) 676-8030. Open mid-Mar–mid-Oct Mon–Sat 1130–2100*) for authentic wood-smoked meats and enormous slabs of home-made pie. **Bryce Canyon Lodge Restaurant $$** is the only restaurant in the park open all year. **The General Store $$, Sunrise Point**, sells snacks and drinks (*mid-Apr–Oct*).

GRAND CANYON NATIONAL PARK

ⓘ Grand Canyon National Park $$
PO Box 129; tel: (928) 638-7888; www.nps.gov/grca. Ask for The Guide, free at visitor centres, or find online: www.nps.gov/grca/parknews/ newspaper.htm

The Grand Canyon is larger than it appears. The popular South Rim and the less-frequented North Rim are just 10 miles straight across the canyon and 215 miles by highway. It is possible to see the Grand Canyon in a day, less if on a flightseeing package from Las Vegas, but the ever-changing colours and the utter vastness of the canyon beg to be absorbed at leisure, far from the vast crowds who stop at the South Rim and Grand Canyon Village. At the very least, skirt the crowds by walking or cycling the **South Rim Trail** from **Hopi Point** east to Grand Canyon Village and **Mather Point**. A free shuttle (*www.nps.gov/grca/planyourvisit/shuttle-buses.htm*) on five South Rim routes eases the return.

Bright Angel Trail began as a Native American trail from the rim down to the springs at Indian Gardens. Private developers widened the trail in 1891 and began the mule rides that remain one of Grand Canyon's most popular organised activities.

ⓘ Canyon View Information Plaza
South Rim 6 miles north from the South Entrance. Open daily winter 0800–1700; summer 0800–1800. Access is by shuttle bus, walking or by bicycle.

Desert View Information Center, Verkamp's Visitor Center, Kolb Studio, Yavapai Observation Station and Tusayan Museum *keep similar hours, i.e. 0800 or 0900–1700. Verify hours online.*

Road and Fire Conditions or **Arizona Road Conditions** *Tel: (888) 411-7623; www.az511.gov/hcrsweb/hcrsweb.jsp*

North Rim Visitor Center *Near Grand Canyon Lodge. Open mid-May–mid-Oct daily 0800–1800.*

ⓗ Grand Canyon Railway $–$$$
233 N. Grand Canyon Blvd, Williams; tel: (800) 843-8724; www.thetrain.com. Operates daily.

ⓠ The park runs a **free shuttle bus** system year-round through the Village and the West Rim. Shuttle routes, seasons of operation and times can change. Check *www.nps.gov/grca/planyourvisit/shuttle-buses.htm*

Bright Angel Bicycle Rentals $ *Canyon Visitor Information Plaza; tel: (928) 814-8704; www.bikegrandcanyon.com. Rents bicycles, adult tricycles (handicapped) and bicycle trailers in summer*

The **Grand Canyon Railway** *(tel: (800) 843-8724)* runs to the South Rim from Williams, 65 miles south of the park. The 1901 line, originally run by the Santa Fe Railway, provided the easy access that turned the Grand Canyon from geographic curiosity into an American icon. A vintage steam locomotive engine sometimes pulls the restored 1920s Harriman carriages in summer; a 1950s diesel does the duty in winter.

Grand Canyon Village Historic District is the central section of Grand Canyon Village from **Bright Angel Trailhead** east to **Verkamp's Visitor Center** and the First National Park Service Administration Building. Many Village structures are historic landmarks, including the **Kolb Studio** and **Lookout Studio**, perched on the canyon rim, **Red Horse Station, Bright Angel Lodge, El Tovar Hotel**, the **Santa Fe Railway Station, Verkamp's (Curios)** and the **First National Park Service Administration Building**. **Hopi House**'s Native American rugs, jewellery, pottery and tourist souvenirs are museum-class, as is the Southwest-style adobe building.

Mule Trips *(Xanterra Parks & Resorts®; tel: (303) 297-2757 or (888) 297-2757; year-round one-day rides $$ and 1–2 nights overnight to Phantom Ranch $$$)* have been popular for generations. Riders must be at least 4ft 7in tall and weigh less than 200lb. Advance booking is essential year-round, but there *may* be last-minute cancellations the morning of the ride *(tel: (928) 638-2631; www.grandcanyonlodges.com/mule-trips-716.html)*.

One-day trips lead from the stone corral at the head of Bright Angel Trail to Tonto Platform and Plateau Point, 3,200ft below. The blue-green Colorado River twinkles another 1,300ft down. The ride takes about 7 hours.

Phantom Ranch rides stay overnight or two nights at Phantom Ranch cabins on Bright Angel Creek at the bottom of the canyon. Two-night trips take a different return route.

The **North Rim**, 1,000ft higher than the South Rim, is a different world. While the South Rim bakes in desert heat, the North Rim enjoys a cooler, mountain summer with spruce, fir and quaking aspen. And when the South Rim is dusted with snow, the North Rim is frozen beneath 25ft of white. The Grand Canyon Lodge and other North Rim facilities are open mid-May–mid-October; the park itself remains open longer, snow permitting.

A shorter season and more roundabout access mean that North Rim crowds are a tenth of South Rim mobs. The quickest way to enjoy the relative serenity is on foot. Easiest walks are the ½-mile Bright Angel Trailhead and the 1½-mile **Transcept Trail**. **Mule Rides $$–$$$** are another option; **Canyon Trail Rides** *(Grand Canyon Lodge Trail Rides Desk; tel: (435) 679-8665)* offer hour and half-day rides along the Canyon Rim or half-day rides into the canyon.

Rafting the Colorado River remains the most adventurous way to see the Grand Canyon. Allow a full day for a smooth-water float, including a picnic lunch. Water trips last from between one and

Above
The North Rim of the Grand Canyon

for use on all park roads and the 2.8-mile Hermit's Rest road Greenway Trail (*www.nps.gov/grca/parkmgmt/hermit.htm*), away from vehicles.

Grand Canyon Field Institute
Offers classes, some with in-park lodging, most months of the year. Check schedules, itineraries and costs on *(866) 471-4435* or *(928) 638-2485; www. grandcanyon.org/fieldinstitute*

Canyon Trail Rides $$$
Tel: (435) 679-8665; www.canyonrides.com. Uses mules for various-length rides in Bryce, Grand Canyon North Rim and Zion National Parks.

eighteen days. Most outfitters depart from Lees Ferry, upstream from the park. A few outfitters ride the river all year. Check detailed park information online (*www.nps.gov/grca/planyourvisit/whitewaterrafting.htm*) for contact information for approved concessionaires, details on length and put-in and take-out points and permits. Summer trips book up early in the season. The waiting time for private 'non-commercial' river-running permits can be several years.

Outside park boundaries, the **Hualapai Nation** in **Grand Canyon West** (*tel: (888) 868-9378* or *(928) 769-2636; www.grandcanyonwest. com*) offers tours of the **Skywalk**, suspended 4,000ft above the canyon floor, an Indian village, flightseeing, riding, rafting and lodging. Beautiful, sacred **Havasu Falls** is on the **Havasupai Indian Reservation** (*Havasupai Tourism Office; tel: (928) 448-2121; www.havasupaitribe.com*). Access the tribal centre by hiking, riding a horse or taking a helicopter from Hualapai Hilltop to Supai Village, where tourists camp or stay in a lodge and take a tour to several waterfalls.

Accommodation and food in Grand Canyon National Park

Book as early as possible (6–12 months) to ensure a place to sleep at America's most popular national park. South Rim is open year-round; North Rim is open mid-May–mid-October. All South Rim park accommodation and restaurants are operated by **Xanterra Parks & Resorts®**, *tel: (303) 297-2757* or *(888) 297-2757; www. grandcanyonlodges.com*

Queen of the seven accommodation options (including Phantom Ranch, *see opposite*) is the historic **El Tovar Hotel $$$** near the railway station. **Bright Angel Lodge and Cabins $$$$** is near the Rim; **Thunderbird Lodge $$$** and **Kachina Lodge $$$** offer a choice of canyon-side or park-side rooms. **Maswik Lodge $$–$$$** and **Yavapai Lodge $$** are removed from the Village. Accommodation is also available in **Tusayan** (just outside the park's South Entrance), **Valle, Williams, Flagstaff** and **Sedona**.

All of the park hotels have restaurants, from the casually formal **El Tovar Dining Room $$$** to the ever-popular **Bright Angel Fountain $** with long midday queues for ice cream. Best stop for picnic and other supplies is **Canyon Village Marketplace**, in the Market Plaza.

The North Rim hotel is **Grand Canyon Lodge $$$** *(tel: (877) 386-4383 or (480) 337-1320; www.grandcanyonlodgenorth.com. Open mid-May–mid-Oct)*. Outside-the-park possibilities are **Kaibab Lodge $$** *(HC 64, Box 30, Fredonia; tel: (928) 638-2389; www.kaibablodge.com. Open mid-May–Oct)* and **Jacob Lake Inn $$** *(40 miles north of the park's North Rim at the junction of Hwys 67 and 89; tel: (928) 643-7232; www.jacoblake.com)*. The only North Rim restaurant is the **Grand Canyon Lodge Dining Room $$$** but the lodge also has a deli and a snack shop. The **General Store** *(North Rim Campground)* carries picnic supplies.

ZION NATIONAL PARK

Zion Canyon Visitor Center
½ mile north of the South Entrance; tel: (435) 772-3256. Open daily 0800–1700, 1800 or 2000, depending on season.

Kolob Canyons Visitor Center *Park Entrance near I-15. Open daily 0800–1630 or 0800–1700.*

Zion National Park $$$ *Springdale; tel: (435) 772-3256; www.nps.gov/zion*

Zion Human History Museum *½ mile north of park's South Entrance. Open mid-Mar–mid-Nov daily 1000–1700. Interpretive exhibits on Native American culture, local pioneer settlement and water's influence on the park's geography.*

Like Grand Canyon, Zion has two units: **Zion Canyon** (south) and **Kolob Canyons** (north). It is possible to combine the two in a single exhausting day, but more rewarding to allow at least a day for each.

Kolob Canyons is best known to backcountry hikers, but the easy 5-mile drive up Hurricane Fault to the picnic area at **Kolob Canyons Viewpoint** is not to be missed. Look for stunning views of mesa formations dropping sheer to the Lower Kolob Plateau. The *Kolob Canyons Road Guide $* at the visitor centre offers excellent explanations of Kolob geography and geology.

Zion Canyon is filled with names like Abraham, Isaac, Jacob and Moroni (the Mormon angel). The biblical names for the imposing formations were actually chosen by a Methodist minister, Frederick Vining Fisher, who explored the North Fork of the Virgin River.

The **Zion Canyon Scenic Drive** follows Fisher's route up the canyon, starting from **The Watchman** (6,546ft), a mountain wedge standing sentinel near the South Entrance. A short path leads from the car park to the **Court of the Patriarchs**, the aforementioned **Mounts Abraham, Isaac, Jacob** and **Moroni** to the west.

Almost directly across from the Zion Lodge Complex lie the **Emerald Pools**, the lower pool at the base of a waterfall an easy ½-mile from the road. A more strenuous 1-mile trail leads to a larger pool at the base of the cliffs.

The natural hanging gardens of **Weeping Rock** are a ¼ mile from the car park. The gardens are watered by mists and rivulets seeping from the sandstone. Take a moment to duck beneath a well-watered overhang to see Zion's serrated peaks shimmer through the mist.

Zion Park Shuttle
(*www.nps.gov/zion/
planyourvisit/zion-shuttle-
system.htm*) is the only
access to the 6-mile Zion
Canyon Scenic Drive
(*Apr–Oct*), with stops at
scenic viewpoints and
trailheads. Shuttle routes
begin at car parks in
Springdale and the park
Visitor Center. *Zion Canyon
Scenic Drive is open to
private vehicles Nov–Apr. The
remainder of the park is open
to private vehicles all year.*

**Cedar City-Brian
Head Tourism and
Convention Bureau** *581
N. Main St, Cedar City; tel:
(435) 586-5124 or (800)
354-4849; www.
scenicsouthernutah.com*

**Zion Canyon Visitors
Bureau** *PO Box 331,
Springdale; tel: (888) 518-
7070; www.zionpark.com*

**St George Area
Chamber of Commerce**
*97 E. St George Blvd, St
George; tel: (435) 628-1658;
www.stgeorgechamber.com*

**Grand Circle
Association** *PO Box
750392, Torrey;
tel: (888) 254-7263;
www.grandcircle.org*

Climbers cling like ants to the cliffs beyond Weeping Rock that lead to the **Temple of Sinawava**, end of the road and start of a 1-mile **Riverside Walk** along the Virgin River to another hanging garden.

Accommodation and food in Zion National Park

Zion Lodge $$$ (*4 miles north of the South Entrance; tel: (888) 297-2757 or (435) 772-7700; www.zionlodge.com*) is the only indoor accommodation in the park. Reservations are essential.

Other accommodation is available in Springdale, just beyond the South Entrance, and the nearby towns of Hurricane and St George. Most convenient accommodation for Kolob Canyons' visitors is in Cedar City.

The **Castle Dome Café $** and the **Red Rock Grill $$$** (*tel: (435) 772-7760*) are the only park restaurants. Picnic supplies can be purchased in nearby towns.

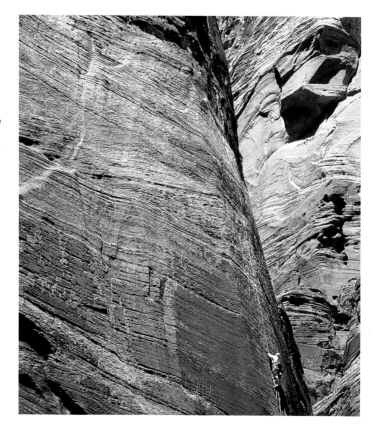

Right
Pitting human strength and agility against sheer rock in Zion National Park

Language

How To Talk Californian

Alternate: Means 'alternative', not 'every other' – sometimes a source of confusion when reading timetables.

Bed & Breakfast (or 'B&B'): Overnight lodging in a private home, usually with private facilities and almost always more expensive than nearby hotels and motels.

Brewpub: A tavern that brews its own beer.

Buffalo wings: Chicken wings, usually fried and served with a spicy sauce as an appetiser or as bar food.

California cuisine: Anything the chef wants it to mean, as long as it's expensive, but usually based on fresh, organically grown foods.

Chilli dog or chilli burger: Hot dog or hamburger disguised with chilli, onions and cheese.

Chimichanga: A pseudo-Mexican concoction of a fried tortilla filled with meat, beans, cheese, tomatoes and lettuce.

Chips: Crisps, usually made from potatoes, but also from corn, taro, casava, rice or other starches.

Corn dog: Hot dog dipped in corn meal and fried. Usually served hot on a stick.

Dead head: Fans of the band the Grateful Dead; also a term for hippies.

Designer water: Pejorative term for bottled water.

Downtown: City or town centre.

Holiday: A public holiday, such as Labor Day, not a private holiday, which is a vacation.

Lodging: The usual term for accommodation.

Natural ingredients: Food that has been grown, processed and prepared without pesticides or other chemical additives.

Outlet shopping: Shopping at large stores specialising in factory overruns at reduced prices. Sometimes, factory outlets are simply low-priced retail stores selling direct from the factory.

Resort: A fancy hotel which specialises in leisure activities such as golf, tennis and swimming.

Road kill: Literally, animals killed by passing cars, but usually used to describe bad restaurant food.

Californian driving terms

Big rig: A large lorry, usually a tractor pulling one or more trailers.

Boulevard stop: Slowing at a stop sign, but not stopping.

CHP California: Highway Patrol, the state road police force.

CNG: Liquefied petroleum gas used as fuel.

Connector: A minor road connecting two freeways.

Crosswalk: Pedestrian crossing.

Curve: Bend.

Divided highway: Dual carriageway.

DUI: Driving Under the Influence of alcohol or drugs, aka Drunk Driving. The blood alcohol limit in California and Nevada is 0.08% and is very strictly enforced.

Fender: Bumper.

Freeway: Motorway.

Garage or parking: Garage car park.

Gas(oline): Petrol.

Grade: Gradient, hill.

Highway: Trunk road.

Hood: Bonnet.

Metering lights: Traffic signals controlling access to bridges, freeways, etc.

Motor home: Motor caravan.

Pavement: Road surface. A UK 'pavement' is a US sidewalk.

Ramp: Slip road.

Rent: Hire.

Rubbernecking: Slowing down to peer while driving past the scene of an accident or some unusual event.

RV (recreational vehicle): Motor caravan.

Shift (stick): Gear lever.

Shoulder: Verge.

Sidewalk: Pavement.

Sig-alert: An official warning of unusually heavy traffic, usually broadcast over local radio stations.

Switchback: Serpentine road.

Traffic cop: Traffic warden.

Trunk: Boot.

Yield: Give way.

Index

Acknowledgements

Project management: Cambridge Publishing Management Limited
Project editor: Karen Beaulah
Series design: Fox Design
Cover design: Liz Lyons Design
Layout: Cambridge Publishing Management Limited
Map work: PCGraphics (UK) Ltd
Repro and image setting: PDQ Digital Media Solutions Ltd/Cambridge Publishing Management Limited
Printed and bound in India by: Replika Press Pvt Ltd

We would like to thank the following photographers and organisations for the photographs used in this book, to whom the copyright in the photograph belongs:

Maxine Cass (pages 4, 6, 10, 11, 14, 15, 16, 18, 20, 21, 22, 28, 30, 31, 32, 33, 34, 37, 40, 43, 46, 47, 49, 50, 51, 57, 58, 60, 62, 64, 68, 71, 74, 76, 83, 84, 87, 88, 92, 99, 100, 102, 107, 108, 119, 120, 125, 126, 132, 134, 137, 140, 141, 144, 146, 150, 152, 155, 157, 162, 164, 166, 169, 170, 174, 176, 179, 181, 184, 186, 189, 192, 194, 197, 198, 201, 204, 212, 214, 216, 217, 219, 224, 227, 233, 236, 238, 241, 244, 246, 250, 256, 260, 265, 268, 272, 274 and 279);
Ethel Davies (page 277);
Dreamstime.com (pages 1a, 79 Sprokop, 1b, 96 Bart Everett, 158 Harris Shiffman);
Fred Gebhart (pages 52, 56, 72, 112, 116, 122, 128, 248, 254, 262, 264, 267 and 271);
UPPA/Photoshot (page 95).

Feedback form

We're committed to providing the very best up-to-date information in our travel guides and constantly strive to make them as useful as they can be. You can help us to improve future editions by letting us have your feedback. Just take a few minutes to complete and return this form to us.

When did you buy this book? ....
....

Where did you buy it? (Please give town/city and, if possible, name of retailer)
....
....

When did you/do you intend to travel in California? ....
....

For how long (approx)? ....

How many people in your party? ....

Which cities, national parks and other locations did you/do you intend mainly to visit?
....
....
....
....

Did you/will you:
❏ Make all your travel arrangements independently?
❏ Travel on a fly-drive package?
Please give brief details: ....
....

Did you/do you intend to use this book:
❏ For planning your trip?   ❏ Both?
❏ During the trip itself?

Did you/do you intend also to purchase any of the following travel publications for your trip?
A road map/atlas (please specify) ....
Other guidebooks (please specify) ....

Have you used any other Thomas Cook guidebooks in the past? If so, which?

....

....

Please rate the following features of *driving guides California* for their value to you (circle VU for 'very useful', U for 'useful', NU for 'little or no use'):

The *Travel facts* section on pages 12–21	VU	U	NU
The *Driver's guide* section on pages 22–27	VU	U	NU
The *Highlights* on pages 38–39	VU	U	NU
The recommended driving routes throughout the book	VU	U	NU
Information on towns and cities, National Parks, etc	VU	U	NU
The maps of towns and cities, parks, etc	VU	U	NU

Please use this space to tell us about any features that in your opinion could be changed, improved, or added in future editions of the book, or any other comments you would like to make concerning the book:

....

....

....

....

....

....

....

Your age category: ❑ 21–30   ❑ 31–40   ❑ 41–50   ❑ over 50

Your name: Mr/Mrs/Miss/Ms ....

(First name or initials) ....

(Last name) ....

Your full address (please include postal or zip code):

....

....

....

....

....

Your daytime telephone number: ....

Please detach this page and send it to: driving guides Series Editor, Thomas Cook Publishing, PO Box 227, Coningsby Road, Peterborough PE3 8SB.

Alternatively, you can e-mail us at: *books@thomascook.com*